The
BLACKBIRCH
Kid's Almanac
of Geography

Packed with information; crammed with full-color photos,
maps, charts, and graphs; and bursting with statistics,
trivia, and fun facts about our world!

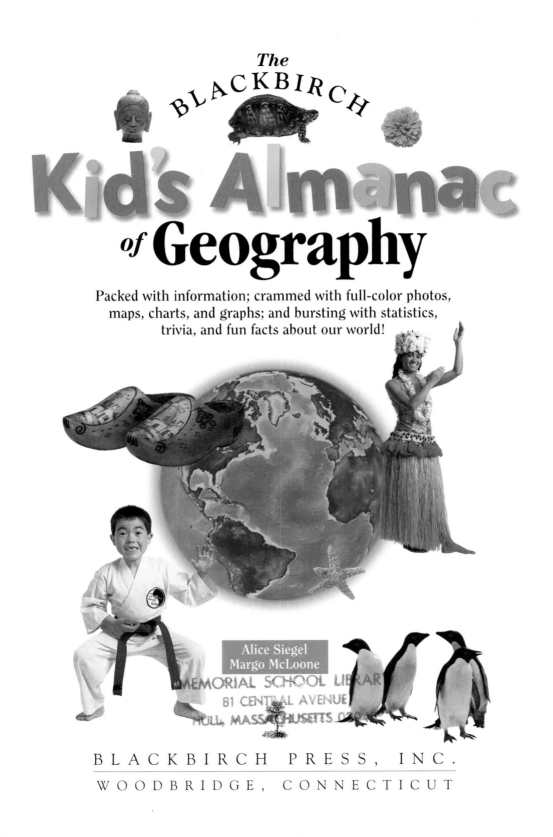

Alice Siegel
Margo McLoone

BLACKBIRCH PRESS, INC.
WOODBRIDGE, CONNECTICUT

For my students, in the Class of 2000, IS 123 in the Bronx, who brought spirit and joy into the classroom.
— Margo McLoone

This book is dedicated to my husband, George, and my three sons, Andrew, Howard and James.
— Alice Siegel

Published by Blackbirch Press, Inc.
260 Amity Road
Woodbridge, CT 06525

©2000 by Blackbirch Press, Inc.
First Edition

e-mail: staff@blackbirch.com
Web site: www.blackbirch.com

Printed in Singapore

10 9 8 7 6 5 4 3 2 1

The Kid's Almanac of Geography Staff
Executive Editor: Bruce S. Glassman
Editorial Director: Beverly Larson
Editor/Photo Research: Jenifer Morse
Assistant Editor: Emily Kucharczyk
Copy Editor: Barbara Bakowski
Cover Design: Nancy Raver
Art Director/Book Design: Calico Harington
Graphic Designer: Mindi Englart
Indexer: Kathleen Rocheleau

Library of Congress Cataloging-in-Publication Data
Siegel, Alice.
    The kid's almanac of geography / by Alice Siegel and Margo McLoone.
        p.   cm.
Includes index.
        ISBN 1-56711-300-1 (hardcover : alk. paper)
        1. Geography—Juvenile literature. 2. Almanacs, Children's. [1. Geography. 2. Almanacs.]
        I. McLoone, Margo. II. Title.
G133 .S58 2000
910—dc21   00-009399
                                                                                                          CIP
                                                                                                           AC

TABLE OF CONTENTS

(Italic = map)

Animal A.P.B. (All Points Bulletin)   6

Unique Animals of the World • Animal Champions Around the World • Animals of the Chinese Calendar • World Animal Extinction and Endangerment • Animals at Risk • Selected Endangered Species of the World • Dinosaur Digs • World Zoos and Wildlife Preserves • World Wildlife Watching Centers • Regions of Wildlife • Far-Flung Animal Facts • U.S. State Animals

Cash Flow (World Money)   22

Selected Countries and Currencies • Money in the World • Far-Out Money from Far-Flung Places • Twenty-One Unusual Kinds of Money • Dollars and Cents in the United States • Money Milestones • Who's on U.S. Currency?

Continental Divides (All About Landmasses)   34

Earth's Tectonic Plates • From Supercontinent to Seven Continents • *Timeline of Continental Drift* • Profile of Earth • *Continental Movement* • Earthquakes • Volcanoes • *Asia* • Sizing Up Asia • Highlights of Asia • *Africa* • Sizing Up Africa • Highlights of Africa • *North America* • Sizing Up North America • Highlights of North America • *South America* • Sizing Up South America • Highlights of South America • *Antarctica* • Highlights of Antarctica • Sizing Up Antarctica

Countries of the World   52

Countries of the World • *Countries of Africa* • *Countries of Asia* • *Countries of Oceania* • *Countries of Europe* • *Countries of North America* • *Countries of South America* • Countries of the World (1999) • Country Name Meanings • Old Names and New Names • Country Nicknames • Countries with the Most... • *World Population Density* • Country Neighbors • Peninsular Neighbors

Daily Planet (Calendar of World Events)   80

Calendars of the World • Months of the Year • Periods of Time • January • February • March • April • May • June • July • August • September • October • November • December

Daring Dwellers (Nomads and Semi-nomads)   106

Indigenous Peoples of the World • Nomads of the World • Indigenous People Around the World • Pygmies: Fire Carriers of the Forest • Lapps: Reindeer Herders of the Tundra • The Bajau: Boat Dwellers of the Sea • The Guajiro: Indian Wanderers of Colombia • The Al Murrah: "Nomads of Nomads" • The Tuareg of the Sahara • The Chipaya of Bolivia • The Penan of Sarawek on the Island of Borneo • Traditional Life of the Inuit

Global Beauty (Clothing and Adornment)   120

Traditional Clothing from Around the World • Clothing • The Meanings and Uses of Color • Garbs and Their Geography • Kente Cloth • Global Headwear • Religious Hats • The Story of Hair • Jewelry • Body Painting • Tattoos • Body Piercing and Pulling

Global Gab (World Languages) 132

World Languages • Language Families • The Indo-European Family of Languages • The Growth of English • Fifteen Most-Spoken World Languages • Countries with the Most English-Language Speakers • The Language and Meaning of Place Names • Geographic Terms in World Languages • English Words Borrowed from World Languages • Words in Different Languages

Global Gourmet (The Geography of Tastes) 148

Gourmet Capitals of the World • Food Facts • Country Beverages • Spices • Cereal Grains of the World • Exotic or Unusual Foods of the World • The Geography of Tastes in the United States • Breakfast Around the World • Staple Foods • Origins of Food • The Global Table • City Specials

Globally Green (The World of Plants) 162

World Biomes • Major Land Biomes • Twenty Terrific Tree Flavors • Connecting Sports with Trees • Amazing Trees Around the World • Famous Trees of the United States • Naming Trees and Plants • State Trees and Flowers of the United States • Plants as Potions and Poisons • Poison Plants in History • Healing Plants • Twenty Common Poisonous Plants • Meat-Eating Plants • World Conservation Union's Red List • Most Endangered National Parks in the United States

International Flags 180

Fabulous Flag Facts • Nicknames of National Flags • Storm Warning Flags • International Flags • World Flags • International Flag Code

Mapping the World 188

Elements of a Map • Highlights of Mapmaking • Marvelous Map Collections • Latitude and Longitude • Famous Lines of Latitude • Sizing Up Longitude • Kinds of Maps • Physical Maps • Geographical Terms Found on a Physical Map • Political Maps • Geographical Terms Found on a Political Map • Thematic Maps • Useful Thematic Maps • The Compass: An Explorer's Tool • Centuries of Instruments

Water Wonders (Oceans, Seas, Lakes, and Rivers) 202

Oceans of the World • Oceans • Awesome Ocean Facts • Surfing Earth's Surface • Ocean Investigation • The Ocean Floor • Sizing Up the World's Oceans • Pacific Ocean • Pacific Ocean Currents • Atlantic Ocean • Atlantic Ocean Currents • Indian Ocean • Indian Ocean Currents • Arctic Ocean • Who Owns the Oceans? • Coastlines • Seas, Bays, and Gulfs • Sizing Up Seas, Bays, and Gulfs • Lakes • Rivers • Anatomy of a River • Rivers with the Greatest Amount of Water • World's Longest Rivers • Glaciers—The World's Longest Rivers of Ice • The 10 Most Endangered Rivers of the United States, 1998 • River Words • Famous Rivers of the World • Waters Named After Explorers • Water Words

World Beat (Music and Dance) 224

Origins of Selected Musical Styles and Instruments • Animals and Music • National Dance, Music, and Instruments • Music and Dance Capitals of the World • Musical Instruments: Kinds to Know • World Music • Selected Music Capitals of the United States

World Cities (From Katmandu to Timbuktu) 240

Selected Major Metropolitan Areas of the World • Awesome Ancient Cities • World's Fastest-Growing Cities • World's Most Densely Populated Cities • Cities by World Regions • City Nicknames • City Name Origins • World Cities Named After People • U.S. Cities by the Numbers • Island Cities • Confusing Capitals • World's Highest Cities • Five World Cities Lend Their Names • City Celebrities • City Name Changes • Ten Most Popular U.S. City Names • Ten Biggest U.S. Cities • U.S. City Shorts • Unusual U.S. City Names • "People" Cities • Great Lakes Cities • U.S. State Capital Cities

World Landmarks (Natural and Human-Made Wonders) 258

Wonders and Landmarks Around the World • Seven Natural Wonders of the World • Famous Mountains of the World • Seven Wonders of the Ancient World • Great Spans, Dams, and Canals • World's Largest Sports Stadiums • World's Highest Dams • Worldwide Wonders • World's Longest Suspension Bridges • World Cities with the Most Skyscrapers • The 10 Tallest Buildings in the World Today • Down Below: Notable Caves of the World • International Icons

World Religions (Spiritual Beliefs and Practices) 272

Religion Around the World • Major World Religions • Understanding Religious Calendars and Dates • The Jewish Calendar • The Islamic Calendar • Timeline of World Religions, 3500 B.C.-A.D. 1 • Timeline of World Religions, A.D. 1-1000 • Timeline of World Religions A.D. 1001-2000 • Major Religious Books • Christianity • Christian Holy Days • The Twelve Apostles • Other Christian Groups • The Protestant Reformation • Judaism • The Ten Commandments • Holy Days • Five Women of the Old Testament • Old Testament Pairs • Other Notable Old Testament Characters • The Geography of Judaism • Islam • Holy Days of Islam • Buddhism • Places in Buddhist History • Key Terms of Buddhism • The Four Noble Truths of Buddhism • Buddhist Festivals • The Dalai Lama of Tibet • Hinduism • The Language of Hinduism • Hindu Beliefs • Hindu Festivals • Tanscendental Meditation • Other Religions in Brief • Indigenous Religions • Ceremonies in Indigenous Religions

World Weather (Winds, Currents, and Storms) 308

Local Wind Names • Atmosphere • Winds • Wind Belts • Regional Winds • Local Winds • Measuring Winds • Wind Facts • Beaufort Wind Scale • El Niño and La Niña • A Kid's Scale for Measuring Wind Speed • Wind Word Bank • Storm Degrees • Tropical Storms • The World's Deadliest Tropical Cyclones • Hurricane Hunters • Naming Hurricanes • Hurricane Facts • How a Hurricane Forms • The Five Deadliest Hurricanes in the Continental United States, 1900-1999 • The Five Costliest Hurricanes in the Continental United States, 1900-1999 • The Five Most Intense Hurricanes in the Atlantic Ocean, 1900-1999 • Global Warming • Tornadoes • Tornado Facts • How a Tornado Forms • Measuring Tornadoes • Tornado Safety Tips • World Weather Extremes

Appendix 322
For More Information 325
Index 327

Animal A.P.B.
(All-Points Bulletin)

Earth is about 4.6 billion years old. Life as we know it appeared some 4 billion years ago, making Earth a living planet. In this chapter, we celebrate one of Earth's most important life-forms—animals. Although mammals are the largest and most intelligent life-forms, they are few in number compared to other species of living things. As for sheer numbers, insects are the world champions! They inhabit the entire Earth, from the frosty Arctic to the steamy equator. Consider beetles, which alone account for 35,000 species. In fact, beetles make up one-fifth of all known forms of life! Animals inhabit oceans, deserts, salt lakes, hot springs, glaciers—every possible earthly niche. Let's look at some of the wonders of our world's wildlife.

UNIQUE ANIMALS OF THE WORLD

Bald eagle

Giant panda

Arctic Ocean

NORTH AMERICA
- Bald eagle
- Chuckwalla
- Snowshoe hare
- Mountain beaver
- American red squirrel

Atlantic Ocean

EUROPE
- Pine marten
- Chamois
- White-toothed shrew
- Greater horseshoe bat
- Alpine marmot

ASIA
- Giant panda
- Sloth bear
- Hog badger
- Large Indian civet
- Leopard cat

AFRICA
- Giraffe
- Cheetah
- Galago
- Meerkat
- Aardvark

Pacific Ocean

Pacific Ocean

SOUTH AMERICA
- Capybara
- Guanaco
- Common marmoset
- Patagonian cavy
- Spectacled bear

Indian Ocean

AUSTRALIA
- Koala
- Kangaroo
- Quokka
- Echidna
- Duckbill platypus

Meerkat

◄ Kangaroo

Animal Count

It is difficult to make a precise count of all the animal life on Earth because some habitats, such as deep oceans, are largely unexplored. We know there are about 6 billion people in the world today, but humans are just one of the 4,500 known species of mammals. All those mammals are only a tiny fraction of the many living things that inhabit our planet. In fact, if you look at the chart to the right, you'll see that it is the very small things that rule Earth.

Animal Group	Known Species*
Insects	963,000
Protozoans	80,000
Mollusks	70,000
Crustaceans	40,000
Worms	25,000
Fish	22,000
Reptiles/Amphibians	10,500
Birds	10,000
Jellyfish/Corals	10,000
Sponges	10,000
Mammals	4,500

*Approximate

Animal Champions Around the World

We celebrate and admire animal intelligence, diversity, habitat adaptation, and other wonders of existence and survival. Here are some animal recordholders and their titles.

Largest

The **largest mammal** is the blue whale of the Southern Hemisphere oceans. The male is 79 feet (24 m) long and weighs 83.5 tons (75.8 metric tons).

The **largest land mammal** is the African elephant. The male is 10.6 feet (3.2 m) at the shoulder and weighs 6 tons (5.4 metric tons).

The **tallest living animal** is the giraffe of Africa, measuring 18 feet (5.5 m) and weighing 4,000 pounds (1,800 kg).

Ostrich

About 1.75 million species of animals and plants have been classified. Some scientists estimate the total number of species at around 100 million!

World Wise

The **largest fish** is the whale shark at 40 feet (12 m) long, and weighing 15 tons (14 metric tons). It inhabits the tropical waters of the Atlantic, Pacific, and Indian oceans.

The **largest freshwater fish** is the Russian sturgeon of the Black and Caspian seas and the Volga and Danube rivers. It measures 24 feet (7.3 m) long and can weigh about 2,000 pounds (906 kg).

The **largest nonflying bird** is the ostrich of northern Africa. It is 8 feet (2.4 m) tall and weighs 280 pounds (127 kg).

Trumpeter swan

The **largest waterfowl** is the trumpeter swan of North America. It weighs 40 pounds (18 kg) and has a wingspan of 8 feet (2.4 m).

The **largest reptile** is the saltwater crocodile of India, southern China, New Guinea, and the Philippines. The male is 16 feet (4.9 m) long and weighs up to 1,150 pounds (521 kg).

The **largest turtle** is the Pacific leatherback, measuring 6.7 feet (2.1 m) from the tip of the beak to the tip of the tail. It weighs 1,000 pounds (453 kg).

The **heaviest snake** is the anaconda of South America, which weighs 600 pounds (272 kg) and measures up to 25 feet (7.6 m) long.

The **largest amphibian** is the giant salamander of central China. It is 3.3 feet (1 m) long and weighs up to 66 pounds (30 kg).

The **largest frog** is the goliath frog of western Africa at a length of 2 feet (61 cm) and a weight of 8 pounds (5.9 kg).

Longest

The **longest insect**— the stick insect—lives in tropical areas of the world and measures 13 inches (33 cm) long.

The **longest snake** is the reticulated python at 28 feet (8.5 m). It inhabits parts of Southeast Asia.

◄ Stick insect

Smallest

The **smallest mammal** is the Kitti's hog-nosed bat of Thailand. Its head and body measure a little more than an inch (29 mm), and it has a wingspan of 6 inches (15 cm).

The **smallest nonflying mammal** is the Savi's white-toothed pygmy shrew of Africa. It measures 2 inches (52 mm) and weighs 0.09 ounces (2.5 g).

The **smallest bird** is Helena's hummingbird of Cuba. It measures 2.3 inches (58 mm) from the beak to the tail and weighs 0.07 ounces (2 g).

The **smallest waterfowl** is the pygmy goose of Africa. It is less than 1 foot (30 cm) long and weighs half a pound (0.22 kg).

The **smallest reptile** is the gecko of the Virgin Islands, West Indies. From snout to vent, it is 0.71 inches (18 mm) long, with an equally long tail.

The **smallest amphibian** is the poison-arrow frog of Cuba. It measures 0.48 inches (12.4 mm) long.

The **smallest fish** is the dwarf pygmy goby, which inhabits fresh water in the Philippines. It weighs 0.0021 ounces (59 mg) and is 0.43 inches (11 mm) long.

The **smallest shark** is the long-faced dwarf shark of the Gulf of Mexico at 6 inches (15.2 cm).

The **smallest insect** is the hairy-winged dwarf beetle at 0.0098 inches (0.25 mm).

Fastest

The **fastest land mammal** is the cheetah of eastern Africa, Iran, Turkey, and Afghanistan. It can reach a speed of 60 miles (96 km) per hour.

The **fastest marine mammal** is the sei whale, found from Norway to Tasmania. It can travel 34.5 miles (55.2 km) per hour.

The **fastest flying mammal** is the noctule bat, which flies at 31 miles (49.6 km) per hour.

The **fastest fish** is the sailfish of all tropical waters. It swims at a speed of 18 miles (29 km) per hour.

The **fastest bird** is the spine-tailed swift of Asia. This bird reaches speeds of 106 miles (170 km) per hour.

The **fastest-swimming bird** is the gentoo penguin of Antarctica, which swims at speeds of 22.3 miles (35.6 km) per hour.

Gentoo penguin

The **fastest power diver** is the peregrine falcon of North America, with flying dives reaching 200 miles (320 km) per hour.

The **fastest-swimming, four-legged animal** is the marine turtle of the Atlantic Ocean, which swims at 22 miles (35.2 km) per hour.

The **fastest land reptile species** is the six-lined race runner lizard of the United States, which runs at 18 miles (29 km) per hour.

The **fastest land snake** is the African black mamba at 10 to 15 miles (16–24 km) per hour.

Slowest

The **slowest mammal** is the three-toed sloth of South America, which moves at 0.15 miles (0.24 km) per hour.

The **slowest fish** is the sea horse, which moves at 0.01 miles (0.02 km) per hour.

The **slowest reptile** is the tortoise, which moves at 0.17 miles (0.25 km) per hour.

Other champions

The **longest-lived land mammal**, other than the human, is the Asiatic elephant, which may live to 70 years.

Some of the world's deadliest snakes are the black mamba of Africa (95% to 99% of bites are fatal), the common krait of Southeast Asia (77% to 93%), and the Indian cobra of South Asia (33%).

World Wise

The **longest-lived ocean mammals** are the blue and fin whales. They live from 90 to 100 years.

One of the **shortest-lived animals** is the mayfly, with a lifespan of only 2 hours.

The **longest gestation period for a mammal** is that of the African elephant, which takes about 22 months to develop.

The **farthest frog jumper** is the South African sharp-nosed frog. It can jump 9 feet (3 m).

The **most aerial bird** is the common swift, which can stay aloft for up to 2 to 4 years.

The **most poisonous snake** of the world is the fierce snake of Australia. Its most toxic venom has enough poison (110 mg) to kill more than 100 people in a single bite.

The **heaviest poisonous snake** in the world is the Eastern diamond-back rattlesnake of the United States. It weighs 12 to 15 pounds (5.5–7 kg) and is up to 6 feet (1.83 m) in length.

The **only poisonous lizards** in the world are the Gila monster of the United States and the beaded lizard of Mexico. A Gila monster's poison is more deadly than a rattlesnake's.

The **most electric animal** is the electric eel, which can emit 400 volts.

Elephant ➤

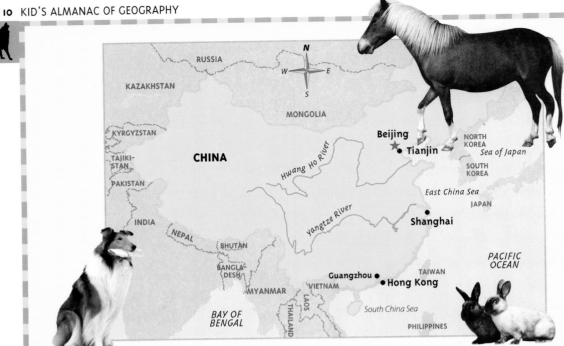

ANIMALS OF THE CHINESE CALENDAR

The Chinese calendar is divided into 12-year cycles, and each year is named for an animal. People born in the year of a particular animal are said to share the characteristics of that animal.

Animal	Characteristics	Years
Dragons	lucky, full of energy, and focused	1964, 1976, 1988, 2000
Snakes	wise and good secret-keepers	1953, 1965, 1977, 1989
Horses	lively company and love to travel	1954, 1966, 1978, 1990
Goats	art lovers and perfectionists	1955, 1967, 1979, 1991
Monkeys	clever, especially in moneymaking	1956, 1968, 1980, 1992
Cockerels	intelligent and efficient	1957, 1969, 1981, 1993
Dogs	loyal and kind	1958, 1970, 1982, 1994
Pigs	popular and jovial	1959, 1971, 1983, 1995
Rats	friendly and sociable	1960, 1972, 1984, 1996
Oxen	serious, quiet, and short-tempered	1961, 1973, 1985, 1997
Tigers	adventurous and daring	1962, 1974, 1986, 1998
Rabbits	quiet, peaceful, and successful	1963, 1975, 1987, 1999

World Animal Extinction and Endangerment

Extinction is a natural process. Thousands of animal species no longer exist on Earth because they have lived out their natural timespan. However, there is a quickened pace of extinction today. This rapid rate of extinction and the endangerment of animals and other life-forms is mostly the result of human actions. The greatest threat to animals is the destruction of their homes, or habitats. Humans have plowed up grasslands, cut down rain forests, drained wetlands, and paved woodlands. Humans have also polluted rivers, streams, and oceans. They have altered the Earth's protective ozone layer. Humans have hunted too many rare species and have introduced other species into unnatural habitats, which can damage local ecosystems.

Elephant seal

Extinct

Extinct means these animals will never live on Earth again. Tasmanian tigers, woolly mammals, ivory-billed woodpeckers, and West Indian monk seals are just a few of the animals that will never return.

Endangered

Endangered means that the species is in immediate danger of becoming extinct. It means the plant or animal is low in number and needs special protection in order to survive. Asian elephants, clouded leopards, and green sea turtles are endangered. So are black rhinos, whose population in Africa has decreased from 65,000 in 1970 to 2,500 today.

World Wise

Up to 100 plant and animal species become extinct every day. Researchers say the total number of species lost may have already climbed to 40,000.

Threatened

Threatened means that a species is not yet endangered but is likely to become so. These plants or animals are low in population and live in threatened habitats. Some threatened animals include moths, bees, butterflies, and other plant pollinators from remote areas. Of the 1,035 known species of pollinators, 103 birds, 82 mammals, and 1 reptile are threatened.

ANIMALS AT RISK

Africa
Elephant

Asia
Clouded leopard
Elephant
Malayan tapir
Orangutan
Red panda
Ruffled lemur
Rusty spotted cat
Sumatran rhino

Australia
Freshwater crocodile
Koala
Northern hairy-nosed
  wombat
Princess parrot
Tree kangaroo

Europe
Siberian tiger

South America
Elephant seal
Galapàgos turtle
Three-toed sloth

North America
Beluga whale
Caribou
Grizzly bear
Wolverine

Koala ➤

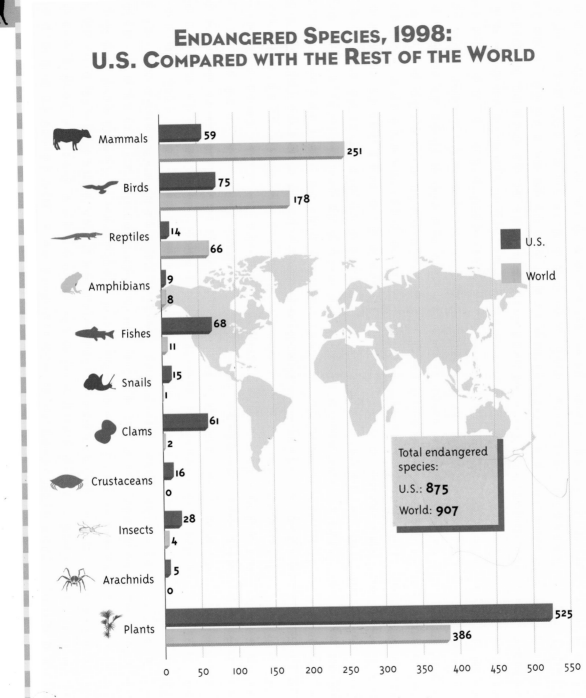

ENDANGERED SPECIES, 1998:
U.S. COMPARED WITH THE REST OF THE WORLD

Mammals
- U.S.: 59
- World: 251

Birds
- U.S.: 75
- World: 178

Reptiles
- U.S.: 14
- World: 66

Amphibians
- U.S.: 9
- World: 8

Fishes
- U.S.: 68
- World: 11

Snails
- U.S.: 15
- World: 1

Clams
- U.S.: 61
- World: 2

Crustaceans
- U.S.: 16
- World: 0

Insects
- U.S.: 28
- World: 4

Arachnids
- U.S.: 5
- World: 0

Plants
- U.S.: 525
- World: 386

U.S.

World

Total endangered species:
U.S.: **875**
World: **907**

0 50 100 150 200 250 300 350 400 450 500 550

Number of endangered species

Source: U.S. Fish and Wildlife Service

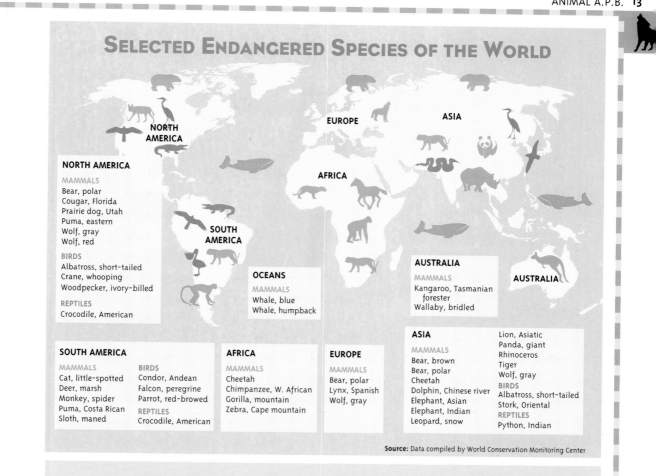

SELECTED ENDANGERED SPECIES OF THE WORLD

NORTH AMERICA

MAMMALS
Bear, polar
Cougar, Florida
Prairie dog, Utah
Puma, eastern
Wolf, gray
Wolf, red

BIRDS
Albatross, short-tailed
Crane, whooping
Woodpecker, ivory-billed

REPTILES
Crocodile, American

OCEANS

MAMMALS
Whale, blue
Whale, humpback

AUSTRALIA

MAMMALS
Kangaroo, Tasmanian forester
Wallaby, bridled

SOUTH AMERICA

MAMMALS
Cat, little-spotted
Deer, marsh
Monkey, spider
Puma, Costa Rican
Sloth, maned

BIRDS
Condor, Andean
Falcon, peregrine
Parrot, red-browed

REPTILES
Crocodile, American

AFRICA

MAMMALS
Cheetah
Chimpanzee, W. African
Gorilla, mountain
Zebra, Cape mountain

EUROPE

MAMMALS
Bear, polar
Lynx, Spanish
Wolf, gray

ASIA

MAMMALS
Bear, brown
Bear, polar
Cheetah
Dolphin, Chinese river
Elephant, Asian
Elephant, Indian
Leopard, snow
Lion, Asiatic
Panda, giant
Rhinoceros
Tiger
Wolf, gray

BIRDS
Albatross, short-tailed
Stork, Oriental

REPTILES
Python, Indian

Source: Data compiled by World Conservation Monitoring Center

10 SPECIES REMOVED FROM THE ENDANGERED AND THREATENED LISTS

Brown pelican

- Brown pelican (Atlantic coast and eastern Gulf)
- Palau dove
- Palau fantail (Old world flycatcher)
- Palau owl
- American alligator
- Rydberg milk vetch
- Arctic peregrine falcon
- Eastern gray kangaroo
- Red kangaroo
- Western gray kangaroo

ENDANGERED SPECIES FACTS

- Scientists estimate that at least 500 plant and animal species have become extinct in the United States since the 1500s.

- The Wilderness Society reported in 1995 that if current trends continue, up to 20% of the world's plant and animal species could already be extinct.

- Thirteen species have been removed from the endangered list—7 of them because they are now extinct.

- The states with the greatest number of endangered species are California, Hawaii, and Florida.

- Of all the known endangered species of plants, 97% can be found somewhere in the United States.

- The U.S. National Wildlife Refuge System, which in 1994 included some 499 refuges covering more than 91 million acres, comprises the only federal lands managed primarily for the benefit of wildlife.

- In 1996, the World Conservation Monitoring Center listed 1,096 mammals—almost one-fourth of all mammals—as threatened species.

- The United States is home to all of the known endangered species of crustaceans and arachnids and almost all endangered species of snails and clams.

Clam and snail

TOP 5 PIG COUNTRIES
Millions of pigs in 1998

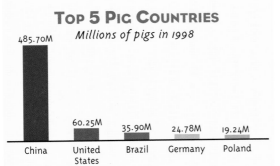

China	United States	Brazil	Germany	Poland
485.70M	60.25M	35.90M	24.78M	19.24M

Source: Food and Agriculture Organization of the United States

TOP 5 CATTLE COUNTRIES
Millions of cattle in 1998

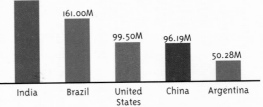

India	Brazil	United States	China	Argentina
209.08M	161.00M	99.50M	96.19M	50.28M

Source: Food and Agriculture Organization of the United States

TOP 5 HORSE COUNTRIES
Millions of horses in 1998

China	Brazil	Mexico	United States	Argentina
8.85M	6.39M	6.25M	6.15M	3.30M

Source: Food and Agriculture Organization of the United States

TOP 5 CAMEL COUNTRIES
Millions of camels in 1998

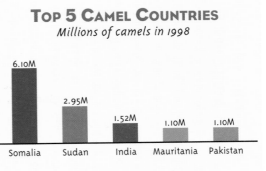

Somalia	Sudan	India	Mauritania	Pakistan
6.10M	2.95M	1.52M	1.10M	1.10M

Source: Food and Agriculture Organization of the United States

Dinosaur Digs

Dinosaurs lived on Earth 230 million years ago, but they became extinct only 65 million years ago. Their fossils have been found all over the world. If you were to dig for dinosaur bones, here are some places you might find fossils.

Albertosaurus

In Dinosaur Provincial Park in Alberta, Canada, you can see the bones of *Albertosaurus* preserved in the sandstone where they were found.

Arctosaurus

In the islands north of the Arctic Circle, *Arctosaurus* fossils were found. *Arctosaurus* means "Arctic lizard."

Austrosaurus

A giant plant eater named *Austrosaurus* once lived on the continent of Australia.

Cryolophosaurus

Cryolophosaurus, or "frozen-crested reptile," was a large early meat eater of Antarctica. It was nicknamed "Elvis" for its crest hairstyle, which swept up on its forehead like a pompadour.

Giganotosaurus

In the Patagonia area of Argentina, *Giganotosaurus* once lived. Scientists believe that this giant meat eater lived in family groups.

Giraffatitan

One of the tallest dinosaurs, *Giraffatitan*, could be found in Tanzania. Its name means "gigantic giraffe."

Iguanodon

You can look for *Iguanodon* all over the world. Fossils of this peaceful plant eater have been found worldwide.

Indosaurus

Indosaurus, a member of the family known as the "tigers of the Dinosaur Age," lived in India.

Itemirus

Itemirus, a small, two-legged dinosaur with excellent balance, once lived in Russia.

Kagasaurus

Kagasaurus, a large meat eater with very sharp teeth, inhabited parts of Japan.

Lobocania

A smaller version of *Tyrannosaurus rex*, known as *Lobocania*, dwelled in Mexico.

Spinosaurus

Spinosaurus, which had a giant, sail-like fin on its back, once roamed in Egypt. Scientists think that this fin was used by the dinosaur to defend itself, or to control body temperature.

Szechuanosaurus

You can find more types of dinosaurs in China than anywhere else in the world. Look in the southern Szechuan area for *Szechuanosaurus*.

Triceratops

Scientists think that *Triceratops*, a three-horned dinosaur, once roamed in great herds in the Montana region of the United States.

World Zoos and Wildlife Preserves

A zoo, or zoological park, is a collection of living animals. In early history, there were some private zoos in China, Egypt, and Greece. These zoos were kept for the pleasure of their owners. Modern zoos are meant to be sanctuaries for animals. Endangered animals are bred and born in zoos. The mission of modern zoos is wildlife education and appreciation. Here are some of the world's most notable zoos.

Penguin enclosure

Alaska Zoo
Anchorage, Alaska

This zoo is thought to be the northernmost zoo in the world. It features a wide variety of Arctic animals, such as the blue glacier bear.

Arizona-Sonora Desert Museum
Tucson, Arizona

Zebra ▼

This zoo is located on 186 acres of desert and has a unique display of desert life. The museum features a hummingbird exhibit and 4,000 animals, with 250 species native to the southwestern United States.

Bermuda Aquarium Museum and Zoo
Bermuda

This small island in the Atlantic has nearly 8,000 species of animals! Many reached the island by way of the Gulf Stream. The museum is dedicated to protecting the fragile ecology of the island.

Bronx Zoo
Bronx, New York

This 265-acre zoo is run by the World Conservation Society. It

started the world's first animal hospital in 1916. Today the zoo is known for its realistic habitats and exotic animals.

Chilkat Bald Eagle Preserve
Haines, Alaska

This protected home for wildlife is just north of Juneau. The salmon run in the Chilkat River and attract as many as 4,000 bald eagles in a season. The birds stay from mid-September through January.

World Wise

The first wildlife sanctuary in Africa was the Pongola Reserve, which was established in 1894 to protect elephants.

Edinburgh Zoo
Edinburgh, Scotland

The largest collection of animals in Scotland lives in this zoo, which is located on 80 acres of parkland. The world's largest penguin enclosure is located here.

Hummingbird

Marwell Zoo Park
Hampshire, England
Marwell's specialty is hoofed animals, including zebras, giraffes, and white rhinoceroses.

Perth Zoo
Western Australia
Opened in 1898, it is home for 1,200 animals from 230 different species. The Perth Zoo features an African savanna for elephants. It also has herons and other waterfowl.

▼ Monarch butterfly

Rachel Carson National Wildlife Reserve
Wells, Maine
Thousands of migratory waterfowl join native species of herons, egrets, and other birds in this bird-watching heaven.

San Diego Zoo and Wild Animal Park
San Diego, California
This zoo runs the Center for Reproduction of Endangered Species (CRES). It features the Panda Research Station and works closely with China to study the bears and breed them in captivity.

Zoo Negro Malaysia
Ulu Kelang, Malaysia
This national zoo is located on a jungle reserve in the Klang Valley. It opened in 1963 and is the center of wildlife education in the country.

Bog turtles of the United States rank among the world's top 10 most wanted endangered species. Their shells are highly valued in world pet markets.

World Wildlife Watching Centers

◄ Giraffe

Butterfly town
The area of Pacific Grove, California, is a stopover for millions of monarch butterflies. They usually arrive in October from Alaska. They continue their migration in January to southern Mexico. Monarchs, which weigh about as much as a penny, don't fly in cold weather. Instead, they fold their wings together and shiver to keep warm.

Firefly heaven
The island of Jamaica in the Caribbean Sea is famous for its diverse firefly population. More than 50 firefly species flicker and light up the night skies.

Gooney bird nest
More than 70% of the world's gooney birds, or Laysan albatrosses, are born and bred on the Midway island group in the Pacific Ocean.

Polar bear lodge
Hundreds of polar bears live part-time at the edge of Churchill, Manitoba, in the Hudson Bay in Canada.

Reindeer run
Hundreds of thousands of reindeer breed on the tundra of northern Siberia and move south to live in the forests of Russia.

Whale pad
Hundreds of killer whales live year round in the ocean waters of the San Juan Islands near the state of Washington.

Regions of Wildlife

Gecko

Marine habitat

The Bering Sea is a region for migrating marine life, including bowhead and gray whales. It also supports a vast number of seabirds.

Mountain forest habitat

Northern Rocky Mountain forests sustain North America's richest population of bears, wolves, lynx, and caribou.

Bird habitat

The Ecuador-Colombia border in the Andean forest has high, single mountain peaks, which are home to several species of birds found nowhere else. The Andean condor nests here.

Fish habitat

The reefs of New Guinea harbor 525 species of fish and 450 species of coral.

Reptile habitat

New Caledonia is the home of the world's largest number of species of gecko.

Killer whale

ANIMAL AS SYMBOL

The bald eagle is the national bird of the United States. This animal was chosen to symbolize the country because it is thought to represent courage, independence, and endurance. The following list includes eight countries and the animals that are their national symbols.

Eagle

COUNTRY	ANIMAL
Chile	Condor
El Salvador	Motmot
Guinea	Dove
Iraq	Eagle
Laos	White elephant
Senegal	Lion
Sri Lanka	Lion
Vanuatu	Pig

Toad

FAR-FLUNG ANIMAL FACTS

- All toads are poisonous.

- The sea anemone may look like an under-water flower, but it is really a poisonous animal. Its tentacles are used to paralyze fish and drag them into its mouth.

- Most elephants (99%) are born at night.

- A giraffe's tongue is blue, possibly to prevent it from getting sunburned while it is eating.

- Each hair of a polar bear is hollow in the middle in order to insulate the bear from the cold of its Arctic home.

- Ant species have been on the planet for 92 million years! Their survival may be due to special glands, which secrete juices that kill harmful fungi and bacteria.

- The highest-living mammal is the yak, which inhabits the southern parts of China and former Tibet. It lives 20,000 feet (6,096 m) above sea level.

- Instead of a "man in the moon," the Japanese see the profile of a rabbit in the moon.

- The country with the largest number of snakebite deaths annually is Sri Lanka.

- In China, it is considered good luck to see a bat in flight.

◄ Emerald tree snake

- The Weddell seal of Antarctica is the southernmost-dwelling mammal in the world.

- Bald eagles mate for life. They add sticks and woody debris to their nests yearly. Some of these nests weigh as much as 2 tons (1.8 metric tons)!

◄ Polar bear

Sea anemone

U.S. STATE ANIMALS

◄ Raccoon

Buffalo

Washington
State fish
Steelhead trout

Montana
State fish
Western meadowlark

North Dakota
State fish
Northern pike

Oregon
State insect
Swallowtail butterfly

Idaho
State horse
Appaloosa

Wyoming
State bird
Meadowlark

South Dakota
State animal
Coyote

Nevada
State animal
Desert bighorn sheep

Utah
State animal
Elk

Nebraska
State animal
White-tailed deer

Calfornia
State reptile
California desert tortoise

Colorado
State animal
Bighorn sheep

Kansas
State animal
American buffalo

Tortoise

Arizona
State bird
Cactus wren

New Mexico
State animal
Black bear

Oklahoma
State animal
American buffalo

Alaska
State marine mammal
Bowhead whale

Texas
State bird
Mockingbird

Hawaii
State bird
Nene
(Hawaiian goose)

Coyote

◄ Black bear cub

Swallowtail butterfly

Honeybee ➤

Chesapeake Bay retriever

Beaver

New Hampshire
State reptile
Red spotted newt

Maine
State cat
Maine coon cat

Minnesota
State bird
Common loon

Vermont
State bird
Hermit thrush

Massachusetts
State fish
Cod

Wisconsin
State peace symbol
Mourning dove

District of Columbia
State bird
Wood thrush

New York
State animal
Beaver

Rhode Island
State bird
Rhode Island red chicken

Michigan
State insect
Dragonfly

Pennsylvania
State dog
Great Dane

Connecticut
State animal
Sperm whale

Iowa
State bird
Eastern goldfinch

New Jersey
State insect
Honeybee

Illinois
State animal
White-tailed deer

Indiana
State bird
Cardinal

Ohio
State insect
Ladybug

Delaware
State insect
Ladybug

Missouri
State insect
Honeybee

West Virginia
State animal
Black bear

Virginia
State dog
American foxhound

Kentucky
State animal
Gray squirrel

Maryland
State dog
Chesapeake Bay retriever

Arkansas
State bird
Mockingbird

Tennessee
State animal
Raccoon

North Carolina
State reptile
Box turtle

Ladybug

South Carolina
State fish
Striped bass

Louisiana
State crustacean
Crawfish

Mississippi
State fish
Black bass

Alabama
State fish
Tarpon

Georgia
State fish
Largemouth bass

Gray squirrel

Florida
State marine mammal
Manatee

Manatee

Mourning dove

Cash Flow
(World Money)

What is money, and why is it important to people? By definition, money is anything people will accept for the work they do or for the goods they exchange. There have been many kinds of money in the world. The concept of money is that the value of it is a set amount and is agreed upon by everyone. This is true whether people exchange salt, gold, or coins.

In early times, before coins and paper money were introduced, people bartered goods. Cattle were very valuable but cumbersome to trade. Money in the form of paper and coins made trading easier. Today, money is mainly paper, plastic (credit cards), or simply a balance on a computer system. The paper itself is not valuable—its worth is purely due to the fact that everyone accepts it as payment for anything.

World Wise

"Bucks" is a slang term for money or bills. Before paper money was made in the United States, buckskins (male deer hide) were a common form of currency.

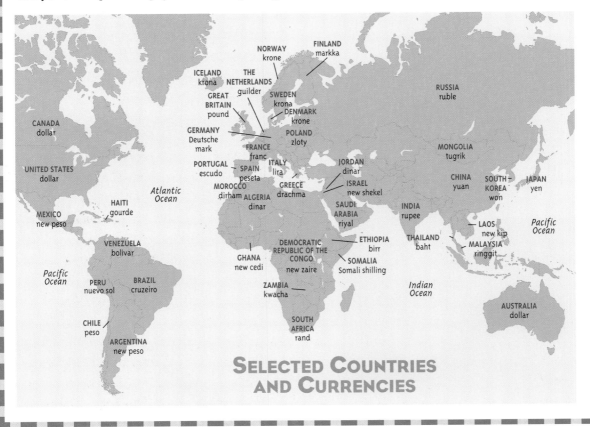

SELECTED COUNTRIES AND CURRENCIES

Money in the World

In the United States, the money system is based on a unit of currency called the dollar. Each country in the world has its own equivalent of the U.S. dollar. On bills and coins, each country prints its own languages, pictures, and symbols of people and things it honors. The following lists give the names of the money that various countries use as their main unit of currency.

AFRICA

Country	Currency
Algeria	Algerian dinar
Angola	Kwanza
Benin	CFA franc
Botswana	Pula
Burkina Faso	CFA franc
Burundi	Burundi franc
Cameroon	CFA franc
Cape Verde Islands	Cape Verdean escudo
Central African Republic	CFA franc
Chad	CFA franc
Comoros	Comoron franc
Congo	CFA franc
Côte d'Ivoire	CFA franc
Djibouti	Djiboutian franc
Egypt	Egyptian pound
Equatorial Guinea	CFA franc
Eritea	Birr
Ethiopia	Birr
Gabon	CFA franc
Gambia	Dalasi
Ghana	New cedi
Guinea	Guinean franc
Guinea-Bissau	Guinean-Bissauan peso
Kenya	Kenyan shilling
Lesotho	Loti
Liberia	Liberian dollar
Libya	Libyan dinar
Madagascar	Malagasy franc
Malawi	Malawian kwacha
Mali	CFA franc
Mauritania	Ouguiya
Mauritius	Mauritian rupee
Morocco	Moroccan dirham
Mozambique	Metical
Namibia	Namibian dollar
Niger	CFA franc
Nigeria	Naira
Rwanda	Rwandan franc
São Tomé & Príncipe	Dobra
Senegal	CFA franc
Seychelles	Seychelles rupee
Sierra Leone	Leone
Somalia	Somali shilling
South Africa	Rand
Sudan	Sudanese pound
Swaziland	Lilangeni
Tanzania	Tanzanian shilling
Togo	CFA franc
Tunisia	Tunisian dinar
Uganda	Ugandan shilling
Democratic Rep. of the Congo	New zaire
Zambia	Zambian kwacha
Zimbabwe	Zimbabwean dollar

ASIA

Afghanistan	Afghani
Bahrain	Bahraini dinar
Bangladesh	Taka
Bhutan	Ngultrum
Brunei	Bruneian dollar
Cambodia	New riel
China	Yuan

Japanese bills

Chinese bills

Cyprus	Cypriot pound
India	Indian rupee
Indonesia	Indonesian rupiah
Iran	Iranian rial
Iraq	Iraqi dinar
Israel	New Israeli shekel
Japan	Yen
Jordan	Jordanian dinar
Kuwait	Kuwaiti dinar
Laos	New kip
Lebanon	Lebanese pound
Malaysia	Ringgit
Maldives	Rufiyaa

Mongolia	Tugrik
Myanmar	Kyat
Nepal	Nepalese rupee
North Korea	North Korean won
Oman	Omani rial
Pakistan	Pakistani rupee
Philippines	Philippine peso
Qatar	Qatari riyal
Saudi Arabia	Saudi riyal
Singapore	Singapore dollar
South Korea	South Korean won
Sri Lanka	Sri Lankan rupee
Syria	Syrian pound
Taiwan (Republic of China)	New Taiwan dollar

South Korean bills

BANK OF ISRAEL

Israeli bills

Thailand	Baht
Turkey	Turkish lira
United Arab Emirates	Emirian dirham
Vietnam	New dong
Yemen	Yemeni rial

AUSTRALIA AND THE SOUTH PACIFIC

Australia	Australian dollar
Fiji	Fijian dollar

Australian bill

Kiribati	Australian dollar
Marshall Islands	United States dollar
Micronesia	United States dollar
Nauru	Australian dollar
New Zealand	New Zealand dollar
Palau	United States dollar
Papua New Guinea	Kina
Solomon Islands	Solomon Islands dollar
Tonga	Pa'anga
Tuvalu	Tuvaluan dollar or Australian dollar

New Zealand bills

Vanuatu	Vatu
Western Somoa	Tala

COMMONWEALTH OF INDEPENDENT STATES (CIS)

Armenia	Dram
Azerbaijan	Manat
Belarus (Byelorussia)	Belarusian ruble

Byelorussian bills

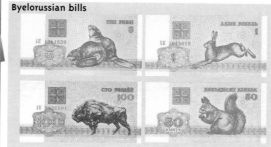

Georgia	Lari
Kyrgyzstan	Kyrgyzstani som
Moldova	Leu
Russia	Ruble

Russian bills

Tajikistan	Tajik ruble
Turkmenistan	Manat
Ukraine	Hryvnia
Uzbekistan	Som

EUROPE

Albania	Lek
Andorra	French franc
Austria*	Austrian schilling/Euro

Cinquante Francs

BANQUE de FRANCE

French bill

Belgian bills

France*	French franc/Euro
Germany*	Deutsche mark/Euro

German bills

Belgium*	Belgium franc/Euro
Bosnia-Herzgovina	Dinar
Bulgaria	Lev
Croatia	Croatian kuna
Czech Republic	Koruna

Danish bills

Greece	Drachma

Greek bills

Denmark	Danish krone
Estonia	Estonian kroon
Finland*	Markka or finmark/Euro

Hungary	Forint
Iceland	Icelandic krona
Ireland*	Irish pound/Euro

Finnish bills

Irish bills

Italian bill

Italy*	Italian lira/Euro
Latvia	Lat
Liechtenstein	Swiss franc
Lithuania	Litas
Luxembourg*	Luxembourg franc/Euro
Macedonia	Denar
Malta	Maltese lira
Monaco	French franc

Netherlands bills

Netherlands*	Netherlands guilder/Euro
Norway	Norwegian krone

Norwegian bills

Poland	Zloty
Portugal*	Portuguese escudo/Euro
Romania	Leu
San Marino	Italian lira

Slovakia	Koruna
Slovenia	Tolar

Spanish bills

Spain*	Peseta/Euro
Sweden	Swedish krona

Swiss bills

Switzerland	Swiss franc
United Kingdom	British pound

British bills

Vatican City	Vatican lira

* These 11 member states of the European Monetary Union are in a transitional period. On January 1, 1999, the Euro was adopted as the single currency of the European Monetary Union. Both Euros and old national currencies will remain legal tender until July 1, 2002, when the local notes and coins will no longer be valid for everyday use. (Euro notes and coins will begin distribution on January 1, 2002.)

NORTH AND CENTRAL AMERICA

Antigua and Barbuda	East Caribbean dollar
Bahamas	Bahamian dollar
Barbados	Barbadian dollar
Belize	Belizean dollar
Nicaragua	Gold cordoba
Panama	Balboa
Saint Kitts and Nevis	East Caribbean dollar
Saint Lucia	East Caribbean dollar
Saint Vincent and the Grenadines	East Caribbean dollar
United States of America	United States dollar

Canadian bill

Canada	Canadian dollar
Costa Rica	Costa Rican colón
Cuba	Cuban peso
Dominica	East Caribbean dollar
Dominican Republic	Dominican peso
El Salvador	Salvadoran colón
Grenada	East Caribbean dollar
Guatemala	Queztal
Haiti	Gourde
Honduras	Lempira
Jamaica	Jamaican dollar
Mexico	New Mexican peso

United States bills

Mexican bill

SOUTH AMERICA

Argentina	Nuevo peso argentino
Bolivia	Boliviano
Brazil	Cruzeiro
Chile	Chilean peso
Colombia	Colombian peso
Ecuador	Sucre
Guyana	Guyanese dollar
Paraguay	Guarani
Peru	Nuevo Sol
Suriname	Surinamese guilder, or florins
Trinidad and Tobago	Trinidad and Tobago dollar
Uruguay	Uruguayan peso
Venezuela	Bolivar

Far-Out Money from Far-Flung Places

Before and after paper money and coins were used, many other things served as money throughout the world.

Africa

Some items that have been used as money in Africa are: manillas, which were objects made of metal and worn as jewelry; cowrie shells, which are shiny seashells; knives; and spearheads.

Asia

In Asia, horses are still a form of money, and are used by the Kirghiz. The Kirghiz are a tribe who live on the grasslands of Russia. Small change is given in lambskins.

In China, spades, hoes, and other metal tools were used as money. Tea bricks were another unusual form of money. They were made from tea that had been mixed with animal blood, then molded into bricks and dried. Bits were then broken off to make a cup of tea.

North America

Wampum made from the shells of a certain type of clam was the best-known form of money used by Native Americans in North America. Beads made from these shells were strung as long as 6 feet (1.8 m).

Oceania (Pacific Islands)

Whales' teeth were used as currency in Fiji. In Yap, fei stones—varying in size from saucers to huge millstones—were taken from the quarries in Palau, 260 miles (418 km) away.

Islanders in the Philippines traded C-shaped metal bracelets, while in Vanuatu people swapped pigs.

South America

Cocoa beans were used as money on this continent. The ancient Aztecs placed a high value on these beans. Approximately 100 beans would buy a shawl. Only the very rich could afford to actually drink the chocolate made from cocoa beans.

Cocoa beans

Twenty-One Unusual Kinds of Money

Eggs

Amber
Axes
Drums
Eggs

Feathers
Gongs
Hoes
Ivory
Jade
Kettles
Leather
Mats
Nails

Oxen
Pigs
Quartz
Rice
Salt
Thimbles
Vodka
Yarn

Rice

Nails

Amber

Dollars and Cents in the United States

All the money in the United States carries the country's official motto, "In God We Trust." Here are some fun facts about U.S. money.

- The largest denomination of a U.S. bill was the $100,000 bill once used by U.S. government banks. It pictured Woodrow Wilson.

- Money that has been damaged will be replaced if 51% of the bill is intact. The Office of Currency Standards in Washington, D.C., provides this service.

- In the early 1900s, the U.S. government washed and ironed dirty money and then re-issued the bills.

- The Bureau of Printing and Engraving in Washington, D.C., and Fort Worth, Texas, together have 16 presses that print money. In one day, 2.5 million bills may be printed at the bureau.

U.S. dollars

- It costs 4 cents to make a $1 bill. It costs the same amount to make a $100 bill.

- The average lifespan of a $1 bill is 18 months.

- The number of $1 bills destroyed in a year would make a stack 200 miles (322 km) high.

- Today, worn-out money is shredded and buried, but in the past it was burned. This was discontinued, however, because the lead used in the ink polluted the environment when ignited.

- The Secret Service was established by the Department of the Treasury in 1865 to combat the counterfeiting of money.

Money Milestones

Money has no single place of origin. The use of money developed over time in many different parts of the world. Here are some highlights of the history of money.

9000–6000 B.C. Cattle, probably the oldest form of money, are traded in many parts of the world.

3000–2000 B.C. The first banks grow out of the use of temples and palaces to store valuables such as grain, cattle, and metals.

1200 B.C. Cowrie shells are used throughout the world as money. In Chinese writing, the symbol for money is a cowrie shell.

640–630 B.C. The first coins are made in Lydia—now Turkey—from electrum, a combination of gold and silver.

390 B.C. The word *money* originates in ancient Rome, after the Gauls attacked the Roman Empire to steal Roman valuables. Forewarned, the Romans build a shrine to Moneta, the goddess of warning. From the name *Moneta* comes the word *money*.

323–230 B.C. Grain is the form of money in Egypt. The Ptolemy family, who rule Egypt at the time, make a central bank in Alexandria.

118 B.C. Leather, in the form of white deerskin, is used in China as money. One square foot equaled 40,000 cash. *Cash* was the name for the Chinese base metal coin.

A.D. 806–821 The first use of paper as money takes place in China. A copper shortage delays

Red pepper

the minting of coins, so store owners give people paper receipts.

A.D. 1124 In England, the quality of silver money decreases. On Christmas Day, all the mint masters are punished by having their right hands cut off.

A.D. 1282 In England, the purity of gold and silver is tested in public.

A.D. 1519–1521 The Aztecs and Mayas of South America use gold dust and cocoa beans as money.

A.D. 1532 The Incas of Peru have an advanced civilization without the use of money, despite huge stores of gold and silver.

A.D. 1599 In Europe, pepper and other spices are literally worth their weight in gold.

A.D. 1619 Tobacco is used as money in the colony of Virginia and continues for nearly 200 years.

Cowrie shells

▲ Gold bars

WHO'S ON U.S. CURRENCY?

Bill	Face		Reverse
$1	George Washington		Great Seal of the United States
$2	Thomas Jefferson		Signing of the Declaration of Independence
$5	Abraham Lincoln		Lincoln Memorial
$10	Alexander Hamilton		U.S. Treasury
$20	Andrew Jackson		White House
$50	Ulysses S. Grant		U.S. Capitol
$100	Benjamin Franklin		Independence Hall

The Great Seal of the United States depicts a bald eagle—the national symbol—on the front. On the reverse, there is a pyramid, which represents strength and permanence. The pyramid is unfinished, to show future growth. The eye surrounded by light represents God. The Latin inscriptions are Annuit Coeptis—"He has favored our undertakings;" and Novus Ordo Seclorum— "a new order of the ages."

BITS AND BUCKS

Wampum was a common form of money in the American colonies. Both Dutch and British colonists traded wampum.

The pine tree shilling was the first coin made in the colonies. Minted in **Massachusetts** in 1657, it was a silver coin with a picture of a pine tree stamped on it.

Pine tree shilling

Bits were pieces of a Spanish dollar made in **Mexico** and circulated in the American colonies in the 1700s. The coin could be broken into eight pieces called bits or four pieces (quarters) called two bits. Today some people still refer to a quarter as "two bits."

Continentals were the first paper bills issued in the colonies. Paul Revere engraved the plates for these bills, which were used to pay American soldiers during the Revolutionary War.

"Greenbacks" was the nickname for the first U.S. government bills because of the color of ink used in printing. The paper bill was first made in 1861 in order to pay soldiers for fighting in the Civil War.

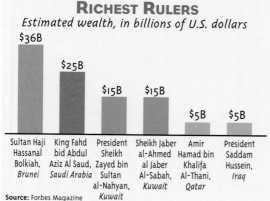

RICHEST RULERS
Estimated wealth, in billions of U.S. dollars

Sultan Haji Hassanal Bolkiah, *Brunei*	King Fahd bid Abdul Aziz Al Saud, *Saudi Arabia*	President Sheikh Zayed bin Sultan al-Nahyan, *Kuwait*	Sheikh Jaber al-Ahmed al Jaber Al-Sabah, *Kuwait*	Amir Hamad bin Khalifa Al-Thani, *Qatar*	President Saddam Hussein, *Iraq*
$36B	$25B	$15B	$15B	$5B	$5B

Source: Forbes Magazine

COUNTRIES WITH THE MOST BILLIONAIRES
Number of billionaires

United States	Germany	Japan	China (Hong Kong)	France/ Mexico/ Saudi Arabia (3-way tie)
70	18	12	8	7

Source: Forbes Magazine

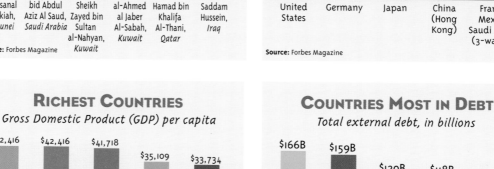

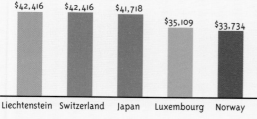

RICHEST COUNTRIES
Gross Domestic Product (GDP) per capita

Liechtenstein	Switzerland	Japan	Luxembourg	Norway
$42,416	$42,416	$41,718	$35,109	$33,734

Source: World Bank

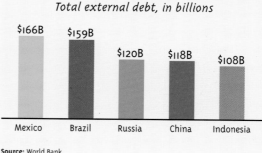

COUNTRIES MOST IN DEBT
Total external debt, in billions

Mexico	Brazil	Russia	China	Indonesia
$166B	$159B	$120B	$118B	$108B

Source: World Bank

Continental Divides
(All About Landmasses)

Continents are the great landmasses of Earth. All of today's continents were once joined in one huge supercontinent called Pangaea more than 200 million years ago. Over time, the land broke up and drifted apart so that today we have seven continents. Underneath the oceans and the continents are massive sections of Earth's crust. These sections are called tectonic plates, and they fit together like huge pieces of a jigsaw puzzle. When these plates move, the shift can create disasters, such as earthquakes, volcanoes, and tidal waves up on Earth's surface. The continents of the world are: Asia, Africa, North America, South America, Antarctica, Australia, and Europe. Technically, Europe is not a continent. It is a peninsula of Asia and is part of the Eurasian continent.

The Atlantic Ocean grows wider by an inch (2.5 cm) each year. In 50 million years, it will be 775 miles (1,250 km) wider than it is today.

World Wise

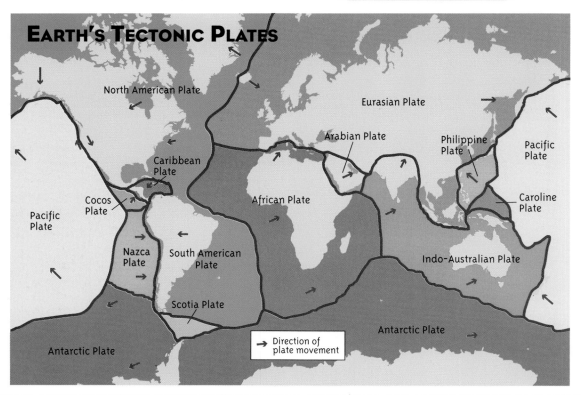

EARTH'S TECTONIC PLATES

North American Plate

Eurasian Plate

Arabian Plate

Philippine Plate

Pacific Plate

Caribbean Plate

Cocos Plate

Caroline Plate

Pacific Plate

African Plate

Nazca Plate

South American Plate

Indo-Australian Plate

Scotia Plate

Antarctic Plate

→ Direction of plate movement

Antarctic Plate

From Supercontinent to Seven Continents

Earth is covered with a hard outer layer called the crust. Beneath the oceans, the crust is only 5 miles (8 km) thick. But beneath the continents the crust may be as much as 45 miles (72 km) thick. This crust is broken into huge slabs called plates. The continents are embedded in these plates. Under Earth's crust is the mantle, a layer of hot, melting rocks that moves in currents of its own. The land plates float on currents of the mantle. The movement is so

The plate tectonics theory is the name given to the study of how Earth moves.

slow—about 2 inches (5 cm) a year—that it barely seems noticeable. However, it is the power of this movement that explains the continuous drifting of continents over millions of years.

TIMELINE OF CONTINENTAL DRIFT

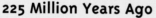

225 Million Years Ago
Pangaea, one supercontinent, is afloat on one huge ocean of water.

180 Million Years Ago
Pangaea splits into two continents, and India breaks away from Africa.

65 Million Years Ago
Australia and Antarctica have drifted apart. South America has separated from Africa. Asia and North America are still connected.

Present
India bumped into Asia, which created the Himalaya Mountains. Asia and North America have separated. The continents exist as we know them today.

PROFILE OF EARTH

Age:	4.6 billion years old
Weight:	Six sextillion*, 588 quintillion** tons
Diameter at the equator:	7,926.4 miles (12,756 km)
Diameter at the poles:	7,899.8 miles (12,714 km)
Distance around the equator:	24,901.55 miles (40,074 km)
Distance from pole to pole:	24,859.82 miles (40,008 km)
Land surface area:	57,259,000 square miles (148,300,000 sq km), which is 29% of the total surface area
Water surface area:	139,692,000 square miles (361,800,000 sq km), which is 71% of the total surface area
Highest point on land:	Mt. Everest in Asia at 29,035 feet (8,850 m)
Lowest point on land:	Dead Sea in Asia at 1,339 feet (408 m) below sea level
Deepest point in the ocean:	Mariana Trench in the Pacific Ocean at 32,827 feet (9,848 m) below sea level
Rotation:	Rotates on its axis once every 23 hours, 56 minutes, and 4.09 seconds
Revolution:	Makes one revolution around the sun every 365 days, 6 hours, 9 minutes, and 9.54 seconds

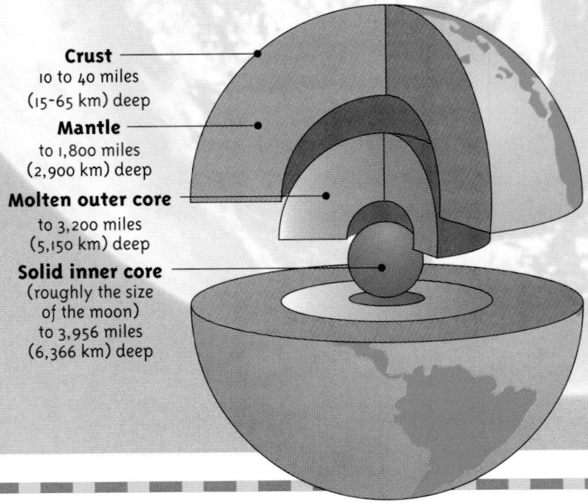

Crust
10 to 40 miles
(15-65 km) deep

Mantle
to 1,800 miles
(2,900 km) deep

Molten outer core
to 3,200 miles
(5,150 km) deep

Solid inner core
(roughly the size
of the moon)
to 3,956 miles
(6,366 km) deep

* sextillion = a billion trillions
** quintillion = a million trillions

World Wise

Is Earth a big planet? If the sun were the size of a soccer ball, Earth would be the size of a peppercorn!

Continental Movement

The movement of Earth's plates causes volcanoes to erupt and the ground to quake. Over a million earthquakes and about 50 volcanic eruptions occur yearly. Most of these take place around the edges of Earth's plates. These edges are known as the "Ring of Fire." The Ring of Fire is a line around the rim of the Pacific Ocean that runs through the Philippines, Japan, New Zealand, and along the coasts of North and South America.

EARTHQUAKES

Earthquakes result when two plates slide past each other, creating intense friction along a fault line. These are some major earthquakes that have occurred in recent history.

LOCATION	YEAR	DEATH TOLL
U.S.A. (San Francisco)	1906	700
Italy	1908	75,000
Japan	1923	143,000
Peru	1970	67,000
China	1976	242,000
India	1993	30,000
Turkey	1999	35,000

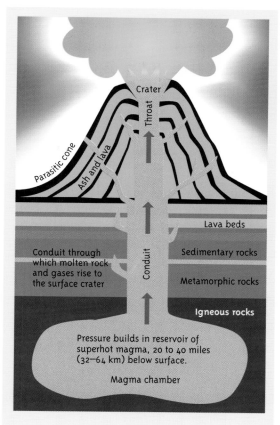

Pressure builds in reservoir of superhot magma, 20 to 40 miles (32–64 km) below surface.

Magma chamber

VOLCANOES

Volcanoes erupt when pressure builds up in the magma, causing lava, hot gases, and rocks to blast through an opening in Earth's surface. Most volcanoes are formed where two plates collide, and one plate is forced under the other. The heat and friction of the collision causes pressure to build, which causes an eruption. Here are some major eruptions from recorded history.

LOCATION	YEAR	DEATH TOLL
Vesuvius (Italy)	79	20,000
Tambora (Indonesia)	1815	92,000
Krakatau (Indonesia)	1883	36,000
Mt. Pelée (Martinique)	1902	30,000
Ruiz (Colombia)	1985	25,000

HOW AN EARTHQUAKE OCCURS

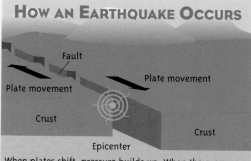

When plates shift, pressure builds up. When the pressure becomes too great, Earth's crust breaks, causing an earthquake. This forms a fault that can be many miles long. The epicenter is the spot where the crust first cracks.

Asia

Asia is the largest continent in size, population, and diversity of land regions. It covers more land area than North America, Europe, and Australia combined. More people live in Asia than live in all the rest of the world. Yet, the uninhabited parts of Asia take up more space than the parts of the continent where people live. Asia extends from Europe and Africa in the west to the Pacific Ocean in the east. It reaches north to the frosty Arctic and south to the steamy tropics near the equator. Earth's highest mountains and lowest lands are both in Asia.

Asia is the birthplace of civilization and a place of many firsts. For example, the first cities were developed in Asia. Writing and literature were created there as well. The first farmers, lawyers, and merchants were Asian.

SIZING UP ASIA

Area:	17 million square miles (44 million sq km)—one-third of Earth's total land area
Coastline:	80,205 miles (129,074 km)—three times the distance around Earth at the equator
Greatest distances:	East to west—6,000 miles (9,656 km); north to south—5,400 miles (8,690 km)
Elevations:	Highest: Mount Everest, Nepal/China at 29,035 feet (8,85 m) Lowest: Dead Sea, Israel/Jordan at 1,310 feet (400 m) below sea level These are the highest and lowest points in the world
Population:	3.6 billion—more than 60% of Earth's total population

All of the world's major religions began in Asia. They include Buddhism, Christianity, Confucianism, Hinduism, Islam, Judaism, Shinto, and Taoism.

HIGHLIGHTS OF ASIA

Himalayan peaks, Nepal

- Home of the "cradle of civilization" because humans first progressed from primitive to civilized ways of life in the Tigris-Euphrates River valley (also called the Fertile Crescent). Around 3500 B.C., the Sumerians invented a system of writing called cuneiform. They also developed laws for measuring, weighing, and trading.

- Home of the Caspian Sea, the world's largest lake.

- Home of the Plateau of Tibet, the world's highest plateau.

- Home of the Himalayas, the world's highest mountain range.

- Home of thousands of islands, including Cyprus, Sri Lanka, Indonesia, the Philippines, Taiwan, and Japan.

- Home of countless great inventions, including the magnetic compass, (300 B.C.) in China; paper, (A.D. 105) in China; and the compact disc, (1982) in Japan.

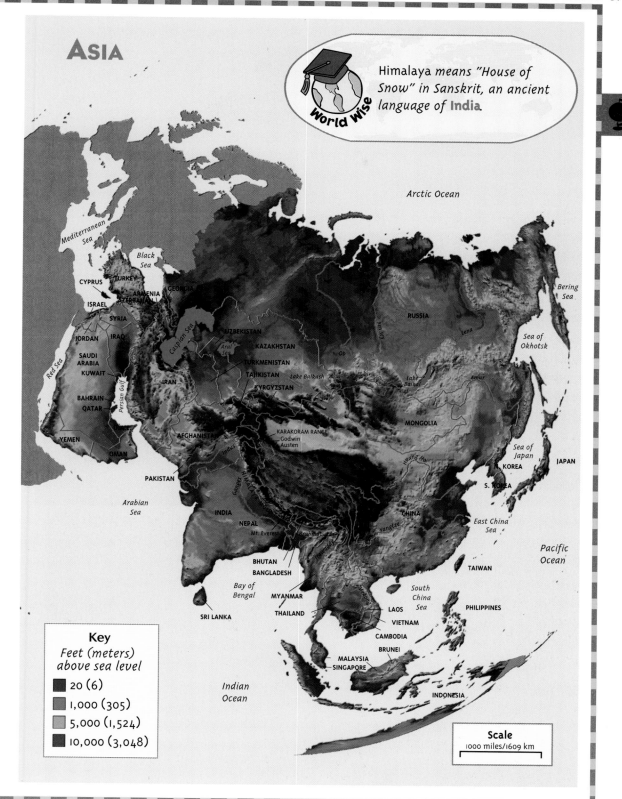

ASIA

Himalaya *means "House of Snow" in Sanskrit, an ancient language of* **India**.

World Wise

Arctic Ocean

Mediterranean Sea

Black Sea

CYPRUS
TURKEY
ARMENIA
GEORGIA
AZERBAIJAN
ISRAEL
SYRIA
JORDAN
IRAQ
SAUDI ARABIA
KUWAIT
BAHRAIN
QATAR
YEMEN
OMAN

Red Sea
Persian Gulf

Caspian Sea
Aral Sea

UZBEKISTAN
KAZAKHSTAN
TURKMENISTAN
TAJIKISTAN
KYRGYZSTAN
IRAN
AFGHANISTAN
PAKISTAN

RUSSIA

Yenisey
Lena
Ob
Lake Balkash
Lake Baikal
Amur

Sea of Okhotsk

Bering Sea

MONGOLIA

Sea of Japan

N. KOREA
S. KOREA
JAPAN

Haang Ho

KARAKORAM RANGE
Godwin Austen

Indus
Ganges
Brahmaputra

INDIA
NEPAL
Mt. Everest
BHUTAN
BANGLADESH

CHINA
Yangtze

East China Sea

TAIWAN

Pacific Ocean

Arabian Sea

Bay of Bengal

SRI LANKA

MYANMAR
THAILAND
LAOS
VIETNAM
CAMBODIA

Mekong

South China Sea

PHILIPPINES

MALAYSIA
SINGAPORE
BRUNEI

Indian Ocean

INDONESIA

Key
Feet (meters) above sea level

- 20 (6)
- 1,000 (305)
- 5,000 (1,524)
- 10,000 (3,048)

Scale
1000 miles/1609 km

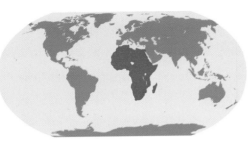

Africa

Africa is the second-largest continent. It covers one-fifth of the world's land area. It is the only continent through which the equator and both the Tropic of Cancer and the Tropic of Capricorn run. The world's largest desert—the Sahara—stretches across the north of Africa. Tropical rain forests extend through the central part of the continent. Vast grasslands cover the areas north and south of the rain forests. The world's longest river— the Nile—flows through northeastern Africa.

This continent is the third most populous, with one-eighth of the world's people. Africans belong to several races and more than 800 ethnic groups. Nearly 1,600 different languages are spoken there.

Africa is divided into 53 countries. The largest in area is Sudan; the smallest is Seychelles. Nigeria is the most populated country, with about 117 million people.

SIZING UP AFRICA

Area:	11.6 million square miles (30.3 million sq km)
Coastline:	22,921 miles (36,888 km)
Greatest distances:	East to west: 4,700 miles (7,564 km) North to south: 5,000 miles (8,047 km)
Elevations:	Highest: Kilimanjaro in Tanzania at 19,340 feet (5,895 m) Lowest: Lake Assal in Djibouti at 509 feet (155 m) below sea level
Population:	670 million, and more than half are under 15 years old

Mount Kilimanjaro

HIGHLIGHTS OF AFRICA

Home of the Sahara, the largest desert in the world. The Sahara is about 3.5 million square miles (9 million sq km) and covers an area nearly as large as the continental United States.

Sahara Desert

Home of the Nile River, the longest river in the world. The Nile River is more than 4,000 miles (6,437 km) long.

Home of the largest tropical area in the world. The equator runs through the middle of the continent, and 90% of Africa is within the tropics.

Home of the the Great Rift Valley, a chain of valleys with volcanoes and elongated lakes, which indicate cracks in the continent.

Home of underground riches of gold and diamonds in South Africa.

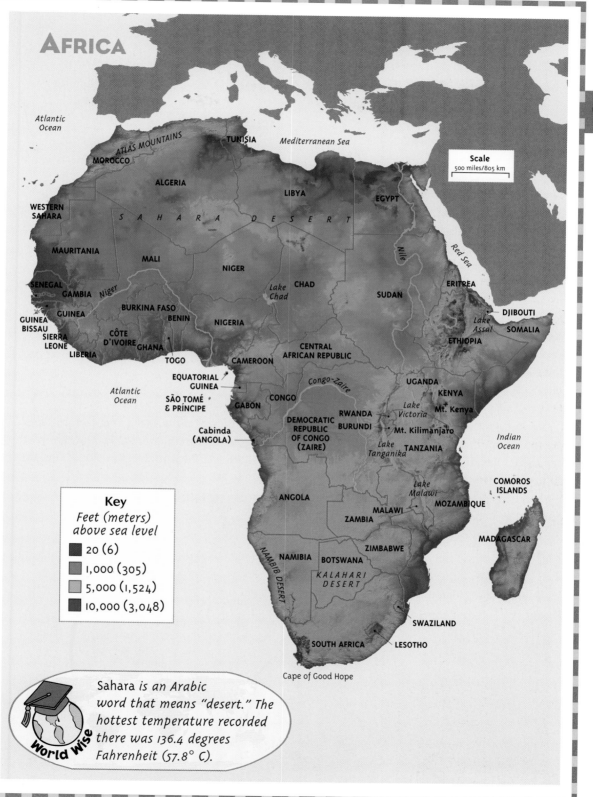

AFRICA

Atlantic Ocean

ATLAS MOUNTAINS

TUNISIA

Mediterranean Sea

MOROCCO

ALGERIA

LIBYA

EGYPT

S A H A R A   D E S E R T

Scale
500 miles/805 km

WESTERN SAHARA

MAURITANIA

MALI

NIGER

Niger

CHAD

Lake Chad

SUDAN

Nile

Red Sea

ERITREA

SENEGAL

GAMBIA

Niger

BURKINA FASO

BENIN

NIGERIA

DJIBOUTI

Lake Assal

SOMALIA

GUINEA BISSAU

GUINEA

SIERRA LEONE

LIBERIA

CÔTE D'IVOIRE

GHANA

TOGO

CAMEROON

CENTRAL AFRICAN REPUBLIC

ETHIOPIA

Atlantic Ocean

EQUATORIAL GUINEA

SÃO TOMÉ & PRÍNCIPE

GABON

CONGO

Congo-Zaire

DEMOCRATIC REPUBLIC OF CONGO (ZAIRE)

RWANDA

BURUNDI

UGANDA

KENYA

Lake Victoria

Mt. Kenya

Mt. Kilimanjaro

TANZANIA

Lake Tanganika

Indian Ocean

Cabinda (ANGOLA)

COMOROS ISLANDS

Lake Malawi

MALAWI

MOZAMBIQUE

ANGOLA

ZAMBIA

MADAGASCAR

Key
Feet (meters) above sea level

- 20 (6)
- 1,000 (305)
- 5,000 (1,524)
- 10,000 (3,048)

NAMIB DESERT

NAMIBIA

BOTSWANA

ZIMBABWE

KALAHARI DESERT

SWAZILAND

SOUTH AFRICA

LESOTHO

Cape of Good Hope

World Wise

Sahara is an Arabic word that means "desert." The hottest temperature recorded there was 136.4 degrees Fahrenheit (57.8° C).

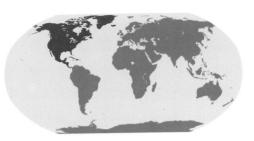

North America

This is the third-largest continent in size, but ranks fourth among the continents in population. North America includes Greenland, Canada, the United States, Mexico, the countries of Central America, and the islands of the Caribbean Sea.

North America has the most varied climate of all the continents. In fact, it is the only continent with every kind of climate. The northern stretches are ice-covered polar regions, and the southern areas are warm and tropical. In between, there are temperate, subtropical, and semi-arid regions.

North America is shaped somewhat like a downward-pointing triangle. It is bordered by the Arctic, Pacific, and Atlantic oceans on three sides. Two huge mountain ranges run

parallel down the western and eastern sides. The younger and higher Rocky Mountains are on the west. The Appalachian Mountains are on the east.

SIZING UP NORTH AMERICA

Area:	9.4 million square miles (24.4 million sq km)
Coastline:	190,000 miles (305,767 km)
Greatest distances:	East to west: 4,000 miles (6,437 km) including islands The narrowest parts, in Panama, are only 30 miles (48 km) wide North to south: 5,400 miles (8,690 km)
Elevations:	Highest: Mt. McKinley in Alaska at 20,320 feet (6,194 m) Lowest: Death Valley in California at 282 feet (86 m) below sea level
Population:	432 million, about 8% of the world's people

HIGHLIGHTS OF NORTH AMERICA

- Home of Greenland, the largest island in the world.
- Home of the Great Lakes, which are located

Lake Superior

on the border of Canada and the United States. These five lakes include: Superior (the largest freshwater lake in the world), Huron, Ontario, Michigan, and Erie.

- Home of Niagara Falls—the world-famous waterfall located between Lake Erie and Lake Ontario. Niagara Falls is made up of two falls, the Horseshoe Falls and the American Falls. More water flows over Horseshoe Falls than any other North American waterfall.

- Home of the Mississippi-Missouri-Ohio River system, the longest on the continent. This river system flows 4,700 miles (7,563 km) to the Gulf of Mexico.

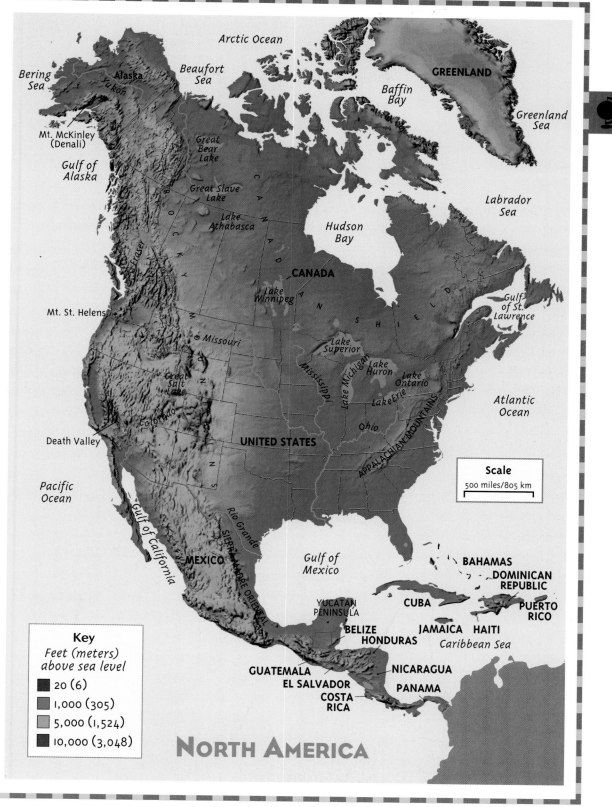

Arctic Ocean

Bering
Sea

Alaska

Yukon

Beaufort
Sea

GREENLAND

Baffin
Bay

Greenland
Sea

Mt. McKinley
(Denali)

Gulf of
Alaska

Great
Bear
Lake

Great Slave
Lake

Lake
Athabasca

Hudson
Bay

Labrador
Sea

Fraser

ROCKY

CANADA

Lake
Winnipeg

SHIELD

Gulf
of St.
Lawrence

Mt. St. Helens

Missouri

Lake
Superior

Lake Michigan

Lake
Huron

Lake
Ontario

Lake Erie

Mississippi

Atlantic
Ocean

Great
Salt
Lake

Colorado

UNITED STATES

Ohio

APPALACHIAN MOUNTAINS

Scale

500 miles/805 km

Death Valley

Pacific
Ocean

Gulf of California

Rio Grande

SIERRA MADRE ORIENTAL

MEXICO

Gulf of
Mexico

BAHAMAS

**DOMINICAN
REPUBLIC**

YUCATAN
PENINSULA

CUBA

**PUERTO
RICO**

BELIZE
HONDURAS

JAMAICA

HAITI

Caribbean Sea

GUATEMALA
EL SALVADOR
**COSTA
RICA**

NICARAGUA

PANAMA

Key

*Feet (meters)
above sea level*

20 (6)

1,000 (305)

5,000 (1,524)

10,000 (3,048)

NORTH AMERICA

Boat on Lake Titicaca

South America

South America is the fourth-largest continent. It covers about 12% of the world's land area. It ranks fifth among the continents in population, with about 6% of the world's people. There are 12 independent countries in South America.

South America is shaped like a gigantic triangle that stretches from the equator to the southern tip of Cape Horn, only 600 miles (965 km) from Antarctica. Up until 3 million years ago, South America was not connected to North America. Unusual animals, such as the giant anteater and the giant tortoise of the Galàpagos Islands, evolved in isolation there.

South America has everything from tropical rain forests, to dry deserts, to rolling grass-lands. It also has some of the world's most spectacular waterfalls, lakes, and islands.

SIZING UP SOUTH AMERICA

Area:	6.8 million square miles (17.6 million sq km)
Coastline:	20,000 miles (32,186 km)
Greatest distances:	East to west: 3,200 miles (5,150 km) North to south: 4,750 miles (7,645 km)
Elevations:	Highest: Mt. Aconcagua in Argentina at 22,832 feet (6,959 m) Lowest: Valdes Peninsula in Argentina at 131 feet (40 m) below sea level
Population:	Estimated 302 million people

HIGHLIGHTS OF SOUTH AMERICA

- Home of the world's largest tropical rain forest, covering more than one-third of the continent.

- Home of the world's largest river—the Amazon—which carries more water than any other river. The Amazon is the second-longest river in the world.

- Home of the world's longest mountain chain—the Andes. These mountains extend 4,500 miles (7,242 km) along the western coast of the continent. More than 40 peaks rise 20,000 feet (6,096 m) or higher.

- Home of the Atacama Desert, the world's driest desert (not including Antarctica).

Rain has not fallen in some areas of this desert for hundreds of years.

- Home of Lake Titicaca, the world's highest lake used for transportation. This lake lies on the Peru-Bolivia border at an elevation of 12,507 feet (3,812 m).

Giant Galápagos turtle

Caribbean Sea

SOUTH AMERICA

Orinoco

VENEZUELA

GUYANA
SURINAME

FRENCH
GUIANA

COLOMBIA

G U I A N A
H I G H L A N D S

ECUADOR

PERU

Amazon

BRAZIL

B R A Z I L I A N
H I G H L A N D S

Lake
Titicaca **BOLIVIA**

A
N
D
E
S

M
O
U
N
T
A
I
N
S

ATACAMA DESERT

PARAGUAY

Paraná

Pacific
Ocean

Paraguay

Uruguay

Mt. Aconcagua

ARGENTINA

URUGUAY

Atlantic
Ocean

P A M P A

Rio de la
Plata

Scale

500 miles/805 km

CHILE

Valdes Peninsula

FALKLAND ISLANDS

SOUTH
GEORGIA

Cape Horn

Key

Feet (meters)
above sea level

■ 20 (6)

■ 1,000 (305)

■ 5,000 (1,524)

■ 10,000 (3,048)

Antarctica

Antarctica is the fifth-largest continent. Its land is covered by a huge ice cap, which is 1.2 miles (2 km) thick. With its ice cap, Antarctica is larger than Europe and Australia, and twice the size of the contiguous United States. Without its ice cap, Antarctica would be the smallest continent.

Antarctica is cold and dry. Temperatures rarely climb above 32 degrees Fahrenheit (0° C), and in winter can plummet to -112 degrees F (-80° C). The inland plateau has the driest climate in the world.

Antarctica has mountains, lowlands, and valleys beneath its cover of snow and ice. The Transantarctic Mountains cross the entire continent. High mountain peaks make up the only visible land.

The only people on the continent are scientists who work at research stations, and tourists who visit. Though only a few plants and insects can survive in Antarctica, the icy seas that surround the continent are full of fish and mammals.

HIGHLIGHTS OF ANTARCTICA

- Home of the South Pole, which is located in the center of the continent.
- Home of the world's greatest supply of fresh water. The ice cap holds 70% of the world's supply.
- Home of the only continent without a country.
- Home of the world's deepest ice. At 15,700 feet (4,785 m), it is more than 10 times the height of the Sears Tower in Chicago.
- Home of the midge, a wingless type of fly that is no more than 1/2 inch (12 mm) long. The midge is the continent's largest land animal.
- Home of the quietest place on Earth.

SIZING UP ANTARCTICA

Area:	5.4 million square miles (14 million sq km)
Coastline:	19,800 miles (31,864 km)
Elevation:	Highest: Vinson Massif at 16,864 feet (5,140 m) Lowest: Sea level. The average elevation makes this the highest continent in the world
Population:	Uninhabited

Iceberg in Antarctica

Ice breaking up

The South Pole is slightly colder than the North Pole. The North Pole is in the Arctic Ocean, while the South Pole is on land in **Antarctica**.

World Wise

ANTARCTICA

ANTARCTIC CIRCLE

Pacific Ocean

Ross Sea

Amundsen Sea

Indian Ocean

Bellingshausen Sea

ANTARCTICA

Vinson Massif

South Pole

Prydz Bay

Weddell Sea

Scale
1000 miles/1609 km

Atlantic Ocean

Key
Feet (meters) above sea level

- 20 (6)
- 1,000 (305)
- 5,000 (1,524)
- 10,000 (3,048)

Europe

Europe is the sixth-largest continent. It occupies one-fifth of Earth's greatest land-mass. Asia occupies the rest. This landmass is sometimes referred to as Eurasia. Europe extends from the Arctic Ocean in the north to the Mediterranean Sea in the south, and from the Atlantic Ocean in the west to the end of Russia in the east.

Although Europe is the second-smallest continent, it has more people than any continent except Asia. Because these people live in

HIGHLIGHTS OF EUROPE

- Home of the world's most irregular coastline. The coastline's pattern of interlocking fingers of land and sea makes it unusually long—over one and a half times the distance around the equator!

- Home of many peninsulas. They are: the Scandinavian Peninsula (Norway and Sweden), the Jutland Peninsula (Denmark), the Iberian Peninsula (Portugal and Spain), the Apennine Peninsula (Italy), and the Balkan Peninsula (Albania, Bulgaria, Greece, and parts of Turkey and Yugoslavia).

- Home of the lost forests. Many European forests were cleared for farmland or to provide timber for ships and charcoal for industry. Most of the surviving forests are in cold or mountainous places.

- Home of the birthplace of western civilization. The ancient Greeks and Romans developed western traditions for art, science, and law.

- Home of Vatican City, the world's smallest country.

SIZING UP EUROPE

Area:	4.1 million square miles (10.6 sq km)
Coastline:	37,887 miles (60,973 km)
Greatest distances:	East to west: 4,000 miles (6,437 km); North to south: 3,000 miles (4,827 km)
Elevations:	Highest: Mount Elbrus at 18,481 feet (5,633 m) Lowest: shore of the Caspian Sea at 92 feet (28 m) below sea level
Population:	697 million people

such a small area, Europe is one of the world's most densely populated places, with 172 persons per square mile (66 per sq km). The average number of persons per square mile in the world is 93 (36 per sq km). More than 50 languages are spoken in the many countries of Europe.

Europe has a variety of climates, but has mostly mild weather. Mountain ranges, including the Pyrenees and the Alps, protect parts of the continent from cold winds from the north. Much of the coastal land is bathed in warm winds brought from the equator by the powerful Gulf Stream.

Much of Europe is covered by the Great European Plain, which has been turned into rich farmland. The Rhine, the Danube, and other rivers and canals make up a vast network of inland waterways.

Apennine Peninsula coastline

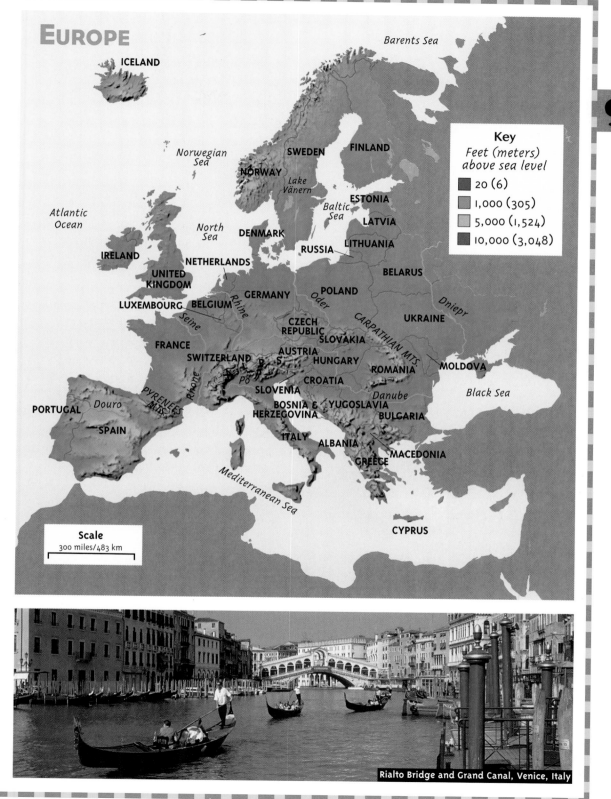

EUROPE

ICELAND

Barents Sea

Norwegian Sea

SWEDEN   FINLAND

NORWAY

Lake Vänern

ESTONIA

Baltic Sea

LATVIA

Atlantic Ocean

North Sea

DENMARK

LITHUANIA

RUSSIA

IRELAND

NETHERLANDS

BELARUS

UNITED KINGDOM

LUXEMBOURG   BELGIUM

GERMANY

Rhine

Oder

POLAND

Dniepr

UKRAINE

Seine

CZECH REPUBLIC

CARPATHIAN MTS

MOLDOVA

FRANCE

SLOVAKIA

SWITZERLAND

AUSTRIA   HUNGARY

ROMANIA

Rhone

Po

CROATIA

SLOVENIA

Danube

Black Sea

PYRENEES MTS

Douro

BOSNIA & HERZEGOVINA

YUGOSLAVIA

BULGARIA

PORTUGAL

SPAIN

ITALY

ALBANIA

MACEDONIA

GREECE

Mediterranean Sea

CYPRUS

Key
Feet (meters) above sea level
- 20 (6)
- 1,000 (305)
- 5,000 (1,524)
- 10,000 (3,048)

Scale
300 miles/483 km

Rialto Bridge and Grand Canal, Venice, Italy

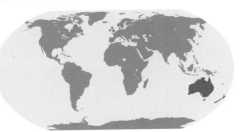

Australia

Australia is the smallest and flattest continent. It is the only continent that is also a country. Australia was once part of a super-continent called Gondwana. South America, Africa, India, Madagascar, New Zealand, and Antarctica were all part of Gondwana too. Australia broke free from Antarctica 150 million years ago. It slowly drifted north at a rate of 3 inches (7.6 cm) a year. Today, Australia is located completely within the Southern Hemisphere—between the Pacific and Indian oceans. It is about 7,000 miles (11,265 km) southwest of North America, and about

The Great Barrier Reef

HIGHLIGHTS OF AUSTRALIA

- Home of the world's largest coral reef, the Great Barrier Reef, which extends 1,250 miles (2,000 km) along the northeast coast of the continent.

- Home of 45 species of kangaroos.

- Home of Ayers Rock (called Uluru by Aborigines), a massive rock that stands in central Australia. It is about 1.5 miles (2.4 km) long and 1,000 feet (305 m) high, with many small caves. The rock is considered sacred by the Aborigines.

- Home of "three dog nights," an Aborigine term for nights in the desert that are so cold, one needs to curl up with three dogs in order to stay warm.

SIZING UP AUSTRALIA

Area:	2.9 million square miles (7.5 million sq km)
Coastline:	17,366 miles (27,948 km)
Greatest distances:	East to west: 2,475 miles (3,983 km) North to south: 1,950 miles (3,138 km)
Elevations:	Highest: Mount Kosciusko at 7,310 feet (2,228 m) Lowest: Lake Eyre at 52 feet (16 m) below sea level
Population:	16.9 million people

2,000 miles (3,218 km) southeast of mainland Asia.

Small, dry, and flat, Australia has been worn down by 3 billion years of exposure to rain and wind. Four great deserts cover the center of Australia: the Simpson, Gibson, Great Sandy, and Great Victoria deserts. These deserts are made up mostly of swirling sands that make giant dunes. Some dunes are more than 200 miles (322 km) long!

The first people to live in Australia were the Aborigines. They lived on this continent for thousands of years before settlers from England arrived in the 1700s. Today, people of Irish and British descent make up most of the population.

Kangaroo

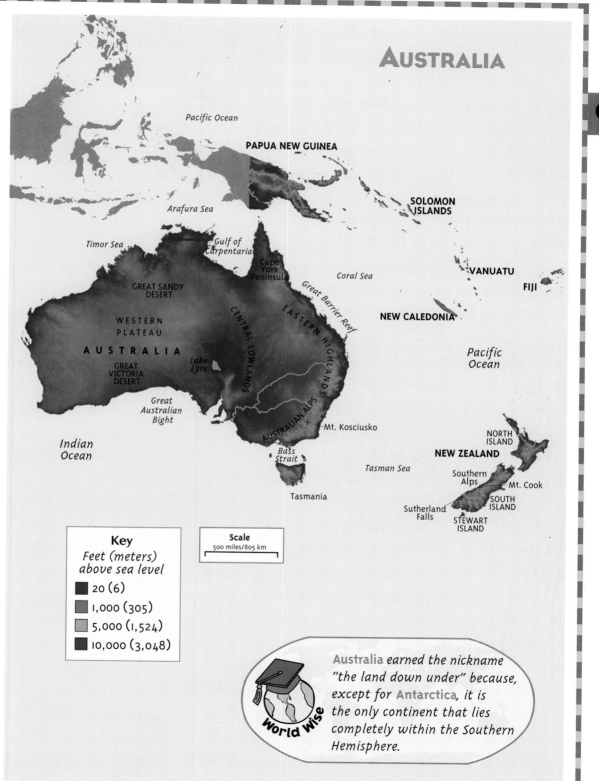

AUSTRALIA

Pacific Ocean

PAPUA NEW GUINEA

Arafura Sea

SOLOMON ISLANDS

Timor Sea

Gulf of Carpentaria

Cape York Peninsula

Coral Sea

VANUATU

FIJI

Great Barrier Reef

NEW CALEDONIA

GREAT SANDY DESERT

WESTERN PLATEAU

CENTRAL LOWLANDS

EASTERN HIGHLANDS

AUSTRALIA

Pacific Ocean

GREAT VICTORIA DESERT

Lake Eyre

Great Australian Bight

AUSTRALIAN ALPS

✕ Mt. Kosciusko

NORTH ISLAND

NEW ZEALAND

Indian Ocean

Bass Strait

Tasman Sea

Southern Alps

Mt. Cook

Tasmania

Sutherland Falls

SOUTH ISLAND

STEWART ISLAND

Key
Feet (meters) above sea level

- 20 (6)
- 1,000 (305)
- 5,000 (1,524)
- 10,000 (3,048)

Scale
500 miles/805 km

World Wise

Australia *earned the nickname "the land down under" because, except for* **Antarctica***, it is the only continent that lies completely within the Southern Hemisphere.*

Countries of the World

All of the land on Earth, except for Antarctica, has been claimed by a country. A country is a nation of people and the land on which they live. Every country has its own boundaries, government, name, and flag. The number of countries in the world is ever changing. Fifty years ago, there were 82 countries. By 1999, there were more than 190. How did this number change so quickly? Some countries, like East Timor, voted for independence from their mother country (Indonesia). Other countries, like Tibet, were taken over by larger countries, like China. One of the greatest changes in world countries took place in 1991, when the former Union of the Soviet Socialist Republics (U.S.S.R.) ceased to be and broke up into 15 smaller countries.

Antarctica is protected by a treaty among 42 different nations, which outlines how the continent is managed. The treaty was signed on December 1, 1959, and went into effect on June 23, 1961.

World Wise

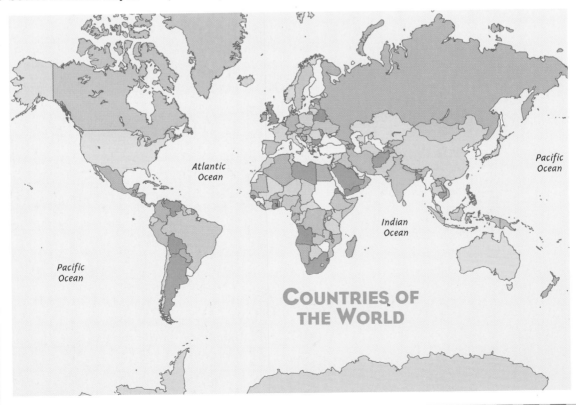

Atlantic Ocean

Pacific Ocean

Indian Ocean

Pacific Ocean

COUNTRIES OF THE WORLD

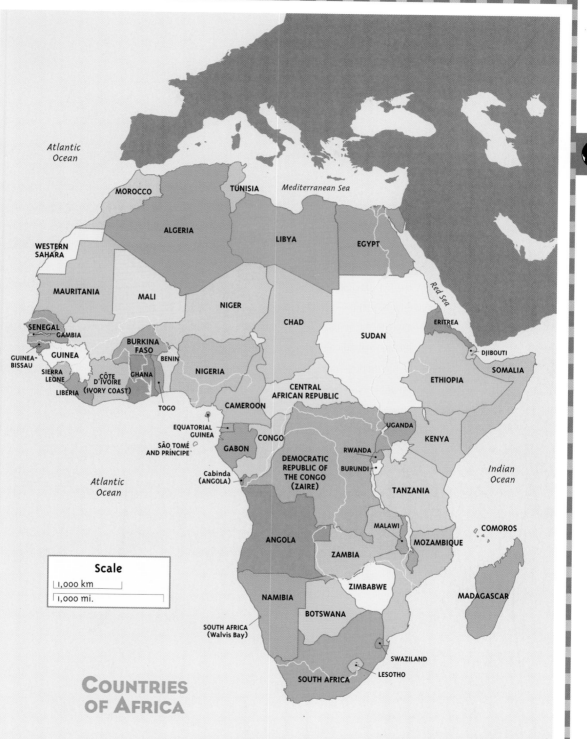

Atlantic
Ocean

MOROCCO

TUNISIA

Mediterranean Sea

ALGERIA

LIBYA

EGYPT

WESTERN
SAHARA

Red Sea

MAURITANIA

MALI

NIGER

CHAD

ERITREA

SENEGAL

SUDAN

DJIBOUTI

GAMBIA

BURKINA
FASO

GUINEA-
BISSAU

GUINEA

BENIN

SIERRA
LEONE

CÔTE
D'IVOIRE
(IVORY COAST)

GHANA

NIGERIA

CENTRAL
AFRICAN REPUBLIC

SOMALIA

ETHIOPIA

LIBERIA

TOGO

CAMEROON

EQUATORIAL
GUINEA

UGANDA

KENYA

SÃO TOMÉ
AND PRÍNCIPE

GABON

CONGO

RWANDA

Cabinda
(ANGOLA)

DEMOCRATIC
REPUBLIC OF
THE CONGO
(ZAIRE)

BURUNDI

TANZANIA

*Indian
Ocean*

Atlantic
Ocean

MALAWI

COMOROS

ANGOLA

ZAMBIA

MOZAMBIQUE

Scale

ZIMBABWE

MADAGASCAR

1,000 km

1,000 mi.

NAMIBIA

BOTSWANA

SOUTH AFRICA
(Walvis Bay)

SWAZILAND

**COUNTRIES
OF AFRICA**

SOUTH AFRICA

LESOTHO

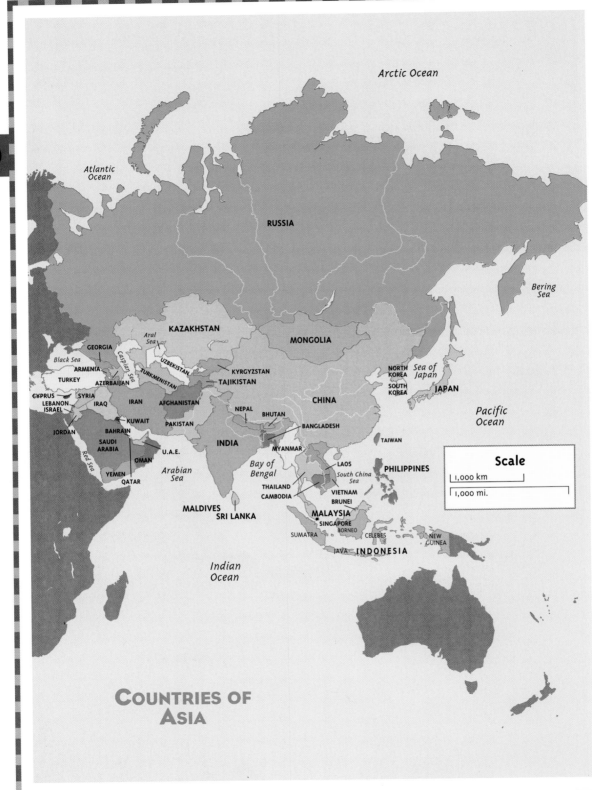

Arctic Ocean

Atlantic
Ocean

Bering
Sea

RUSSIA

KAZAKHSTAN

*Aral
Sea*

MONGOLIA

GEORGIA

Black Sea

ARMENIA

Caspian Sea

UZBEKISTAN

KYRGYZSTAN

NORTH
KOREA

*Sea of
Japan*

TURKEY

AZERBAIJAN

TURKMENISTAN

TAJIKISTAN

SOUTH
KOREA

JAPAN

CYPRUS

SYRIA

LEBANON
ISRAEL

IRAQ

IRAN

AFGHANISTAN

CHINA

Pacific
Ocean

JORDAN

KUWAIT

BAHRAIN

PAKISTAN

NEPAL

BHUTAN

Red Sea

SAUDI
ARABIA

U.A.E.

OMAN

INDIA

BANGLADESH

TAIWAN

YEMEN

QATAR

*Arabian
Sea*

MYANMAR

LAOS

PHILIPPINES

MALDIVES

SRI LANKA

*Bay of
Bengal*

THAILAND

CAMBODIA

*South China
Sea*

VIETNAM

BRUNEI

MALAYSIA

SINGAPORE

SUMATRA

BORNEO

CELEBES

NEW
GUINEA

*Indian
Ocean*

JAVA

INDONESIA

Scale

1,000 km

1,000 mi.

**COUNTRIES OF
ASIA**

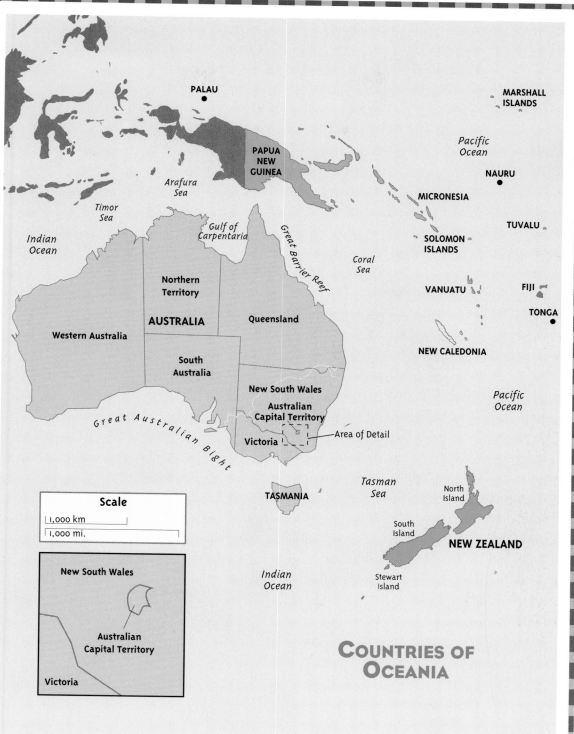

PALAU

MARSHALL
ISLANDS

*Pacific
Ocean*

PAPUA
NEW
GUINEA

NAURU

*Arafura
Sea*

MICRONESIA

*Timor
Sea*

SOLOMON
ISLANDS

TUVALU

*Indian
Ocean*

*Gulf of
Carpentaria*

*Coral
Sea*

Great Barrier Reef

Northern
Territory

VANUATU

FIJI

AUSTRALIA

Queensland

TONGA

Western Australia

South
Australia

NEW CALEDONIA

New South Wales

Australian
Capital Territory

*Pacific
Ocean*

Great Australian Bight

Victoria

Area of Detail

TASMANIA

*Tasman
Sea*

North
Island

Scale

| 1,000 km |
| 1,000 mi. |

South
Island

NEW ZEALAND

New South Wales

*Indian
Ocean*

Stewart
Island

Australian
Capital Territory

Victoria

**COUNTRIES OF
OCEANIA**

COUNTRIES OF EUROPE

ICELAND

NORWAY

SWEDEN

FINLAND

Atlantic
Ocean

North
Sea

Baltic
Sea

ESTONIA

LATVIA

LITHUANIA

DENMARK

UNITED
KINGDOM

IRELAND

1

GERMANY

POLAND

BELARUS

2

3

16

AUSTRIA

8

7

UKRAINE

FRANCE

4

HUNGARY

9

6

5

ROMANIA

ITALY

10

13

15

18

19

BULGARIA

TURKEY
(partial)

Black Sea

14

11

12

PORTUGAL

SPAIN

GREECE

17

Mediterranean
Sea

Red Sea

Key

1. NETHERLANDS
2. BELGIUM
3. LUXEMBOURG
4. SWITZERLAND
5. CROATIA
6. SLOVENIA
7. SLOVAKIA
8. CZECH REPUBLIC
9. MOLDOVA
10. BOSNIA & HERZEGOVINA

11. ALBANIA
12. MACEDONIA
13. YUGOSLAVIA (SERBIA & MONTENEGRO)
14. ANDORRA
15. MONACO
16. LIECHTENSTEIN
17. MALTA
18. SAN MARINO
19. HOLY SEE

Scale

1,000 km

1,000 mi.

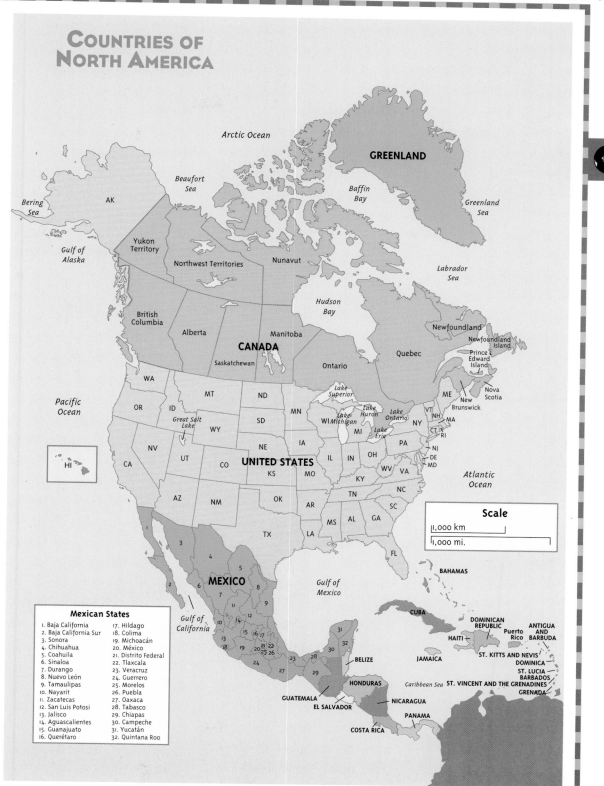

COUNTRIES OF NORTH AMERICA

Arctic Ocean

GREENLAND

Beaufort Sea

Baffin Bay

Greenland Sea

Bering Sea

AK

Gulf of Alaska

Yukon Territory

Northwest Territories

Nunavut

Labrador Sea

British Columbia

Alberta

Manitoba

CANADA

Saskatchewan

Hudson Bay

Newfoundland

Newfoundland Island

Ontario

Quebec

Prince Edward Island

Nova Scotia

Pacific Ocean

WA

MT

ND

Lake Superior

ME

New Brunswick

OR

ID

Great Salt Lake

WY

SD

MN

WI

Lake Michigan

Lake Huron

Lake Ontario

NY

VT

NH

MA

CT

RI

NV

UT

CO

NE

IA

MI

Lake Erie

PA

NJ

DE

MD

CA

UNITED STATES

KS

MO

IL

IN

OH

WV

VA

Atlantic Ocean

HI

AZ

NM

OK

AR

KY

TN

NC

SC

TX

LA

MS

AL

GA

Scale

|1,000 km|

|1,000 mi.|

FL

BAHAMAS

MEXICO

1

3

2

6

5

7

8

11

9

Gulf of Mexico

Gulf of California

10

14

12

13

15

16

17

18

19

20

21

25

22

26

24

23

28

31

32

30

29

27

CUBA

DOMINICAN REPUBLIC

HAITI

Puerto Rico

ANTIGUA AND BARBUDA

ST. KITTS AND NEVIS

JAMAICA

DOMINICA

ST. LUCIA

BARBADOS

BELIZE

ST. VINCENT AND THE GRENADINES

GRENADA

HONDURAS

Caribbean Sea

GUATEMALA

EL SALVADOR

NICARAGUA

PANAMA

COSTA RICA

Mexican States

1. Baja California
2. Baja California Sur
3. Sonora
4. Chihuahua
5. Coahuila
6. Sinaloa
7. Durango
8. Nuevo León
9. Tamaulipas
10. Nayarit
11. Zacatecas
12. San Luis Potosi
13. Jalisco
14. Aguascalientes
15. Guanajuato
16. Querétaro
17. Hildago
18. Colima
19. Michoacán
20. México
21. Distrito Federal
22. Tlaxcala
23. Veracruz
24. Guerrero
25. Morelos
26. Puebla
27. Oaxaca
28. Tabasco
29. Chiapas
30. Campeche
31. Yucatán
32. Quintana Roo

COUNTRIES OF SOUTH AMERICA

Caribbean Sea

TRINIDAD AND TOBAGO

VENEZUELA

GUYANA

FRENCH GUIANA

SURINAME

COLOMBIA

ECUADOR

PERU

BRAZIL

BOLIVIA

Pacific
Ocean

PARAGUAY

CHILE

Atlantic
Ocean

URUGUAY

ARGENTINA

Scale

1,000 km

1,000 mi.

FALKLAND
ISLANDS

Countries of the World (1999)

This handy guide will show you the world's countries, their capital cities, their location by continent, and the names given to their citizens.

COUNTRY	CAPITAL	CONTINENT	NATIONALITY
Afghanistan	Kabul	Asia	Afghan
Albania	Tirana	Europe	Albanian
Algeria	Algiers	Africa	Algerian
Andorra	Andorra la Vella	Europe	Andorran
Angola	Luanda	Africa	Angolan
Antigua and Barbuda	Saint John's	North America	Antiguan, Barbudan
Argentina	Buenos Aires	South America	Argentine
Armenia	Yerevan	Asia	Armenian
Australia	Canberra	Australia	Australian
Austria	Vienna	Europe	Austrian
Azerbaijan	Baku	Asia	Azerbaijani
Bahamas, The	Nassau	North America	Bahamian
Bahrain	Manama	Asia	Bahraini
Bangladesh	Dhaka	Asia	Bangaldeshi
Barbados	Bridgetown	North America	Barbadian
Belarus	Minsk	Europe	Belarusian
Belgium	Brussels	Europe	Belgian
Belize	Belmopan	North America	Belizean
Benin	Porto-Novo	Africa	Beninese
Bhutan	Thimphu	Asia	Bhutanese
Bolivia	La Paz; Sucre	South America	Bolivian
Bosnia and Herzegovina	Sarajevo	Europe	Bosnian, Herzegovinian
Botswana	Gaborone	Africa	Botswana
Brazil	Brasília	South America	Brazilian

Australian man

Austrian man

Butanese woman

Brazilian girl

Canadian man

Chinese woman

Croatian couple

COUNTRY	CAPITAL	CONTINENT	NATIONALITY
Brunei	Bandar Seri Begawan	Asia	Bruneian
Bulgaria	Sofia	Europe	Bulgarian
Burkina Faso	Ouagadougou	Africa	Burkinabe
Burundi	Bujumbura	Africa	Burundian
Cambodia	Phnom Penh	Asia	Cambodian
Cameroon	Yaoundé	Africa	Cameroonian
Canada	Ottawa	North America	Canadian
Cape Verde	Praia	Africa	Cape Verdean
Central African Republic	Bangui	Africa	Central African
Chad	N'Djamena	Africa	Chadian
Chile	Santiago	South America	Chilean
China	Beijing	Asia	Chinese
Colombia	Bogotá	South America	Colombian
Comoros	Moroni	Africa	Comoran
Congo, Democratic Republic of (Zaire)	Kinshasa	Africa	Congolese
Congo, Republic of	Brazzaville	Africa	José
Costa Rica	San José	North America	Costa Rican
Côte d'Ivoire	Abidjan; Yamoussoukro	Africa	Ivorian
Croatia	Zagreb	Europe	Croatian
Cuba	Havana	North America	Cuban
Cyprus	Nicosia	Europe	Cypriot
Czech Republic	Prague	Europe	Czech
Denmark	Copenhagen	Europe	Dane
Djibouti	Djibouti	Africa	Djiboutian
Dominica	Roseau	North America	Dominican
Dominican Republic	Santo Domingo	North America	Dominican
Ecuador	Quito	South America	Ecuadoran

COUNTRY	CAPITAL	CONTINENT	NATIONALITY
Egypt	Cairo	Africa	Egyptian
El Salvador	San Salvador	North America	Salvadoran
Equatorial Guinea	Malabo	Africa	Equatorial Guinean
Eritrea	Asmara	Africa	Eritrean
Estonia	Tallinn	Europe	Estonian
Ethiopia	Addis Ababa	Africa	Ethiopian
Fiji	Suva	Oceania	Fijian
Finland	Helsinki	Europe	Finn
France	Paris	Europe	French
Gabon	Libreville	Africa	Gabonese
Gambia, The	Banjul	Africa	Gambian
Georgia	T'bilisi	Asia	Georgian
Germany	Berlin	Europe	German
Ghana	Accra	Africa	Ghanaian
Greece	Athens	Europe	Greek
Grenada	St. George's	North America	Grenadian
Guatemala	Guatemala	North America	Guatemalan
Guinea	Conakry	Africa	Guinean
Guinea-Bissau	Bissau	Africa	Guinea-Bissauan
Guyana	Georgetown	South America	Guyanese
Haiti	Port-au-Prince	North America	Haitian
Holy See	Vatican City	Europe	
Honduras	Tegucigalpa	North America	Honduran
Hungary	Budapest	Europe	Hungarian
Iceland	Reykjavik	Europe	Icelander

Guatemalan man

Fijian couple

French man

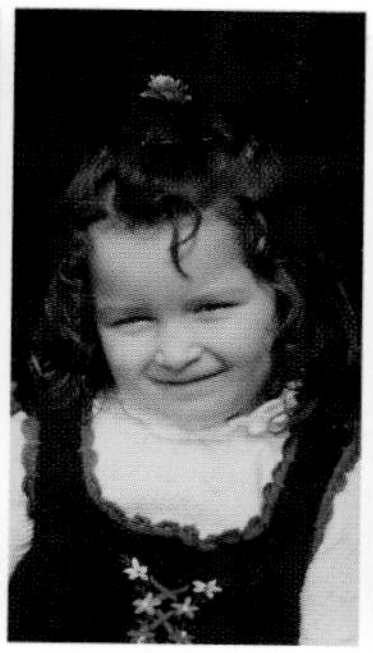

German girl

Greek man

Irish boy

Indian woman

Japanese woman

Kenyan man

COUNTRY	CAPITAL	CONTINENT	NATIONALITY
India	New Delhi	Asia	Indian
Indonesia	Jakarta	Asia	Indonesian
Iran	Tehran	Asia	Iranian
Iraq	Baghdad	Asia	Iraqi
Ireland	Dublin	Europe	Irish
Israel	Jerusalem	Asia	Israeli
Italy	Rome	Europe	Italian
Jamaica	Kingston	North America	Jamaican
Japan	Tokyo	Asia	Japanese
Jordan	Amman	Asia	Jordanian
Kazakhstan	Astana	Asia	Kazakhstani
Kenya	Nairobi	Africa	Kenyan
Kiribati	Tarawa	Oceania	I-Kiribati
Korea, North	P'yŏngyang	Asia	North Korean
Korea, South	Seoul	Asia	South Korean
Kuwait	Kuwait	Asia	Kuwaiti
Kyrgyzstan	Bishkek	Asia	Kyrgyz

Indonesian
child

I-Kiribati child

Korean man

Kuwaiti man

COUNTRY	CAPITAL	CONTINENT	NATIONALITY
Laos	Vientiane	Asia	Laotian
Latvia	Riga	Europe	Latvian
Lebanon	Beirut	Asia	Lebanese
Lesotho	Maseru	Africa	Basotho
Liberia	Monrovia	Africa	Liberian
Libya	Tripoli	Africa	Libyan
Liechtenstein	Vaduz	Europe	Liechtensteiner
Lithuania	Vilnius	Europe	Lithuanian
Luxembourg	Luxembourg	Europe	Luxembourger
Macedonia	Skopje	Europe	Macedonian
Madagascar	Antananarivo	Africa	Malagasy
Malawi	Lilongwe	Africa	Malawian
Malaysia	Kuala Lumpur	Asia	Malaysian
Maldives	Male	Asia	Maldivian
Mali	Bamako	Africa	Malian
Malta	Valletta	Europe	Maltese
Marshall Islands	Majuro	Oceania	Marshallese
Mauritania	Nouakchott	Africa	Mauritanian
Mauritius	Port Louis	Africa	Mauritian
Mexico	Mexico City	North America	Mexican
Micronesia	Palikir	Oceania	Micronesian
Moldova	Chisinau	Europe	Moldovan
Monaco	Monaco	Europe	Monacan
Mongolia	Ulaanbaatar	Asia	Mongolian
Morocco	Rabat	Africa	Moroccan

Malaysian man

Malian man

Mexican man

Moroccan man

Norwegian woman   Pakistani elder   Peruvian child   Filipino woman   Rwandan woman

COUNTRY	CAPITAL	CONTINENT	NATIONALITY
Mozambique	Maputo	Africa	Mozambican
Myanmar (Burma)	Yangon (Rangoon)	Asia	(Burmese)
Namibia	Windhoek	Africa	Namibian
Nauru	Yaren District	Oceania	Nauruan
Nepal	Kathmandu	Asia	Nepalese
Netherlands	Amsterdam	Europe	Dutch
New Zealand	Wellington	Oceania	New Zealander
Nicaragua	Managua	North America	Nicaraguan
Niger	Niamey	Africa	Nigerian
Nigeria	Abuja	Africa	Nigerian
Norway	Oslo	Europe	Norwegian
Oman	Muscat	Asia	Omani
Pakistan	Islamabad	Asia	Pakistani
Palau	Koror	Oceania	Palauan
Panama	Panama	North America	Panamanian
Papua New Guinea	Port Moresby	Oceania	Papua New Guinean
Paraguay	Ascunción	South America	Paraguayan
Peru	Lima	South America	Peruvian
Philippines	Manila	Asia	Filipino
Poland	Warsaw	Europe	Pole
Portugal	Lisbon	Europe	Portuguese
Qatar	Doha	Asia	Quatari
Romania	Bucharest	Europe	Romanian
Russia	Moscow	Europe and Asia	Russian
Rwanda	Kigali	Africa	Rwandan
St. Kitts and Nevis	Basseterre	North America	Kittsian; Nevian

COUNTRY	CAPITAL	CONTINENT	NATIONALITY
St. Lucia	Castries	North America	St. Lucian
St.Vincent and the Grenadines	Kingstown	North America	St. Vincentian
Samoa	Apia	Oceania	Samoan
San Marino	San Marino	Europe	San Marinese
São Tomé and Principe	São Tomé	Africa	São Toméan
Saudi Arabia	Riyadh	Asia	Saudi
Senegal	Dakar	Africa	Senegalese
Seychelles	Victoria	Africa	Seychellois
Sierra Leone	Freetown	Africa	Sierra Leonean
Singapore	Singapore	Asia	Singaporean
Slovakia	Bratislava	Europe	Slovak
Slovenia	Ljubljana	Europe	Slovene
Solomon Islands	Honiara	Oceania	Solomon Islander
Somalia	Mogadishu	Africa	Somali
South Africa	Pretoria*	Africa	South African
Spain	Madrid	Europe	Spanish
Sri Lanka	Colombo	Asia	Sri Lankan
Sudan	Khartoum	Africa	Sudanese
Suriname	Paramaribo	South America	Surinamer
Swaziland	Mbabane	Africa	Swazi
Sweden	Stockholm	Europe	Swedish
Switzerland	Bern	Europe	Swiss
Syria	Damascus	Asia	Syrian
Taiwan	Taipei	Asia	Chinese

*Administrative capital

Saudi man

Senegalese man

Singaporean woman

Swedish man

Thai woman

Tongan woman

Turkish man

Uzbek elder

Zimbabwean woman

COUNTRY	CAPITAL	CONTINENT	NATIONALITY
Tajikistan	Dushanbe	Asia	Tajik
Tanzania	Dar es Salaam	Africa	Tanzanian
Thailand	Bangkok	Asia	Thai
Togo	Lomé	Africa	Togolese
Tonga	Nuku'alofa	Oceania	Tongan
Trinidad and Tobago	Port-of-Spain	South America	Trinidadian; Tobagonian
Tunisia	Tunis	Africa	Tunisian
Turkey	Ankara	Asia and Europe	Turk
Turkmenistan	Ashgabat	Asia	Turkmen
Tuvalu	Funafuti	Oceania	Tuvaluan
Uganda	Kampala	Africa	Ugandan
Ukraine	Kiev	Europe	Ukrainian
United Arab Emirates	Abu Dhabi	Asia	Emirian
United Kingdom	London	Europe	Briton
United States	Washington, D.C.	North America	American
Uruguay	Montevideo	South America	Uraguayan
Uzbekistan	Tashkent	Asia	Uzbek
Vanuatu	Port-Vila	Oceania	Ni-Vanuatu
Venezuela	Caracas	South America	Venezuelan
Vietnam	Hanoi	Asia	Vietnamese
Yemen	Sanaa	Asia	Yemeni
Yugoslavia (Serbia and Montenegro)	Belgrade	Europe	Yugoslav; Serb; Montenegrin
Zambia	Lusaka	Africa	Zambian
Zimbabwe	Harare	Africa	Zimbabwean

THE NAME GAME

Most of us are familiar with the English names for countries, but how many of us know what certain countries call themselves? Here are 13 countries and their official names.

English Name	Official Name	English Name	Official Name
Albania	Shaiperi	Ireland	Hibernia
Belgium	Belgique	Israel	Yisrael
Ethiopia	Eritrea	Japan	Nippon
Germany	Deutschland	The Netherlands	Nederland
Greece	Hellas	Poland	Polska
Greenland	Kalatdlit-Nunat	Spain	España
India	Bharat		

COUNTRY NAME MEANINGS

Indus River

Albania means "white land" from the Latin *albus*, or white.

Argentina means "silvery" from the Latin *argentum*, or silver.

Australia is named for an ancient Greek mythical place, *Terra Australis*, or southern land.

Austria comes from *ostreich*, which means "eastern kingdom."

Belgium is named for the *Belgae*, a Celtic tribe, who were early inhabitants.

Bolivia is named for Simon Bolivar, a South American independence fighter.

Congo is from *kong*, which means "mountain" in Bantu.

India was named after the Indus River.

Ireland is from *Eire*, the country's Gaelic name.

Jamaica means "island of water springs" in the Arawak language.

Maldives is from the Sanskrit language. *Mal* means "thousand," and *diva* means "island."

Myanmar means "strong and honorable."

Pakistan means "land of the Paks, the spiritually pure and clean."

Sri Lanka means "splendid thing."

Tierra del Fuego means "the land of the fires." This island group was named by explorers at sea who first sighted land by the blaze of bonfires. Located at the tip of **South America**, Tierra del Fuego belongs partly to **Chile** and partly to **Argentina**.

Vatican City is from *vaticinatio*, which is Latin for "prophesy."

Venezuela means "little Venice," after Venice, a city in **Italy**.

Zimbabwe means both "dwelling place of a chief," and "a great stone building."

The Vatican

The name Pakistan was composed by a group of Cambridge University students from the names of their home-lands: Punjab, Afghania, Kashmir, Iran, Sindh, Tukharistan, Afghanistan, and Balochistan.

Old Names and New Names

As countries gained their independence from colonial or political power, they often changed their names. Here is a sampling of old and new names of the same places.

Old Name	New Name
British Guiana	Guyana
British Honduras	Belize
Burma	Myanmar
Ceylon	Sri Lanka
French Equatorial Africa	Gabon
New Hebrides	Vanuatu
Northern Rhodesia	Zambia
Malagasy Republic	Madagascar
Siam	Thailand
Zaire	Democratic Republic of the Congo

COUNTRY NICKNAMES

- **Canada**, the **United States** (**Alaska**), **Norway**, **Finland**, **Sweden**, **Greenland**, **Siberia**, **Russia**, and **Kazakhstan** are all in the "Land of the Midnight Sun." In this region, the sun does not set from late March to late September. These countries are located north of 60° north latitude.

- **India** was called "the Jewel in the Crown" by the British who controlled the country from 1757 to 1947.

- **Ireland** is called the "Emerald Isle" because it is an island country with an emerald green countryside. The green landscape results from the underlying limestone and frequent rains that bathe the country.

Himalayan mountains

- **Japan** is called the "Land of the Rising Sun," which is a transliteration of a Chinese phrase and a description of its location in the east, where the sun rises.

- **Tibet**, a former country, is now part of **China**. It is known as "the Rooftop of the World" because it is on a plateau 13,000 feet (4,000 m) above sea level in the Himalayan Mountains.

Irish countryside

Siam means "Land of the Sacred White Elephant." Today in Thailand (modern Siam) the white elephant is worshiped as sacred.

ANIMAL COUNTRY

Certain animals or breeds have been named after their country or place of origin.

Australian terrier

Irish setter

Tasmanian devil

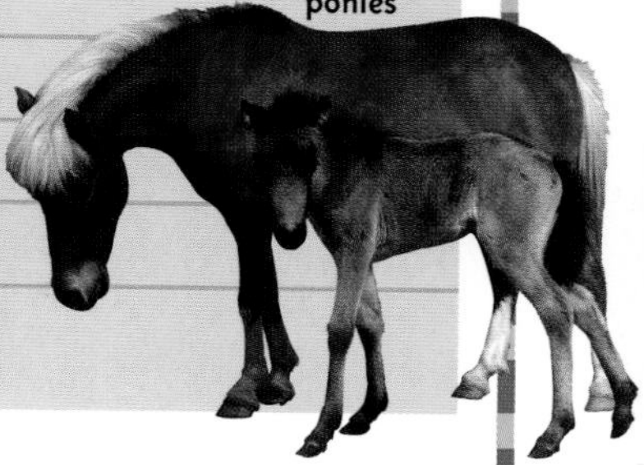

Shetland ponies

Animal	Country
Australian terrier	Australia
Bengal tiger	Bangladesh
German shepherd	Germany
Irish setter	Ireland
Irish wolfhound	Ireland
Japanese beetle	Japan
Komodo dragon	Indonesia, Komodo Island
Norwegian elkhound	Norway
Shetland pony	Scotland, Shetland Islands
Tasmanian devil	Australia, Tasmania Island
Tasmanian tiger	Australia, Tasmania Island

American Beauty rose

COUNTRY THINGS

You've probably seen a Hawaiian shirt, and it's likely that you've tasted Canadian bacon and French toast. These are common things with country names. Here are more:

Name	Object	Country
American Beauty	rose	United States of America
Australian crawl	swim stroke	Australia
Chinese lantern	paper light	China
English muffin	bread	England
French door	pair of middle-opening doors	France
German measles	viral disease	Germany
Irish moss	seaweed	Ireland
Swedish massage	massage technique	Sweden
Swiss dot	fabric	Switzerland
Turkish delight	candy	Turkey

Chinese lantern

SPORTING COUNTRIES

The following sports originated in these countries.

Baseball	United States
Basketball	United States
Bowling	Germany
Boxing	Italy (ancient Rome)
Chess	India
Cricket	England (United Kingdom)
Croquet	France
Football	United States
Golf	Scotland
Ice Hockey	Canada
Jai Alai	Mexico
Karate	Ryukyu Islands (east of China)
Lacrosse	Canada
Marathon running	Greece
Polo	Iran (ancient Persia)
Rugby	England (United Kingdom)
Soccer	England (United Kingdom)
Speed skating	Netherlands
Volleyball	United States
Water skiing	United States

*Both the highest golf course
and ski run in South America
are located in Bolivia*

World Wise

Chinese bicycles

Egyptian casket

COUNTRIES WITH THE MOST...

Bicycles	China	Over 130 million (30 million new ones each year)
Daily newspapers	India	800 printed in a variety of languages
Encyclopedias	China	11,000 volumes written 600 years ago
Islands	Indonesia	More than 13,000
Moviegoers	India	9 million tickets sold a day
Mummies	Egypt	10,000 in the Valley of the Golden Mummies near Cairo
Endangered treasures	Italy	57,000 treasures threatened by floods and earthquakes

COUNTRIES WITH THE LONGEST...

Fence	Australia	Sheep farmers built a dog fence 6,000 miles (9,600 km) long to keep dingoes, or wild dogs, out of sheep-grazing land.
Beach	Bangladesh	The beach extends 357 miles (575 km) along the coastline of the Bay of Bengal.
Coastline	Canada	Its 151,485-mile (243,791-km) coastline includes the mainland and the islands.
Place name	Bangkok, Thailand	The city's full name is Krungthep Mahanakhon Bovorn Ratanakosin Mahintharayutthaya Mahadilokpop Noparatratchathani Burirom Udomratchanivet Mahasathan Amornpiman Avatarnsathit Sakkathattiyavisnukarmprasit.

Coast of Canada

Chinese people

COUNTRIES WITH THE MOST PEOPLE

1. China — 1.23 billion
2. India — 970 million
3. United States — 268 million
4. Indonesia — 204 million
5. Brazil — 160 million
6. Russia — 147 million
7. Pakistan — 138 million
8. Japan — 126 million
9. Bangladesh — 122 million
10. Nigeria — 107 million

India is expected to surpass **China** as the most populous country by the year 2050.

World Wise

COUNTRIES WITH THE MOST LAND

In millions of square miles/(kilometers)
(area is rounded for comparison)

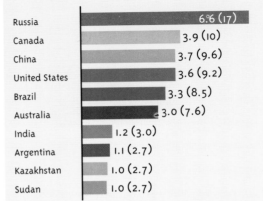

Country	Area
Russia	6.6 (17)
Canada	3.9 (10)
China	3.7 (9.6)
United States	3.6 (9.2)
Brazil	3.3 (8.5)
Australia	3.0 (7.6)
India	1.2 (3.0)
Argentina	1.1 (2.7)
Kazakhstan	1.0 (2.7)
Sudan	1.0 (2.7)

Source: CIA World Factbook

Canadian farmland

Key	
Inhabitants per square mile	*Inhabitants per square kilometer*
Under 2	Under 1
2–25	1–10
25–60	10–25
60–125	25–50
125–250	50–100
Over 250	Over 100

WORLD POPULATION DENSITY

Great Wall of China

COUNTRIES WITH THE MOST TOURISTS

These countries had the most visitors of all the countries of the world in 1998, according to a world organization for tourists.

1. France
2. United States
3. Spain
4. Italy
5. United Kingdom
6. China
7. Poland
8. Mexico
9. Canada
10. Austria

Louvre Museum, Paris, France

COUNTRIES WITH THE MOST SCHOOL DAYS PER YEAR

China	251 days
Japan	243 days
Korea	220 days
Israel	215 days
Germany	210 days
Russia	210 days
Switzerland	207 days
The Netherlands	200 days
The United States	180 days

Chinese schoolchildren

Countries with the Most Happy People

After 20 years of studying the happiness factor in people by country, social scientists have come up with the following results, which were printed in *The New York Times*, September 1999.

Irish girl

Top rank
Iceland, Ireland, Denmark, Finland, Norway, Netherlands, Sweden, Switzerland

Middle rank
Canada, Germany, France, Italy, United States

Bottom rank
Bangladesh, Nigeria, Portugal, Spain, Russia

Japanese woman at an ATM

COUNTRIES WITH THE MOST MONEY

This rating is based on having the world's highest income per person by country.

1. United States
2. Norway
3. Canada
4. Monaco
5. Luxembourg
6. United Arab Emirates
7. Australia
8. Liechtenstein
9. Denmark
10. Japan

COUNTRIES WITH THE LEAST MONEY

The people of these countries have the lowest incomes per person.

1. Congo
2. Rwanda
3. Ethiopia
4. Somalia
5. Eritrea
6. Bosnia and Herzegovina
7. Burundi
8. Chad
9. Mali
10. Niger

COUNTRIES WITH THE MOST MONEY IN EDUCATION

These countries spent the most money, in proportion to their economies, on education. (1995)

1. Botswana
2. Uzbekistan
3. Namibia
4. Tajikistan
5. Zimbabwe
6. Maldives
7. Denmark
8. Norway
9. Swaziland
10. Sweden

COUNTRIES WITH THE MOST TELEVISIONS

These countries have the most television sets per person.

1. United States
2. Monaco
3. Malta
4. Canada
5. El Salvador
6. Japan
7. Oman
8. France
9. Denmark
10. Germany

COUNTRIES IN WHICH WOMEN MOST OUTNUMBER MEN
Women per 100 men

- Latvia — 116.7
- Ukraine — 115.2
- Russia — 113.3
- Belarus — 112.9
- Estonia/Lithuania (2-way tie) — 112.5

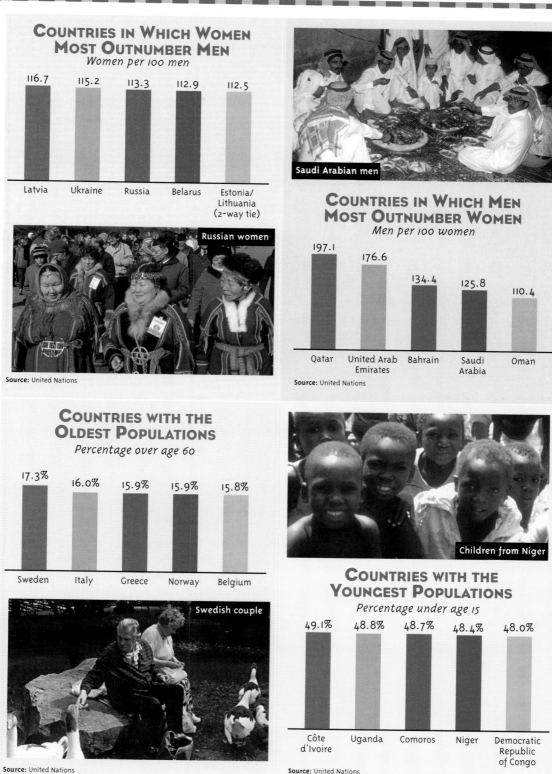

Saudi Arabian men

Russian women

Source: United Nations

COUNTRIES IN WHICH MEN MOST OUTNUMBER WOMEN
Men per 100 women

- Qatar — 197.1
- United Arab Emirates — 176.6
- Bahrain — 134.4
- Saudi Arabia — 125.8
- Oman — 110.4

Source: United Nations

COUNTRIES WITH THE OLDEST POPULATIONS
Percentage over age 60

- Sweden — 17.3%
- Italy — 16.0%
- Greece — 15.9%
- Norway — 15.9%
- Belgium — 15.8%

Swedish couple

Source: United Nations

Children from Niger

COUNTRIES WITH THE YOUNGEST POPULATIONS
Percentage under age 15

- Côte d'Ivoire — 49.1%
- Uganda — 48.8%
- Comoros — 48.7%
- Niger — 48.4%
- Democratic Republic of Congo — 48.0%

Source: United Nations

Country Neighbors

When countries have common borders, they are considered neighbors. Consider these facts about the world's neighbors.

China and Russia

These countries have the most neighbors, each with 14.

Russia's 13 neighbors are: Azerbaijan, Belarus, China, Estonia, Finland, Georgia, Kazakhstan, Latvia, Lithuania, Mongolia, North Korea, Norway, Poland, and Ukraine.

China's 13 neighbors are: Afghanistan, Bhutan, India, Kazakhstan, Kyrgyzstan, Laos, Mongolia, Myanmar, Nepal, North Korea, Russia, Tajikistan, and Vietnam.

There are 42 landlocked countries in the world.

South Pacific

The South Pacific is home to a large group of islands. These island neighbors have the Pacific Ocean as their common border: American Samoa, Australia, Fiji, French Polynesia, Guam, Indonesia, Japan, Kiribati, Marshall Islands, Micronesia, Nauru, New Caledonia, New Zealand, Northern Mariana Islands, Palau, Papua New Guinea, Pitcairn Islands, Singapore, Solomon Islands, Taiwan, Tonga, Tuvalu, Vanuatu, and Western Samoa.

Liechtenstein and Uzbekistan

These are two double-landlocked countries. A double-landlocked country is one that is completely surrounded by other landlocked countries. In other words, at least two countries block it from an ocean or bay on all sides.

Canada and the United States

These countries have the longest border between world neighbors. The border runs on the 49° north line of latitude. It is 2,635 miles (4,250 km) long.

All continent names begin and end with the same letter: America (North and South), Asia, Australia, Antarctica, Africa, and Europe.

Peninsular Neighbors

A peninsula is a piece of land that projects into a body of water and is connected to the mainland by an isthmus (a narrow strip of land). These countries are neighbors within peninsulas.

Arabian Peninsula

This peninsula is made up mainly of desert lands. Saudi Arabia occupies most of the peninsula. Its neighbors are Yemen, Oman, United Arab Emirates, Qatar, and Kuwait.

Balkan Peninsula

The Balkans are in the southeast corner of Europe. Albania, Bulgaria, Croatia, Bosnia, Macedonia, Serbia and Montenegro (Republic of Yugoslavia), mainland Greece, and part of Turkey make up these peninsular neighbors.

The Balkans are called "the powder keg of Europe" because of the many wars that began there.

Iberian Peninsula

Spain and Portugal occupy this peninsula. The Iberians were one of the oldest groups of people in Europe. The word *Iberian* is still used to describe literature and other aspects of the people of Spain and Portugal.

The countries of Norden include Denmark, Norway, Sweden, Iceland, and Finland—where Scandinavian people live.

Scandinavian Peninsula

Norway and Sweden are located on this peninsula. However, the term *Scandinavian* also refers to nearby Denmark.

FROM EMPIRE TO COUNTRY

Have you ever wondered where in the world ancient empires were located? This chart will help you put those empires in their places. It gives the current names of most of the countries within the boundaries of ancient empires.

Ancient Empire	Current Country Names	Time Frame
Aztec	Central and south Mexico	A.D. 1300 to 1500
Inca	Colombia, Ecuador, Peru, Bolivia, Chile, and Argentina	A.D. 1300 to 1500
Maya	Mexico, Guatemala, Honduras, El Salvador, and Belize	A.D. 250 to 900
Mongol	Cambodia, China, Russia, Iran, Korea, Thailand, Vietnam, Burma, Turkestan, Armenia, and India	A.D. 1200 to 1700
Roman	United Kingdom, Netherlands, Belgium, France, Spain, Portugal, Italy, Greece, Romania, Turkey, Syria, Lebanon, Israel, Egypt, and parts of northern Africa.	275 B.C. to A.D. 476

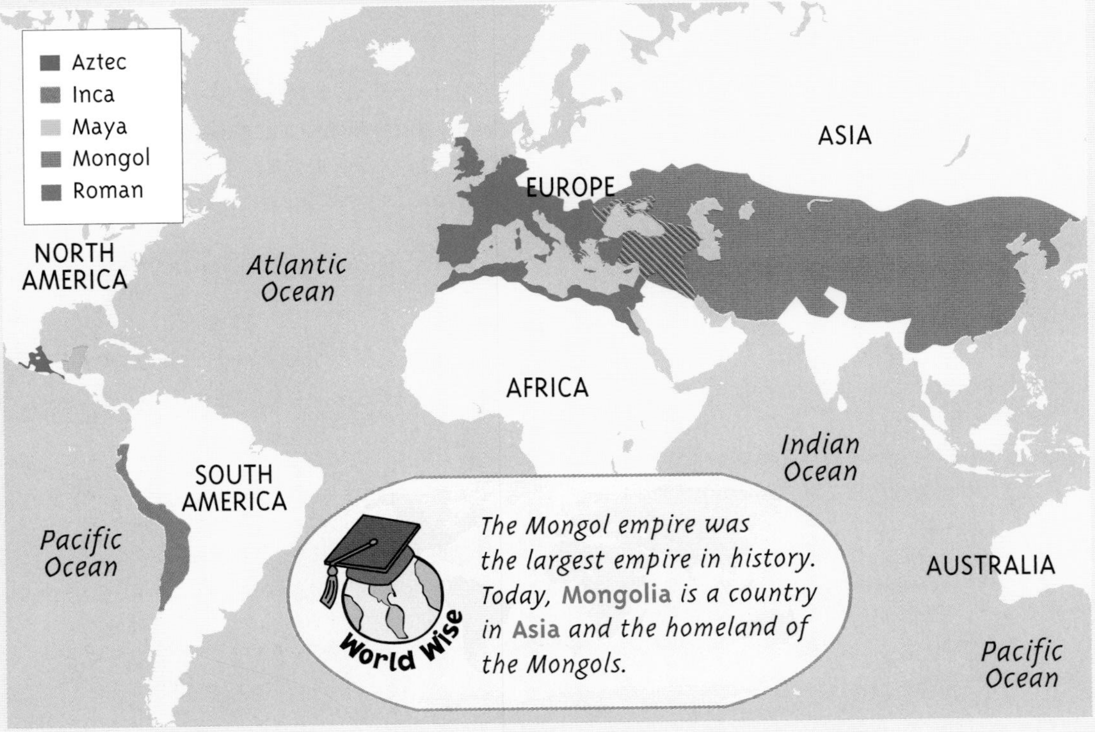

Legend:
- Aztec
- Inca
- Maya
- Mongol
- Roman

NORTH AMERICA
Atlantic Ocean
EUROPE
ASIA
AFRICA
Indian Ocean
SOUTH AMERICA
Pacific Ocean
AUSTRALIA
Pacific Ocean

World Wise

The Mongol empire was the largest empire in history. Today, Mongolia is a country in Asia and the homeland of the Mongols.

Country Confusion?

Several countries have recently divided into new nations. Some are still the same, but a bit confusing. The following are some of those easily confused countries.

Wales, U.K.

United Kingdom (U.K.)

The country that is called the United Kingdom consists of England, Scotland, and Wales, which together make up the island of Great Britain. It also includes Northern Ireland, which is part of the island of Ireland. The Republic of Ireland, or Ireland, is a separate country.

The suffix -stan means "country" in Hindu and Persian.

U.S.S.R.: From one country to many

After 69 years as the Union of Soviet Socialist Republics (U.S.S.R.), this nation broke up into 15 countries in 1991. Those countries are: **Russia, Kazakhstan, Kyrgyzstan, Tajikistan, Uzbekistan, Turkmenistan, Azerbaijan, Armenia, Georgia, Moldova, Ukraine, Belarus, Lithuania, Latvia,** and **Estonia.**

Armenia

Berlin Wall

BREAKS AND BONDS

- The former country of Czechoslovakia divided into the Czech Republic and Slovakia in 1993.
- Tanganyika and Zanzibar united to become Tanzania in 1964.
- In 1990, the Berlin Wall was torn down, and East Germany and West Germany united to form Germany.
- Serbia and Montenegro is the official name of the Federal Republic of Yugoslavia, which was created in 1992 by the union of Serbia and Montenegro.

Daily Planet
(Calendar of World Events)

Earth is a busy place. Every day people celebrate and commemorate holidays and events everywhere on the planet.

The most widely adopted system for keeping track of months and days is known as the Gregorian calendar. It was named after Pope Gregory XIII, who decreed this calendar in the 16th century. His system was first adopted by countries in Europe. These governments spread its use to many places around the world.

World Wise

A century is made up of 100 consecutive calendar years. The 1st century consists of years 1 through 100. The 20th century was made up of years 1901 through December 31, 2000. The 21st century technically begins January 1, 2001.

Eventually, most nations adopted the Gregorian calendar for official purposes. However, many cultures and religions mark time with their traditional calendars. Here you can find a daily guide to worldwide events.

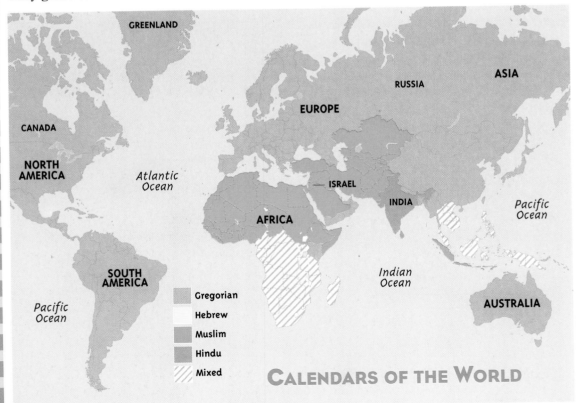

GREENLAND

ASIA

RUSSIA

EUROPE

CANADA

NORTH AMERICA

Atlantic Ocean

ISRAEL

INDIA

Pacific Ocean

AFRICA

SOUTH AMERICA

Indian Ocean

AUSTRALIA

Pacific Ocean

- Gregorian
- Hebrew
- Muslim
- Hindu
- Mixed

CALENDARS OF THE WORLD

MONTHS OF THE YEAR

Gregorian	Hebrew	Hindu	Muslim
January	Shebat	Magha	Muharram
February	Adar	Phalguna	Safar
March	Nisan	Caitra	Rabi I
April	Iyar	Vaisakha	Rabi II
May	Sivan	Jyaistha	Jumada I
June	Tammuz	Asadha	Jumada II
July	Av	Sravana	Rajab
August	Elul	Bhadra	Shaban
September	Tishri	Asvina	Ramadan
October	Heshvan	Karitka	Shawwal
November	Kislev	Agrahayana	Dhu'l-Qa'dah
December	Tebet	Pausa	Dhu'l-hijjah

PERIODS OF TIME

Term	Definition	Term	Definition
annual	yearly		
bi-annual	twice a year (at unequally spaced intervals)		
bicentennial	marking a period of 200 years		
bi-ennial	marking a period of two years	quinquennial	marking a period of five years
bimonthly	every two months; twice a month	semi-annual	every six months
biweekly	every two weeks; twice a week	semicentennial	marking a period of 50 years
centennial	marking a period of 100 years	semidiurnal	twice a day
decennial	marking a period of 10 years	semiweekly	twice a week
diurnal	daily; of a day	septennial	marking a period of seven years
duodecennial	marking a period of 12 years	sesquicentennial	marking a period of 150 years
millennial	marking a period of 1,000 years	sexennial	marking a period of six years
novennial	marking a period of nine years	thrice weekly	three times a week
octennial	marking a period of eight years	tricennial	marking a period of 30 years
perennial	occurring year after year	tri-ennial	marking a period of three years
quadrennial	marking a period of four years	trimonthly	every three months
quadricentennial	marking a period of 400 years	triweekly	every three weeks; three times a week
quincentennial	marking a period of 500 years	undecennial	marking a period of 11 years
quindecennial	marking a period of 15 years	vicennial	marking a period of 20 years

January

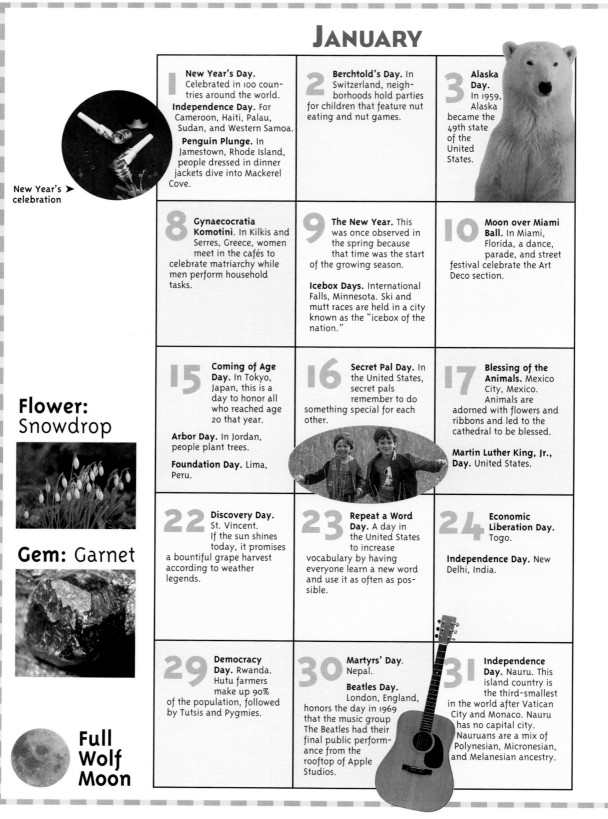

New Year's ➤ celebration

1 New Year's Day. Celebrated in 100 countries around the world.
Independence Day. For Cameroon, Haiti, Palau, Sudan, and Western Samoa.
Penguin Plunge. In Jamestown, Rhode Island, people dressed in dinner jackets dive into Mackerel Cove.

2 Berchtold's Day. In Switzerland, neighborhoods hold parties for children that feature nut eating and nut games.

3 Alaska Day. In 1959, Alaska became the 49th state of the United States.

8 Gynaecocratia Komotini. In Kilkis and Serres, Greece, women meet in the cafés to celebrate matriarchy while men perform household tasks.

9 The New Year. This was once observed in the spring because that time was the start of the growing season.
Icebox Days. International Falls, Minnesota. Ski and mutt races are held in a city known as the "icebox of the nation."

10 Moon over Miami Ball. In Miami, Florida, a dance, parade, and street festival celebrate the Art Deco section.

Flower: Snowdrop

15 Coming of Age Day. In Tokyo, Japan, this is a day to honor all who reached age 20 that year.
Arbor Day. In Jordan, people plant trees.
Foundation Day. Lima, Peru.

16 Secret Pal Day. In the United States, secret pals remember to do something special for each other.

17 Blessing of the Animals. Mexico City, Mexico. Animals are adorned with flowers and ribbons and led to the cathedral to be blessed.
Martin Luther King, Jr., Day. United States.

Gem: Garnet

22 Discovery Day. St. Vincent. If the sun shines today, it promises a bountiful grape harvest according to weather legends.

23 Repeat a Word Day. A day in the United States to increase vocabulary by having everyone learn a new word and use it as often as possible.

24 Economic Liberation Day. Togo.
Independence Day. New Delhi, India.

29 Democracy Day. Rwanda. Hutu farmers make up 90% of the population, followed by Tutsis and Pygmies.

30 Martyrs' Day. Nepal.
Beatles Day. London, England, honors the day in 1969 that the music group The Beatles had their final public performance from the rooftop of Apple Studios.

31 Independence Day. Nauru. This island country is the third-smallest in the world after Vatican City and Monaco. Nauru has no capital city. Nauruans are a mix of Polynesian, Micronesian, and Melanesian ancestry.

Full Wolf Moon

JANUARY

4 Independence Day. Myanmar. A celebration of freedom from British rule. The country's name change reflects the many ethnic groups who, along with the Burmans, populate the Union of Myanmar.

5 Black and White Carnival Popayan. In Colombia, people celebrate the racial diversity of the Three Wise Men by smearing themselves in black grease. The following day they cover themselves in white flour or powder.

6 Hashigo-nori. In Tokyo, Japan, firemen dress in traditional clothing of the Edo period and perform acrobatic stunts on tall ladders.

Children's Day. Uruguay.

7 Panama Canal Day. For the United States and Panama, a commemoration of the building of the Panama Canal.

Panama Canal ➤

11 Republic Day. Albania.

Unification Day. Nepal.

12 Revolution Day. Tanzania.

13 Liberation Day. Togo.

Saint Knut's Day. Sweden. The end of the Christmas season is marked by parties to dismantle Christmas trees.

14 Hindu Harvest Festival Day. India. Farmers put aside grain to appease any bad spirits that may be in the harvest.

18 Polar Bear Jump-Off. In Seward, Alaska, people participate in ice bowling and dog weight-pulling contests, plus a plunge into Resurrection Bay.

19 Tamborrada. In San Sebastian, Spain, a Procession of Drummers fiesta begins at midnight on the 19th and ends at midday on the 20th.

20 Award Day. Mali.

Babin Day. In Bulgaria, women who help deliver babies are called babins, or grandmothers. Parents give flowers to babins on this day.

21 Altagracia Day. The people of the Dominican Republic celebrate with processions to the shrine of St. Altagracia.

25 International Snow Sculpture. In Breckenridge, Colorado, teams from Austria to Singapore compete.

26 Australia Day. Australia.

Liberation Day. Uganda.

Republic Day. India. *Bharat* is the official name for the Union of India.

27 Apollo I spacecraft fire. 1967.

Mozart's Birthday. This leading classical composer was born in 1756.

28 Vietnam Day. In Vietnam, *Tet,* or first day, marks the new year. New Year's trees are brought into homes to ward off evil spirits.

◄ Sydney, Australia

FEBRUARY

Flower:
Violet

Gem:
Amethyst

Full Old Moon

1 **National Freedom Day.** United States. Slavery was abolished in the United States in 1865 with the 13th Amendment to the Constitution.

2 **Candlemas Day.** A Christian feast at which candles are blessed.

Groundhog Day. The city of Punxsutawney, Pennsylvania, celebrates the legend of the groundhog emerging from its burrow (see below).

Heroes Day. Mozambique.

3 **Independence Day.** Sri Lanka.

8 **Culture Day.** Slovenia.

Revolution Anniversary. Iraq.

Youth Day. Congo.

9 **Feast of St. Maron.** Lebanon. Apples, cherries, grapes, lemons, oranges, and peaches are the fruits of Lebanon and are eaten on feast days.

10 **Feast of St. Paul's Shipwreck.** Malta.

Pero Palo Festival. In Caceres, Spain, a dummy of the devil is beaten by dancing villagers.

15 **Chinese Spring Festival.** Mauritius.

Folklore Day. South Korea.

Revolution Day. Iran.

16 **Lantern Festival.** In Taiwan, this festival occurs on the full moon of the first lunar month when celestial spirits are about and easily seen by lantern light.

17 **Geronimo Day.** Geronimo, an Apache leader who fought to prevent his people from being put on reservations, was born in 1829 in the United States.

22 **Independence Day.** St. Lucia.

Union Day. Egypt.

23 **National Day.** Brunei.

Republic Day. Guyana.

24 **Buergsonndeg.** On this day in Luxembourg, young people build bonfires in the countryside to celebrate the sun.

29 **Leap Year.** February has 29 days once every four years.

◀ Groundhogs

FEBRUARY

4 **Constitution Day.** Mexico.

5 **President's Day.** Congo.

Meteorologists Day. United States. The first U.S. weatherperson, John Jeffries, was born in Boston in 1774.

6 **Great Sami (Lapp) Winter Fair.** The people of Jokkmokk, Sweden, celebrate a 400-year-old reindeer festival (see below).

Waitangi Day. New Zealand commemorates the treaty signed by the Maoris and Great Britain.

7 **Independence Day.** Grenada.

11 **National Foundation Day.** Japan.

Youth Day. Cameroon.

12 **Lost Penny Day.** United States. In honor of the birth in 1809 of Abraham Lincoln (who appears on a penny), people collect pennies for worthy causes.

13 **White Turf.** This annual horse race is held on snow in St. Moritz, Switzerland.

14 **Valentine's Day.** Celebrated in various European and North American countries by exchanging love tokens.

18 **Independence Day.** Gambia. Gambia is one of Africa's smallest countries. It exports peanuts to the world. Rice, grown only by Gambian women, is an important family food.

National Day. Nepal.

19 **Nicholas Copernicus's Birthday.** Celebrates the astronomer, born in 1473, who stated that Earth revolved around the sun.

20 **Celtic Flame Festival.** A national festival of music and song is celebrated in Cork and Kilkenny, Ireland.

21 **Shaheed Day** (Martyrs' Day). Bangladesh.

Presidents' Day. Third Monday of the month honors U.S. presidents Washington and Lincoln.

◀ Lincoln

25 **People Power Day.** Philippines. Filipinos celebrate the overthrow of President Ferdinand Marcos in 1986.

26 **Grand Canyon National Day.** Commemorates the first national park established in the United States, in 1919 (see below).

27 **Independence Day.** Dominican Republic. Located on the eastern part of the island of Hispaniola, it shares the island with the country of Haiti.

28 **Kalevala Day.** A Finnish national holiday that honors the *Kalevala*, the epic poem of Finland.

◀ Grand Canyon, Arizona

MARCH

Flower:
Daffodil

Gem:
Aquamarine

Full Crust Moon

1 **Procession of the Swallow.** In Greece, children in villages fill baskets with ivy leaves for the swallows.
Independence Day. South Korea.
Heroes' Day. Paraguay.
National Pig Day. United States.

2 **Peasants' Day.** Burma.
Festival of Colors (also called Holi). Celebrated in late February or early March, in India. People smear one another with colored powders to celebrate the triumph of good over evil.

3 **Independence Day.** Morocco.
Discovery Day. Guam.
Liberation Day. Bulgaria.
National Unity Day. Sudan.
Girls' Day (Hina Matsuri). A national festival of dolls in Japan.

8 **International Woman's Day.** In Russia, this national holiday is marked by giving gifts and flowers for working women.
Youth Day. Zambia.
Decoration Day. Liberia.

9 **Commonwealth Day.** Gibraltar. Located on the tip of Spain, the Rock of Gibraltar is a huge limestone rock that takes up most of the land.

10 **Labor Day.** South Korea. A holiday for farmers, fishers, factory workers, and other workers.

15 **Ides of March.** Julius Caesar was assassinated in Rome in 44 B.C. Ides was a day near the middle of the month in the old Roman calendar.
Buzzard's Day. The annual return of the buzzards to Hinckley, Ohio.

16 **Saint Urho's Day.** The patron saint of Finland, who reportedly drove the grasshoppers out of the country, is honored.

17 **St. Patrick's Day.** Ireland, Canada, and the United States celebrate the patron saint of Ireland, who drove the snakes out of the country, according to legend.

22 **Tulip Day.** In Lisse, the Netherlands, millions of tulips bloom in Keukenhof Gardens.

23 **Pakistan Day.** Pakistan.

24 **Africa Day.** Zambia.

29 **Boganda Day.** Central African Republic. In honor of Barthelemy Boganda, the country's first prime minister who died in an air accident in 1959.

30 **Seward's Day.** The United States celebrates its purchase of Alaska from Russia on this day in 1867.

31 **Freedom Day.** Malta.

MARCH

4 **Constitution Day.** United States.

March 4 Yourself Day. United States. A day to march wherever you go to show determination and personal responsibility.

5 **Atlas Day.** Mercator Gerhardus, who first called a collection of maps an *atlas*, was born in 1512. Atlas was a Greek god shown holding Earth on his shoulders.

6 **Independence Day.** Ghana.

Victory Day. Ethiopia.

7 **Burbank Day.** Luther Burbank, the botanist who bred more than 800 kinds of plants, was born in the United States in 1849.

11 **National Day.** Lithuania.

12 **Independence Day.** Mauritius.
Canberra Day. The official birthday of the capital of Australia, celebrated with a hot-air balloon fiesta (see below).
Elephant Festival. A procession of elephants in Jaipur, India.

13 **National Day.** Grenada. Located in the Caribbean Sea, this island nation grows nutmeg, mace, and other spices.

14 **Albert Einstein Day.** International birthday celebration for the German-Swiss-American physicist born in 1879.

◄ **Einstein**

18 **International Kite Festival.** This event is held yearly in Bangkok, Thailand. The festivities include kite-flying contests and competitions for kite design and painting.

19 **Las Fallas de San José.** At the stroke of midnight, gigantic cardboard caricatures of politicians, movie stars, and demons are set on fire in the streets of Valencia, Spain.

20 **Independence Day.** Tunisia. The northernmost country in Africa, Tunisia, won independence from France in 1956.

21 **Vernal Equinox.** In Chichen Itza, Mexico, a shadow serpent descends the steps of the Inca pyramid of Kukulkan, marking the beginning of spring. In Mexico City, thousands gather at the Aztec Pyramid of the Sun at dawn to welcome spring (see below).

25 **Independence Day.** Greece.

26 **Independence Day.** Bangladesh. In 1971, East Pakistan separated from West Pakistan and became the independent country of Bangladesh.

27 **Victory Day.** Angola. Marks the end of a bloody civil war in Angola.

28 **Teacher's Day.** Czech Republic. Teachers are honored in a country where nearly all people can read and write.

◄ **Pyramid of the Sun, Mexico**

Hot-air balloons, Australia ►

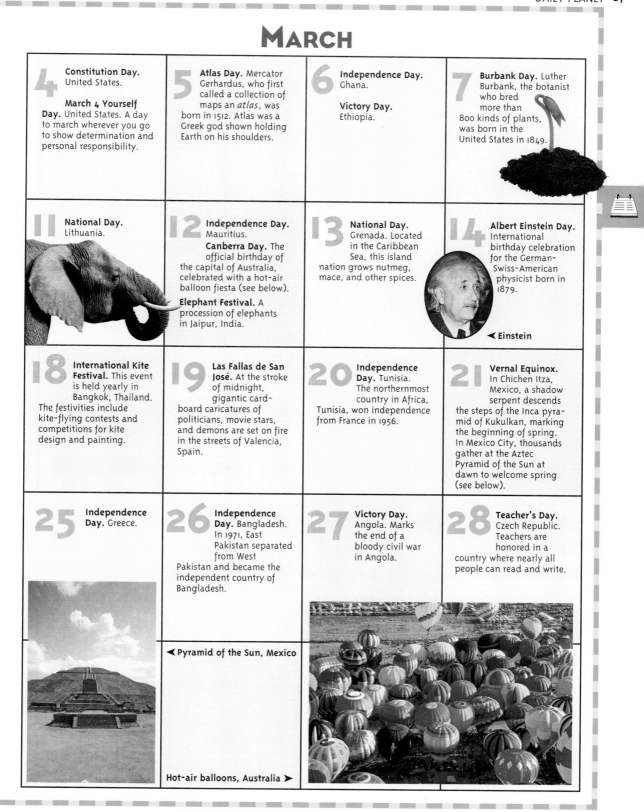

APRIL

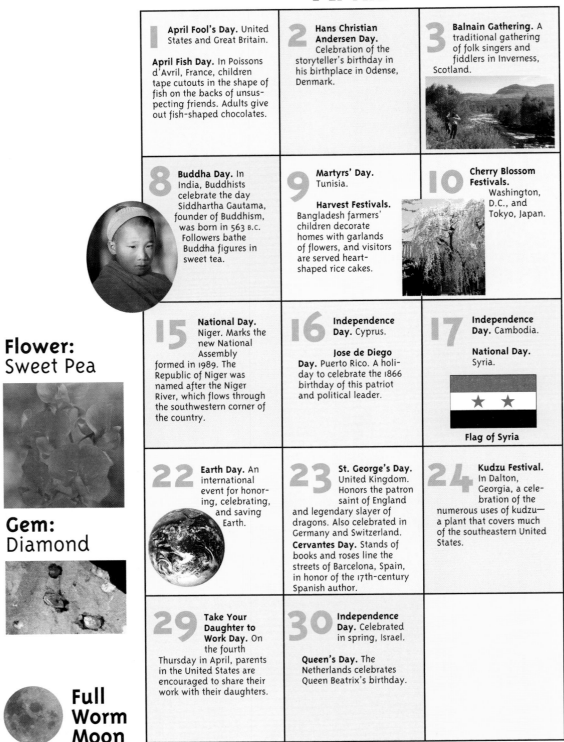

1 April Fool's Day. United States and Great Britain.

April Fish Day. In Poissons d'Avril, France, children tape cutouts in the shape of fish on the backs of unsuspecting friends. Adults give out fish-shaped chocolates.

2 Hans Christian Andersen Day. Celebration of the storyteller's birthday in his birthplace in Odense, Denmark.

3 Balnain Gathering. A traditional gathering of folk singers and fiddlers in Inverness, Scotland.

8 Buddha Day. In India, Buddhists celebrate the day Siddhartha Gautama, founder of Buddhism, was born in 563 B.C. Followers bathe Buddha figures in sweet tea.

9 Martyrs' Day. Tunisia.

Harvest Festivals. Bangladesh farmers' children decorate homes with garlands of flowers, and visitors are served heart-shaped rice cakes.

10 Cherry Blossom Festivals. Washington, D.C., and Tokyo, Japan.

15 National Day. Niger. Marks the new National Assembly formed in 1989. The Republic of Niger was named after the Niger River, which flows through the southwestern corner of the country.

16 Independence Day. Cyprus.

Jose de Diego Day. Puerto Rico. A holiday to celebrate the 1866 birthday of this patriot and political leader.

17 Independence Day. Cambodia.

National Day. Syria.

Flag of Syria

22 Earth Day. An international event for honoring, celebrating, and saving Earth.

23 St. George's Day. United Kingdom. Honors the patron saint of England and legendary slayer of dragons. Also celebrated in Germany and Switzerland.

Cervantes Day. Stands of books and roses line the streets of Barcelona, Spain, in honor of the 17th-century Spanish author.

24 Kudzu Festival. In Dalton, Georgia, a celebration of the numerous uses of kudzu—a plant that covers much of the southeastern United States.

29 Take Your Daughter to Work Day. On the fourth Thursday in April, parents in the United States are encouraged to share their work with their daughters.

30 Independence Day. Celebrated in spring, Israel.

Queen's Day. The Netherlands celebrates Queen Beatrix's birthday.

Flower:
Sweet Pea

Gem:
Diamond

Full Worm Moon

APRIL

4 **Tomb Sweeping Day.** In Taipei, Taiwan, families tend the graves of their ancestors and make offerings of food and wine.

5 **Arbor Day.** South Korea.

Burial of the Sardine. People in Spain celebrate this holiday on Ash Wednesday. It symbolizes the burial of worldly joys during Lent.

6 **Ougadi Day.** In Mauritius, this day commemorates the end of slavery in 1833.

Founders Day. South Africa.

7 **Women's Day.** Mozambique.

World Health Day.

11 **Heroes Day.** Costa Rica.

Liberation Day. Uganda.

12 **Songkran Festival.** The old Thai lunar New Year starts in the new moon of this month. Celebrations include throwing water on passersby.

13 **National Day.** Chad.

Demon Dances. In Kyoto, Japan, processions and dancing take place to ward off sickness at the Imamiya Shrine.

14 **Fast and Prayer Day.** Liberia.

Pan American Day. Honduras. A day set aside to foster friendly economic and cultural links with other Central and South American countries.

18 **Independence Day.** Zimbabwe.

19 **King's Birthday.** Swaziland.

Republic Day. Sierra Leone.

20 **Feria de Abril.** A festival with horses, traditional dress, bullfights, and flamenco dancing in Seville, Spain (see below).

21 **Shellfish Gathering Day.** In Japan, families gather shellfish from the seashore on the lowest tide day of this month.

25 **National Flag Day.** Swaziland.

ANZAC Day. WWI soldiers of the Australia and New Zealand Army Corps are honored.

26 **Union Day.** Tanzania. In 1964, Tanganyika and Zanzibar united to become Tanzania.

27 **Independence Day.** Afghanistan, Sierra Leone, and Togo.

Freedom Day. South Africa. A national holiday celebrating the 1994 election. For the first time all citizens could vote.

28 **Arbor Day.** United States. The last Friday in April is a special day for tree planting.

◄ Bullfight, Spain

MAY

1 **Lei Day.** People exchange fresh leis (garlands of flowers worn around the neck) in Hawaii as symbols of friendship and goodwill.

May Day. Northern Europe.

2 **King's Birthday.** Lesotho.

3 **Bass Islands Birdathon.** In Bass Islands, Ohio, a contest is held to see who can count the most species of migrating birds flying over this Lake Erie island.

8 **National Windmill Day.** The Netherlands.

Helston Furry Dance. Wales. A day of dancing in the city of Cornwall, highlighted by the Helston furry dance, a line dance that winds through the streets at noon.

9 **Peter Pan Day.** Author Sir James Barrie was born in Scotland on this day in 1860.

10 **Matsu Day.** In Taiwan, people honor Matsu, the goddess of the sea.

15 **Hollyhock Festival.** Kyoto, Japan. This costumed procession honoring the hollyhock flower was started in the 7th century.

16 **Lily of the Valley Day.** This month's flower, which symbolizes the return of happiness, is honored today.

17 **Discovery Day.** Cayman Islands. Grand Cayman, Little Cayman, and Cayman Brac are the three islands of this British dependency.

National Be a Millionaire Day. United States.

Flower: Lily of the Valley

22 **Detective Day.** Sir Arthur Conan Doyle, creator of the fictional detective Sherlock Holmes, was born on this day in England in 1859.

Heroes Day. Sri Lanka.

23 **Labor Day.** Jamaica.

24 **Bermuda Day.** Bermuda.

Culture Day. Bulgaria. A national holiday celebrated by students, scientists, and artists.

Gem: Emerald

29 **International Jazz Day.** Music lovers worldwide celebrate this original American music.

30 **Dragon Day.** People in Mons, Belgium, re-enact the battle of St. George and the dragon. Spectators try to snatch hair and ribbons from the dragon's tail for good luck.

31 **Republic Day.** South Africa.

Memorial Day Prayer for Peace. United States. Presidential proclamations from 1948 call for prayers for permanent peace in the world.

Full Pink Moon

MAY

4 Mother's Day. Mothers in the United States are honored in the month of May, which was named after Maia, the Greek goddess honored as the "good mother."

5 Cinco de Mayo Day. Celebration of the defeat of the French armies in 1862, with dances and fireworks in Puebla, Mexico.

6 Martyrs' Day. Syria.

Procession of the Holy Blood. In Bruges, Belgium, floats enacting biblical scenes are featured in this religious festival.

7 Water Day. Celebrates the life-giving force of water, which makes up 75% of our planet.

11 International Mother's Day.

12 Limerick Day. Write and celebrate the humorous five-lined verse named after Limerick, Ireland.

13 Sir Arthur Sullivan's birthday. A day to celebrate this British composer, born in 1842, who was famous for his light operas.

14 Carabao Festival. Water buffalo are washed, adorned with flowers, and led to church to be blessed in Luzon, Philippines.

18 Canadian Tulip Festival. In Ottawa, Canada, 3 million tulips are featured in this annual event.

19 Atatürk Youth Day. Turkey. The independence movement of 1919 is celebrated with sports and play.

20 Party Day. Zaire.

Amelia Earhart Day. On this day in 1932, the American aviator became the first woman to fly solo across the Atlantic Ocean from Canada to Ireland.

21 Buddha's Day. South Korea.

25 National Day. Argentina.

Liberation of African Continent Day. Gabon.

Independence Day. Eritrea and Jordan.

26 Independence Day. Guyana.

Constitution Day. Denmark.

27 Warbler Wave Week. A celebration of the return of migrating thrushes, tanagers, orioles, warblers, and other birds to Deer Isle, Maine (see below).

Golden Gate Bridge Day. San Francisco, California, commemorates the opening of the bridge in 1937.

28 Day of the Republic. Azerbaijan.

Amnesty International Day. A day to work to free prisoners of conscience, abolish torture, and support human rights around the world.

◀ Guards marching, Denmark

▲ Warblers in nest

JUNE

1 International Children's Day.

Independence Day. Samoa.

2 Republic Day. Ireland and Italy.

Hristo Botev Day. Bulgaria. Honors the poet and national hero who died on this day in 1876.

Coronation Day. The United Kingdom commemorates the crowning of Queen Elizabeth II.

3 Foundation Day. Australia.

Eel Festival. Denmark. The city of Jyllingue holds an annual festival in which fried eel is served.

8 Barunga Cultural Festival. In Barunga, Australia, Aboriginal people from the Northern Territory gather for dancing, athletics, and arts.

9 Independence Day. Argentina, the second-largest country in South America, declared independence from Spain in 1816.

10 Portugal Day. A national holiday to remember the death of Portugal's national poet Luis Vaz de Camões in 1524.

15 Admission Day. Arkansas was admitted as the 25th state in the Union in 1836.

16 Soweto Day. To commemorate the uprisings against apartheid in South Africa.

17 Magna Carta Day. England's anniversary of the document of 1215.

Independence Day. Iceland.

22 Sun Day. A celebration of Earth's star.

Vancouver Day. Canada. The English explorer George Vancouver, after whom the city and island of Vancouver in British Columbia were named, was born in England on this day in 1757.

23 Midsummer's Eve. A European holiday celebrating the return of summer. Maypoles, music, and dancing are part of the celebration.

24 Saint John's Day. Celebrated in many countries, this festival celebrates the summer solstice and name day of Janis, or John.

29 Independence Day. Seychelles. Seychelles is an African country consisting of 90 islands in the Indian Ocean. Great Britain granted it independence in 1976.

30 Sunflower Day. Celebrates the great bird feeder, the sunflower.

Flower:
Rose

Gem:
Pearl

Full Flower Moon

JUNE

4 **Independence Day.** Tonga.

5 **Constitution Day.** Denmark.

World Environment Day. The United Nations designated this day to campaign for a healthy biosphere.

6 **Constitution Day.** Sweden.

Women's Vote Day. United States. On this day in 1872, American suffragist Susan B. Anthony was fined for voting in a public election.

7 **Firefly Day.** Festivals are held this month in South Korea, where prayers are said for the proliferation of fireflies.

11 **National Day.** Libya.

12 **Independence Day.** Philippines. More than 7,000 islands make up this nation. In 1898, Spain gave this country to the United States. In 1946, the United States granted independence.

13 **Feast of St. Anthony.** In Lisbon, Portugal, city newspapers hold a party for children of the poor.

14 **Flag Day.** United States.

18 **Independence Day.** Egypt.

19 **Labor Day.** Trinidad and Tobago.

Juneteenth. United States. This holiday marks the 1865 freeing of slaves in Texas with a reading of the Emancipation Proclamation, sermons, songs, picnics, and games.

20 **Flag Day.** Argentina. The flag of Argentina was adopted in 1818. The sun represents freedom from Spain. The blue and white colors were worn by patriots who fought British invaders in 1806.

21 **Summer Solstice.** Northern Hemisphere.

Hurricane Agnes Day. United States. This 1972 hurricane dumped more than 28.1 trillion tons of water on the eastern seaboard of the United States.

25 **Independence Day.** Croatia, Mozambique, and Slovenia.

Battle of Little Bighorn Anniversary. United States. Lakota (Sioux) chiefs Sitting Bull and Crazy Horse defeated attacking U.S. troops under the command of Custer in 1876.

26 **Independence Day.** Madagascar and Somalia.

27 **Independence Day.** Djibouti.

Johannus Day. Finland.

28 **Birthday of Kuan Kong** (God of War). Taiwan.

Treaty of Versailles. Signed in France on this day in 1919, this treaty marked the end of World War I.

Festival, ➤ Madagascar

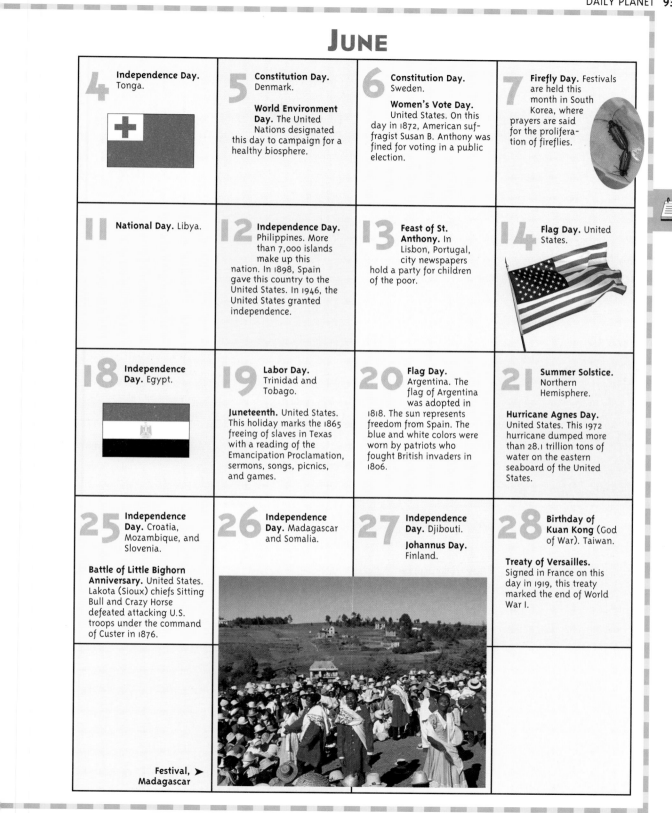

JULY

1 Canada Day. Canada.

2 Festa del Palio (Festival of the Palio). Horse-racing and flag-throwing competitions are held around the town square in Siena, Italy.

3 Water Lily Day. The water lily symbolizes purity of heart. It grows in shallow water in both temperate and hot climates.

8 Declaration of Independence. Pennsylvania. First public reading in 1776 by Colonel John Nixon.

9 Independence Day. Argentina.

Sewing Machine Day. United States. Elias Howe, the American inventor of the sewing machine, was born on this day in Massachusetts in 1819.

10 Independence Day. Bahamas.

15 St. Swithin's Day. United Kingdom. Folklore says if this day is fair, it will not rain for the next 40 days.

16 Four-Day Walking Marathon. In Nijmegen, in the Netherlands, this annual event draws more than 35,000 participants who walk 124 miles.

17 Independence Day. Slovakia.

Munoz-Rivera Day. Puerto Rico. A public holiday to mark the birth of the patriot, poet, and journalist who was born in 1859.

22 Mary Magdalene Day. Men on stilts make a spectacular downhill race from the Anguiano village church in Spain.

23 Guelaguetza Dance Festival. This pre-Columbian corn harvest celebration features singing and dancing by indigenous villagers in Oaxaca, Mexico.

24 Simon Bolivar Day. Ecuador and Venezuela. Birthday of Simon Bolivar in Venezuela in 1783. He defeated the Spanish to win independence for Bolivia, Colombia, Ecuador, Peru, and Venezuela.

29 World Eskimo-Indian Olympics. Events include muktuk, or raw whale skin, eating contests and mouth-pull matches in Fairbanks, Alaska.

30 Forbidden City Day. This walled enclosure of Beijing once held the palaces of Chinese emperors.

31 Soap-and-Water Day. The first U.S. patent was granted in 1790 to Samuel Hopkins for a process for making soap.

Flower: Water lily

Gem: Ruby

Full Strawberry Moon

JULY

4 Independence Day. United States.

5 Independence Day. Algeria, Cape Verde, and Venezuela.

Caribbean Day. A national holiday to mark the treaty of the Caribbean community of Barbados, Guyana, Jamaica, and Trinidad and Tobago.

6 Independence Day. Comoros. In 1975, the African country of Comoros, consisting of several islands in the Indian Ocean, claimed independence from France. The four main islands of Comoros are Anjouan, Grand Comore, Mayotte, and Moheli.

7 Independence Day. Solomon Islands.

Running of the Bulls. Pamplona, Spain (see below).

11 Revolution Day. Mongolia. Mongolia was ruled by Genghis Khan and his grandson Kublai Khan in the 1200s and 1300s. This country's first free elections were held in 1974.

12 National Day. São Tomé and Principe.

13 Lions Camel Cup. Annual camel race and polo games on camels in Alice Springs, Australia.

14 Bastille Day. France.

18 Candle Festival. In Ubon Ratchathani, Thailand, the Buddhist Rains Retreat is marked by parades of carved beeswax candles, some of them several feet high.

19 Independence Day. Laos.

Women's Rights Day. United States. Anniversary of the Seneca Falls, New York, convention led by Lucretia Mott and Elizabeth Cady Stanton in 1848, which called for the right for women to vote.

20 Day of the Sea. Japan.

Independence Day. Colombia.

21 Coldest Day. Vostok, Antarctica. The lowest temperature, −129° Fahrenheit (−89° Celsius), was recorded here on this day in 1983.

25 Constitution Day. Puerto Rico.

26 Independence Day. Liberia and Maldives.

Revolution Day. Cuba.

27 Ring of Fire Day. Japan. Earth's most volcanically active area is called the "Ring of Fire." All of Japan's 3,000 islands are located within this ring.

28 Independence Day. Peru.

◄ Pamplona Festival, Spain

AUGUST

Flower:
Poppy

Gem: Onyx

Full Thunder Moon

1 Confederation Day. Switzerland. The anniversary of the founding of the Swiss Confederation in 1291 is celebrated with parades, bonfires, and fireworks.

2 Wolf Howl Nights. Canada. Thursday nights in August are for public wolf howls in Algonquin Provincial Park, Canada. Naturalists imitate wolf howls and wait for wolves to howl back.

3 Independence Day. Niger.

8 Peace Day. Iraq.
Arctic Explorer Day. Celebrates the 1866 birthday of American explorer Matthew Henson in Maryland. Henson accompanied Robert Perry to the North Pole.

9 National Day. Singapore.

10 Independence Day. Ecuador. Celebrates the Declaration of Independence in 1809.
International Theater Festival. Finland. Annual festival of plays and performances in Tampere.

15 Independence Day. India. Celebrates freedom from British rule in 1947.
Foundation Day. Panama. Celebrates the founding of Panama City with cultural festivities.

16 Discovery Day. Yukon, Canada. Marks the anniversary of the discovery of gold at Bonanza Creek in the Klondike region of the Yukon.
Menachim Begin Day. Israel. Celebrates the 1913 birthday of this former prime minister.

17 Independence Day. Gabon. National holiday celebrates independence from France in 1960.
Independence Day. Indonesia. Proclaimed independence from the Netherlands on this day in 1945

22 Junk Day. Many children grow up on these Chinese boats, which are used as homes, fishing boats, and transportation for passengers and cargo.

23 National Day. Romania. Celebrates the 1944 peace in Romania proclaimed by King Michael.

24 Independence Day. Russia.
National Day. Ukraine.

Flag of Ukraine

29 Independence Day. Uzbekistan.
Potato Feast. United States. Houlton, Maine, hosts its annual potato feast supper, parade of dolls, and potato games at the end of August.

30 Children's Day. Afghanistan.

31 National Day. Malaysia. Malaysia became independent from Britain in 1957.
Montessori Day. Birthday of educator Maria Montessori in Italy, in 1870.

AUGUST

4 **Coast Guard Day.** United States. The anniversary of the founding of the U.S. Coast Guard in 1790.

Independence Day. Jamaica.

5 **Republic Day.** Burkina Faso (Upper Volta). Celebrates this country's freedom from France in 1960.

Workers' Day. Iceland.

International Busker Festival. Canada. Annual festival of street performers from around the world at Halifax, Nova Scotia.

6 **Farmer's Day.** Zambia.

Independence Day. Bolivia. A national holiday that celebrates freedom from Spain, 1825.

Peace Festival. Japan. Held in Hiroshima, Japan, in memory of the victims of the 1945 atomic bomb explosion.

7 **Republic Day.** Côte d'Ivoire.

Shop and Office Day. Ireland. Workers are treated to a day off. Celebrated on the first Monday in August.

11 **Independence Day.** Chad. National holiday celebrating independence from France in 1960.

Festival of Hungry Ghosts. China. During the seventh lunar month, prayers, food, and ghost money are offered to the spirits of the dead.

12 **Queen's Birthday.** Birthday celebrations honoring Queen Sirkit in Thailand.

13 **Independence Day.** Central African Republic and Congo.

14 **Independence Day.** Pakistan.

18 **Jashn.** Afghanistan. A week-long celebration of liberation from British control.

19 **Bon Festival.** In Japan, a religious rite held in memory of the dead. Buddhists believe the dead revisit the Earth at this time of year.

20 **Istvan's (St. Stephen's) Day.** Celebrations mark the formation and culture of Hungary.

Independence Day. Senegal.

21 **Independence Day.** Balkans, Estonia, Latvia, and Lithuania.

25 **Independence Day.** Uruguay and Belarus. Uruguay declared independence from Brazil in 1825.

Kiss-and-Make-Up Day. United States. A day to mend friendships.

26 **Women's Equality Day.** North America.

27 **Independence Day.** Moldova. Moldova became independent in 1991.

Mother Teresa Day. India.

28 **Nile Festival.** In Egypt, a yearly celebration of the river's life-giving qualities.

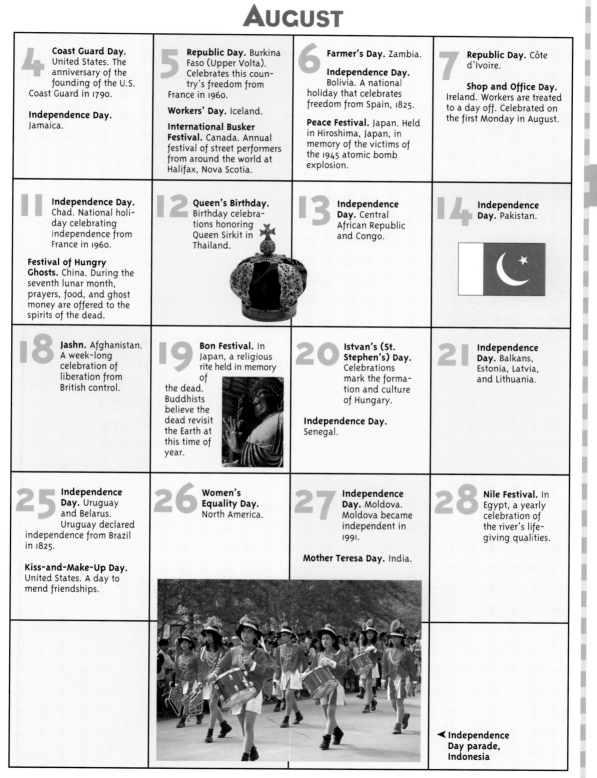

◄ Independence Day parade, Indonesia

SEPTEMBER

Flower: Morning glory

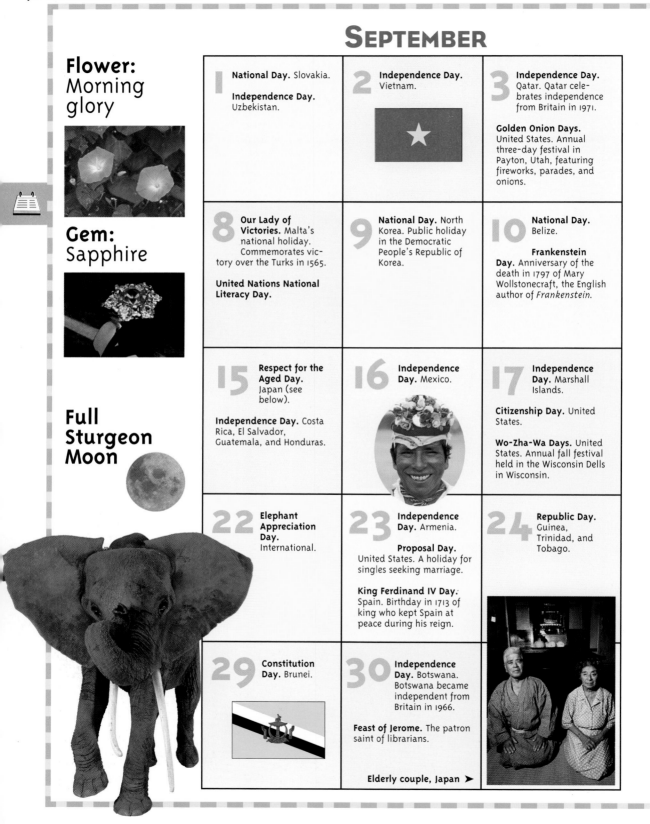

Gem: Sapphire

Full Sturgeon Moon

1
National Day. Slovakia.

Independence Day. Uzbekistan.

2
Independence Day. Vietnam.

3
Independence Day. Qatar. Qatar celebrates independence from Britain in 1971.

Golden Onion Days. United States. Annual three-day festival in Payton, Utah, featuring fireworks, parades, and onions.

8
Our Lady of Victories. Malta's national holiday. Commemorates victory over the Turks in 1565.

United Nations National Literacy Day.

9
National Day. North Korea. Public holiday in the Democratic People's Republic of Korea.

10
National Day. Belize.

Frankenstein Day. Anniversary of the death in 1797 of Mary Wollstonecraft, the English author of *Frankenstein*.

15
Respect for the Aged Day. Japan (see below).

Independence Day. Costa Rica, El Salvador, Guatemala, and Honduras.

16
Independence Day. Mexico.

17
Independence Day. Marshall Islands.

Citizenship Day. United States.

Wo-Zha-Wa Days. United States. Annual fall festival held in the Wisconsin Dells in Wisconsin.

22
Elephant Appreciation Day. International.

23
Independence Day. Armenia.

Proposal Day. United States. A holiday for singles seeking marriage.

King Ferdinand IV Day. Spain. Birthday in 1713 of king who kept Spain at peace during his reign.

24
Republic Day. Guinea, Trinidad, and Tobago.

29
Constitution Day. Brunei.

30
Independence Day. Botswana. Botswana became independent from Britain in 1966.

Feast of Jerome. The patron saint of librarians.

Elderly couple, Japan ➤

SEPTEMBER

4 **Civil Servants' Day.** Venezuela.

Newspaper Carrier Day. United States. Honors 10-year-old Barney Flaherty of New York City, the first child in the country to sell newspapers.

5 **Morning Glory Day.** The United States celebrates this climbing summer flower that has heart-shaped leaves.

6 **Independence Day.** Swaziland.

7 **Independence Day.** Brazil.

11 **Enkutatsh.** New Year celebration in Ethiopia marked by the end of the rainy season. Children go from house to house singing songs and leaving small bouquets of flowers.

12 **National Revolution Day.** Ethiopia.

Buckeye Tree Festival. United States. A celebration of the Ohio State Tree in Utica, Ohio.

13 **Paper Day.** Honors the invention of paper by the Chinese in A.D. 105.

Charlie and the Chocolate Factory Day. Birthday in South Wales of author Roald Dahl in 1916.

14 **International Cross-Cultural Day.** To celebrate diversity in cultures and heritages and to promote international goodwill.

18 **Independence Day.** Chile.

19 **Independence Day.** St. Kitts.

20 **Alexandria World Festival.** In Alexandria, Egypt, an annual celebration of the 35 cities around the world with the same name (see below left).

21 **Independence Day.** Malta.

25 **Pacific Ocean Day.** On this day in 1513, Spanish explorer Vasco Nuñez de Balboa sighted the Pacific Ocean.

26 **Mid-Autumn Day.** China, Hong Kong, and Taiwan.

27 **Ancestor Appreciation Day.** A day for celebrating the cultural diversity of the United States (see below).

28 **Confucius's Birthday and Teachers' Day.** Taiwan. National holiday honors Confucius, who taught for 40 years.

◄ Alexandria, Egypt

Cultural diversity, ►
United States

OCTOBER

1 **National Day.** An official celebration takes place in the Great Hall of the People while performances are held in theaters throughout China.

Goodwill Day. Namibia.

Independence Day. Nigeria and Tuvalu.

2 **"Mahatma" Gandhi Birthday.** Honoring the birth in 1869 of the Indian nationalist and spiritual leader who practiced nonviolent disobedience.

Independence Day. Guinea.

3 **German Unity Day.** Germany.

Francisco Morazan Day. Honduras. Public holiday to honor the national hero born in 1799.

8 **Akan-Machi.** The Ainu, the aboriginal people of Japan, celebrate a round green floating plant, the marimo, with ancient dances on the shores of Lake Akan.

9 **Independence Day.** Uganda.

National Dignity Day. Peru.

10 **Independence Day.** Fiji. National holiday to commemorate freedom from Bristish rule in 1970.

15 **Independence Day.** Bosnia.

16 **Oyster Sound Off.** United States. A celebration of the beginning of the oyster season and restoration of shellfish beds in Puget Sound in Washington.

17 **Sweetest Day.** A day for sweet foods and kind acts in the United States.

Dessalines' Day. In Haiti, this day commemorates the assassination of Jean Jacques Dessalines in 1806.

22 **Copycat Day.** The first xerographic image was produced by Chester Carlson in 1938 in the United States.

23 **National Liberation Day.** Egypt.

National Mole Day. United States.

Chulalongkorn Day. Thailand. Honors the king of Thailand who abolished slavery.

24 **Independence Day.** Zambia.

United Nations Day.

29 **National Youth Day.** Liberia.

30 **Zoo Day.** Zoos celebrate with Halloween themes.

Mischief Night. United States. Harmless pranks are played by youngsters before Halloween.

31 **Halloween.** Ireland and United States.

Flower: Calendula

Gem: Opal

Full Harvest Moon

OCTOBER

4 **Independence Day.** Lesotho.

Independence Day. Cyprus.

5 **Sports Day.** Lesotho.

6 **Food of the Gods Festival.** Chocolate tastings and classes on the pre-Hispanic use of medicinal plants in Oaxaca, Mexico.

7 **Children's Day.** The United Nations has declared the first Monday in October as a day to honor children (see below).

11 **Revolution Day.** Panama.

Native American Day. A legal holiday in South Dakota to honor great Native American leaders.

12 **Columbus Day.** Spain, United States, South America, and Central America.

13 **Thanksgiving Day.** This observance is on the second Monday of October in Canada.

14 **Columbus Day.** Belize. A public holiday to honor the explorer Christopher Columbus.

William Penn Day. Birthday of William Penn, founder of the state of Pennslvania, 1644.

18 **Lord of the Miracles Day.** Lima, Peru.

Persons Day. Canada. The anniversary of the 1929 ruling that declared women to be persons.

19 **Pumpkin Day.** United States. A day to prepare foods with pumpkins, and to carve jack-o-lanterns.

20 **Kenyatta Day.** Honors Jomo Kenyatta, Kenya's first president.

21 **Overseas Chinese Day.** Taiwan. Thousands of Chinese from overseas visit Taiwan to celebrate Chinese culture.

Dynamite Day. Birthday of Alfred Nobel, the inventor of dynamite, in Sweden, 1833.

25 **Mothers' Day.** Malawi.

26 **National Day.** Austria (see below).

Mule Day. United States. Anniversary of first mules in the United States given by King Charles III of Spain.

27 **Independence Day.** St. Vincent and Turkmenistan.

28 **Dedication of the Statue of Liberty.** United States. The Statue of Liberty was a gift from France in 1886.

◄ Austria

Children's Day ►

NOVEMBER

Flower:
Chrysanthemum

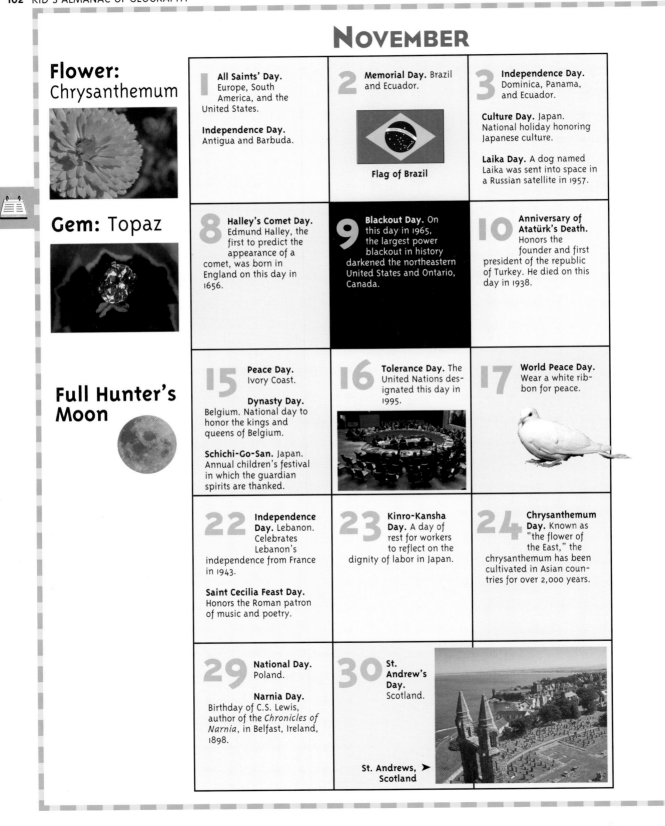

Gem: Topaz

Full Hunter's Moon

1 **All Saints' Day.** Europe, South America, and the United States.

Independence Day. Antigua and Barbuda.

2 **Memorial Day.** Brazil and Ecuador.

Flag of Brazil

3 **Independence Day.** Dominica, Panama, and Ecuador.

Culture Day. Japan. National holiday honoring Japanese culture.

Laika Day. A dog named Laika was sent into space in a Russian satellite in 1957.

8 **Halley's Comet Day.** Edmund Halley, the first to predict the appearance of a comet, was born in England on this day in 1656.

9 **Blackout Day.** On this day in 1965, the largest power blackout in history darkened the northeastern United States and Ontario, Canada.

10 **Anniversary of Atatürk's Death.** Honors the founder and first president of the republic of Turkey. He died on this day in 1938.

15 **Peace Day.** Ivory Coast.

Dynasty Day. Belgium. National day to honor the kings and queens of Belgium.

Schichi-Go-San. Japan. Annual children's festival in which the guardian spirits are thanked.

16 **Tolerance Day.** The United Nations designated this day in 1995.

17 **World Peace Day.** Wear a white ribbon for peace.

22 **Independence Day.** Lebanon. Celebrates Lebanon's independence from France in 1943.

Saint Cecilia Feast Day. Honors the Roman patron of music and poetry.

23 **Kinro-Kansha Day.** A day of rest for workers to reflect on the dignity of labor in Japan.

24 **Chrysanthemum Day.** Known as "the flower of the East," the chrysanthemum has been cultivated in Asian countries for over 2,000 years.

29 **National Day.** Poland.

Narnia Day. Birthday of C.S. Lewis, author of the Chronicles of Narnia, in Belfast, Ireland, 1898.

30 **St. Andrew's Day.** Scotland.

St. Andrews, ➤ Scotland

November

4 **Flag Day.** Panama.

5 **Guy Fawkes Day.** Bonfires are lit to recall Guy Fawkes's attempt to blow up England's Houses of Parliament in 1605.

6 **Basketball Day.** Today is the birthday (1861) of Canadian-American James Naismith, who invented basketball.

7 **National Peanut Festival.** Annual week-long festival in Dothan, Alabama, featuring recipe contests for peanuts.

11 **Independence Day.** Angola.

Veterans Day. United States.

12 **Sun Yat-sen's Birthday.** In Taiwan, people celebrate the founder of the Chinese Nationalist Party, who was born on this day in 1866.

13 **Treasure Island Day.** Today is the birthday of Scottish author Robert Louis Stevenson, who was born in 1850.

14 **Children's Day.** India. A holiday to honor the children of India.

18 **Independence Day.** Morocco.

Mickey Mouse's Birthday. Walt Disney's cartoon character first appeared in the movies on this day in New York City.

19 **Discovery Day.** Puerto Rico. To commemorate Christopher Columbus in Puerto Rico on his second voyage in 1493.

Lincoln's Gettysburg Address Day. United States. Anniversary of the famous speech in 1863.

20 **Revolution Day.** Mexico.

21 **Hello Day.** The word *hello* was introduced in the United States as a telephone greeting.

25 **Thanksgiving Day.** The fourth Thursday of November in the United States. The first Thanksgiving was three days of prayer and feasting in Plymouth, Massachusetts, in 1621.

26 **Sojourner Truth Memorial Day.** Honors this former slave who spoke out against slavery and for equal rights for women in the United States.

27 **Chaim Weizman Day.** Honors the 1874 birth of the first president of Israel.

28 **Independence Day.** Albania, Mauritania, and Panama.

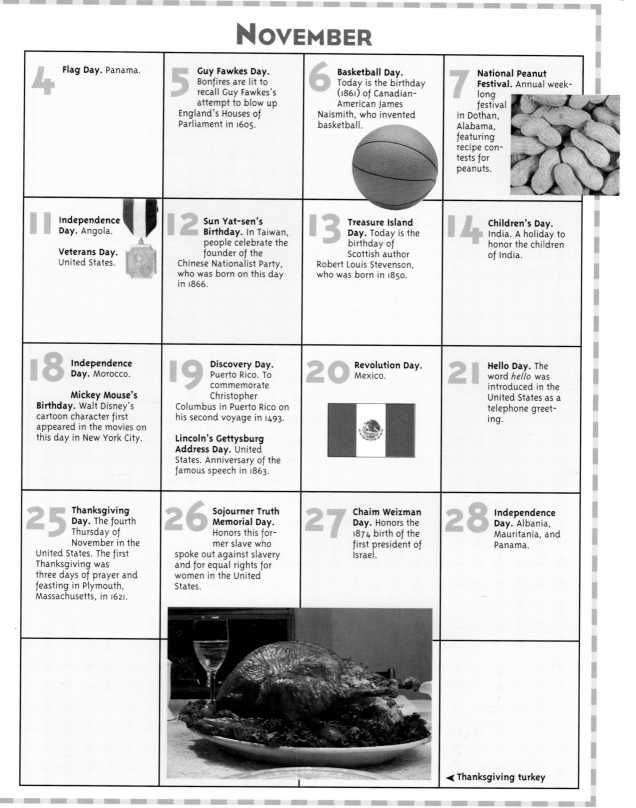

◄ Thanksgiving turkey

DECEMBER

Flower:
Poinsettia

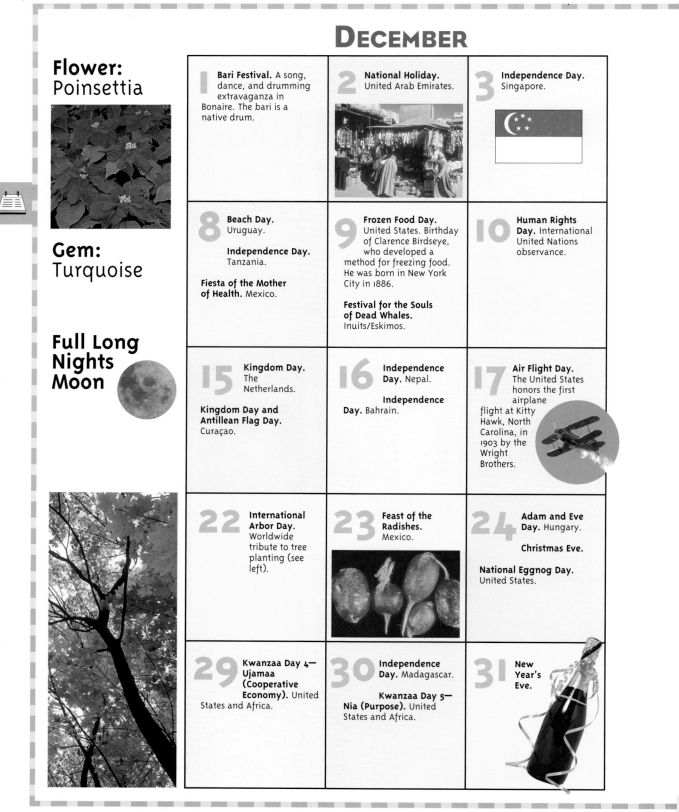

Gem:
Turquoise

Full Long Nights Moon

1 Bari Festival. A song, dance, and drumming extravaganza in Bonaire. The bari is a native drum.

2 National Holiday. United Arab Emirates.

3 Independence Day. Singapore.

8 Beach Day. Uruguay.

Independence Day. Tanzania.

Fiesta of the Mother of Health. Mexico.

9 Frozen Food Day. United States. Birthday of Clarence Birdseye, who developed a method for freezing food. He was born in New York City in 1886.

Festival for the Souls of Dead Whales. Inuits/Eskimos.

10 Human Rights Day. International United Nations observance.

15 Kingdom Day. The Netherlands.

Kingdom Day and Antillean Flag Day. Curaçao.

16 Independence Day. Nepal.

Independence Day. Bahrain.

17 Air Flight Day. The United States honors the first airplane flight at Kitty Hawk, North Carolina, in 1903 by the Wright Brothers.

22 International Arbor Day. Worldwide tribute to tree planting (see left).

23 Feast of the Radishes. Mexico.

24 Adam and Eve Day. Hungary.

Christmas Eve.

National Eggnog Day. United States.

29 Kwanzaa Day 4— Ujamaa (Cooperative Economy). United States and Africa.

30 Independence Day. Madagascar.

Kwanzaa Day 5— Nia (Purpose). United States and Africa.

31 New Year's Eve.

December

4 **Pallas Athena Day.** Honors the Greek goddess of wisdom.

5 **King's Birthday.** In Thailand, this day is celebrated with colorful pageantry during the day and spectacular illuminations at night.

6 **Independence Day.** Ireland, Denmark, and Finland.

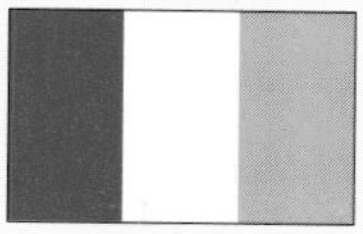

Flag of Ireland

7 **Waterloo Day.** Napoleon was defeated by the British at Waterloo, Belgium, on this day in 1815.

11 **Republic Day.** Upper Volta.

12 **National Day.** Kenya.

Fiesta of Our Lady of Guadalupe. Mexico (see below).

13 **St. Lucia Day.** A holiday observed in Sweden, where the oldest daughter serves a breakfast of sweet rolls to her family.

14 **St. Spyridon's Feast.** Corfu, Greece.

South Pole Discovery Day. Antarctica.

18 **Republic Day.** Niger.

19 **Almanac Day.** *Poor Richard's Almanac,* by Benjamin Franklin, was first published in the United States on this day in 1732.

Franklin ➤

20 **Longest Night of the Year Day.** In Iran, bonfires, storytelling, and treats of fruits and nuts mark this celebration.

21 **Water Festival.** A three-day celebration of life-giving water in Cambodia.

25 **Christmas Day.**

Children's Day. Congo.

26 **Day of Goodwill.** South Africa.

Kwanzaa Day 1— Umoja (Unity). United States and Africa.

Day of the Wren. Ireland honors the wren, a small bird.

Wren

27 **Feast of Marimba (Goddess of Musical Happiness).** South Africa.

Kwanzaa Day 2— Kuichagulia (Self-Determination). United States and Africa.

28 **Kwanzaa Day 3— Ujima (Collective Work and Responsibility).** United States and Africa.

◄ Christmas

Guadalupe ➤ festival, Mexico

Daring Dwellers
(Nomads and Semi-nomads)

Daring dwellers are people who live in some of the most extreme climates in the world. They survive by following the rhythms of nature, and by living off, and with, the Earth. Throughout the world, very old cultures persevere in harsh climates. From the high desert region of Bolivia to the rain forest of Borneo, there are at least 5,000 indigenous, or native, cultures trying to survive the pressures of the modern world. Some, like the Penan peoples of Borneo, are being driven from their rain forest homes by large logging companies. Others, like the Chipaya of Bolivia, struggle to survive in barren land.

Some 300 million people continue to follow the old ways of their culture in the places where they and their ancestors were born. Sadly, these may become the vanishing cultures of the world. *Ethnocide* is the word used by geographers to describe the destruction of a people's way of life.

Geographers help to enhance our understanding of the world's indigenous peoples by taking risks. Whether they spend the summer in Antarctica studying the climate and habitat or forge the horizonless deserts of Arabia to learn the ways of people, geographers are also daring dwellers in their own right.

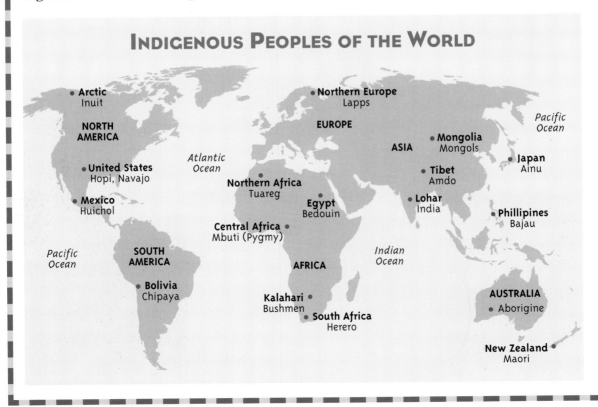

INDIGENOUS PEOPLES OF THE WORLD

Arctic
Inuit

Northern Europe
Lapps

NORTH AMERICA

EUROPE

Pacific Ocean

ASIA

Mongolia
Mongols

Atlantic Ocean

Japan
Ainu

United States
Hopi, Navajo

Tibet
Amdo

Northern Africa
Tuareg

Egypt
Bedouin

Lohar
India

Mexico
Huichol

Phillipines
Bajau

Central Africa
Mbuti (Pygmy)

Indian Ocean

Pacific Ocean

SOUTH AMERICA

AFRICA

Bolivia
Chipaya

Kalahari
Bushmen

AUSTRALIA
Aborigine

South Africa
Herero

New Zealand
Maori

Nomads of the World

Nomads never settle in one place for very long. They travel to new grounds when the seasons change. Some nomads journey thousands of miles to move their herds to seasonal grazing lands. Other nomads move only a few miles away to change hunting camps. Some trade and barter with settled people as they travel.

The Lohar nomads of Rajasthan in India often keep their old ways. Government housing is used for storing grain and equipment, but the people continue to live outside of the houses.

Australian outback boy hunter

All nomads carry whatever they need with them, including their shelter and food. Whether they move camp a few miles away, as the Mbuti (Pygmies) of the Ituri Forest in Africa do, or travel thousands of miles, like the Lapp nomads of northern Europe, these traveling people move from place to place as a way of life.

Anthropologists call nomadic farmers "shifting cultures."

SURVIVING ON THE MOVE

Carry weapons and hunt for food

- Akuriyos of Suriname
- Aborigines of Australia
- Bushmen of the Kalahari
- Mbuti of Africa

Trade goods or offer services

- Gypsies of Europe
- Lohars of Rajisthan, India

Herders

- Mongols of northern Asia
- Lapps of northern Europe

Farmers

- Iban of Sarawak
- Masai of Africa

Lohar man

INDIGENOUS PEOPLE AROUND THE WORLD

Some 300 million people worldwide are members of an indigenous culture. That is roughly 5% of the global population. An indigenous culture is one that originally comes from a particular region or area.

Ainu elder

Aboriginal elder

Africa

(Northern): Berber, Kabyle, Mozabite, Shluh, Tuareg

(Eastern central): Afar, Beja, Dinka, Fulanil, Nuer, Tigre

(Southeastern): Ariaal, Barabaig, Hadza, Himba, Karamojong, Masai, Ovambo, Rendille, Samburu, Somali, Turkana

(Central): Baka, Batwa, Bongo, Efe, Ijaw, Mbuti, Ogoni, Twa

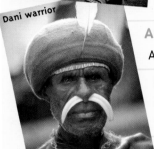
Dani warrior

Australia

Aborigine

Brazil, and into Bolivia

Chipaya, Kayapo, Makuxi, Nambikwara, Tukano, Xavante, Yanomani

Canada

Cree, Dene, Innuit, Metis, Micmac

(Western): Ahapaskan, Bella Coola, Haida, Tlingit, Tsimshian

Masai woman

Caribbean woman

Caribbean Islands

Carib

Central America

Garifuna, Lenca, Maya (Choi, Chuj, K'iche', Q'eq'chi, and other Maya), Miskito, Pipil, Sumu

Chile

Ache, Guarani, Mapuche, Toba, Wichi

China

(Northern): Chukchi, Evenk, Khanty, Koryak, Nenets, Yakut

(Middle): Hui, Miao, Mongol, Naga, Tibetan, Uygur, Zhuang

Mayan children

Navajo weaver

India

Bhil, Gond, Ho, Munda, Santal

Indonesia

Bontoc, Chamorro, Ibaloy, Ifugao, Kalinga

Japan

Ainu

Malaysia

Asmat, Dani, Iban, Penan

Mexico

Huichol, Lacandon, Maya, Mazatec, Nahuati, Tarahumara, Zapotec

New Zealand

Maori

Scandinavia

Sami (Lapps)

South America

(Northern region): Achuar, Aguaruna, Arakmbut, Ashaninka, Panare, Quichua, Shuar, U'wa, Waorani, Wayana

Southeast Asia

Chakma, Chin, Kachin, Kuoy, Marma, Mru, Shan, Tai

United States

(Southwest): Hopi, Navajo (Dine'), Zuni

(Northwest): Nez Perce

(Central): Apache, Arapaho, Cheyenne, Comanche, Crow, Oglala, Pawnee, Shoshone, Sioux

(Alaska): Aleut, Inuit (Inupiat, Yupik, and other Inuit)

Tibetan monks

Zapotec mother and daughter

Maori warrior

Pygmies: Fire Carriers of the Forest

The Mbuti are the Pygmy nomads of the African forest. Their home is the Ituri Forest— a wild, deep tropical rain forest. Neighboring Bantu tribes fear the dangers of the forest, but for the Mbuti it is a safe haven that provides food, shelter, clothing, and medicine for their people. Bands of Mbuti move their camp in order to hunt animals and locate mushrooms and berries. They travel short distances within the forest, staying for a few months in each place. Neighboring Bantu farmers trade tools, bananas, and sweet potatoes with the Mbuti in order to obtain game meat.

The Mbuti are a small people. An average 11-year-old child grows to about 3.25 feet (99 cm) tall, while a mature adult is 4.5 feet (137 cm) tall. Their small bodies enable them to move quickly through the forest. The Mbuti find all their needs for survival there. They hunt game animals and gather roots and berries for food. The Mbuti construct shelters from tree branches and make their clothes

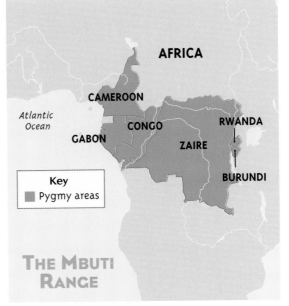

THE MBUTI RANGE

Key
■ Pygmy areas

from the bark of fig trees. Drums and flutes are fashioned from animal skins and forest wood. The Mbuti believe in the supernatural forces of the forest and often dance and sing their praises.

Pygmy *was the name of a race of dwarfs in Greek mythology. Many small people and animals are often called "pygmy," as in pygmy parrot (bird) and pygmy goat.*

Pygmy hut

WORLD'S WETTEST INHABITED PLACES

Average annual rainfall, in inches (millimeters)

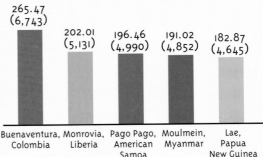

Buenaventura, Colombia	Monrovia, Liberia	Pago Pago, American Samoa	Moulmein, Myanmar	Lae, Papua New Guinea
265.47 (6,743)	202.01 (5,131)	196.46 (4,990)	191.02 (4,852)	182.87 (4,645)

ON THE MOVE WITH THE MBUTI

Roaming region

The Ituri Forest, a tropical rain forest in the Congo region of central Africa. The temperatures average 70 degrees Fahrenheit (21° C) at night and 80 degrees Fahrenheit (27° C) during the daytime.

Pygmies prepare poison arrows

Packing to go

Bands of Pygmies, usually numbering about 50, live and travel together. They may shift camp every two months or so. They move when food is scarce, or when their roofs become leaky. The Mbuti always carry their fire with them, even when they are hunting. The fire is usually in the form of smoldering ashes held in leaves. The men usually carry bows and arrows and wear flutes around their necks. The women wear backpacks (made of woven palm leaves) held by a strap that is secured across the forehead. The backpack holds cooking pots, a mortar for making arrow poison, and a hammer for beating tree bark into clothing. The women wear knives in their belts, which they use for digging roots along the way. The big girls carry smaller children on their backs. The young boys carry bows and arrows.

Road food

Whether they are hunting or moving, Mbuti carry fire, which they use to roast fruit, meat, vegetables, or fish. Children enjoy chewing fresh tree twigs, similar to chewing gum.

Setting up camp

It takes about two hours to set up a new camp. First, a central campfire is made to keep biting insects away. Then, shelters are made from vines, saplings, and leaves. Each home has its own fire, which keeps the inhabitants warm and dry at night. Beds are made from leafy branches. There are no bed covers.

Child's life

Pygmy children play by climbing trees, swinging from vines, and dancing with hoops made from the pliable liana vine (similar to western-style Hula-Hoops). Some children have pet monkeys. Although monkey meat is eaten by the Mbuti, they do not kill the animals they tame as pets.

The hunt

The men hunt antelope, birds, elephants, monkeys, and other animals, mostly using nets, spears, bows, and poison arrows. The hunters are very skilled at shooting bows and arrows. Mbuti use dogs for tracking wounded animals. Women and children often join the hunt, making noises to drive wild animals toward the hunters.

WORLD'S DRIEST INHABITED PLACES

Average annual rainfall, in inches (millimeters)

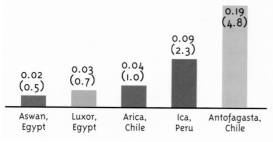

Aswan, Egypt	Luxor, Egypt	Arica, Chile	Ica, Peru	Antofagasta, Chile
0.02 (0.5)	0.03 (0.7)	0.04 (1.0)	0.09 (2.3)	0.19 (4.8)

WORLD'S COLDEST INHABITED PLACES

Average temperature, in degrees Farenheit (Celsius)

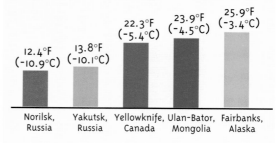

Norilsk, Russia	Yakutsk, Russia	Yellowknife, Canada	Ulan-Bator, Mongolia	Fairbanks, Alaska
12.4°F (-10.9°C)	13.8°F (-10.1°C)	22.3°F (-5.4°C)	23.9°F (-4.5°C)	25.9°F (-3.4°C)

Lapp woman weaving

Lapps: Reindeer Herders of the Tundra

Lapps, also known as Sami, live in a region of northern Europe called Lapland. Lapland is within the Arctic Circle and belongs to the countries of Norway, Sweden, Finland, and Russia. At one time, all Lapps were were nomads and herders of reindeer across the Arctic regions.

Lapps are some of the smallest people in Europe. The average adult Lapp is about 5 feet (152 m) tall.

There are about 67,000 Lapps: 40,000 live in Norway, 20,000 in Sweden, 4,400 in Finland, and 2,000 in Russia.

THE LAPP RANGE

LAPLAND
Arctic Ocean
NORWAY
FINLAND RUSSIA
Atlantic Ocean
SWEDEN

Today, some Lapps—known as Sea Lapps—have settled into fishing villages. Others, called Forest Lapps or River Lapps, have settled near forests, where they work as lumberjacks or farmers. The smallest group of Lapps, about 5,000 people, still herd reindeer. These nomads continue the traditional life by herding reindeer across the frigid Arctic in a seasonal search for grazing land. Families of Lapps travel with the herd, but most herders today are single men. Reindeer are prized for their meat as well as for being sturdy pack animals.

ON THE MOVE WITH THE LAPPS

Roaming region

Northern Europe within the Arctic Circle. Winter is spent in the southern region, and summer is spent in the northern area.

Habitat

Vast, treeless plains with moss and lichen cover; scattered areas of forest with birch, spruce, and pine trees.

Lapp man

Weather

Winter temperatures of -45 degrees Fahrenheit (-43° C) inland. Winter lasts from October through May. For two of the winter months, the sun never rises above the horizon. For two summer months the sun never goes down. Daylight lasts all day, and the sky never darkens.

Packing to go

Clothing is made of wool and trimmed with reindeer fur. Portable cone-shaped tents are used. Sleds are pulled by reindeer, and skis are used by scouts to find stray animals.

Road food

Dried reindeer meat, bread, and butter (made from reindeer milk).

Drink of choice

Coffee made from melted snow.

Travel time

It takes about a month for a herd to travel 100 miles (159 km). The reindeer determine the travel time. Lapps, like other herders, stop to rest and eat only where grazing food is available.

The Bajau: Boat Dwellers of the Sea

The Bajau, who live on boats in the seas of the Philippine Islands, number about 1,600 people. They inhabit the Tawi Tawi Islands in the Sulu Province of the **Philippines**. The Bajau are a very gentle people who live by fishing. They moor at harbors on the islands—singing as they settle—and reunite with friends and relatives.

ON THE MOVE WITH THE BAJAU

Roaming region

The Bajau fish in the Sulu and Celebes seas, which are sprinkled with many islands providing calm waters. They move with the moon because its tides and currents affect the movement of fish. The Bajau know the waters as well as urban dwellers know streets of a city. They name areas of water the same way land dwellers name valleys, rivers, or mountains.

Bajau boats

Houseboats

The Bajau call their houseboats *lipas*. The *lipas* are dugout canoes with space for sleeping, cooking, and eating. The living space may be as small as 6 by 4 feet (1.8 by 1.2 m) for a family of five. A clay hearth is used for cooking. The roof is made of palm-leaf matting, which can be rolled up when the sails are hoisted. Sails are often made of rice flour sacks. The family sleeps and sits on mats laid out on planks inside the boat. A branch of driftwood may serve as a drying rack for clothes and fishing nets. Smaller canoes called *boggohs*—which are used for fishing and short trips—are attached to the houseboat. These may also serve as garden space for growing fresh herbs.

Fishing for survival

The Bajau are superb fishers. They know the cycle of wind shifts, tides, and currents, and the movement of schools of fish. To attract sharks, they shake a rattle made of coconut shells in the water. When sharks approach the boat, the Bajau fishers spear them. The Bajau also use hooks, lines, and nets to catch fish. Their catch is traded with land people for rice and cassava, which are their staple foods.

Child's play

Babies swing in small cradlelike hammocks. Children fashion homemade stilts to play in the shallow waters. Children and mothers often sing lullabies and play songs.

The Guajiro: Indian Wanderers of Colombia

The Guajiro Indians live on the Guajira Peninsula of South America. About 44,000 Guajiro live in small clans. These people are classified as semi-nomadic because their movement is erratic and not based on the seasons. In Spanish, these people are described as *andariego*, or "roving." They move freely across the national borders of Venezuela and Colombia, fishing, herding goats, and harvesting salt.

THE GUAJIRO RANGE

HONDURAS

Caribbean Sea

Guajira Peninsula

NICARAGUA

PANAMA

VENEZUELA

COSTA RICA

Pacific Ocean

GUYANA

COLOMBIA

ECUADOR

PERU

BRAZIL

ON THE MOVE WITH THE GUAJIRO

Roaming region

The Guajiro live on the Guajira Peninsula. They live by herding goats and fishing for turtles and other seafood near the coast. Twice a year, they harvest salt from salt pans near Manaure, just as their ancestors did. Here seawater evaporates under the tropical sun, leaving beds of salt.

Sea turtle in the Caribbean

Packing to go

When they travel, women first paint their faces black to protect their skin from wind and sun. Donkeys are used as pack animals. They are saddled with pots, clothing, and hammocks. The hammocks are their homes. The Guajiro live and sleep in hammocks strung from scrubby trees around campfires. They are born and die in hammocks as well.

Road food

Dried sea turtle, rabbits caught along the way, and corn gruel are travel foods for the Guajiro.

Clothing

The women of the tribe wear brightly colored mantas, which are square-necked dresses made of cotton. The men wear aproned *guayucos* adorned with colorful pompoms.

Culture

The Guajiro celebrate life with song and dance. Goats are roasted for celebration, and *chichamaya* dancers perform intricate steps to the beat of snare drums and maracas. Each Guarjiro has three names. One is a social name, which is most often used. The second is the private name given at birth and kept secret. The last name is a baptismal name given when an individual becomes a church member.

Child's life

Children who misbehave are dealt with in a stern fashion. Young girls may be chained to a tree for misbehavior. Boys who try to run away are hung by their heels and spun around until they become sick.

World Wise

In the past, Guajiro women wore face paint to show their age and status.

The Al Murrah: "Nomads of Nomads"

The Al Murrah are camel-herding nomads of the desert. They travel and live in the harshest area of the Arabian Desert, known as the Rub' al Khali, or "Empty Quarter." Other desert inhabitants call the Al Murrah the "Nomads of Nomads" because of their lifestyle. The Al Murrah may lead their herds 1,200 miles (1,910 km) through harsh habitat in a search for the best grasses for camel grazing.

The Al Murrah consider the desert as the place of the purest camels, cleanest sands, and

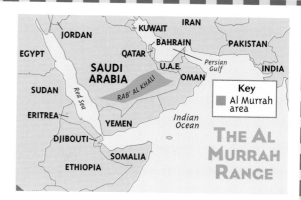

THE AL MURRAH RANGE

freshest air. They value their sense of freedom and relish the independence that their lifestyle offers them.

ON THE MOVE WITH THE AL MURRAH

Roaming region

The Rub' al Khali encompasses 200,000 square miles (518,000 sq km) of desert in southern Arabia. This region is a vast "ocean" of sand where summer temperatures reach as high as 130 degrees Fahrenheit (54° C). Only the most skilled and daring dwellers live in this region.

Packing to go

Women pack the camels for travel. They carry ropes, black tents made of goat hair, and rugs, on which the Al Murrah sleep, work, and eat. Men herd the camels, and women and children follow in groups.

Road food

Dates, rice, and camel's milk are the staples of the desert. Mint tea and coffee (which is ground and roasted over fires) are drunk daily. Small desert animals, hares, and gazelles provide a variety of meat. The Al Murrah carry water in goatskin bags, which are now often replaced by leakproof inner tubes.

Child's play

Young girls learn to weave and make carpets. At the age of 10, most boys learn how to herd camels. Kids play games of racing and wrestling. Reciting poetry and singing are

Al Murrah nomad

important forms of entertainment for all. Tent schools are set up in oases for educating children. The schools consist of a white umbrella and a chalkboard. There is no furniture.

The Tuareg of the Sahara

Berber nomads of the Sahara Desert of Africa are herders of sheep, goats, cattle, and camels. They also transport valuable salt by camel from the salt beds at Bilma hundreds of miles to southern Niger. The men wear a *tagilmust*, or turban veil, which protects their eyes and keeps their mouths from drying. Before a migration, the holy men of the tribe bless the water. The travelers drink the holy water to protect them from becoming lost, dying of thirst, or losing herd animals.

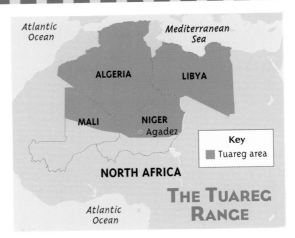

THE TUAREG RANGE

ON THE MOVE WITH THE TUAREG

Roaming region

The Tuareg live in North Africa in an area that covers parts of Algeria, Libya, Niger, and Mali. The people live in groupings that are called confederations. People in the north live totally in the desert. Those in the south live in areas that combine steppes and savannas. They are mostly camel-herding nomads.

Packing to go

Most Tuareg live in tents made from goatskins that have been sewn together and dyed a red color. Some tents in the south are dome-shaped and made from palm fronds.

Some Tuareg in Niger live in square houses made of stone. Modern tents are even made of plastic. Droughts throughout the area have affected their nomadic ways. Famine has also reduced the Tuareg population.

Clothing

Adult males cover their heads with a blue veil when they are with women or strangers.

Culture

The Tuareg social structure is feudal (class-oriented). Leaders are nobles. The common person is a laborer. The city of Agadez, Niger, is the main center of the Tuaregs.

Tuareg nomads holding council

THE CHIPAYA OF BOLIVIA

- About 2,000 people of the Chipaya tribe still live in Altiplano, a high plateau between the two ranges of the Andes Mountains.

- The Chipaya live by farming quinoa, a staple grain, and by herding sheep to produce wool for clothes and blankets.

- Each planting season, Chipaya farmers must channel water from the Lauca River to irrigate and desalt the soil. Years of drought have made survival difficult. More and more, the people leave the high plains to work on farms or as housekeepers in other parts of Bolivia and Chile.

- Chipaya women still wear the hairstyle of their ancestors (who were contemporaries of the Incas of Peru). They braid their hair into a hundred ribbon-tied braids.

- Religious beliefs help the people in difficult times. The Chipaya blend Christianity with ancient Andean ritual. They call on their gods and ancestors to bless their crops and the tasks of their daily life. They continue to drink a ritual toast of alcohol and dried coca leaves to honor their gods and ancestors.

The Andes

Bako National Park, Sarawak

THE PENAN OF SARAWAK ON THE ISLAND OF BORNEO

- The Penan way of life has changed in modern times because the government has allowed companies to log the trees of the Borneo rain forest.

- Of the 7,000 people of the Penan tribe, fewer than 300 still live in the rain forest. Those who remain in the forest now struggle to survive. From the beginning, the people preserved the trees and animals of the forest. They hunted and gathered food, which was always plentiful. The Penan practiced a tradition of sharing food with each other. Today, they are losing the tradition, because there is never enough food to go around. Most Penan have moved to resettlement camps, where, after 30 years, they still wait for promised schools to be built. Boredom, squalor, and hunger are the hallmarks of these camps.

- The staple food of the Penan is sago, which is a pasty starch made from the sago palm. The Penan have 40 words in their language for sago.

- The main meat of the Penan is wild pig. There are fewer pigs because loggers cut down the fruit trees, which were food for the animals.

Traditional Life of the Inuit

Eskimos live in the **Arctic**. In **Canada**, they are the Inuit; in **Alaska**, they are the Inupiat and Yupik; and in Siberia, they are the Yuit. The word *Eskimo* is a Native American word that means "eaters of raw meat." Eskimos prefer to be called *Inuits*, meaning "the people."

For thousands of years, these people have lived a unique way of life in order to survive in their cold, harsh environment.

Modern life of the Inuit

The way of life for the Inuit began to change in the mid 1900s. In Siberia, the government took over control of all native communities and encouraged the sale and export of reindeer hides, soapstone carvings, and other handicrafts. In **Alaska**, hunting with rifles and trapping animals reduced the number of game animals. The Inuit worked part-time in fishing and construction industries. In **Canada**, the decline in fur trade and the decrease in the caribou population led the Inuit to move to government communities. In **Greenland**, a change in climate that warmed the coastal waters drove seals north and attracted other fish. The Inuit then began working in the fishing industry.

The traditional way of life has ended for most Inuits. Many live in wooden houses with modern appliances. They wear modern clothing instead of clothes made of animal skin. Motorboats have replaced the kayak and umiak. Snowmobiles have replaced dog teams.

Inuit couple on dogsled

Modern Inuit constantly blend old and new lifestyles into daily life. Although they are open to modern conveniences, Inuit and other Native Americans work to keep their cultures alive. This practice is called tribal movement. Its goal is to protect land and to solve social problems brought about by modern life. It also seeks to preserve their unique tribal heritage. This involves their languages, music, folktales, and arts.

Inuit woman and child

On the Move with the Inuit

Food

Most Inuits live near the sea, which provides food. They hunt seals, whales, walruses, and polar bears. They eat raw meat because they have no fuel for cooking. Usually, they eat several small meals a day. Favorite foods include walrus liver and the skin of whales. They drink soup made by mixing hot water and seal blood.

Clothing

Animal skins are used to make clothing. The Inuit favor caribou skin because it is warm and lightweight. Men, women, and children wear the same type of clothes: hooded jackets, trousers, socks, boots, and mittens. In winter, they wear two suits of clothing. They wear the inner suit with the fur next to their skin. They wear the outer skin with the fur on the outside. The air between the suits acts as a layer of insulation—it keeps in body heat and allows perspiration to evaporate. In order to reduce the glare of sunlight on snow, they often wear goggles made of wood or bone.

Inuit elder

Shelter

Most central Inuit families have a summer home and a winter home. In winter, they live in a snow house or a sod house. A snow house is built of snow that has been packed and hardened by wind and frost. The Inuit can build a snow house in a few hours. They use a snow knife to cut blocks of snow. The blocks are stacked in continuous, circular rows until a dome-shaped house is made. The snow houses are heated and lighted with soapstone lamps, which are also used for cooking. Snow houses are temporary shelters.

Most sod houses are built for several winters. The base is a sunken dirt floor 1 to 2 feet (30–61 cm) deep. The home is framed with whalebone, stone, or wood and covered with sod (earth). A large dirt platform is used as a bed and a seat. Smaller platforms serve as tables.

Transportation

Sleds made of wood, whale jawbones, frozen animal skins, or frozen meat are pulled by dogs to travel over land. Boats called kayaks and umiaks made of wood, sealskin, or caribou skin are used to travel over water. Modern transportation also involves airplane and snowmobile travel.

Homeland

Nunavut is the Canadian province that belongs to the Inuit.

Global Beauty
(Clothing and Adornment)

Human clothing and adornment is closely tied to the world around us. Most humans who beautify themselves imitate elements from the natural world and take inspiration from the beauty of the Earth. Color, line, and texture are found everywhere in nature—from the majestic beauty of a male peacock's showy fan of feathers to the brilliant hues of a dramatic sunset.

People also use many earthly elements to make themselves more beautiful. Both clothing and cosmetics grew out of a basic human need to find protection from the natural elements of sun, wind, rain, and cold. To do this, humans have utilized plants, minerals, and various parts of animals to make everything from coats to cold cream.

The human practice of body painting and tattooing grew mostly out of important ceremonies or rituals, such as harvest festivals, birth celebrations, or weddings—special events for which people wished to make themselves beautiful in order to give thanks.

Holy man in South India

TRADITIONAL CLOTHING FROM AROUND THE WORLD

Bunad Norway

Hupa Iceland

Tuque Quebec, Canada

EUROPE

ASIA

Kilt Scotland

Dirndl Germany

Fez Turkey

Shanghai gown China

NORTH AMERICA

Feathered headdress Native American

Mantilla Spain

Huke Malta

Tarboosh Iran

Sari India

Kimono Japan

Grass skirt Hawaii

Galabia Egypt

Atlantic Ocean

Pacific Ocean

Sombrero Mexico

Kanga Kenya

Boubou Nigeria

AFRICA

Indian Ocean

Sarong Indonesia

Pacific Ocean

Panama hat Ecuador

SOUTH AMERICA

AUSTRALIA

Gaucho hat Argentina

Clothing

The traditional clothing of a people often has a lot to do with where they live and what they do to survive. People wear clothing to cover and protect their bodies. In the Arabian desert, women and men wear long, loose gowns to protect them from sand and sun during the day. In tropical climates, people wear light-colored clothes to reflect the hot sun, and open sandals to keep their feet cool. In the frozen Arctic, the Inuit wear thick furs and skins to stay warm. All around the globe, in every climate, humans make and wear clothes for personal decoration as well. Even early human warriors wore their animal skins both as protection and as a trophy.

Weaver at Bunratty folk park

Making clothes

Animal skins (leather), tree bark, leaves, and grass have been used to make clothes for many thousands of years. About 25,000 years ago, people began to sew these materials into clothing.

Fisherman's sweater and cap

• In ancient Egypt, linen was a popular fabric. Linen is woven from the stems of the flax plant. Mummified dead bodies were wrapped in linen.

• In parts of Asia, silk fabric was first woven from the cocoons of silkworms as early as the 27th century B.C.

• In Europe, wool from sheep, goats, and other fleecy animals is woven into fabric.

• In South America, people first made fabric from the cotton of the boll seed pod more than 5,000 years ago.

Warm Inuit coat ➤

• In Guatemala, weavers create designs based on Mayan traditions. Many designs have birds and animals mixed in with geometric elements. One end of the loom is attached to the weaver's waist with a strap. The other end is tied to a tree.

• The traditional Aran fisherman's sweater is knit from sheep's wool from the Aran Islands off the west coast of Ireland. The natural oil from sheep helps to make the sweaters waterproof.

• In Scotland, a tartan kilt is made from about 6 yards of material that is pleated into a 1-yard length.

• The people of Persia (now Iran) originated the modern style of dress. They were the first to cut and fit fabric to the body, which was more comfortable for horse riding.

Huli dancer

The Color of Wealth

Earth is colorful. All the colors and hues humans use to beautify themselves originated from the Earth. For centuries, the sources of colors were closely guarded secrets. Pigments for purple, yellow, and ultramarine blue were literally worth their weight in gold. In ancient times, cities were built on the fortunes made from the color purple. High prices were paid for purple dye because it was the color of royalty. Tyrian purple (the royal purple) was extracted from certain sea mollusks found only in the Mediterranean Sea, near Tyre, an ancient Phoenician city.

Colorful clothing is a trademark of the Lapp people who live in the Arctic regions of Europe. Children lost on the snowy tundra can be easily spotted in their brightly colored clothing.

World Wise

The Meanings and Uses of Color

Black

• In Japan, an inky black color is made from the pitch and soot of burned pine trees.

• Women in India use kohl, a black cosmetic preparation, to darken and outline the rims of their eyelids.

• Native Americans used black body paint to signify death.

Blue

• The Ashanti people of Africa wear blue as the color of mourning.

• Since 1748, "navy blue" has been the color used by the British for their navy uniform.

• Ultramarine blue was first made by grinding precious lapis lazuli stones.

• Blue is the national color of Scotland.

• Native Americans wore blue paint to show trouble.

Brown

• European artists painted many masterpieces with a brown pigment made from grinding the remains of Egyptian mummies.

American wedding

White

• In Japan, oyster shells are aged for a least 20 years before being crushed into a white pigment used to paint the faces of dolls.

• In the United States, white is worn by brides because it signifies purity.

• In India, white is the color of mourning.

• In Spain, women wear lace mantillas (head veils) of white when attending a bullfight.

Spanish dancer in parade

• Natives of North America were called red-skins by the Europeans because they painted their bodies for tribal rituals and ceremonies. They believed that red was the color of life.

• Many Asians celebrate Chinese New Year by hanging a red banner on their front door.

• In China, red is the color for a bride's dress.

• Tibetan monks wear red-brown robes. The color is made from roots, bark, and wild rhubarb that grow in the area.

• A red pigment used in Japan is made from the cochineal insect.

World Wise

The first synthetic dye (made from chemicals) was manufactured by William Perkin in 1856 in England. Before that time all dyes were made from rocks, stones, plants, and soil.

Red

• Explorers from Portugal used a red and purple pigment that the South American natives found in the brazilwood tree. The Portuguese called the area *Tierra de brazil*, which was later shortened to Brazil.

• In Thailand, mothers dress their babies in headgear with bright red pompoms in order to attract good fortune.

• Most Asians believe that red chases away evil spirits.

Chinese in costume

Purple

• Sea mollusks living around the Canary Islands, and near Oaxaca, Mexico, produce a highly valued shade of purple.

Yellow

• A highly prized yellow substance called saffron is obtained from the stigma of the crocus flower. It is used both as a dye and as a seasoning for food. The orange robes of some Buddhist monks of China are dyed with saffron.

Buddhist monks ➤

Shanghai gown

Garbs and Their Geography

The traditional clothing of people in the world countries is called the national costume. While many people throughout the world wear modern "western-style" clothing for everyday activities, they sometimes wear costumes to celebrate national holidays.

Hong Kong

Here, and in Singapore, a popular dress called the Shanghai gown is worn by many women. The dress is named after Shanghai, a city in China. Locally, the dress is called a *cheongsam*.

Indian saris

India

The sari appears in Hindi literature as early as 3,000 B.C. Today it is worn in many ways. In the south, it is draped between the legs to make pants. In central and south India, the sari looks like a gown. It is usually made from 6 yards of silk or cotton gauze material.

Malta

The women of this country favor a long, black, cloth cloak called a *huke*. The Moors, a people of mixed Arab and Berber descent from northwest Africa, introduced the huke to Malta.

Scotland

There are more than 2,500 tartan patterns. The first one was the Government or Black Watch pattern, which dates back to 1725. Clan tartans began at the end of the 19th century.

The Harris Tweed suit was originally designed as camouflage for hunters. The tweed fabric blends patterns and colors found in the countryside of Scotland. Each hunting estate has its own Harris Tweed, dyed to blend in with the local vegetation.

Nigeria

In Ijebu, the women weave a cloth called *aso olona*. The designs include crocodiles, frogs, and elephants with alternating bands of shaggy pile.

Fulani women of Uano

Germany

The people in Germany wear costumes for festivals. Women wear a Bavarian-style dirndl dress, and men wear lederhosen, leather shorts with suspenders. Many have Alpine flowers embroidered as part of the pattern.

KENTE CLOTH

Kente cloth has its origin in weavings from ancient West African kingdoms. The cloth that is known today comes from the 17th century. Its original use was for royalty. Even today, Kente cloth stands for social status within the community. There are numerous patterns, each with its own name and meaning. The colors of the cloths are also important.

Blue stands for the blue sky, where the Creator lives. In the cloths, it is used to show harmony. Red stands for blood. In the cloths, it is used to show sacrifice and struggle. White stands for the white part of the egg and for purity. Green represents growth and prosperity. Maroon represents the color of the earth, or soil. It is used to show healing.

Woman wearing Kente cloth ➤

Native American

The Kiowa Native Americans were a tribe from the northwestern Great Plains in the **United States**. They mostly wandered from place to place while they hunted bison.

The animals they hunted also provided them with clothing. Both men and women wore buckskin leggings and moccasins. Men's shirts and pants, and women's dresses were made from deerskin. These were decorated with shells, animals' teeth, and sometimes porcupine quills. The robes they wore for warmth during the winter were made from buffalo hides.

Tonga

The people in **Tonga** wear a wraparound skirt called a *tupenu*. Men wear knee-length skirts, and women wear ankle-length ones. All wear a sash at the waist, called a *ta'ovala* or *kie kie*.

Malaysia

The traditional costume in **Malaysia** for women is called the *baju kurung*. It consists of a loose-fitting tunic worn over a sarong, or loose-fitting skirt. The clothing for men is called a *baju melayu*, a loose shirt worn over trousers. Men also wear a velvet banded hat, called a *songkok*.

Woman from Ghana

Girl from Germany

Girl from Thailand

Man from Morocco

Beefeater

England

The guards at the Tower of London, called beefeaters, wear a Tudor costume. They have been the personal bodyguards of the English king or queen since 1485.

Japan

The kimono from Japan is from the Edo period, A.D. 1603—1867. The patterns in the fabric tell about the age of the wearer and the season the kimono is worn. A kimono that is worn in summer often has a water pattern. One that is worn in the fall has chrysanthemums as part of the design. During holidays, the design often shows plum blossoms, a symbol of good luck. Some kimonos have the family crest on them.

The kimono is worn with a sash, called an obi. The obi is made of silk and is usually 12 feet long and 12 inches wide. It is wrapped around the waist and tied

Geisha from Japan

at the back. The colors and way an obi is tied also tell the age of the wearer.

Finland

The country of Finland has two types of folk costumes. One is the West Finnish costume which has a colorful, striped skirt. This is worn with a laced blouse and a hip-length jacket.

The Karelian costume is off-white, black, and blue or red. It is embellished with lace-work and embroidery. The skirts are usually pleated. The headscarf is called a *sorokka*, which is made of linen. The costumes may be worn for a festival or even as a wedding dress.

IF THE SHOE FITS...

The main purpose of a shoe is to protect the wearer's feet. In some cultures, shoes also show one's status. Some ancient people even believed that shoes protected a person from the underworld.

- Dutch wooden shoes have been made for more than 500 years. Most shoes are made from poplar in the eastern part of the Netherlands.

- Mukluks are soft boots made of sealskin or reindeer skin worn by Eskimos. The word mukluk comes from the Yupik word *mak-lak*, meaning "bearded seal."

- Marquis Converse started Converse Rubber Company in 1908. He made the first sneakers and called them "Converse rubber shoes." His company brought out the first "Keds" brand in July 1916.

- The traditional footwear in Japan is a zori. It is a straw or rubber sandal with a flat sole and v-shaped thong that fits between the big and second toe.

Global Headwear

Sombrero ➤

People wear hats and headwear for protection, decoration, and communication. The ancient Egyptians often shaved their heads only to cover them with wigs of wool, plant fiber, and hair. The wigs were like hats. Not only did the hats decorate the head, but they also showed something about the person's place in society. Here are some notable hats from around the world.

Canada

The signature hat of the French-speaking farmers of Quebec is called a tuque.

Coolie hat

China

A coolie hat is worn by Chinese farmers. The hat is made of bamboo or straw. Farmers in Mexico wear similar hats. In China the hat is shaped like an umbrella to keep off the rain, but in Mexico the brim is turned up to hold water for drinking.

Ecuador

Panama hats, or *procesadora de sombreros*, are handwoven straw hats made in Ecuador. The thinner the hat, the better the quality. The Panama hat is named for the country of Panama, which was once the shipping center for these straw hats.

France

The French beret is a woolen hat with a flat top.

▲ Beret

Iceland

The *hupa*, a pancake-shaped hat with a gold cylinder and long black tassel, is considered a symbol of good fortune.

Iran

A tarboosh is a cap with glass cubes hanging from its rim. The glass is thought to be good for the blood and helpful in easing the pains of childbirth.

Mexico

The sombrero is a hat with a high crown for keeping the head cool. The broad brim protects the wearer from the sun and can also hold water and food. This hat is also used in the Mexican hat dance; during his solo, the male dances around and on the brim of the sombrero, which is placed on the dance floor.

Netherlands

The *volendam* cap, or Dutch cap, is a traditional hat worn for housecleaning.

North America

A cowboy hat was a very important possession for a cowboy of the Old West. It protected him from the elements. He also used it for carrying water and fanning a fire. Some cowboys even wore their hats to bed!

▲ Cowboy hat

India

The turban is a head covering worn by Muslim men. The word turban comes from *dulband*, which means "scarf wound around the head." Turbans offer protection from the sun. They can also show rank or status.

◄ Man with turban

Miter

RELIGIOUS HATS

The world's different religions use head coverings to show respect and reverence for God.

Roman Catholic	Bishops wear an official headdress covering called a miter. Some nuns wear a head covering called a coif beneath a veil.
Islam	Muslim women wear a head covering called a *hijab* and a face veil called a *niqab* as prescribed in the Koran.
Judaism	A man wears a hat called a yarmulke as a symbol of humility.
Sikhism	The men of this religion wear a turban to show their faith.

Sikh man

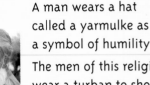
Boy with yarmulke

Muslims

The Story of Hair

The earliest recorded information on hairstyles comes from **Egypt** around 3,000 B.C. Today people in countries around the world wear a vast variety of diverse hairdos.

- In ancient Egypt, wigs were made from human hair or sheep's wool and often decorated with stripes.

- Dreadlocks come from the Caribbean. A religious group called Rastafarians do not believe in cutting their hair.

- Muslims traditionally cover their hair. Men often wear turbans, and women wear veils.

- In ancient **Rome**, wealthy women sprinkled gold dust in their dyed hair.

- In **England**, members of the Royal Court of Justice have a tradition of wearing wigs.

- Cornrows are an African-American style of hair braiding.

Derby

◄ **Girl with cornrows**

THREE HATS NAMED AFTER PEOPLE

- The derby hat is named after an Englishman, Edward Stanley, the Earl of Derby, who organized the English Derby horse race. The derby is also called a bowler and is worn by people throughout the world.

- The Stetson hat is named after John B. Stetson, an American hatmaker from Philadelphia, who created this quality hat for cowboys to wear.

- The "Gandhi hat" is named after "Mahatma" Gandhi, a spiritual and national leader of **India**. The style of this hat originated in his birthplace in western India. Gandhi redesigned the hat using less cloth so poor people could wear it.

Jewelry

All around the world, people use jewelry to adorn their clothes or body. Some jewelry has special significance, such as a diamond engagement ring. Other jewelry is worn just for fun.

Padaung girl, Thailand

- Kono, South Africa, is a valuable source of diamonds. About $5 million worth of diamonds are mined there every week!
- About 40% of the world's diamonds are mined in western Australia.

- Bombay, India, is the world's largest diamond-cutting center.
- In Ireland, a Claddagh ring is given as a token of friendship. The Irish consider it bad luck to buy one of these rings for one-self.
- In parts of southern Italy some men wear a gold horn, called a *cornetta*, on a chain around their necks. The *cornetta* is supposed to keep bad luck away.
- Women who belong to some ethnic groups in Thailand wear gold rings around their necks. More rings are added to gradually stretch and lengthen their necks.

Body Painting

From earliest times, humans have used paint to decorate their bodies, and protect their skin. Some people believe body painting enables them to endow themselves with magical powers.

Indian woman with a *bindi*

- Hindu women of India paint a red dot (*bindi*) on the center of their foreheads as a sign of blessing.
- In India, a paste made of henna leaves, called *mehndi,* is used to decorate the body. Women use henna to paint elaborate designs on their hands and feet, especially for weddings. Black henna is reserved for the soles of the feet. Red henna is used for the tips of fingers and toes. Today, *mehndi* painting is only decorative, but it was once thought to bring good luck and magic. *Mehndi* is a popular style of body decorating in the United States today. A *mehndi* design lasts for up to two weeks and is a pain-less alternative to tattooing.

Mehndi

- On islands in the south Pacific Ocean, women paint their faces with white rice powder to protect them from the sun.
- The Moroni women of the Comoros Islands wear a powder made of crushed coral shells to protect their faces.
- Native Americans have used body paint to repel insects, protect themselves from sun and wind, and show brave deeds, as well as for personal decoration.

- The Maori people of **New Zealand** no longer tattoo themselves. Instead, they paint their bodies in age-old traditional patterns.

- The Bari, Yukpas, and other indigenous people of **Venezuela** paint their bodies in elaborate designs. These designs indicate age and social group.

- Men in **New Guinea** use body and face paint as part of their ceremonial dances.

The Huli Wigman, New Guinea

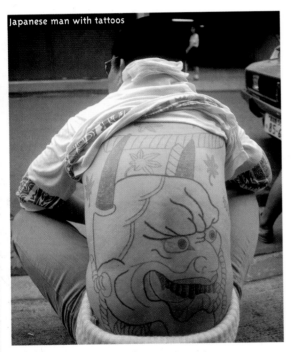
Japanese man with tattoos

In most traditional tattooing, the design and location of tattoos were determined by personal achievement and status.

explorers called the islands "Los Pintados" after the colorful tattoos of the people who lived there. The natives tattooed their bodies, except for forehead and chin, with fish, shells, shark teeth, and other images.

- In **China** and **Japan** during the 6th century, tattoos in the shapes of dogs or stripes were marked on the foreheads and forearms of criminals as a form of punishment.

- In **England** and the **United States** during the 19th century, prisoners were tattooed to identify them as convicts when they were released.

English punk

Tattoos

To tattoo is to pierce the skin with a needle and inject dye under the layer of skin. Tattoos date back as far as 4000–2000 B.C.—possibly even earlier. Tattoos within tribes expressed status, group, personal identity, traditions, and beliefs. Tattoos have traditionally depicted objects of a culture and its world. All around the globe, people try to make themselves more beautiful with tattoos.

The language of tattoos

In 1529, explorers from **Spain** landed on the Marshall Islands of the Pacific Ocean. The

- Tattoos once branded low-caste workers in **China**. These laborers did the "dirty work" of society, such as digging graves, and their tattoos separated them from the upper classes.

- The seafaring Vikings of Scandinavia wore tattoos of tribal symbols and family crests.

- In **Tahiti**, tattooing was a secret art form.

Traditional tattoo tools

➤ Borneo is one of the few places where tribal tattooing is still practiced. Needles are called *tatatau* and are carved from bones or shells. Dye is made from the soot of burned nuts, such as the candlenut.

The Daju people of north central Africa tattoo their eyelids.

Tattoo beliefs

• Women of the Kaya people of Borneo believe that a completely tattooed woman will bathe in a mythical river and collect pearls in her afterlife. A partially tattooed woman will stand on the shores of the river. An untattooed woman cannot approach the river.

TATTOO PROCEDURE OF KAYAN GIRLS OF BORNEO

- At age 10, all of her fingers and toes and the upper part of her feet are tattooed. A year later, her forearms are tattooed.

- At ages 13 and 14, both thighs to just below the knees are tattooed.

• People of Samoa believe a tattooed hand will insure a safe trip to the afterlife.

• The Iban of Borneo believe that a large hook tattooed on the ankle will deter crocodiles. Iban hunters catch crocodiles on hooks.

• Buddhist monks living in Asia in the 17th century tattooed prayers on their backs in calligraphy (a style of writing).

Dayak woman, Borneo

Body Piercing and Pulling

• Among some people of Africa, lip plates were worn to keep slavers away. Today, some Africans wear lip plates because they believe this practice will prevent evil spirits from entering the body through the mouth.

Masai boy in Kenya

• The Mayas of Mexico stretched their earlobes to great lengths in order to wear ear spools and earplugs.

• Among tribes of Borneo, earlobes are stretched to the shoulder by the weight of heavy earrings.

• The Inuit of Alaska wore lip plugs called labrets. Women wore one in the center of the lip. Men wore two—one in each side of the lip.

Scarification is the practice of cutting the skin and making a permanent pattern of raised welts.

Global Gab
(World Languages)

Language is spoken or written human speech. It is the most common means of communication among people. Wherever there is a human society, there is language. Most people learn the patterns of their language by the age of five or six. Language mastery includes reading, writing, speaking, and understanding words and phrases.

People use words to greet each other. The word *hello* was first used as a telephone greeting. When telephones first came into operation in the United States, people were confused about what to say when picking up a call. After experimenting with various telephone greetings, *hello* was adopted. In 1880, the "hello badge" was worn by telephone operators at their first national convention. Only in the United States is a telephone greeting also used in everyday speech.

Other world countries also have their own telephone greetings. In Italy, the greeting is *pronto*. In Japan, people say *moisha moisha* after picking up the phone.

World Wise

The English word talk *is from the Lithuanian language.*

NORTH AMERICA

EUROPE

ASIA

Atlantic Ocean

AFRICA

Pacific Ocean

SOUTH AMERICA

Indian Ocean

AUSTRALIA

- Indo-European
- Dravidian
- Uralic
- Altaic
- Afro-Asiatic
- Niger-Congo
- Nilo-Saharan
- Austro-Asian
- Sino-Tibetan
- Austronesian
- Korean
- Japanese
- Australian Aborigine
- Other groups
- Information unavailable

WORLD LANGUAGES

ANTARCTICA

Language Families

Language families are groups of languages that developed from a parent language. As speakers of a language divide into groups, their language develops in unique ways. After several centuries, the groups may speak languages that are so different, they may not understand one another at all! The languages remain in the same family, however, because they are all based on the same parent language.

Chinese written characters on a billboard

Croatia

France

Norway

THE INDO-EUROPEAN FAMILY OF LANGUAGES

Half of the world's population speaks the languages of the Indo-European family. Here are the eight branches and their languages.

LANGUAGE BRANCH	NAME(S) OF LANGUAGE(S)
German or Teutonic	English, Dutch, German, Danish, Icelandic, Norwegian, Swedish
Romance or Latin Romance	French, Spanish, Portuguese, Italian, Romanian
Balto-Slavic	Russian, Ukrainian, Polish, Czech, Slovak, Serbo-Croatian, Slovenian, Bulgarian, Lithuanian, Latvian
Indo-Iranian	Hindi, Urdu, Bengali, Farsi, Pashto
Greek	Greek
Celtic	Irish Gaelic, Scots Gaelic, Welsh, Breton
Albanian	Albanian
Armenian	Armenian

The Sino-Tibetan family

These are the leading languages of East Asia. They consist of one-syllable words. Word meaning is changed by the tone of voice used for otherwise identical words. The family includes Chinese, Thai, Burmese, and Tibetan.

Hebrew, Arabic, and English characters

The Afro-Asian family

These languages are concentrated in the Near East and in North Africa. The family includes Arabic, Hebrew, Amharic, and Berber.

The Uralic and Altaic family

Most of these languages are spoken in Asia. The family includes Finnish, Hungarian, Turkish, Mongol, and Manchu.

The Japanese and Korean family

These languages are mainly spoken in Japan, North Korea, and South Korea. The family is made up of Japanese and Korean.

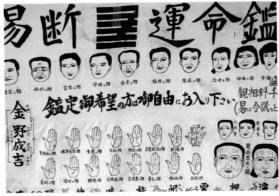

Japanese words and symbols

The Dravidian family

These languages are spoken in southern India and Sri Lanka. The family includes Tamil, Telugu, and others.

At least 600 universal languages have been proposed. Esperanto, created in 1887, is the most successful universal language with about 10 million speakers.

The Malayo-Polynesian family

This family includes the languages of Indonesia, the Philippines, Hawaii, New Zealand, Madagascar, and other Pacific and Indian Ocean islands.

The Mon-Khmer family

This family is sometimes called Austro-Asiatic. These languages are spoken in Southeast Asia and parts of India.

The Black African family

These languages are spoken in areas of Africa south of the Sahara and west of the Sudan. The three main families are Nilo-Saharan, Niger-Kordofanian, and Khoisan.

American Indian dances

The American Indian family

American Indian languages number over 1,000 and are spoken by 20 million people of North, Central, and South America.

Neon signs in China

The Top Two Languages

Chinese

The Chinese language has more than 40,000 different word pictures, or characters. Each one must be memorized individually in order to understand the language. Many Chinese words have similar pronunciations and different meanings. The Chinese determine word meaning by context and by tone of voice. A word may mean one thing when said in a high tone and another when uttered in a low tone.

Few Chinese people learn all the characters of their language. A well-educated adult commonly uses 10,000 of the 40,000 characters. A schoolchild is expected to learn 2,000 by the age of 10.

English is the native language in 34 countries.

English

The English language has a 26-letter alphabet. Words are formed by joining together consonants (closed sounds) and vowels (open sounds). It is estimated that there are 300 million native English speakers, 300 million more who speak English as a second language, and another 100 million who use it as a foreign

language. More people may speak Mandarin Chinese, but the use of English is more widespread throughout the world. English is the language used worldwide in aviation, diplomacy, computing, science, and tourism.

THE GROWTH OF ENGLISH

YEAR	NUMBER OF ENGLISH SPEAKERS	PERCENTAGE OF WORLD POPULATION
1600	5 to 7 million	1%
1960	400 million	13%
1993	750 million	14%

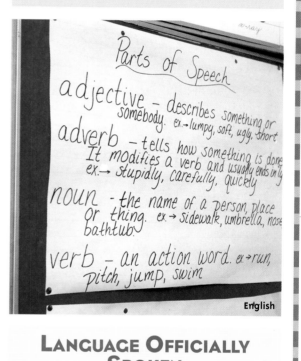

Parts of Speech

adjective – describes something or somebody. ex→ lumpy, soft, ugly, short

adverb – tells how something is done. It modifies a verb and usually ends in ly ex.→ stupidly, carefully, quickly

noun – the name of a person, place or thing. ex→ sidewalk, umbrella, nose, bathtub.

verb – an action word. ex→run, pitch, jump, swim

English

LANGUAGE OFFICIALLY SPOKEN

by number of countries

English	French	Arabic	Spanish	Portuguese
54	33	24	21	8

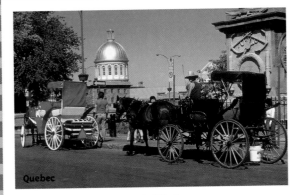
Quebec

Language Tidbits

• Pidgin English is a combination of one or more languages with English. In the Solomon Islands, the people speak a colorful Melanesian pidgin English.

• Creole is a dialect, or form, of French, Spanish, or Portuguese spoken in North and South America.

• A dead language is one that is no longer spoken. Egyptian, Etruscan, Hittite, Latin, and Gothic are dead languages.

• The only major French-speaking region in North America is the province of Quebec in Canada.

FIFTEEN MOST-SPOKEN WORLD LANGUAGES

LANGUAGE	# OF SPEAKERS
Mandarin (Chinese)	900 million
English	700 million
Hindi	320 million
Spanish	310 million
Russian	280 million
Arabic	185 million
Bengali	180 million
Portuguese	175 million
Malay/Indonesian	140 million
Japanese	125 million
German	120 million
French	115 million
Urdu	88 million
Punjabi	75 million
Korean	68 million

NUMBER OF LANGUAGES BY WORLD AREA

Europe
225

Asia
2,165

Americas
(North, Central,
and South)
1,000

Africa
2,011

Oceania
1,300

Switzerland

Do the Swiss Speak Swiss?

Switzerland has three official languages:
German, French, and Italian. All national laws
are published in these three languages. There
are actually four national languages. Romansh
is spoken in the mountain valleys of the
Graubunden canton by about 1% of the Swiss
population. Most Swiss speak a form of
German called Schwyzerdutsch.

COUNTRIES WITH THE MOST ENGLISH-LANGUAGE SPEAKERS

Approximate number of speakers, in millions

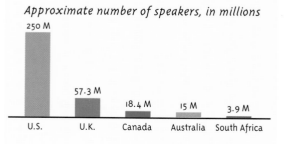

U.S.	U.K.	Canada	Australia	South Africa
250 M	57.3 M	18.4 M	15 M	3.9 M

FORKED TONGUES

Many countries use different languages
for different purposes. One language may
be the "official" language, but another
may be the most widely spoken. In other
countries, one language may be most
commonly spoken, but not as commonly
written. Here are some countries that use
at least two different languages:

China	Mandarin, Yue, Wu, Minbei, Minnan, Xiang, Gan, Hakka
Canada	English, French
Fiji	English, Fijian, Hindustani
India	Urdu, Tamil, Hindi
Israel	Hebrew, Arabic, English
South Africa	11 official languages including Afrikaans, English, Ndebele, Pedi, Sotho, Swazi, Tsonga, Tswana, Venda, Xhosa, and Zulu
Philippines	Pilipino, English
Romania	Romanian, Hungarian, German
Switzerland	German, French, Italian, Romansh
Zimbabwe	English, Shona, Sindebele

Family from Zimbabwe

Florida

Arches National Park, Colorado

THE LANGUAGE AND MEANING OF PLACE NAMES

Alabama	"I clear the land"	Choctaw*
Argentina	"Little silver"	Spanish
Arizona	"Place of the small spring"	Papago*
Canada	"Village"	Iroquois*
Chicago	"Skunk"	Polawatomi
Colorado	"Red rocks"	Spanish
Connecticut	"At the long tidal river"	Mohican*
Costa Rica	"Rich coast"	Spanish
Dakota	"Friend"	Sioux*
Ecuador	"Equator"	Spanish
Ethiopia	"Hot place"	Greek
Florida	"Flower"	Spanish
Idaho	"Light on the mountain"	Shoshone*
Illinois	"Warrior men"	Miami*
Japan	"Rising sun"	Mandarin
Kansas	"Land of the south wind people"	Sioux*

Costa Rica

Canada

Ohio

Japan

Kentucky	"Meadowland"	Iroquois *
Massachusetts	"Place near the big little hills"	Algonquin*
Minnesota	"Sky blue waters"	Sioux*
Mississippi	"Great river"	Ojibwa*
Missouri	"Muddy river"	Algonquin*
Naples	"New city"	Greek
Nebraska	"River in flatness"	Omaha*
Ohio	"Beautiful water"	Iroquois*
Oklahoma	"Red people"	Choctaw*
Pakistan	"Land of the pure"	Urdu
Panama	"Abundance of fish"	Cuna
Saskatchewan	"Rapid current"	Cree*
Trinidad	"Trinity"	Spanish
Venezuela	"Little Venice"	Spanish
Winnipeg	"Swamps"	Cree*
Wisconsin	"Grass place"	Algonquin*
Wyoming	"Place of big flats"	Algonquin*

* American Indian languages

Massachusetts

Wisconsin

GEOGRAPHIC TERMS IN WORLD LANGUAGES

Some commonly used geographic terms in English have different words in other languages. The words for many common geographical characteristics have become familiar in country names, cities, and other topographical features, such as Boca Raton and Puerto Rico.

Archipelago
A group or string of islands.
Japanese: *gunto, shuto*
Spanish: *archipiélago*

Bay

Bay
A body of water partly enclosed by land.
Chinese: *wan*
Portuguese: *bahia*
Swedish: *vik*

Cape
A pointed projection of land into the sea.
Arabic: *ras*
Italian: *capo*
Japanese: *saki*
Turkish: *burnu, baran*

Channel
A narrow waterway.
French, Spanish: *canal*
Malay: *selat*

Coast
The shoreline where land and sea meet.
French: *côte*
German: *land*
Russian: *bereg*
Spanish: *costa*

Desert
Dry, sandy, or pebbly land.
Arabic: *sahra* (sahara, plural)
Italian: *deserto*
Mongol: *gobil*

Estuary
The mouth of a river; where it empties into the sea.
French: *estuaire*
Spanish: *boca, estuario*

Gulf
A large area of sea partially enclosed by land.
Chinese: *won*
Italian, Portuguese, Spanish: *golfo*

Hill
A small elevation of land.
Arabic: *tel*
Japanese: *san*
Turkish: *tepe*

Island of Manhattan

Island
Land totally surrounded by water.
Chinese: *tao*
Italian: *isola*
Spanish: *isla*

Lagoon
A shallow body of water separated from a sea.
French: *étang*
Spanish: *laguna*

Mountain
Land that is elevated.
Dutch: *berg*
French: *mont*, *massif*
Italian, Portuguese, Spanish: *monte*

Pass
A narrow gap between mountains.
French: *col*
German: *pass*
Japanese: *toge*
Spanish: *paso*

Peak
The highest point of a mountain.
German: *spitz*
Italian: *picco*

Peninsula
Land that is almost surrounded by water.
Italian: *penisola*
Japanese: *hanto*
Spanish: *peninsula*

Plain

Plain
A large, rolling, flatland.
German: *feld*
Malay: *padang*
Russian: *step*

Plateau
An elevated flatland or tableland.
French: *plateau*
Italian: *altipiano*
Portuguese: *planalto*
Spanish: *mesa*

Plateau

Port
A place on a waterway for ships to dock.
French: *port*
Spanish: *puerto*

River
A stream or flow of water.
Arabic: *bahr*
Chinese: *kiang*, *ho*, *kong*
Dutch: *rivier*
Portuguese, Spanish: *rio*

Strait
A narrow channel of water between two large bodies of water.
Dutch: *straat*
French: *détroit*
Italian: *stretto*

Valley
A lowland between mountains.
Arabic: *wadi*
Dutch: *dal*
Portuguese, Spanish: *valle*

English Words Borrowed from World Languages

Animals

alligator	Spanish
buffalo	Greek
caribou	Algonquin
cheetah	Hindi
chipmunk	Algonquin
cobra	Portuguese
condor	Incan (Quechua)
coyote	Aztec (Nahuatl)
crocodile	Greek
dinosaur	Greek
elephant	Hebrew
gazelle	Arabic
gecko	Malay
giraffe	Arabic
ibis	Egyptian

iguana	Arawak
jaguar	Guarani
kangaroo	Guugu-Yimidhirr
llama	Incan (Quechua)
maggot	Welsh
monkey	Italian
moose	Cree
opossum	Cree
orangutan	Malay
penguin	Welsh
raccoon	Algonquin
shark	Mayan
skunk	Cree
terrapin	Algonquin
tiger	Farsi
walrus	Norwegian

Clothing

bandana	Hindi
flannel	Welsh
khaki	Farsi
kimono	Japanese
moccasin	Algonquin
pajama	Farsi (Iran, Afghanistan)
parka	Aleut
poncho	Spanish
sandal	Greek
sarong	Malay
sash	Farsi
shawl	Farsi

trousers	Gaelic
turban	Farsi
vest	French

Creatures

banshee	Gaelic
cherub	Hebrew
leprechaun	Gaelic
robot	Czech
spook	Dutch
vampire	Serbian (Balkans)
zombie	Kongo

Food

artichoke	Arabic
avocado	Aztec
banana	Senegalese (Wolof)
barbecue	Caribe
biscuit	French
broccoli	Italian
candy	Sanskrit
chili	Aztec
chocolate	Aztec
cider	Hebrew
cinnamon	Hebrew
cocoa	Incan (Quechua)
coleslaw	Dutch
cookie	Dutch
egg	Norse
guacamole	Aztec
hamburger	German
ketchup	Cantonese
lemon	Farsi
lime	Farsi
macaroni	Italian

marmalade	Portuguese
molasses	Portuguese
orange	Sanskrit
papaya	Caribe
pastrami	Romanian
pecan	Algonquin
pepper	Sanskrit
pickle	Dutch
pistachio	Farsi
pizza	Italian
potato	Taino (Caribbean)
pretzel	German
rice	Farsi
sauce	French
soup	French
spaghetti	Italian
spinach	Farsi
sugar	Sanskrit
tea	Amay (East China)
waffle	Dutch
yam	Senagalese (Wolof)
yogurt	Turkish

Sports

acrobat	Greek
athlete	Greek
billiards	Breton (French)
caddy	French
fumble	Dutch
golf	Gaelic

gymnasium	Greek
jockey	Hebrew
judo	Japanese
jujitsu	Japanese
league	Breton (French)
ski	Norwegian
tackle	German

Name-calling

bandit	Italian
brat	Gaelic
pet	Gaelic
phony	Gaelic
slob	Gaelic
vandal	German

Other words

alcohol	Arabic
algebra	Arabic
assassin	Arabic
attic	Greek
ballot	Italian
bar	Breton
bark	Egyptian

jungle	Hindi
kidnap	Danish
magic	Farsi
pouch	Breton
rock	Breton
shampoo	Hindi
sheriff	Arabic
silhouette	Basque
sofa	Arabic
souvenir	French
stove	Dutch
tan	Breton
tattoo	Tahitian
tobacco	Arawak
window	Norse

bizarre	Basque (Spanish)
branch	Breton (French)
bribe	Breton
career	Breton
coupon	French
diaper	Arabic
dollar	German
duffel	Dutch
elope	Dutch
ghetto	Italian
growl	Dutch
hurt	Breton
job	Breton

Transportation

barge	Egyptian
canoe	Caribe
car	Breton
coach	Hungarian
dinghy	Bengali
kayak	Inuit
toboggan	Micmac
wagon	Dutch

Exclamations

amen	Hebrew
gusto	Italian
hallelujah	Hebrew

"Two Countries Separated by a Common Language"

The English that Americans speak comes directly from the "Queen's English" of Great Britain. Though much of the language is the same, there are some notable differences in word usage. Here is a sampling of American English words and their British counterparts.

AMERICAN	BRITISH	AMERICAN	BRITISH
Apartment	Flat	Gasoline	Petrol
Baby carriage	Pram	Hood	Bonnet
Bathroom	W.C. (water closet)	Pharmacy	Chemist
Dessert	Pudding	Police officer	Bobby
Elevator	Lift	Truck	Lorry
Flashlight	Torch	Sausages	Bangers
French fries	Chips	Sneakers	Plimsolls
Galoshes	Rubbers	Subway	Underground

"Other" English

English-speaking people in Australia and Ireland have a twist to their use of language. Here are some commonly used words and their American English equivalents.

AUSTRALIAN	AMERICAN	IRISH	AMERICAN
Barbie	Barbecue	Bap	Hamburger bun
Bloke	Man	Bangers and mash	Sausage and mashed potatoes
Bonzer	Great	Busker	Street musician
Chook	Chicken	Candy floss	Cotton candy
Dingo	Wild dog	Caravan	Trailer
Dinkim	Honest	Chips	French fries
Jackaroo	Sheep rancher	Coach	Bus used for long distances
Grazier	Rancher		
Outback	Remote bush area	Crisps	Potato chips
Oz	Australia	Dear	Expensive
Sandshoes	Sneakers	Gaol	Jail
Sheila	Woman	Hire	Rental
Ta	Thank you	Hoover	Vacuum cleaner
Tatu	Good-bye	Lav	Bathroom
Tucker	Food	Nappies	Diapers

What's in a Phrase?

Some phrases that Americans commonly use originally came from a variety of other languages. Here are a few:

R.S.V.P.

LATIN PHRASE	MEANING
Ad infinitum	to infinity
Bona fide	genuine
Mea culpa	my fault
Pro bono	free of charge
Persona non grata	unwelcome person

ITALIAN PHRASE	MEANING
Dolce vita	the good life
Nota bene	note well

FRENCH PHRASE	MEANING
Coup de grâce	finishing blow
Carte blanche	unrestricted power to act
Nom de plume	pen name
Faux pas	social mistake
Fait accompli	a foregone conclusion
R.S.V.P. (répondez s'il vous plaît)	please reply

Words in Different Languages

When people travel, they often learn a few words or phrases from the countries they visit. Some of these words may be similar to ones you already know.

"HELLO"

Guten tag	German
Ciao	Italian
Shalòm	Hebrew
Aloha	Hawaiian
Jambo	Swahili
Bonjour	French
Hola	Spanish
Alo	Portuguese
Hallo	Danish
Hej	Swedish
Ha lo	Esperanto
Dobry den	Czech

China

"Good-bye"

Auf widersehen	German
Arrivederci	Italian
Zaijian	Mandarin Chinese
Adios	Spanish
Ma salama	Egyptian Arabic
Hej då	Swedish
Dag	Dutch
Shalom	Hebrew

Egypt

Ha' det godt	Danish
Adiau	Esperanto
Alamsiki	Swahili
Sayonara	Japanese
Adieu	French
Adeus	Portuguese
Sbohem	Czech
Hyvästi	Finnish

"Thank you"

Danke	German
Hao	Mandarin Chinese
Grazie	Italian
Shukran	Egyptian Arabic
To – dà	Hebrew
Dank u	Dutch
Aye	Swahili
Merci	French
Gracias	Spanish
Obrigado	Portuguese
Tak	Danish
Dankon	Esperanto
De' kuji	Czech
Tack tack	Swedish

France

"Please"

Bitte	German
Wees zo goed	Dutch
S'il vous plaît	French
Por favor	Spanish
Por favor	Portuguese
Per favore	Italian
Vaer sa god at	Danish
Bonvolu	Esperanto
Miellyttää	Finnish
Varsågod	Swedish
Tafadah	Swahili

Germany

Global Gourmet
(The Geography of Tastes)

The first celebrations in many cultures began as harvest festivals—giving thanks for the foods of Earth. To this day, food continues to bring people together in celebration, admiration, and remembrance. In many religions, followers believe that food cannot be eaten unless it is first offered to their God. Among most Native American tribes, food is considered a gift. They respect the plant or animal being eaten by asking forgiveness for taking its life. And in Norway, children commonly shake hands with their mother after every meal and thank her for the food she has prepared.

GOURMET CAPITALS OF THE WORLD

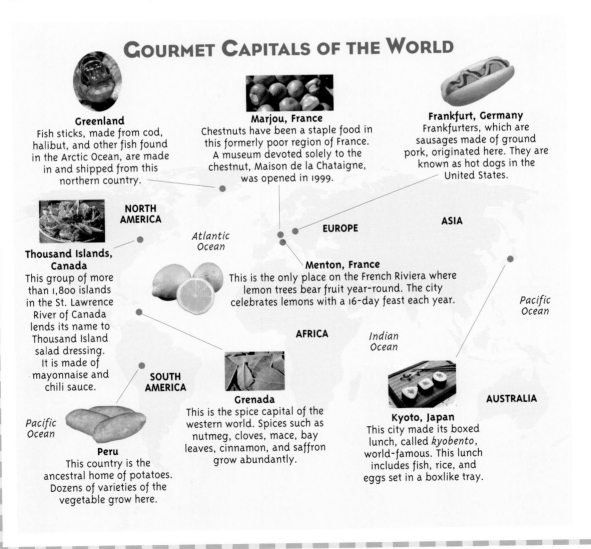

Greenland
Fish sticks, made from cod, halibut, and other fish found in the Arctic Ocean, are made in and shipped from this northern country.

Marjou, France
Chestnuts have been a staple food in this formerly poor region of France. A museum devoted solely to the chestnut, Maison de la Chataigne, was opened in 1999.

Frankfurt, Germany
Frankfurters, which are sausages made of ground pork, originated here. They are known as hot dogs in the United States.

NORTH AMERICA

Atlantic Ocean

EUROPE

ASIA

Thousand Islands, Canada
This group of more than 1,800 islands in the St. Lawrence River of Canada lends its name to Thousand Island salad dressing. It is made of mayonnaise and chili sauce.

Menton, France
This is the only place on the French Riviera where lemon trees bear fruit year-round. The city celebrates lemons with a 16-day feast each year.

Pacific Ocean

AFRICA

Indian Ocean

SOUTH AMERICA

Grenada
This is the spice capital of the western world. Spices such as nutmeg, cloves, mace, bay leaves, cinnamon, and saffron grow abundantly.

Kyoto, Japan
This city made its boxed lunch, called *kyobento*, world-famous. This lunch includes fish, rice, and eggs set in a boxlike tray.

AUSTRALIA

Pacific Ocean

Peru
This country is the ancestral home of potatoes. Dozens of varieties of the vegetable grow here.

Famine Foods

Although there is enough food to feed all of the people living in the world, many people are dying of starvation. Famine, which is a drastic, wide-reaching shortage of food, may be caused by many different situations. Several factors, including pests, plant diseases, and weather disasters such as drought or flooding, can cause crops to fail.

Earthquakes and cyclones also destroy farmland and limit food production. Some human actions can also cause famine. Desertification, which is a combination of deforestation, over-cultivation, and over-grazing, can turn once-fertile land to desert. Wars, which can destroy farmland, also cause farmers to abandon their fields to fight as soldiers. In developing countries, poor transportation and the inability to distribute food can cause famine as well.

Potatoes

World Wise

After 20 years of drought and deforestation in the Sahara region of Africa, the Sahara Desert expanded.

"Hooting at Hunger"

In Ghana, there is a yearly harvest festival known as *Homowo*, which means "to hoot at hunger." It is based on ancient traditions practiced when times of famine were followed by plentiful harvests. People would celebrate the abundance of food and mock the hunger of the past. Today, the rulers of each region walk through villages during the festival and sprinkle the ritual famine food *kpekpele*—cornmeal mixed with palm oil.

Worldwide, victims of famine have commonly eaten dirt and grass for nourishment. This practice is called geophagy. Chinese people, for instance, have eaten a flour made of ground leaves, thistles, or cotton-seeds; oils made from rice husks, grass roots, and corncobs; and juice made from sugar-cane waste. In 1998, the people of South Korea ate meals made from blending twigs, weeds, and dirt. These meals were known as "alternative food for the hungry."

FOOD FACTS

- More foods are made with wheat than with any other cereal grain.
- An average ear of corn (also called maize) has 800 kernels in 16 rows.
- The most important food crops in the world, in order of importance, are wheat, rice, corn, and potatoes.
- Pineapple upside-down cake was the celebratory food of the United States space program, NASA. After every successful launch, this cake was served with coffee.

- Frying foods originated in Africa.
- Ice cream was created in China. This treat then traveled to India, the Middle East, and Italy. It was introduced to the United States by Thomas Jefferson.
- The first freeze-dried foods were made by the people of ancient Peru. They preserved potatoes by freezing them in water at night, and then stomping out the moisture and drying them in the sun.

Ice cream ➤

Country Beverages

Argentina

Yerba maté is served hot or cold. *Yerba*, dried leaves of an ilex tree, are placed in a gourd with boiling water and then sipped through a metal straw.

Tea ➤

China

Soy milk is preferred here. Green and black teas are also drunk throughout the day, but usually not during a meal.

Sake

Egypt

Fragrant hibiscus tea is the favorite beverage in Egypt.

England

The national drink is tea. It is served in late afternoon, usually with biscuits or scones.

Japan

Sake, a wine made from rice, is the national drink.

Kazakhstan

Fermented mare's milk, or *kumiss*, is a popular beverage in this country.

Mexico

Tascalte is a drink that combines chocolate, ground pine nuts, sugar, vanilla, and *achiote* (a flavoring of onions, orange juice, and spices).

Peru

Chich morad is a beverage that has been prepared since ancient times. It is brewed from purple corn and flavored with cinnamon.

Philippines

A milkshake made with avocados is the national treat.

Trinidad

Peanut punch is served at all festive occasions.

United States

In colonial times, Americans drank coffee between meals. Today, coffee is usually drunk with breakfast and after dinner. American adults consume about 400 cups of coffee per year.

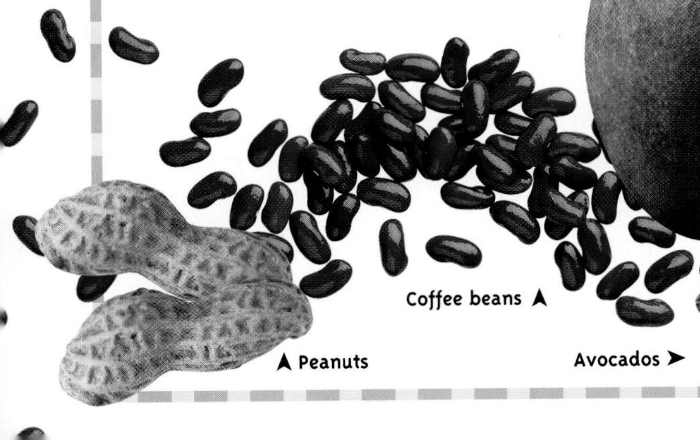

Coffee beans ▲

▲ Peanuts

Avocados ➤

Nutmeg

Paprika

Curry

Ginger

SPICES

For a century, Europeans eagerly pursued the spices of the East Indies. Nutmeg was actually worth more than its weight in gold in 16th- and 17th-century Europe! It was invaluable as an excellent meat preservative before the dawn of refrigeration. Many people thought nutmeg could also cure diseases. Today, spices are shared worldwide. Here are some of the signature spices of national cuisines.

Bhutan
Chili pepper and cheese, known as *asema* and *dachi*, are necessary ingredients for every dish.

Hungary
Paprika is made from dried red peppers.

India
Curry is made from a blend of coriander, turmeric, cumin, onions, chili peppers, and anise seeds.

Mexico
Achiote is a favorite flavoring made of onions, sour orange juice, cilantro, and *habanero* chili peppers.

Nepal
Coriander, cumin, garlic, ginger, and chili peppers are all used in the food.

Peru
A yellow pepper, *aji amarillo*, and a minty licorice-like herb known as *huacatuy* are essential flavorings.

Sri Lanka
Black curry, a seasoning made from roasted curry powder, lemon grass, and cardamom, flavors food in this country.

Vietnam
Nuoc cham is a blend of garlic, red pepper, sugar, lime juice, and fish stock.

Cereal Grains of the World

Rice

The major food grains of the world are: rice, wheat, corn, oats, barley, and rye. They are all part of the grass family.

Rice

The most popular food crop in the world is rice, which is a water grass. It grows in fields called paddies.

• *Arborio* is an Italian rice used for risotto and other Italian dishes.

• Basmati rice is a fragrant rice first grown in the foothills of the Himalayan Mountains in India.

• Black rice has a black outer layer and is commonly eaten in China, Thailand, and Bali.

• Carolina rice is a white, long-grain rice grown in South Carolina. It cooks up dry and fluffy, and is often called American-style rice.

• Louisiana pecan rice is a long-grain rice characterized by its aromatic flavor.

• Puffed rice is widely eaten in India. This rice puffs out after being heated under pressure.

• Wild rice is a ricelike seed of a wild grass that grows in Canada, Minnesota, and Wisconsin.

Wheat

China grows the most wheat in the world, followed by the United States, India, France, Russia, and Canada. Wheat has two

Wheat

growing seasons. Winter wheat is sown in fall and harvested in spring. Spring wheat is planted in spring and harvested in late summer. Wheat types are classified by the hardness, color, and kernel shape.

• Hard red winter wheat is ground into an all-purpose flour used to make breads and sweets.

• Hard red spring wheat has the highest percentage of protein and is a good bread wheat.

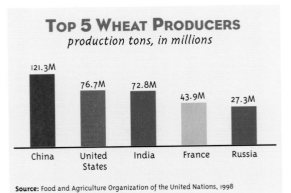

TOP 5 WHEAT PRODUCERS
production tons, in millions

China — 121.3M
United States — 76.7M
India — 72.8M
France — 43.9M
Russia — 27.3M

Source: Food and Agriculture Organization of the United Nations, 1998

TOP 5 RICE PRODUCERS
production tons, in millions

China — 212.7M
India — 134.7M
Indonesia — 51.0M
Bangladesh — 31.1M
Vietnam — 30.4M

Source: Food and Agriculture Organization of the United Nations, 1998

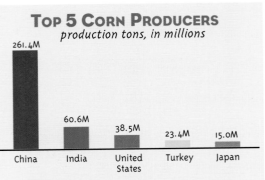

TOP 5 CORN PRODUCERS
production tons, in millions

China — 261.4M
India — 60.6M
United States — 38.5M
Turkey — 23.4M
Japan — 15.0M

Source: Food and Agriculture Organization of the United Nations, 1998

Sweet corn

• Soft red winter wheat is low in protein and is used for flatbreads, cakes, pastries, and crackers.

• Durum wheat is one of the hardest wheats. It is used to make semolina flour for pasta.

• Hard white wheat is mild and rather sweet. It is used for Oriental noodles and tortillas.

• Soft white wheat is low in protein and is used for making cakes, muffins, and pastries.

Corn

Corn first grew in the **Americas**. Today it is grown on every continent except **Antarctica**. In the **United States**, corn is the major grain grown to feed livestock. It is a common ingredient in cereals, peanut butter, and various snack foods. Not only is corn a nourishing food, but it also cleans the air and protects water quality as it grows.

• Dent corn is the most commonly grown corn in the United States. It contains 85% starch and is used to feed livestock, and to make corn syrup, cornstarch, and the fuel ethanol.

• Sweet corn is the most common eating corn. It has a high sugar content and is harvested when the plant is immature and the kernels are still soft. Both canned corn and corn on the cob are sweet corns.

World Wise

Native Americans brought popcorn to the first Thanksgiving feast.

• Popcorn is a special kind of corn that contains moisture inside the kernel. When cooked at high heat, the kernel pops open.

• Food-grade corn may be blue, white, or yellow in color. It is ground into meal and is used to make cornbread, tortillas, and chips.

Corn

Exotic or Unusual Foods of the World

Ant eggs

Found in big clumps on the branches of certain mango trees in the Philippines, these delicacies are fried in butter, leaving the outsides crispy and the insides creamy.

Insects provide about 10% of the protein eaten by humans worldwide.

Bats

These are a popular food in Africa, Asia, Australia, and the South Pacific Islands. They are cooked in underground pits. The 3-pound (1.3-kg) flying fox bat is a favorite.

Birds' nests

In China and the Philippines, the nests of the Asian swift are highly prized in soups.

Blubber

The skin and fat of sea mammals, such as seals, walruses, and whales, is called *muntuk* by the Inuits. The *muntuk* is rolled in herbs and spices and stored in underground pits to ferment before it's eaten.

Costa Rican wood cockroach

◄ Bat

Cockroaches

In Bangkok, Thailand, roaches up to 4 inches (10 cm) long are roasted before being eaten. Roasted locusts and beetles are also enjoyed here.

Dog meat

In the Philippines, *azucena*, or dog meat, is popular, especially in the Mountain Province, where the animals are raised for food.

The Spanish explorers introduced pigs, chickens, and cows to South America, replacing guinea pigs as the staple meat.

Flies

In India, a sugar pastry named *jalebis* is decorated and eaten with flies.

Guinea pigs

In Peru, guinea pigs, or *cuys*, are served with either a peanut sauce or a chili sauce.

Kangaroo

Until recently, kangaroo meat was commonly used as dog food in Australia. Now kangaroo has become a popular game meat in Europe and Australia.

Polar bear

This meat was once eaten raw by coastal Inuits because they lacked cooking fuel.

Prickly pear cactus

Scorpions

In China, these arachnids are eaten fried or cooked in a soup. They are also served live as an appetizer.

Seaweed jelly

Cha hovy is a dish of Cambodia that combines seaweed jelly and coconut milk.

Smuts

This is the name for a fungus parasite that grows on grain. It is gray in color with black spores that look like soot. It is eaten in China and in Mexico (where it's called *huitlacoche*), and by Native Americans in the United States.

Wormwood

In the Philippines, wormwood is taken from driftwood. The wood is chopped so that the pink worms, about 6 to 8 inches (15 to 20 cm) long, can be picked out, washed, and eaten raw.

Prickly pear cactus

The pads of the prickly pear cactus, called *nopals*, are eaten in salads, soups, and casseroles in the southwestern United States. First the needles are carefully removed. The pads are then brushed with garlic, grilled, and eaten.

◄ Scorpion

THE GEOGRAPHY OF TASTES IN THE UNITED STATES

- Americans' favorite sandwich is ham with mayonnaise.
- The favorite American potato dish is French fries.
- Americans prefer vanilla ice cream, and eat it mostly in the month of July and on Sundays.
- Three-quarters of all beef eaten in the United States is in the form of hamburgers.
- Hot dogs are most popular in the East and Midwest.
- Southerners like their chicken fried, while Americans in the Northeast prefer it roasted.
- Most Americans choose creamy peanut butter over chunky, except in the West, where chunky is favored.

French fries

Breakfast Around the World

The first foods eaten in the morning "break" the "fast" of the night before, and are therefore called breakfast. Here are some typical breakfasts from around the globe.

Argentina
Coffee with milk or steamed milk with bittersweet chocolate melted into it; and bread.

Australia
Toast topped with either spaghetti or baked beans and bacon.

Meats and bread

Belize
Egg dishes, chorizo and other sausages, tortillas, sweet breads, and fried plantains.

Bolivia
A mid-morning snack of *saltenas,* or pastries filled with a mixture of meats, peas, potatoes, eggs, raisins, and olives.

Bulgaria
Sesame bread, sheep's milk, cheese, honey, olives, boiled eggs, and yogurt.

China
In northern China, soy milk with steamed wheat buns stuffed with pickles. In southern China, porridge made of rice (*congee*) with pickled turnip or cabbage.

England
An array of meats including bacon, sausages, kidney, and mutton chops, along with eggs, grilled tomato, oatmeal, smoked fish, crumpets, and toast.

◄ Swiss cheese

India
Khichri, a mixture of rice, lentils, and spices; *appam*, a thin rice pancake filled with meat and potatoes; *idi-appam*, rice noodles with sweet coconut milk; *idli*, steamed rice and split peas cakes; or *puttu*, steamed rice and coconut served with bananas and milk.

Ireland
Bacon, sausages, grilled tomato, fried eggs, black pudding, brown bread, soda bread, and toast.

Japan
Miso soup, rice with seaweed flakes, and pickles made from unripe plums.

Madagascar
Cornmeal gruel with *kitoza*, which are thin strips of grilled beef.

Netherlands
Cereal, eggs, breads, cold meats, green herring pickled in brine, and warm milk flavored with anise seed.

Scrambled eggs

Pakistan
Cholla, spicy chickpeas in tamarind gravy.

Russia
Black bread, blini, sausages, fried eggs, cucumber pickles, and kasha (buckwheat cereal) with sour cream and sugar.

White rice ➤

Turkey
Bread with butter and honey; soup of meat broth and cheese; black olives; and sheep's milk cheese.

United States
Coffee, eggs, pancakes, sausage, bacon, toast, cereal, and bagels.

Vietnam
Xoi, sticky steamed rice with peanuts.

Wales
Laverbread (made with seaweed) served plain or mixed with oatmeal; and fried cockles (which are similar to mussels).

STAPLE FOODS

Staple foods are crops that are grown in a region of the world and are basic to the diet of the people of that area.

Africa	Cassavas, yams, corn, sweet potatoes, plantains, bananas, sorghum, millet, legumes (beans), rice, wheat, and potatoes
Asia	Rice, corn, sweet potatoes, cassavas, potatoes, legumes, bananas, plantains, barley, millet, and sorghum
Latin America and the Caribbean	Corn, wheat, rice, potatoes, barley, bananas, plantains, legumes, casssavas, and sweet potatoes
Middle East and North Africa	Wheat, rice, corn, potatoes, legumes, barley, millet, sorghum, bananas, plantains

Legumes

Rice

Lentils

Okra

Cranberries

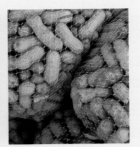
Peanuts

ORIGINS OF FOOD

Even though we think of spaghetti as an Italian food, this pasta/noodle dish actually has its roots in China. The global table now holds foods from all over the world. This is a partial listing of where these foods first grew.

Africa
Coffee, okra, yams, melons, sesame seeds

Asia
Lemons, peaches, rice, black pepper, millet, wheat, barley, water chestnuts, sugarcane, onions

Europe, Mediterranean, Middle East
Apples, asparagus, peas, olives, figs, grapes, dates, lentils, chickpeas

North America
Cranberries, squash, sunflowers, Jerusalem artichokes

South America
Corn, guavas, peanuts, sweet potatoes, white potatoes, peppers (sweet and hot), avocados, pineapples, vanilla, tomatoes, green beans, chocolate

◄ Potatoes

◄ Tomatoes

◄ Pineapples

▲ Asparagus

Apple pie

The Global Table

Apple pie and hamburgers are considered foods of the **United States**. Although apple pie probably originated in **England**, it was the success of apple orchards in the United States that made this a popular American dessert.

The average American eats 141 pounds (64 kg) of potatoes and 3 pounds (1.3 kg) of peanut butter each year.

Hamburgers were first made by immigrants from Hamburg, **Germany**. The buns were added in the United States, and hamburgers were first mass-produced in the 1950s. Now, fast food American-style hamburgers are found throughout the world. Many other countries have foods that are considered their national dishes.

Ham

Albania
The national dish is *pieta*, which is a pie of spinach and cheese.

Argentina
Beef rules in this country and is the basis of the empanada, or meat turnover, which also contain raisins, olives, and onions.

Barbados
The national dish is a pudding, which is made from pig's belly stuffed with sweet sausages, potatoes, beets, spices, and fiery hot peppers.

Stew

Belarus
Draniki, a dish of grated potatoes fried in oil and served with sour cream, is the national dish of this potato-growing country.

Brazil
Feijoada is a stew made of various meats, sausages, and black beans. It is usually prepared on Saturdays and served daily as an accompaniment to other foods, or alone as a main dish.

Costa Rica
Gallo pinto, or spotted rooster, is the national dish. It combines fried rice and black beans, is lightly spiced, and may be served with sour cream.

Shish kebab

Cuba

Picadillo is a hash which combines ham, beef, potatoes, raisins, and olives with rice and fried eggs.

Dominican Republic

Sancocho is the favorite meal, especially for festive occasions. This rich stew combines chicken, pork, plantains, yucca, and vegetables, and is served with rice.

Ethiopia

Enjera is the national dish. It is a gray flatbread made from *tef*, a local grain. Meats and vegetables in a spicy sauce (*wat*) are spread on the pancake-like bread.

France

Escargots, or snails, are cooked in garlic and butter for this famous French dish.

Tortilla

Germany

Many types of sausages, such as frankfurters and bratwursts, and more than 200 varieties of breads distinguish this cuisine.

Hungary

Goulash, a beef and vegetable stew seasoned with paprika, is the national dish.

Korea

Kimchi is the most popular food in Korea. It's made of cabbage and other vegetables combined with garlic, ginger, and hot spices.

Lapland Region

Reindeer is the meat served most often in the Lapland region of northern Sweden, Norway, Finland, and Russia.

Escargots

Lebanon

The national dish is *kibbeh*, which is a paste made of lamb and bulgur wheat.

Liberia

Jolloif is a stew made with rice, tomatoes, spices, and either goat meat, chicken, or pigs' feet.

Mexico

The tortilla, a pancake made of corn or wheat, is filled with meat, vegetables, and cheese. It is this country's signature dish.

Netherlands

The national dish is *rijstafel*, which was borrowed from Indonesia. It consists of rice served with dishes of fish, barbecued meat, pickled vegetables, and salad in peanut sauce.

Romania

Stuffed peppers, or *ardei umpluti*, are sweet peppers stuffed with spiced meat and rice.

Russia

Borscht, or beet soup, is served with piroshki (savory pastries).

Chocolate cake ➤

Scotland

Haggis is the national dish. A mixture of the minced heart, lungs, and liver of a sheep is blended with oatmeal, onions, and seasonings and boiled in the stomach of the sheep.

Spain

Paella is the national dish. It combines a variety of meats, fish, and vegetables atop a saffron-flavored rice. *Jamon serrano*, or ham, is also very popular.

Sweden

The smorgasbord is an array of local delicacies served cold. Smoked salmon, cheeses, eggs, and vegetables are included.

Turkey

Lamb shish kebab grilled on a skewer is the traditional food.

Vienna

Chocolate cakes and pastries, especially the Sacher torte, are world-famous.

Africa is the world leader in cassava, a starchy root, and consumes 80% of what it produces.

CITY SPECIALS

Buffalo, New York	Buffalo wings—deep-fried chicken wings brushed with hot sauce—were created here.
Chicago, Illinois	Deep-dish pizza pies are called "Chicago style" because they were first made popular here.
New Orleans, Louisiana	Gumbo is a spicy seafood stew made with okra. It is often associated with this city because okra is common here.
Key West, Florida	Key lime pie is made with tart, yellowish limes that grow throughout the region.

Key lime pie

Globally Green
(The World of Plants)

Plants are the most amazing living things on Earth because they make all other life-forms possible. They make the air we breathe and the food we eat. Plants—from grasses to trees—grow in almost every part of the world, including deserts, mountaintops, and icy plains.

Humans owe their entire existence to plants. The world's many plants provide us with clothing, shelter, medicines, and other daily needs. Plants also take energy from the sun, carbon dioxide from the air, and water and minerals from the soil to make food and to give off oxygen.

Plants grow in earthly communities called biomes. Biomes are large geographic areas, and each biome has its own climate, plant life, and animal population. The largest biome is the water biome, covering nearly 75% of Earth's surface. All life on Earth began in water more than 3 billion years ago, when microscopic plants first grew in the seas and made all other life possible. Plants found in the oceans supply much of the world's oxygen.

Human activities have drastically changed and threatened many of these biomes. We must now work to preserve these regions to maintain a healthy planet.

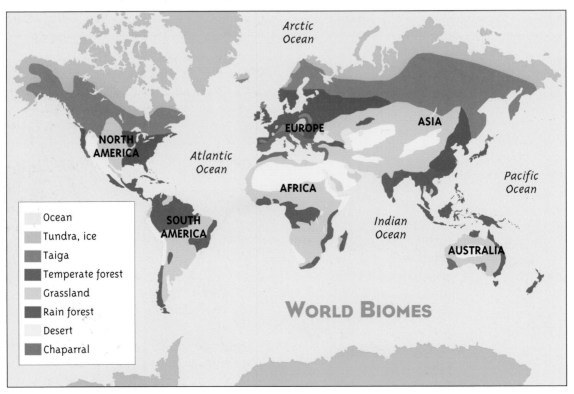

WORLD BIOMES

Legend:
- Ocean
- Tundra, ice
- Taiga
- Temperate forest
- Grassland
- Rain forest
- Desert
- Chaparral

Major Land Biomes

Chaparral

This biome is characterized by thick growths of shrubs and small trees. Chaparrals are found in western **North America**, around the Mediterranean Sea in **Europe** and northern **Africa**, and in southern parts of **Australia**, Africa, and **South America**. When located near mountains, the vegetation of this biome helps prevent flooding and soil erosion. The chaparral is a fire zone where summer fires are common.

Climate: Rainy, mild winters; hot, dry summers.

Plant life: Most plants have tough, crooked branches with leathery leaves that remain throughout the winter. Few plants grow taller than 10 feet (3 m). Frequent fires occur here because some of the shrubs have essential oils that make them burn easily. Other plants resist fire damage, however, or are able to grow back quickly. Some plants' growth is actually stimulated by the heat of the fires.

Common chaparral plants: Chamiso shrub, manzanita, mountain mahogany, sage, scrub and cork oaks, and rare herbs.

⚠ **Threats to the biome:** None.

Desert

Deserts are sandy or rocky regions with very little rainfall. Deserts cover one-fifth of all land. Desert plants grow far apart so that each plant can capture as much rainwater as possible. Oases are parts of deserts where water is

Desert biome

always available and plants are abundant. An oasis is formed by a pool of water trapped in rock layers beneath the desert floor.

Climate: Extremely dry, with an average yearly rainfall of less than 10 inches (25 cm). Most deserts are hot, with daytime temperatures above 100 degrees Fahrenheit (38° C). Some are cold at night. The Gobi Desert of **Asia** is cold most of the time.

Plant life: Deserts are second only to tropical rain forests in their variety of plants. Plants with deep or spreading roots can endure intense heat and dry periods.

Common desert plants: Cactus, mesquite, sagebrush, Joshua trees, palm trees, and yuccas.

⚠ **Threats to the biome:** Human activities have caused many once-fertile areas to turn into desert lands. This process is called desertification. When bordering grasslands are over-grazed, fertile land is destroyed. Improper farming, mining, and destruction of trees also contribute to desertification.

Grassland biome

Grassland

Grasslands are large areas with rolling hills of grasses and wildflowers. The roots of the grasses and small plants make the soil rich.

Welwitschia is a plant that grows in the deserts of **Namibia** *and* **Angola**, *two countries in Africa. It looks like an octopus because it has only two leaves that shred into many long pieces as they grow. The welwitschia can live for 1,000 years.*

World Wise

Grasslands are a transitional biome because they are usually found between the desert and the forest. There are four major areas of grasslands, all with their own names. North America has prairies, Asia has steppes, South America has pampas, and Africa has velds.

Climate: Most grasslands occur in the center of continents where there are hot summers and cold winters. The climate is temperate and subhumid. Rainfall varies widely.

Plant life: There are three types of grasslands. Tall grasslands have grasses up to 5 feet (1.5 m), and about 30 inches (76.2 cm) of rain. Mixed grasslands have grasses 2–3 feet (0.6–0.9 m) high with up to 25 inches (63.5 cm) of rain. Short grasslands have short grass with 10 inches (25.4 cm) of rain each year.

Common grassland plants: Wild grasses (such as prairie cordgrass, bluestem, and wild rye) and cereal grasses (such as oats and wheat) originated in this biome. So did flax, which is used to make linen cloth.

⚠ **Threats to the biome:** Because of their rich soils, many of the world's grasslands have been—or are in the process of being—destroyed. Grasslands have been replaced by ranches and farms.

Savanna

These are lush, tropical grasslands with widely scattered trees and shrubs. Vast areas of Africa, Australia, and South America are covered by savannas. These regions have both dry and rainy seasons.

Climate: Sunny and warm with long, dry seasons. Most savannas receive up to 40 inches (100 cm) of rain a year. However, some have as little as 10 inches (25 cm) of rain annually.

Savanna biome

Plant life: Most of the grasses grow in scattered clumps. In the dry season, these grasses turn brown and stop growing. Trees are widely spaced, and only those that can survive drought conditions grow here.

Common savanna plants: Acacia, baobab, and palms.

⚠ **Threats to the biome:** None.

Taiga

This biome is also called the boreal forest. It is made up mostly of conifer trees. Conifer trees have cones and needles. The needles stay on year round, making them evergreens. These forests are found in northern parts of North America, Europe, and Asia.

Climate: Very cold winters. Short growing season lasting from 50 to 100 days.

Plant life: Very few plants are able to grow on the sandy, acidic forest floors. The trees are pointy and triangular in shape, which helps them shed heavy snows.

Common taiga plants: Balsam firs, black spruce, jack pine, and white spruce.

⚠ **Threats to the biome:** Acid rain and rapid deforestation.

Taiga biome

Temperate coniferous forest

These forests of coniferous trees experience milder and wetter weather than the taiga. They occur in the western part of North America. Sometimes they are called temperate rain forests.

Climate: Coastal areas have mild winters with heavy rainfall. Farther inland, the climate is cool and moist.

Plant life: Coniferous evergreens abound here, and the redwood forests are within this biome.

Common temperate coniferous forest plants: Cedar, Douglas fir, giant sequoia, hemlock, and pine.

⚠ **Threats to the biome:** None.

Temperate deciduous forest

These forests are characterized by their growth of deciduous trees. Deciduous trees have broad, flat leaves. They lose their leaves every autumn and grow new leaves every spring. Large areas of North America, central Europe, and eastern Asia are covered with temperate deciduous forests.

Climate: Moderate to high rainfall occurs in this biome. The warm growing season lasts five to six months, and is followed by cold winters.

Plant life: The floors of these forests are rich in wildflowers and shrubs. Both coniferous and deciduous trees grow in this biome.

Temperate deciduous forest biome

Common temperate deciduous forest plants: Ash, birch, elm, hickory, maple, oak, and walnut trees.

⚠ **Threats to the biome:** This is one of the most altered biomes on Earth. Humans have cleared these forests for farmland and lumber. These activities, along with acid rain, have led to the decline of the forest regions.

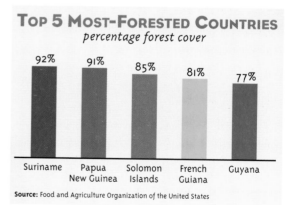

TOP 5 MOST-FORESTED COUNTRIES
percentage forest cover

Suriname	Papua New Guinea	Solomon Islands	French Guiana	Guyana
92%	91%	85%	81%	77%

Source: Food and Agriculture Organization of the United States

Tropical rain forest

Tropical rain forests are sometimes called jungles. They are located close to the equator and have year-round high temperatures with heavy rainfall. The largest tropical rain forest is the Amazon rain forest of South America.

Climate: Warm and wet weather all year round.

Plant life: Millions of species grow in tropical rain forests—more than in any other biome.

Temperate coniferous forest biome

Tropical rain forest biome

More than 50% of the medicines used in the world come from rain forest plants, and 25% of prescription drugs originate here. About 50% of the fruits we eat originally came from here. Sugar originated in the rain forests of India. Chocolate came from Central and South American rain forests. As many as 50,000 different kinds of trees grow in the tropical rain forests each year.

Common tropical rain forest plants: Mahogany, teak, palms, ferns, climbing vines, lianas, orchids, and bromeliads.

⚠️ **Threats to the biome:** The rain forests of the world are being destroyed faster than any other biome. Forested land is being cleared at the rate of one football field per minute. As the rich and valuable trees are taken for lumber, the delicate ecosystem is being destroyed.

Tundra

The tundra is the coldest biome. This treeless area is often described as a polar desert. Tundra stretches across the most northern parts of North America, Europe, and Asia. A layer of soil beneath the tundra stays frozen all year long. This is known as permafrost.

Climate: Annual precipitation, including melting snow, is less than 10 inches (25 cm). The average winter temperature is -30° Fahrenheit (-34° C), and the average summer temperature is 37–54 degrees Fahrenheit (3–12° C).

The word tundra *comes from the Finnish word* tunturia, *meaning "treeless plain."*

World Wise

Summer lasts for 60 days, and the sun shines all the time—even at midnight.

Plant life: In the summer, the top foot (30 cm) of land thaws, leaving marshes and ponds. Plants grow in low clumps, protecting them from wind and cold. About 1,700 different kinds of plants—including 400 varieties of flowers—grow in the tundra. The only tree that grows in the tundra is the dwarf willow, which is only about 4 inches (10 cm) tall.

Common tundra plants: Lichen, sedges, reindeer mosses, and dwarf willow trees.

⚠️ **Threats to the biome:** Industrial activity in the tundra make dirt and grime, which darken the ice. As a result, less heat is reflected from the ice, and global warming is increased.

Tundra biome

Giving Trees

Thousands of things are made from trees. Trees, of course, provide fruits and nuts for eating. Wood from trees is used for building houses and furniture. Newspapers and books are printed on paper made from tree pulp. Gums and resins of trees are used to make cosmetics, mouthwash, paint thinner, perfumes, soap, pill coatings, and chewing gum. Even money is made from trees!

Apple trees

Palm trees

Pineapple

Orange tree

TWENTY TERRIFIC TREE FLAVORS

The fruit, nuts, sap, roots, shoots, and bark of trees give us many flavors for the foods we love to eat. Can you imagine ice cream, soft drinks, and other treats without these flavors?

almond	maple
apple	nutmeg
cherry	orange
chocolate	pecan
cinnamon	pineapple
coconut	pistachio
cola	root beer
lemon	sassafras
lime	vanilla
mango	walnut

CONNECTING SPORTS WITH TREES

Strange but true, most sports would not exist without trees. Most sports equipment is made from tree products. Take, for example, rubber balls, which are made from the sap of rubber trees (*Hevea brasiliensis*). Basketballs, soccer balls, tennis balls, footballs, rugby balls, squash balls, and racquet balls are all made from rubber.

Archery	Arrow	Cedar and pine
	Bow	Yew
Badminton	Shuttlecock	Cork oak
Baseball	Ball (center)	Cork oak
	Bat	White ash
Bowling	Pin	Maple
	Lane	Hickory or pine
Cricket	Bat	Willow
	Wicket	Ash
Croquet	Mallet	Ash and boxwood
Golf	Ball (center)	Rubber tree
	Wooden club	Persimmon
	Tee	Pine
Hockey	Stick	Ash
	Puck	Rubber tree
Lacrosse	Stick	Hickory
Pool	Cue	Ash, maple, or ebony

The now-illegal spitball once thrown by baseball pitchers was made slippery by chewing parts of the slippery elm tree.

Size Supremacy

The largest living things on Earth are from the plant kingdom. Here are some large records from the plant world.

Largest tree

Giant sequoias, which grow only in California on the slopes of the Sierra Nevada mountain range, are truly giants. The trees grow up to 272 feet (83 m) tall. The trunks may measure 30 feet (9 m) wide. A giant sequoia may weigh 6,000 tons (5,442 metric tons), making it the heaviest living thing on Earth.

Tallest tree

The redwood, (a kind of sequoia), can reach up to 350 feet (105 m). These trees grow only on the coast of California.

Giant sequoia

The name sequoia *was given to the trees in honor of Chief Sequoyah, a Cherokee Indian of North America, who created a system of writing for his people.*

Largest leaves

The raffia palm of Madagascar has leaves that extend 40 feet (12 m).

Largest fruit

The jackfruit tree of India and Sri Lanka grows a yellow fruit that can weigh up to 50 pounds (22.5 kg).

Largest flower

The giant rafflesia grows in the tropical rain forests of Southeast Asia. Each flower weighs 15 pounds (7 kg) and may reach up to 3 feet (1 m) in diameter. The rafflesia is a parasitic plant that lives on the roots and vines of other plants.

Largest nut

The coco-de-mer nut grows only in the Seychelles and weighs up to 45 pounds (20 kg).

Longest needle

Longleaf pine needles measure up to 18 inches (45 cm) and are used to make brooms.

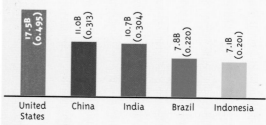

TOP 5 TIMBER-PRODUCING COUNTRIES
in billions of cubic feet (cubic meters)

United States	China	India	Brazil	Indonesia
17.5B (0.495)	11.0B (0.313)	10.7B (0.304)	7.8B (0.220)	7.1B (0.201)

Source: Food and Agriculture Organization of the United States, 1998

Amazing Trees Around The World

Banyan

The banyan tree of India and Sri Lanka is unique—its roots grow down from the tree's branches! One banyan tree in Sri Lanka has 350 large trunks and 3,000 smaller ones, all growing from one tree.

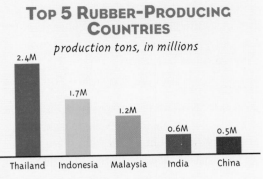

TOP 5 RUBBER-PRODUCING COUNTRIES
production tons, in millions

2.4M	1.7M	1.2M	0.6M	0.5M
Thailand	Indonesia	Malaysia	India	China

Source: Food and Agriculture Organization of the United States, 1998

Baobab trees

Baobab

The baobab tree of Africa has a thick bulging trunk that measures 30–50 feet (9–15 m) around. The white flowers of the tree open at night and are pollinated by bats. The tree bears fruit called monkey bread, which is about a foot (30 cm) long. This fruit is eaten as human food, or used to flavor cool drinks.

Bald cypress

A tree with knees? That's what most people call the bald cypress tree that grows in the swamplands of the United States, particularly Louisiana. The roots make growths, called knees, that stick out above the water and make air for the roots. Unlike other evergreens, these trees shed their leaves each year, making their tops bare or "bald."

Eucalyptus

The eucalyptus tree (also called giant gum) of Australia is one of the world's tallest trees. It grows up to 330 feet (100 m) and provides valuable timber. The bark is used for medicine, and the leaves contain an oil used in deodorants and antiseptics. Koalas sleep in these trees and eat the leaves.

Ginkgo

Ginkgo trees have survived millions of years on Earth. In fact, they were abundant when dinosaurs were alive. Ginkgoes were discovered in China and have been planted throughout the world. The trees are 60 to 80 feet (18 to 24 m) high. The nut is roasted and eaten despite the foul smell of its fleshy covering.

Cork oak

The cork oak tree of Spain and Portugal is the source of cork, commonly used for bulletin boards and bottle stoppers. The cork tree is a live oak tree, which means it stays green all year round. Cork is made from the tree's bark, which is stripped away every 8 to 10 years without damage to the tree.

Koala bear in eucalypus tree

World Wise

Ebony, a black wood from the Diospyros tree of **Africa**, is used to make clarinets, oboes, and piano keys. Various other woods are used to make guitars, flutes, and drums.

Frankincense

The frankincense tree, or *Boswellia*, grows in **Africa**. Resin from the bark of this tree hardens into pale drops called tears. The tears are used as incense in religious services. Frankincense trees were transplanted from southern **Africa** to **Egypt** in 1495 B.C. for Queen Hatshepsut, who valued the perfume of the tree.

Rain

Rain trees grow in tropical climates of **South America**. They have short trunks with very long, spreading branches. They also have branches that measure more than 100 feet (30 m) across. Rain trees got their name from the moisture that drips from their branches, which looks like rain.

Saguaro

The saguaro, or giant cactus, is the largest cactus in the **United States**. It grows as tall as 60 feet (18 m), weighs as much as 10 tons (9 metric tons), and can store hundreds of gallons of water. Saguaros grow in the deserts of **Arizona**, where little rain falls. When it does rain, the cactus soaks up the moisture and stores it. As the cactus stores and then uses the many gallons of water, the grooves and ribs of the plant expand and contract much like an accordion does.

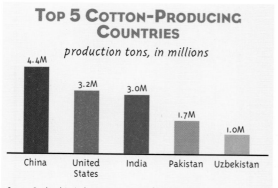

TOP 5 COTTON-PRODUCING COUNTRIES

production tons, in millions

China	United States	India	Pakistan	Uzbekistan
4.4M	3.2M	3.0M	1.7M	1.0M

Source: Food and Agriculture Organization of the United States, 1998

Saguaro cactus

Famous Trees of the United States

DeSoto oak

A mighty live oak tree once stood in Tampa Bay, Florida. It was under this tree that the Spanish explorer Hernando DeSoto made a treaty with Native Americans in 1593 for the king of Spain. The tree was blown down by a hurricane in 1856.

Hernando de Soto

Peter Stuyvesant pear tree

The first memorial tree planted in colonial America was planted by Peter Stuyvesant in front of his Manhattan home. He brought the tree in a tub from his home in Holland. The pear tree stood at the corner of Third Avenue and 13th Street in New York City for 200 years.

Washington elm

In 1775, General George Washington took command of the American Continental Army under a large elm tree in Cambridge, Massachusetts. The tree lived for 204 years.

Hamilton's 13

To celebrate the signing of the Constitution of the United States, Alexander Hamilton planted 13 sweet gum trees, one for each state. They were planted near his former home at Amsterdam Avenue and 143rd Street in New York City. The trees lived from 1787 to 1911, when they were removed to make way for a building.

Arbor Day was created and named by an American from Nebraska. In 1880, Julius Morton (1832–1902) established Arbor Day as a festival in which schoolchildren paraded and planted trees.

World Wise

Council oak

A huge oak tree stands in Sioux City, Iowa. Beneath this tree, explorers Meriwether Lewis and William Clark held council with the Sioux Indians (Lakota). Lewis and Clark had been sent by President Thomas Jefferson to meet with Native Americans in order to get advice on traveling west to the Pacific Ocean.

Methuselah

Bristlecone pine trees are very old trees that grow in Arizona, Nevada, and California. "Methuselah" is the oldest of these trees—it's 4,764 years old. This tree is one of the oldest living things on Earth.

Statue of George Washington ➤

NAMING TREES AND PLANTS

- Bedstraw is a plant that got its name because it was once used to stuff pillows and mattresses.

- *Belladonna* comes from the Italian words for "beautiful lady." At one time, women squeezed the juice in their eyes to make them sparkle. Doctors still use an extract of this plant to enlarge the pupils of the eye during an examination.

- The roots of the bitterroot plant eaten by Native Americans are bitter in taste. This plant also lends its name to the mountains that divide Idaho and Montana.

- *Dandelion* comes from the French *dent de lion*, or "tooth of the lion." The leaves of the plant were thought to look like lions' teeth.

Morning glory

- Morning glory is a twining vine with flowers that open in the morning and close later in the day.

- Spindle trees grow in Europe and North America, and were named for the spindles made from their wood. A spindle is used to wind wool by hand.

- Timothy grass was once called herd grass for its use as cattle feed. After Timothy Hanson of New York took this grass seed into the southern United States it became known as timothy grass.

- *Tulip* comes from a Persian word for "turban." The flower was thought to resemble a turban. Tulips originated in the Middle East, where the turban headdress is commonly worn.

Dandelion ➤

- Death cup is the name of the most poisonous mushroom known to man. Eating even the smallest piece will kill humans and animals. There is no antidote for the poison.

- Firestick is an African shrub. The sticks from the shrub are used to make friction fires.

- Impatiens are plants that grow in damp, shady places all over the world. New Guinea impatiens are one of the largest and most dramatic varieties. They are named for the "impatient" way seed pods explode when touched.

Tulips ➤

STATE TREES AND FLOWERS OF THE UNITED STATES

All 50 states have chosen a special tree and a special flower as state symbols. In many cases, children voted to decide on the state tree and state flower.

STATE	TREE	FLOWER
Alabama	Southern pine	Camellia
Alaska	Sitka spruce	Forget-me-not
Arizona	Paloverde	Saguaro cactus
Arkansas	Shortleaf pine	Apple blossom
California	California redwood	Golden poppy
Colorado	Blue spruce	Columbine
Connecticut	White oak	Mountain laurel
Delaware	American holly	Peach blossom
Florida	Sabal palmetto	Orange blossom
Georgia	Live oak	Cherokee rose
Hawaii	Coconut palm	Yellow hibiscus
Idaho	Western white pine	Syringa
Illinois	Native oak	Native violet
Indiana	Tulip tree	Peony
Iowa	Oak	Wild rose
Kansas	Cottonwood	Sunflower
Kentucky	Tulip poplar	Goldenrod
Louisiana	Bald cypress	Magnolia
Maine	Eastern white pine	White pine cone
Maryland	White oak	Black-eyed Susan
Massachusetts	American elm	Mayflower
Michigan	Eastern white pine	Apple blossom
Minnesota	Red pine	Lady's slipper

Columbine

Saguaro cactus

Redwood

Holly

Peony

Pine sprigs and cones

Sunflower

Lady's slipper

Goldenrod ➤

Mississippi	Great-flowered magnolia	Magnolia
Missouri	Flowering dogwood	Hawthorn
Montana	Ponderosa pine	Bitterroot
Nebraska	Cottonwood	Goldenrod
Nevada	Single-leaf piñon	Sagebrush
New Hampshire	White birch	Purple lilac
New Jersey	Northern red oak	Purple violet
New Mexico	Piñon	Yucca
New York	Sugar maple	Rose
North Carolina	Pine	Dogwood
North Dakota	American elm	Wild prairie rose
Ohio	Buckeye	Scarlet carnation
Oklahoma	American redbud	Mistletoe
Oregon	Douglas fir	Oregon grape
Pennsylvania	Eastern hemlock	Mountain laurel
Rhode Island	Red maple	Violet
South Carolina	Sabal palmetto	Yellow jessamine
South Dakota	Black Hills spruce	Pasqueflower
Tennessee	Tulip tree	Iris
Texas	Pecan	Bluebonnet
Utah	Blue spruce	Sego lily
Vermont	Sugar maple	Red clover
Virginia	Flowering dogwood	Dogwood
Washington	Western hemlock	Rhododendron
West Virginia	Sugar maple	Big rhododendron
Wisconsin	Sugar maple	Wood violet
Wyoming	Plains cottonwood	Indian paintbrush

Golden poppies

Rose

Red maple

Iris

Rhododendron

Plants as Potions and Poisons

Plants can be used to heal as well as to harm. Most plants have both poisonous and medicinal properties. For example, Native Americans used poison ivy to treat snakebites. For thousands of years, humans have experimented with the healing value of plants, as well as using the poisonous parts for hunting and warfare.

Poison Plants in History

Cyanide is a poison obtained from the seeds, leaves, and bark of cherry, apple, and peach trees. They all contain amygdalin, which is harmless in itself. However, amygdalin can be broken down into the compound cyanide.

Monkshood was considered the deadliest poison of ancient Rome and India. Roman armies used it to poison the wells of enemies. Hunters in India applied it to arrows when tracking and killing lions. The character Romeo, of the Shakespearean tragedy *Romeo and Juliet*, took monkshood when he committed suicide. In medieval Europe, this plant was called wolfsbane because it was used to poison wolves. The deadly component of monkshood is aconite.

Despite the name, the poison hemlock plant and the hemlock tree are not related. When the hemlock plant is ingested, it poisons by paralyzing the motor nerves. In ancient Greece, citizens drank hemlock to commit suicide. The famous Greek philosopher, Socrates, was condemned to die by drinking this poison.

HEALING PLANTS

- Willow bark was used as a pain reliever by Native Americans of North America. It's a modern-day source for aspirin.

- Quinine from the bark of the cinchona tree of South America is used to treat malaria. About 250 million people around the world contract malaria each year.

- Foxglove is a flower whose leaves contain digitalis, a chemical used to treat heart disease by slowing down the heartbeat and helping heart muscles work.

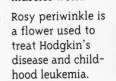
Foxglove

- Rosy periwinkle is a flower used to treat Hodgkin's disease and childhood leukemia.

- Yams, native to Mexico, produce cortisone in their roots. Cortisone is used to treat arthritis and other painful diseases.

- Yew trees found in the Pacific Northwest of the United States produce a drug used to treat ovarian and breast cancers.

- Nearly 5,000 species of plants are used for medicine in China today. About 40% of all prescriptions in the United States are based on compounds found in plants.

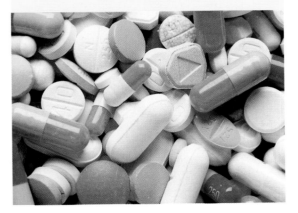

TWENTY COMMON POISONOUS PLANTS

Following is a list of plants found in the home or garden that have toxic potential. They should never be eaten.

FLOWER	PART	RISK
Azalea	All parts	Medium
Boston ivy	Berries (contact)	Medium
Daffodil	All parts	Low
Four-O'Clock	Seeds, roots	Medium
Foxglove	All parts	High ☠
Holly	Berries	High ☠
Honeysuckle	Berries	Low
Hyacinth	All parts	High ☠
Hydrangea	Flowers	Low
Iris	Flowers (contact)	Medium
Ivy, English	All parts	Low
Jimsonweed	All parts	High ☠
Larkspur	All parts	High ☠
Locoweed	All parts	High ☠
Morning glory	Seeds	Low
Oleander	All parts	High ☠
Orange mistletoe	All parts	High ☠
Potato	Green parts	High ☠
Sweet pea	Seeds	Low
Tomato	Leaves (contact)	Low

◄ Sweet pea

◄ Daffodil

Holly ►

Azalea

Iris

English ivy ►

Meat-eating Plants

Venus's-flytrap ➤

There are about 600 species of meat-eating plants. They make most of their own food in the same way other plants do. Most insect-eating plants live in marshes where the soil has an inadequate supply of nitrogen. Insects, however, have plenty of nitrogen. These plants lack teeth to mash their prey. Instead, they secrete juices that slowly digest insects.

The Portuguese sundew plant is so efficient at catching flies that people often use it indoors.

World Wise

Venus's-flytrap

Size: 5–10 inches (12–25 cm) tall.

Habitat: North and South Carolina.

Common prey: Flies, lizards, and sometimes frogs.

Lure: A sweet nectar and reddish interior attract insects when leaves are open.

Trap: Active. When prey brushes against the hairs on the leaves, the leaves fold over and close.

Digestion time: 8 to 10 days.

Nepenthes pitcher plant

Size: 30–40 inches (75–100 cm) tall; pitcher is 12 inches (30 cm) tall.

Habitat: Southeast Asia.

Common prey: Insects, small rodents, frogs, and birds.

Lure: Water collected inside the pitcher, and sweet-scented nectar, attract prey.

Trap: Active. Prey slides down slippery inner walls into a pool of digestive fluids, and lid closes.

Digestion time: one to two weeks.

Greater bladderwort

Size: 3 feet (1 m) or longer, most growth underwater; traps are 0.06–0.2 inches (1.5–5 mm) long.

Habitat: Ponds, bogs, and swamps around the world.

Prey: Water fleas, mosquito larvae, microorganisms, and tadpoles.

Lure: Faint odor attracts insects.

Trap: Active. When prey brushes against hairs near tiny underwater traps, the trap valves open. Water rushes in, carrying the prey.

Digestion time: 15 minutes to two hours.

Sundew

Size: 6 inches–3 feet (15 cm–1m) tall.

Habitat: All continents except Antarctica.

Prey: Ants and other insects.

Lure: Sweet odor and bright red color.

Trap: Passive. Sticky drops on a leaf's tentacles trap insects.

Digestion time: 4 to 5 days.

Pitcher plant

Keeping the Green

One in eight plant species in the world, and nearly one in three in the United States alone, is at risk of extinction. After 20 years of monitoring, conservationists from around the globe compiled the first comprehensive list of threatened plants on a global scale.

The Kew Seed Bank in England keeps 1.5% of the world's plant seeds on deposit. The collection includes 4,000 species, but 34,000 more are at risk.

WORLD CONSERVATION UNION'S RED LIST

Country, Number of Plant Species in Danger

Country	Number	Country	Number
United States	4,669	Spain	985
Australia	2,245	Peru	906
South Africa	2,215	Cuba	888
Turkey	1,876	Ecuador	824
Mexico	1,593	Jamaica	744
Brazil	1,358	Colombia	712
Panama	1,302	Japan	707
India	1,236		

Source: WCU

Most Endangered National Parks in the United States

All of the 378 national parks are troubled by overuse and damage to their ecosystems. Some of the most threatened parks are listed here.

Denali National Park
Alaska

Roads are proposed to run through 80 miles (129 km) of the park, which will destroy both plant and animal habitats.

Everglades National Park
Florida

Development of residential and commercial areas nearby has polluted the water in these wetlands.

Grand Canyon National Park
Arizona

Overcrowding, traffic congestion, air pollution, and air tour flights endanger this area's plant and animal life.

Great Smoky Mountains National Park
Tennessee

Air pollution is damaging trees and other plant life. Landscape views that once reached as far as 60 miles (97 km) are now obscured.

Haleakala National Park
Hawaii

Rare and precious native plants are being crowded out by new plants brought from foreign places.

Mojave National Preserve
California

Human development threatens desert wilderness.

Voyageurs National Park
Minnesota

Increased use of recreational snowmobiles disturbs this peaceful habitat and destroys plant and wildlife.

Yellowstone National Park
Wyoming, Montana, and Idaho

Human waste from a crumbling sewage system has polluted the waters of Yellowstone Lake and Old Faithful.

Flower of the Sacred Datura, Grand Canyon

International Flags

The first flags were probably flown by the Egyptians, who tied streamers to poles and carried them into battle. The flags honored their gods or their rulers.

Today, a national flag represents a country, its land, its people, and its ideals. Most national flags use one or more of seven basic colors: black, blue, green, orange, red, white, and yellow.

There are many other kinds of flags in addition to national ones. Many kings and queens have their own flags. International organizations, such as the United Nations and the Red Cross, have flags. States, cities, provinces, and even ideals may also have their own flags.

Flags and their meanings and origins have always fascinated people. The word *vexillology* means "the study of flags."

FABULOUS FLAG FACTS

Danish flag

Romanian flag

- One of the oldest national flags belongs to Denmark. The 750-year-old flag was inspired by King Valdemar the Victorious, who saw a white cross in a red sky just before he won a battle.

- Libya is the only country with a flag of one color. The flag of this African country is entirely green. Green is the traditional color of Islam, which is the religion of most Libyans.

- The flag of Romania was changed in 1989 to reflect a change in political views. The

Communist crest was removed from the center of Romania's blue, yellow, and red flag. For a brief time, Romanians flew a flag that had a hole where the symbol used to be.

- The Flag Museum in Budapest, Hungary, is the only museum in the world devoted entirely to flags.

- National flags flown at the United Nations Headquarters in New York City are flown for 6 to 12 months before they are considered unfit for display. They are then carefully cut up, and the pieces are burned.

NICKNAMES OF NATIONAL FLAGS

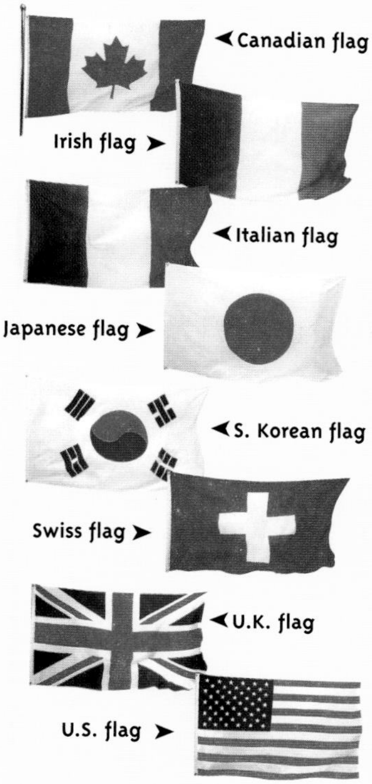

◄ Canadian flag

Irish flag ►

◄ Italian flag

Japanese flag ►

◄ S. Korean flag

Swiss flag ►

◄ U.K. flag

U.S. flag ►

Canada	Maple Leaf Flag
Cuba	La Estrella Solitaria (the lonely star)
Guyana	The Golden Arrow
Ireland	O'Neill's Flag
Italy	Tricolore (tricolor)
Japan	Hinomaru (sun disc flag)
South Korea	Tae-Gheuk-Ghi (great-extreme-flag)
St. Vincent and the Grenadines	The Gems
Switzerland	The Federal Cross
United Kingdom	Union Jack
United States of America	Old Glory; Stars and Stripes

Storm Warning Flags

Flags that warn of dangerous wind and sea conditions fly at stations on shore.

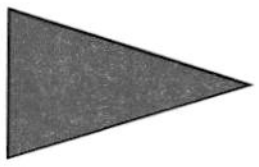

Small-craft advisory: Winds up to 38 mph (61 kph)

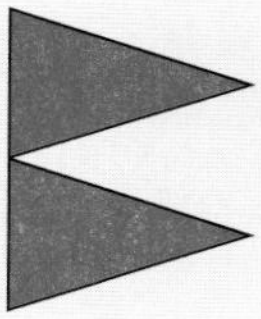

Gale warning: Winds from 39 to 54 mph (63 to 87 kph)

Storm warning: Winds from 55 to 73 mph (89 to 117 kph)

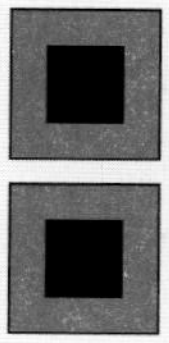

Hurricane warning: Winds that exceed 74 mph (119 kph)

International Flags

Counterclockwise from left:

Earth Flag (designed in 1972 for Earth Day);

United Nations Flag;

Olympic Flag;

Relief Organization Flags (the Red Cross in Christian countries, the Red Crescent in Muslim countries, and the Red Star of David in Israel)

WORLD FLAGS

AFGHANISTAN

ALBANIA

ALGERIA

ANDORRA

ANGOLA

ANTIGUA AND BARBUDA

ARGENTINA

ARMENIA

AUSTRALIA

AUSTRIA

AZERBAIJAN

BAHAMAS

BAHRAIN

BANGLADESH

BARBADOS

BELARUS

BELGIUM

BELIZE

BENIN

BHUTAN

BOLIVIA

BOSNIA & HERZEGOVINA

BOTSWANA

BRAZIL

BRUNEI

BULGARIA

BURKINA FASO

BURUNDI

CAMBODIA

CAMEROON

CANADA

CAPE VERDE

CENTRAL AFRICAN REPUBLIC

CHAD

CHILE

CHINA, People's Rep. of

CHINA, Rep. of (Taiwan)

COLOMBIA

COMOROS

CONGO, DEMOCRATIC REP. OF (formerly Zaire)

CONGO, REPUBLIC OF THE

COSTA RICA

CÔTE D'IVOIRE
(Ivory Coast)

CROATIA

CUBA

CYPRUS

CZECH REPUBLIC

DENMARK

DJIBOUTI

DOMINICA

DOMINICAN REPUBLIC

ECUADOR

EGYPT

EL SALVADOR

EQUATORIAL GUINEA
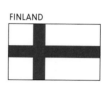

ERITREA

ESTONIA

ETHIOPIA

FIJI

FINLAND

FRANCE

GABON

GAMBIA

GEORGIA

GERMANY

GHANA

GREECE

GRENADA

GUATEMALA

GUINEA

GUINEA-BISSAU
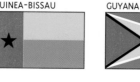

GUYANA

HAITI

HONDURAS

HUNGARY

ICELAND

INDIA

INDONESIA

IRAN

IRAQ
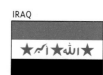

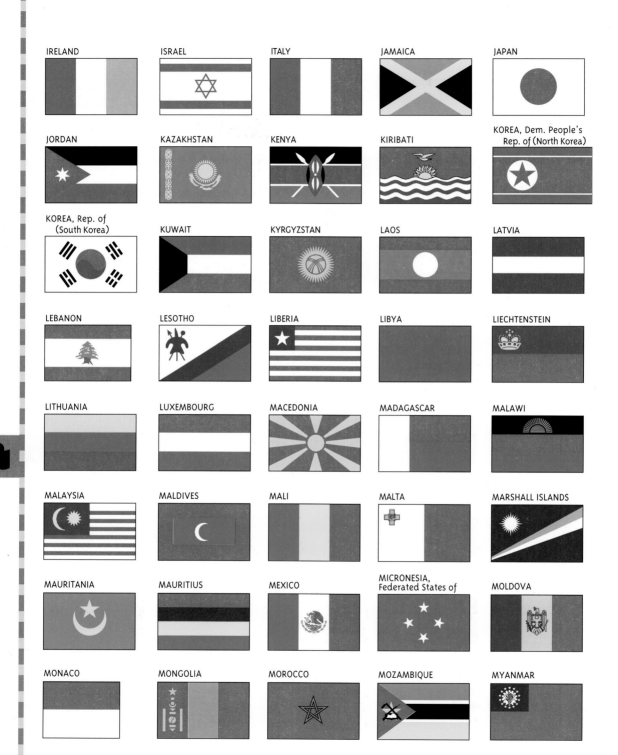

IRELAND

ISRAEL

ITALY

JAMAICA

JAPAN

JORDAN

KAZAKHSTAN

KENYA

KIRIBATI

KOREA, Dem. People's Rep. of (North Korea)

KOREA, Rep. of (South Korea)

KUWAIT

KYRGYZSTAN

LAOS

LATVIA

LEBANON

LESOTHO

LIBERIA

LIBYA

LIECHTENSTEIN

LITHUANIA

LUXEMBOURG

MACEDONIA

MADAGASCAR

MALAWI

MALAYSIA

MALDIVES

MALI

MALTA

MARSHALL ISLANDS

MAURITANIA

MAURITIUS

MEXICO

MICRONESIA, Federated States of

MOLDOVA

MONACO

MONGOLIA

MOROCCO

MOZAMBIQUE

MYANMAR

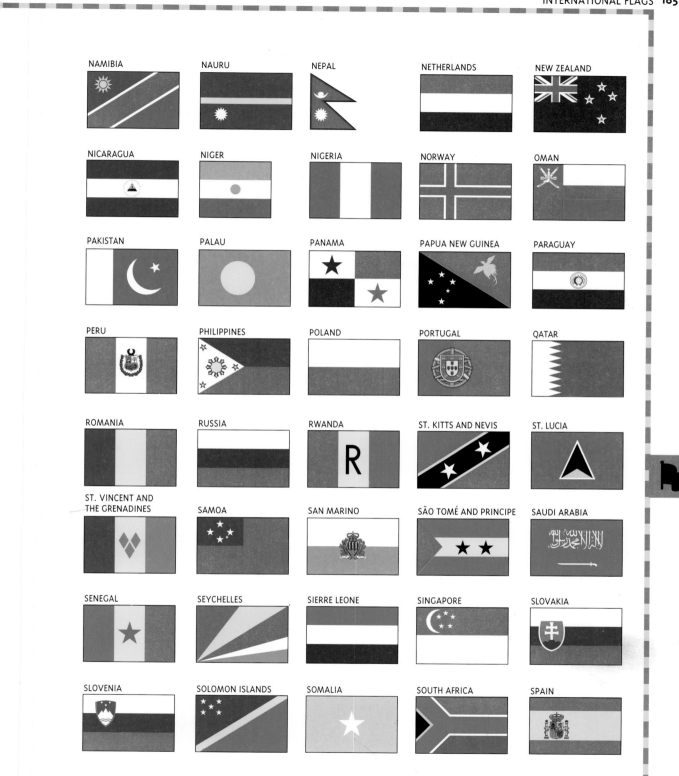

SRI LANKA

SUDAN

SURINAME

SWAZILAND

SWEDEN

SWITZERLAND

SYRIA

TAJIKISTAN

TANZANIA

THAILAND

TOGO

TONGA

TRINIDAD AND TOBAGO

TUNISIA

TURKEY

TURKMENISTAN

TUVALU

UGANDA

UKRAINE

UNITED ARAB EMIRATES

UNITED KINGDOM

UNITED STATES

URUGUAY

UZBEKISTAN

VANUATU

VATICAN CITY

VENEZUELA

VIETNAM

YEMEN

YUGOSLAVIA, Fed. Rep. of
(Serbia and Montenegro)

ZAMBIA

ZIMBABWE

◄ Ceremonial
flag at
Shilla
Festival,
Korea

INTERNATIONAL FLAG CODE

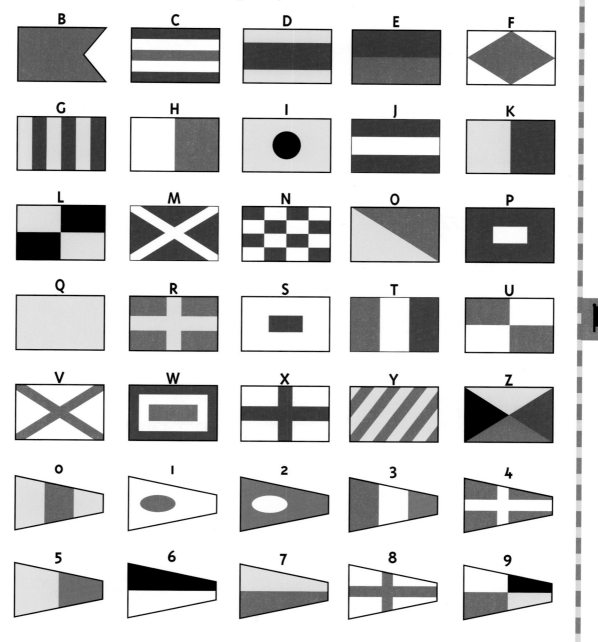

The international flag code is a signaling system used by ships at sea. The system has more than 40 flags. Each flag stands for a letter of the alphabet, and pennants (triangular-shaped flags) stand for numbers. The flags have code meanings, or spell out words.

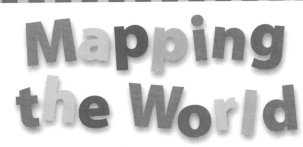

Mapping the World

No one knows who first tried to sketch an area or location on a map. We do know that people around the world have made maps for a very long time. In prehistoric times people drew maps on the walls of caves in Europe. In the Marshall Islands of the Pacific Ocean, people used sticks to make charts of wind and wave patterns. The early Inuits of North America carved maps of coastlines into ivory. The earliest evidence of ancient mapmaking is from 1,000 B.C. The Babylonians made clay tablets that showed Earth as a flat, circular disk.

The Arabs put "north" on the bottom of their maps rather than at the top. Marco Polo used one of these maps around 1290 on his journeys to China.

Maps are very useful tools. They give an idea of where things are in relation to one another. Today, maps enrich our sense of where we are in the world. Using modern tools, cartographers (mapmakers) can map desert sands and polar ice, and even "see" through them with special cameras to map what's underneath.

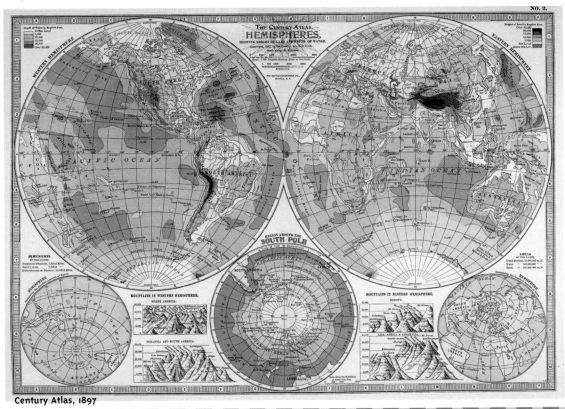

Century Atlas, 1897

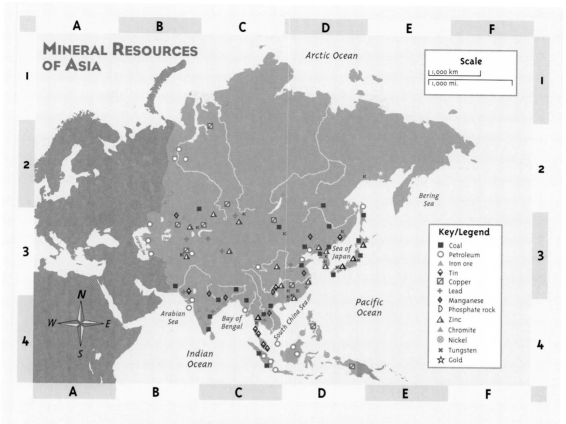

MINERAL RESOURCES OF ASIA

Arctic Ocean

Scale
1,000 km
1,000 mi.

Bering Sea

Aral Sea

Caspian Sea

Sea of Japan

Pacific Ocean

Key/Legend
■ Coal
○ Petroleum
▲ Iron ore
◇ Tin
▨ Copper
✛ Lead
◆ Manganese
▷ Phosphate rock
△ Zinc
▲ Chromite
⊗ Nickel
✳ Tungsten
☆ Gold

Arabian Sea

Bay of Bengal

South China Sea

Indian Ocean

N
W E
S

ELEMENTS OF A MAP

A map **key** or **legend** explains the information shown on a map. The information is the key to understanding the map. The key may include symbols, boundary markers, color graphs, and a scale bar.

The **scale bar** shows how much smaller the map is than the real area it represents. It uses inches to represent miles or centimeters to represent kilometers.

The **compass rose** is a group of directional arrows. The letters on the compass rose are N for north, S for south, E for east, and W for west. North on a map always points toward the North Pole.

The **map index** located in an atlas is an alphabetical listing of the places that appear on the maps. Each place has a letter-number locator and the page number on which it appears. The letter-number is used on the **map grid**, which forms a border around each map. To find the Sea of Japan, for example, the map index would tell you to look at D3 on the map above.

World Wise

An atlas *is a book of maps or charts. Atlas was a character in Greek mythology who was condemned to hold Earth and sky upon his shoulders for eternity.*

HIGHLIGHTS OF MAPMAKING

240 B.C. Eratosthenes, a Greek mathematician, estimated the circumference of Earth without leaving his hometown of Alexandria in northern Africa. He calculated the longitudinal circumference (from pole to pole) at 25,200 miles (40,300 km). He was only off by a mere 340 miles (547 km).

A.D.21 Augustus, a Roman emperor, ordered the first road map to be made. Because the Romans had built an extensive system of roads through their empire, it took 20 years to complete the 21-foot- (6.4-m-) long map.

150 Ptolemy of Greece put together a collection of 27 maps in his book *Geography*. He created a grid system for locating places throughout the known world. This book also included a map index with place names and the latitude and longitude of each place.

1136 After centuries of mapmaking, the Chinese completed a stone map of China and other known lands, showing rivers and the soon-to-be-built Great Wall of China.

1154 The Arab geographer, Al Idrisi, who was employed by a royal court in Sicily, made the first world map. He was influenced by the work of Ptolemy.

Map of pilgrim routes to Jerusalem from the 12th century

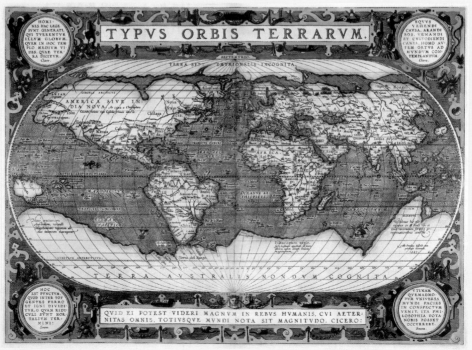

Map of the world, 1588

1280	A priest in **England** created a world map showing the world as a circle surrounded by ocean. The land was divided into three parts: **Europe**, **Africa**, and **Asia**. The map was labeled HEREFORD MAPPA MUNDI.
1492	The first globe was created by Martin Benhaim of Nuremberg, **Germany**. This globe showed Earth as a sphere, even before Columbus set sail.
1500	The first map of the New World and the Old World was drawn by a Spanish sailor Juan de la Cosa after he crossed the Atlantic Ocean.
1507	The first map with the label AMERICA was made by Martin Waldseemuller of **Germany**. It honored Amerigo Vespucci, an Italian navigator who correctly argued that Columbus had reached a new land while trying to sail to **India**.

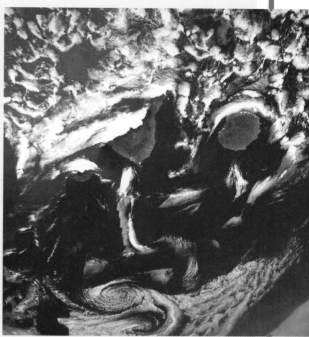

View of Earth's features from space

1569	A new kind of map was created by cartographer Gerardus Mercator. He portrayed the spherical world on a flat map. Mercator used lines of longitude and latitude to show the relationships of places.
1793	**France** became the first country to be completely mapped by using a scientific method called triangulation. Cartographer Jacques-Dominque de Cassini published this physical map of France on 182 sheets of paper. Each sheet was 36 x 36 feet (11 x 11 m) in size.
1858	The first photograph of land from above was taken by Gaspard-Felix Tournachon from a balloon over a village near Paris, **France**. This photograph set the stage for maps made from aerial photos.
1946	The first photographs from rockets were taken by U.S. Army scientists at White Sands, **New Mexico**.
1950	The first computer-made map was published. It was a weather map of **Europe** and **North America**.
1965	The first photographs of the geological features of Earth were taken from space by *Gemini* astronauts.
1997	The *Mars Global Surveyor* spacecraft landed on Mars to do a mapping survey of the planet.

World Wise

Eratosthenes is known as the "father of geography." He was the head of the library at Alexandria, the center of knowledge in the ancient western world.

Marvelous Map Collections

The Gallery of Maps
Vatican City, Rome, Italy

Consists of a long corridor with maps of the world made by Italian mapmakers. The maps are displayed in a hallway longer than a football field.

The Mappararium
Boston, Massachusetts

The Christian Science Publishing Society created this 30-foot (9-m) stained-glass room in the shape of a globe. Standing on the bridge in the middle of the globe allows visitors to experience the world around them. Between the North and South poles, the Earth's landmasses and bodies of water are laid out proportionately. Each of the 608 stained-glass panels represents 10 degrees of longitude and latitude.

The Library of Congress
Washington, D.C.

The Library of Congress is the largest library in the world. The Geography and Map Division holds more than 4.5 million cartographic items. The largest collection is of fire insurance maps for towns and cities throughout the United States. These maps are an excellent reference for the growth of urban America.

Latitude and Longitude

This is a system of imaginary lines that slice Earth into sections. On the vast ocean there is no way to tell your position by looking where the land lies. By means of these imaginary lines, any point on Earth can be located. Lines of latitude are called parallels. Lines of longitude are called meridians. The latitude and longitude system is expressed in degrees.

In order to find absolute location, the degrees are further divided into minutes (') and seconds (''). There are 60 minutes in each degree. There are 60 seconds in each minute.

The Greek geographer Ptolemy set the zero degree latitude at the equator because the sun, moon, and planets pass almost directly overhead at the equator.

Only two continents— North America and Europe— lie completely within the Northern Hemisphere.

Ptolemy set zero degree longitude through the Canary Islands off the coast of west Africa. The prime meridian was moved a number of times, until an international conference officially set it at Greenwich, England, in 1884.

Latitude and longitude lines also divide the spherical Earth into quarters, or hemispheres. They are the Eastern, Western, Northern, and Southern hemispheres.

Latitude and longitude intersect off the west coast of Africa.

Tropic of Cancer

EQUATOR

Tropic of Capricorn

Latitude

Lines of latitude are imaginary lines that circle the globe. They are horizontal lines, also called parallels. A good way to remember latitude is to imagine the horizontal rungs of a ladder as "ladder-tude." Latitude lines are used to measure distance in degrees north or south of the equator. The equator is 0 degrees latitude. The North Pole is 90 degrees north and the South Pole is 90 degrees south. Each degree of latitude is about 69 miles (111 km) apart. There are 17 parallel lines of latitude.

Attitudes about latitudes

During the first century, in the time of Ptolemy, there was a commonly held idea that anyone living below the equator would melt from the intense heat.

Latitude can help us understand why **Alaska** is colder than **Florida**. But latitude doesn't

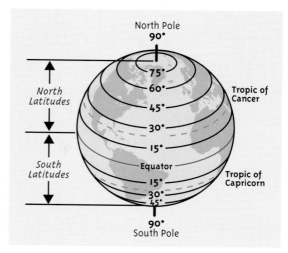

explain why winters in **Montana** (which is south of Alaska) are colder than southern Alaska winters. It is because the Pacific Ocean keeps the southern areas of Alaska warmer with a marine climate—the inland areas of Montana have a continental (landlocked) climate.

FAMOUS LINES OF LATITUDE

- The equator is an imaginary line of latitude that circles Earth halfway between the North and South poles. The equator divides Earth into the Northern Hemisphere and the Southern Hemisphere. At the equator there is no twilight. When the sun goes down at six o'clock, the darkness of the night abruptly takes over.

- The Antarctic Circle is the parallel of latitude at 60 degrees 30 minutes south. It is the southernmost point at which the sun can be seen at the summer solstice on June 22. It is the northernmost point of the southern polar region at which the midnight sun is visible.

- The Arctic Circle is the parallel of latitude at 66 degrees 30 minutes north. It is the northernmost point at which the sun can be seen at the winter solstice on December 22. It is the southernmost point of the northern polar region at which the midnight sun is visible. The arctic region includes the Arctic ocean and all land north of the Arctic Circle:northern **Canada**, **Alaska**, **Russia**, **Norway**, **Iceland**, and most of **Greenland**.

- The Tropic of Cancer is a parallel of latitude 23 degrees 27 minutes north of the equator. It is the northern boundary of the Torrid Zone, which is the most northerly latitude at which the sun can shine directly overhead.

- The Tropic of Capricorn is a parallel of latitude at 23 degrees 27 minutes south of the equator. It is the southern boundary of the Torrid Zone. It is the most southerly latitude at which the sun can shine directly overhead.

Zero-degree longitude (prime meridian) runs from north to south through the cities of Accra, Ghana; Gao, Mali; Reggane, Algeria; and Greenwich, England (near London).

Longitude

Lines of longitude are imaginary lines that run from the North Pole to the South Pole. They are vertical lines that are also called meridians. Longitude lines are used to measure distance in degrees east or west of the prime meridian. The prime meridian is an imaginary line that runs from the North Pole to the South Pole at 0 degrees longitude. The degrees continue 180 degrees east and 180 degrees west, where they meet at the International Date Line in the Pacific Ocean. There are 24 meridians, or lines of longitude.

Any two places that are on diametrically opposite sides of the Earth are called antipodes. The North and South poles are antipodes. Salta, Argentina (65° W longitude and 25° S latitude) and Karachi, Pakistan (65° E longitude and 25° N latitude), are also antipodes.

More about the prime meridian

The prime meridian divides Earth into the Eastern Hemisphere and the Western Hemisphere. The prime meridian was set in Greenwich, England, in 1884. This is the site of the Royal Greenwich Observatory, the world's most prominent astronomical observatory of its time.

Earth is not a perfect sphere. It is slightly egg-shaped, or an oblate ellipsoid.

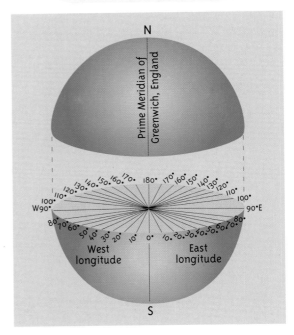

SIZING UP LONGITUDE

At the equator	One degree longitude equals 68 miles (109 km).
At the poles	All degrees merge.
Time	One degree of longitude equals a gain (moving east) or loss (moving west) of four minutes of time the world over.

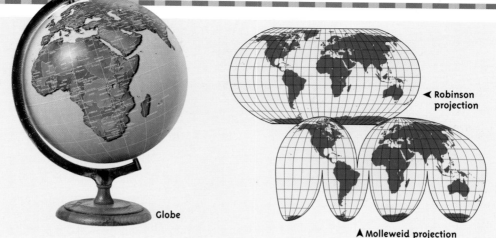

◀ Robinson projection

Globe

▲ Molleweid projection

KINDS OF MAPS

Globes

The most accurate and the most realistic representation of Earth is a globe. One disadvantage of a globe is that only half of the Earth can be viewed at one time. The other disadvantage is that globes are not easily portable.

Flat maps

A map projection is a way of representing the rounded earth on a flat surface. Flat maps are called projections. There are many different kinds of projections. The most common are Robinson, Mercator, and Molleweid.

Mercator

On this kind of map, the lines of longitude are equally spaced vertical lines. The lines of latitude are parallel horizontal straight lines, spaced farther and farther apart as they move away from the equator. This projection is commony used for navigation charts to plot a straight course. It is less practical for world maps because the scale does not accurately show the size of the landmasses in relation to one another.

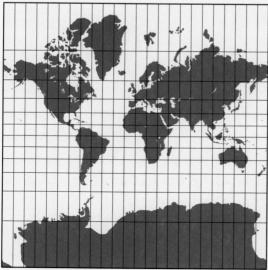

Mercator projection

World Wise

The "Greenland problem" refers to the expansion of Greenland as seen at the top of the Mercator map. The island appears to be bigger than the continent of South America.

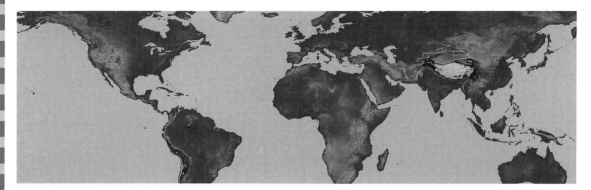

Physical Maps

Physical maps are also called topographical maps. These kinds of maps show different physical features, such as mountains and lakes. Physical maps can also show land elevation and ocean depths. *Topography* is another word for the physical features of the Earth's surface as shown on maps. Contours, which appear on physical maps, are lines that connect all points of land with equal elevation on a map. Reliefs are the differences in elevations or heights of landforms as shown on physical maps.

GEOGRAPHICAL TERMS FOUND ON A PHYSICAL MAP

Water

Archipelago	A chain of islands.
Aquifer	An area of underground water.
Atoll	A low island made of coral reefs.
Basin	A low region of land surrounded by higher land.
Beach	The shore of a body of water, especially when sandy or pebbly.
Bight	A crescent-shaped indentation of a coastline; usually wider and more open than a bay.
Bog	A wetland where water is near the surface.
Cape	A point or head of land projecting into a body of water.
Dam	A wall built to control the flowing water of rivers.
Dike	A special wall built to control floods.
Island	A piece of land surrounded by water.
Isthmus	A narrow piece of land that joins two larger sections of land.
Peninsula	An area of land that is surrounded on three sides by water.
Sea level	The level of the ocean's surface, especially between high and low tide. Used as a standard for measuring land elevation and ocean depth.
Tidewater	A low-lying coastal plain with many waterways.
Wetland	Land where water is often at or near the surface.

▲ Atoll

Elevation

Butte	A hill that rises abruptly from the surrounding area, with sloping sides and a flat top.
Canyon	A deep, narrow valley with high, steep slopes.
Dune	A hill of sand formed by the wind.
Escarpment	A steep cliff.
Gorge	A deep, narrow passage with steep, rocky sides.
Gulch	A small ravine usually cut by a torrent.
Gully	A deep ditch or channel cut in the earth by running water after a prolonged rainfall.
Highland	A large area of mountains or elevated lands.
Hill	A small area of land, higher than the land around it.
Mesa	A broad, flat-topped elevation with one or more cliff-like sides.
Mountain	Land that rises much higher than the land around it.
Mountain range	A row of mountains that are joined together.
Plain	A large area of land that is almost flat; gently rolling.
Plateau	A large, high land area that is generally flat.
Prairie	A gently rolling plain covered with tall, thick grass.
Ravine	A deep, narrow valley worn by running water.
Terrace	A large flat area of land built into the side of a hill for planting crops.
Upland	An area of high ground, usually with a hilly surface.
Valley	The lower land between hills or mountains, often with a stream or river.

Butte

Gorge

Biome

Desert	A dry, often sandy region with little rainfall.
Tundra	A region where small ground plants cover a cold and frozen ground.

Vegetation

Dell	A small, secluded wooded valley.
Dingle	A small wooded valley.
Forest	A large land area covered with trees.
Mixed forest	A region where both conifers and broadleaf trees grow.
Savanna	A land area with long, thick grass and short trees.
Scrubland	A region of short trees and shrubs in a semi-arid region.
Swamp	Wetlands where water is often at or near the surface.

Sand dunes

Political Maps

A political map shows political units, such as countries, states, and cities, and their boundaries.

Political maps are always changing as different countries expand, contract, or reorganize their borders. Country names often change, as well.

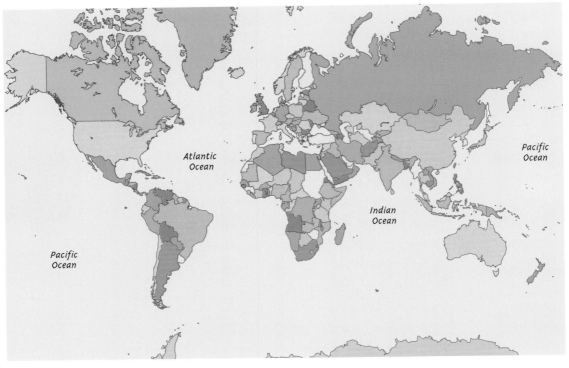

TERMS FOUND ON A POLITICAL MAP

Canton	A small division within a country, especially Switzerland.
City	A center of population.
Country	A nation or state and the land of the nation.
County	A smaller division within a state, as in the United States, or within a country, as in Ireland.
Federal district	An area reserved for the capital of a country such as the District of Columbia in the United States.
Municipality	A city or town with self-government.
Possession	An area of land controlled by a separate, distant country.
Province	A division of land governed by a country, as in Canada.
State	A smaller political territory within a country.
Territory	A geographic region, such as a colony, that is under the control of an external government.

Thematic Maps

A map that gives information about specific topics or themes is called a thematic map. A weather map is one example of a thematic map. Many different kinds of weather information can be plotted on a map, including climate, wind currents, or ocean currents. Another example of a thematic map is a historical map that shows something about the past or where events took place. A map of the United States that shows the locations of all the major battles of the Civil War is an example of a historical thematic map.

Large-scale maps show a small area in great detail. Small-scale maps show a large area without great detail.

Caribbean Sea

Pacific Ocean

Atlantic Ocean

South American Climate Zones

Key
- ◼ Tropical wet
- ◻ Tropical dry
- ◻ Semi-arid
- ◼ Arid
- ◼ Marine west coast
- ◻ Humid sub-tropical
- ◼ Warm summer
- ◼ Highland
- ◻ Upland

Natural Hazards
- ◞ Tsunamis

USEFUL THEMATIC MAPS

Medical mysteries

In 1854, a doctor named John Snow tried to find the source of an outbreak of cholera in London. He drew a thematic map of London. A dot marked the site of each death from the disease, and a cross marked the site of each water pump. When the map was done, the answer was clear—people who drank from a pump on Broad Street were the same people who contracted cholera.

Crime solvers

The police in large U.S. cities often use thematic maps in their efforts to solve crimes. Using a system called Comstat (short for "computer statistics") and a computer map, officials plot out the locations of crimes or evidence, analyze the results, and then use the information to locate criminals.

THE COMPASS: AN EXPLORER'S TOOL

The compass is an instrument used to show geographic direction. It consists of a magnetic needle, suspended and free to pivot until lined up with Earth's magnetic field. The cardinal directions (north, south, east, and west) are shown on the face of the compass. The Chinese invented the first compass to use a magnetic needle. They were using the compass to explore the world's oceans by the year 1000.

The face of a compass

- North is 0 degrees at the meridian 90 degrees, directly opposite south.
- South is 180 degrees clockwise from north, directly opposite north.
- East is 90 degrees clockwise from due north, directly opposite west.
- West is 270 degrees clockwise from due north, directly opposite east.

Getting directions

- The cardinal directions are north, south, east, and west.
- The intermediate directions are north-northeast, north-northwest, south-southeast, south-southwest.

Finding directions

- North is the direction to the left of the sunrise.
- South is the direction to the right of the sunrise.
- Polaris, or the North Star, is in line with the Earth's axis. For that reason it is called the "stay-put star."

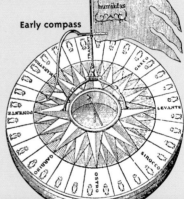

Early compass

Sunset behind trees

CENTURIES OF INSTRUMENTS

Astrolabe

This instrument was used in medieval times to determine the altitude of the sun and other celestial bodies. It was replaced by a sextant.

Astrolabe

Benchmark

Early quadrant

This is a standard by which something can be measured. A benchmark is usually a bronze plaque that is cut into rocks and other stable points on Earth. Altitude and other measurements are recorded on a benchmark.

Chronometer

This instrument was invented to measure exact longitude at sea. It is a clock that is exact to the second. John Harrison of **England** invented the chronometer in 1765.

Geodolite

An instrument that uses lasers to measure exact distance. It was created by a company in **California** in 1960.

Global Positioning System

This tool was developed by the U.S. military in the 1970s. GPS is a network of satellites orbiting more than 12,000 miles (20,000 km) above Earth's surface. The satellites constantly send out radio signals. The GPS receiver can exactly locate the position of something or someone.

Inclinometer

This is an instrument used to find the angle of the Earth's magnetic field in relation to the horizon. Using this instrument, one can measure the distance to the North Pole from any location.

Quadrant

This early instrument was made for measuring the altitude of the sun and other planetary bodies.

Sextant

This is a tool used by sailors to measure the altitude of the sun and other planetary bodies.

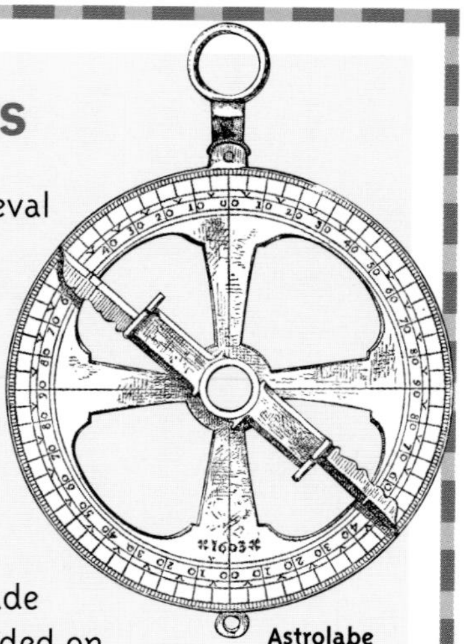

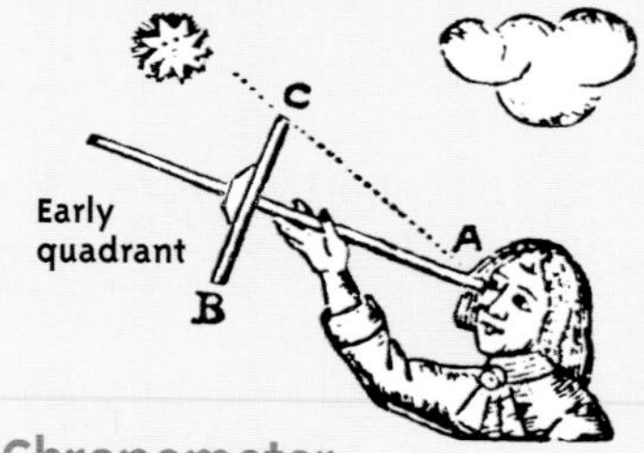

Sextant

Water Wonders
(Oceans, Seas, Lakes, and Rivers)

The Earth is a big ball of water. Water covers 70% of our planet's surface. Earth's water is mainly found in its oceans, which hold 97% of the world's supply. The remaining 3% is fresh water found in lakes and rivers. Three-quarters of all the fresh water is frozen in ice caps and glaciers at the northernmost and southernmost ends of the Earth.

All living things need water. Where water is scarce, life is limited. Drinking water is taken from rivers, freshwater lakes, and underground wells. Water is also used for washing things, manufacturing goods, and growing crops. The oceans, lakes, and rivers provide valuable food for plants and fish. These bodies of water also serve as important transportation routes.

Earth's landscape is always being changed by the forces of water. It cuts away at Earth's surface as rivers and glaciers carve out valleys and push great amounts of soil, stones, and sand over the Earth. People have also used the force of moving water to generate power and electricity.

World Wise

All of the water on or near Earth—including the moisture in the air—makes up the hydrosphere.

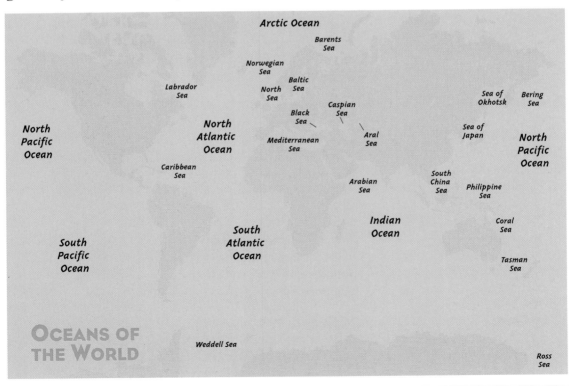

OCEANS OF THE WORLD

AWESOME OCEAN FACTS

- Earth is actually covered by one body of water. The oceans are all connected, one flowing into the other.

- There are 361 quintillion gallons, or 328 million cubic miles, of water in the ocean.

- The average temperature of all ocean water is 34° Fahrenheit (1.1° C).

- The average ocean depth is 12,523 feet (3,817 m). By comparison, the average height of land is 2,772 feet (845 m).

- The pressure at the deepest ocean point is 8 tons per square inch, which is equivalent to the pressure of one person trying to hold up 50 jumbo jets.

- The sea level has risen at an average of 4 to 10 inches (10 to 25 cm) over the past 100 years.

- Vents, or openings, occur on the ocean floor. Here, water temperatures get as high as 254° Fahrenheit (123° C).

- There are currents that flow like rivers, carrying warm water through the oceans.

- There may be as many as 6 million diatoms (floating plants) in 1 cubic foot of seawater.

The world has two vast ice caps, which cover most of Greenland and Antarctica. This is permanent ice that is at least 10,000 feet (3,048 m) thick.

Oceans

One huge body of water covers 75% of Earth. This expanse of salty water is divided by scientists and geographers into four oceans: the Pacific, the Atlantic, the Indian, and the Arctic. The waters of the ocean move constantly and freely. If you were to scoop a cupful of water from the Pacific Ocean off the shores of California, the water in the cup may have once flowed through the Indian Ocean off the coast of Madagascar.

Benjamin Franklin studied the Atlantic to learn why sailors took longer to cross from west to east. He found that ships had to sail against the powerful Gulf Stream current when sailing westward.

SURFING EARTH'S SURFACE

Total area of Earth's surface:
196,951,000 square miles
(510,100,000 sq km)

Total area of water:
139,692,000 square miles
(361,800,000 sq km)

Total area of land:
57,259,000 square miles
(148,300,000 sq km)

Ocean Investigation

Where are mountains also islands?

The ocean floor has abyssal plains (flat areas), valleys (that are called trenches), and mountains. The tops of these underwater mountains are islands.

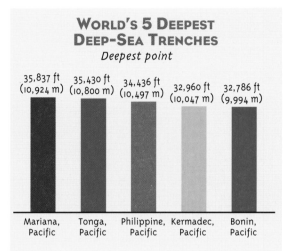

WORLD'S 5 DEEPEST DEEP-SEA TRENCHES
Deepest point

35,837 ft (10,924 m)	35,430 ft (10,800 m)	34,436 ft (10,497 m)	32,960 ft (10,047 m)	32,786 ft (9,994 m)
Mariana, Pacific	Tonga, Pacific	Philippine, Pacific	Kermadec, Pacific	Bonin, Pacific

Where do oceans meet land?

On the coastlines of the continents, there is a layer of slanting land called a continental shelf. A steep cliff that follows a shelf is called a continental slope.

Why does sand cover the shores?

The force of water breaking against rocks makes sand. Sand is actually tiny, broken-down pieces of rock washed up with the tide.

How do waves roll?

Most ocean waves are caused by winds. A tidal wave occurs when wind blows over the highest tides. A tsunami is a huge wave that results from an underwater earthquake.

Atlantic seawater is heavier than Pacific seawater because the Atlantic is saltier.

World Wise

THE OCEAN FLOOR

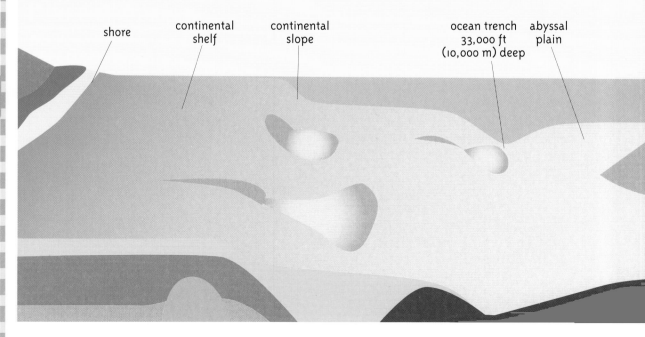

shore

continental shelf

continental slope

ocean trench 33,000 ft (10,000 m) deep

abyssal plain

Sand is created by the force of water on rocks

How does ocean water move?

A tide is the movement of water toward and away from the shores. Ocean tides are caused mostly by the pull of the moon's gravity on Earth's water. Ocean currents are powerful rivers or streams that move through the ocean waters.

Why are the oceans salty?

Seawater contains about 3% salt. Much of the salt comes from land. During the early years of Earth, salt was dissolved by heavy rains and washed into the sea in a process that continues today. Salt also comes from beneath the seafloor. It is brought up along with other minerals that spurt from underwater volcanoes.

How much salt is in the oceans?

If all the salt in the oceans was spread over Earth's land surface, it would form a wall 500 feet (152 m) high—the height of a 50-story building!

A tsunami can move as fast as 500 miles (800 km) per hour and be as high as 50 feet (15 m).

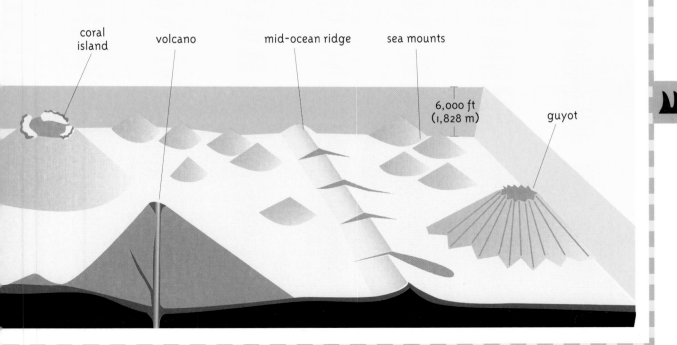

coral island

volcano

mid-ocean ridge

sea mounts

6,000 ft (1,828 m)

guyot

SIZING UP THE WORLD'S OCEANS

In square miles

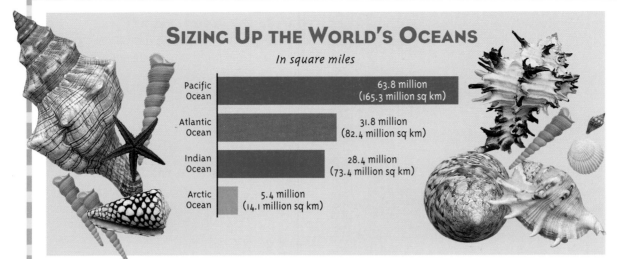

Pacific Ocean	63.8 million (165.3 million sq km)
Atlantic Ocean	31.8 million (82.4 million sq km)
Indian Ocean	28.4 million (73.4 million sq km)
Arctic Ocean	5.4 million (14.1 million sq km)

Pacific Ocean

The Pacific Ocean is the largest and deepest ocean. It holds more than half the seawater on Earth, which is almost as much as the Atlantic and Indian oceans combined. This amazing body of water covers more than one-third of Earth's surface. It is larger in area than all the land in the world combined! The Pacific Ocean is sometimes divided into the North Pacific (north of the equator) and the South Pacific (south of the equator). The Pacific Ocean is

If there are only four oceans, what are the seven seas? The seven seas refers to the waters of the North Atlantic, South Atlantic, North Pacific, South Pacific, Arctic, Antarctic, and Indian oceans.

bounded on the east by the continents of North America and South America; on the west by Asia and Australia; and on the south by Antarctica. Ferdinand Magellan, a Portuguese explorer who sailed for Spain, had good weather when his expedition crossed the Pacific in an attempt to circumnavigate (sail entirely around) Earth. Because of this calm weather, Magellan named this ocean Pacific, which means "peaceful" in Spanish.

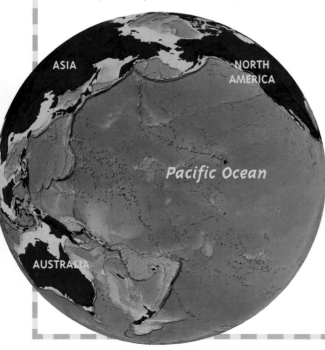

ASIA

NORTH AMERICA

Pacific Ocean

AUSTRALIA

Ferdinand Magellan was killed during a war in the Philippines. The remaining 18 members of his crew returned home to complete the first circumnavigation of the Earth in 1521.

Pacific Ocean, Chile

PACIFIC OCEAN CURRENTS

- The **Alaska** Current is a warm water current in the North Pacific.
- The **California** Current is a cool water current in the North Pacific.
- The Kuroshio Current is a warm water current in the North Pacific near **Japan**.
- The Oyashio, or Kamchatka, Current is a cool water current in the North Pacific.
- The North Pacific Drift is a warm water current in the North Pacific.
- The Equatorial Current is a warm current in the Pacific, near the equator.
- The East Australian Current is a warm current in the South Pacific.
- The Humboldt, or **Peru**, Current is a cool current in the South Pacific.
- The West Wind Drift is a cool current in the South Pacific.

Features of the Pacific

The East Pacific Rise is a mid-ocean mountain ridge that extends from the Gulf of **California** to the southern tip of **South America**. The Mariana Trench in the Pacific is the deepest point on Earth. It is deeper than the highest mountain is tall.

World Wise

The Kuroshio Current is the world's largest ocean current. It travels between 25 and 75 miles (40 to 120 km) a day. It has a depth of 3,300 feet (1,005 m).

PROFILE OF THE PACIFIC

Surface Area	About 64 million square miles (165 million sq km)
Gallons of Water	3,496 trillion
Average Depth	12,925 feet (3,940 m)
Deepest Point	The Mariana Trench at 35,837 feet (10,924 m)
Islands	More than 30,000

Lagoon, French Polynesia

The world's largest island is Greenland, at 840,000 square miles (2,175,600 sq km). To be a continent, it would have to measure about 3 million square miles (7.8 million sq km).

The Atlantic Ocean is thought to have been named by the ancient Romans. The Atlas Mountains, which rose at the western end of the Mediterranean Sea, marked the limits of their known world. The word *Atlantic* refers to the ocean found beyond these mountains.

Atlantic Ocean

The Atlantic is the world's second-largest ocean. It is also the busiest ocean, with the greatest amount of ship travel. This ocean is thought to be the world's youngest ocean—only 100 million years old. The Atlantic covers 20% of the Earth's surface in an S-shape. It is bounded on the west by North America and South America, and on the east by Europe and Africa. The Atlantic meets the Indian Ocean south of Africa. To the north, it is bounded by the Arctic Ocean. The northern border line extends from Greenland to northern Norway. Like the Pacific, the Atlantic Ocean is divided at the equator, into the North Atlantic and the South Atlantic.

PROFILE OF THE ATLANTIC

Average Depth	11,730 feet (3,575 m)
Deepest Point	Puerto Rico Trench at 28,374 feet (8,648 m)
Width	Varies from 1,769 miles (2,847 km) between Brazil and Liberia, to about 3,000 miles (4,828 km) between the United States and northern Africa.
Islands	There are relatively few islands in the Atlantic. They include: Svalbard, Greenland, Iceland, the British Isles, the Azores, the Madeira, the Canaries, the Cape Verde Islands, Bermuda, the West Indies, Ascension, St. Helena, Tristan de Cunha, the Falklands, and the South Georgia Islands.

Iceland coastline

West Indies

ATLANTIC OCEAN CURRENTS

- The Gulf Stream is a river of warm water in the Atlantic Ocean that flows from the Gulf of Mexico north to the coast of Ireland in Europe.
- The Labrador Current is a cold current that comes from the Arctic Ocean between Greenland and Canada and meets up with the end of the Gulf Stream.
- The North Atlantic Drift is a warm water current in the North Atlantic.
- The Brazil Current carries warm water south along the coast of South America.
- The Falkland, or Benguela, Current is both a warm and a cool current that flows north to meet the Brazil Current in the South Atlantic.

The Magical Lagoon in Mexico is where gray whales who have migrated from the Arctic Ocean spawn and raise calves.

Underwater mountains
The Mid-Atlantic Ridge extends from Iceland to about 58° south latitude. Its widest point is 1,000 miles (1,609 km). The Great Rift Valley extends along this ridge for most of its length.

The Walvis Ridge is another mountain ridge located in the South Atlantic.

The Atlantic Intracoastal Waterway
This is a sheltered water route along the Atlantic Coast of the United States. It consists of inland bays, rivers, estuaries, sounds, and inlets, all linked by canals to form one large

The Gulf Stream moves at a rate of 60 miles (96 km) a day and carries 100 times as much water as all the rivers on Earth.

waterway. This waterway is used by barges and smaller vessels to travel from Boston, Massachusetts, to Key West, Florida.

The Bermuda Triangle
This imaginary triangle is also called the Devil's Triangle. The three points of the triangle are Miami, Florida; Puerto Rico; and Bermuda. This area is popularly known for unexplainable disappearances of ships and airplanes. Close study has shown that this part of the Atlantic is not any more dangerous than other open-ocean areas.

St. George, Bermuda

INDIAN OCEAN CURRENTS

- The Agulhas Current is a warm water current.
- The West Australian Current is a cool water current.

Indian Ocean

The Indian Ocean is the third-largest ocean. It is less than half the size of the Pacific Ocean. The Indian Ocean is bordered on the west by Africa, and on the east by Australia and Indonesia. Its northern border is Asia, and its southern border is Antarctica. Most of this ocean is in a tropical climate, which prevents icebergs and heavy fog from forming.

Shallows of the Indian Ocean

The ocean floor rises almost to the surface in areas around the middle of the ocean. These include the Genista Shallow and the Hallbank Shallow.

Underwater mountain ridge

A Y-shaped ridge extends from the southern Arabian Sea to the edge of Antarctica. Several islands are cone-shaped mountains of this ridge. They are the Cocos Islands and Tromelin Island.

Seychelles beach

PROFILE OF THE INDIAN OCEAN

Surface Area	About 29 million square miles (75 million sq km)
Average Depth	12,598 feet (3,840 m)
Deepest Point	Java Trench at 25,344 feet (7,725 m)
Islands	Notable islands include Madagascar, Sri Lanka, the Seychelles, the Maldives, Prince Edward Island, and Christmas Island.

Sea ice and iceberg

Arctic Ocean

The Arctic Ocean is the smallest ocean. It holds a tiny amount of Earth's seawater—just 1%. Despite its small size, the Arctic Ocean still holds more than 25 times the water in all the world's rivers and freshwater lakes combined. Antarctica has as much ice as the Atlantic Ocean has water. The Arctic is bounded on the north by the North Pole, on the east by Asia and Europe, and on the west by North America. The Arctic ice is so vast in winter that one could walk from Greenland to Norway's Svalbard Islands! The areas of open water in the Arctic are called polynyas. These openings are habitats for migrating waterfowl and polar bears.

Arctic ice

Three forms of ice are found in the Arctic Ocean: land ice, river ice, and sea ice. Land ice enters the ocean in the form of icebergs, created by parts of glaciers that have broken off. River ice is found near shore as rivers transport frozen fresh water into the ocean. Sea ice, which is formed by the freezing of seawater, is the most common ice in the Arctic. In winter, a permanent cap of sea ice covers most of the Arctic Ocean's surface.

Laurentian Divide

This rocky region, also called the Canadian Shield, covers land around the Hudson Bay and other parts of Canada. All rivers run north emptying into the Arctic Ocean at the Laurentian Divide. At this point, all waters then flow north into the Arctic Ocean.

PROFILE OF THE ARCTIC OCEAN

Surface Area	About 5.4 million square miles (14 million sq km)
Average Depth	3,407 feet (1,038 m)
Deepest Point	Eurasia basin at 17,881 feet (5,450 m)
Islands	Canada's Arctic Islands form the largest archipelago in the world.

The world's fastest-moving glacier is Jakobshavns Glacier in Greenland. It can move more than 100 feet (30.5 km) a day. Most glaciers move at a speed of less than 1 foot (0.3 km) a day.

ASIA

Arctic Ocean

NORTH AMERICA

Surfer's paradise, Queensland, Australia

Hopland, Norway

WHO OWNS THE OCEANS?

Countries can claim territorial waters. These are the seas near their coastlines. The 10 largest areas of ocean claimed by world countries are listed below in square kilometers.

1. Australia	28,500,000
2. Russia	21,500,000
3. United States	20,000,000
4. Canada	12,400,000
5. China	11,400,000
6. Brazil	11,000,000
7. France	6,000,000
8. Indonesia	6,000,000
9. India	5,700,000
10. New Zealand	5,500,000

Coastlines

Coastlines are the most obvious boundaries between land and ocean. The world's coastlines are about 312,480 miles (502,874 km) long. If stretched out, they would circle the equator 12 times!

Canada has the longest coastline of any country: 151,766 miles (244,191 km). This is about six times the circumference of Earth.

Spectacular seacoasts include the White Cliffs of Dover in England; the fjords of Norway, Chile, and New Zealand; and the Diamond Coast of southwest Africa.

It is estimated that two-thirds of the world's population lives within a few miles of the coastlines.

Seas, Bays, and Gulfs

Bodies of water connected to oceans are called seas, bays, or gulfs. They all contain salt water. Seas are smaller than oceans. A sea may be partially attached to an ocean, like the Mediterranean Sea, which is partially surrounded by land, but attached to the Atlantic Ocean. A sea may also be part of an ocean, like the Sargasso Sea, which is completely surrounded by the waters of the Atlantic Ocean.

A bay is a body of water partially enclosed by land, with a wide mouth that easily connects it to the ocean.

A gulf is larger than a bay, and cuts farther into land. Both bays and gulfs are known as inlets.

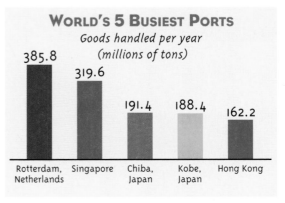

WORLD'S 5 BUSIEST PORTS
Goods handled per year (millions of tons)

Rotterdam, Netherlands	Singapore	Chiba, Japan	Kobe, Japan	Hong Kong
385.8	319.6	191.4	188.4	162.2

SIZING UP SEAS, BAYS, AND GULFS

Bodies of salt water, in order from the largest to the smallest:

1. **Coral Sea** — Part of the Pacific Ocean near Australia
2. **Arabian Sea** — Part of the Indian Ocean between India and Arabia
3. **China Sea** — Part of the Pacific Ocean near Japan, often divided into the South China Sea and the East Sea
4. **Caribbean Sea** — Part of the Atlantic Ocean near Central America
5. **Mediterranean Sea** — An inland sea partially enclosed by Europe, Asia, and Africa
6. **Bering Sea** — Part of the Pacific Ocean connecting to the Arctic Ocean
7. **Bay of Bengal** — Part of the Indian Ocean
8. **Sea of Okhotsk** — An inlet of the Pacific Ocean
9. **Gulf of Mexico** — Part of the Atlantic Ocean on the southeast coast of North America
10. **Gulf of Guinea** — An inlet of the Atlantic Ocean near Africa
11. **Barents Sea** — Part of the Arctic Ocean near Norway
12. **Norwegian Sea** — Part of the Arctic Ocean between Greenland and Iceland
13. **Gulf of Alaska** — An arm of the Pacific Ocean near Alaska
14. **Hudson Bay** — An inlet on the eastern coast of Canada
15. **Greenland Sea** — Part of the Arctic Ocean
16. **Arafura Sea** — Between Australia and Indonesia
17. **Philippine Sea** — Part of the western Pacific Ocean
18. **Sea of Japan** — Part of the Pacific Ocean near Japan
19. **East Siberian Sea** — Part of the Arctic Ocean
20. **Kara Sea** — Part of the Arctic Ocean

Fishing boats, French West Indies

Lake Tahoe, Nevada

Lakes

American writer Henry Thoreau described a lake as "Earth's eye." Geographically speaking, a lake is a body of water surrounded by land. Lakes can be found all over the world. Some large lakes are called seas. For example, the Caspian Sea in western Asia and the Dead Sea in Israel are actually saltwater lakes. The Sea of Galilee in the Middle East is a freshwater lake. Most lakes were formed from glaciers. The word *lake* is a Greek word that means "hole" or "pond."

The Great Lakes

This is a group of five large lakes in North America. From west to east, they are Lake Superior, Lake Michigan, Lake Huron, Lake Erie, and Lake Ontario. Lake Michigan is the only Great Lake that lies entirely within the United States. The other lakes form part of the border between Canada and the United States. The combined surface area of the Great Lakes is 94,460 square miles (244,650 sq km). The St. Lawrence Seaway is a system of channels, canals, and locks that make it possible for oceangoing vessels to sail from the Great Lakes to the Atlantic Ocean.

World Wise

Although Lake Baikal in Siberia, Russia, is only the world's eighth-largest lake, it holds the most fresh water (one-fifth of the world's supply) of all the lakes because it is so deep.

Lake Superior is the largest of the Great Lakes. In fact, it is the largest freshwater lake in the world. It covers an area as large as the states of Massachusetts, Connecticut, Rhode Island, Vermont, and New Hampshire combined! Lake Superior is 350 miles (563 km) long and 160 miles (256 km) wide. Its shoreline is 1,826 miles (2,921 km) long. The lake holds 10% of the world's fresh surface water, about 3 quadrillion gallons. The average time a drop of

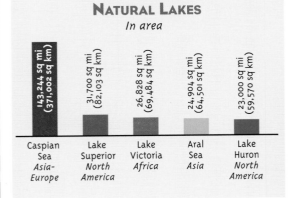

WORLD'S 5 LARGEST NATURAL LAKES
In area

	143,244 sq mi (371,002 sq km)	31,700 sq mi (82,103 sq km)	26,828 sq mi (69,484 sq km)	24,904 sq mi (64,501 sq km)	23,000 sq mi (59,570 sq km)
	Caspian Sea *Asia-Europe*	Lake Superior *North America*	Lake Victoria *Africa*	Aral Sea *Asia*	Lake Huron *North America*

Lake Victoria, Tanzania

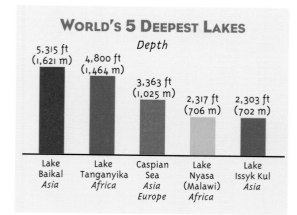

World's 5 Deepest Lakes
Depth

Lake Baikal *Asia*	5,315 ft (1,621 m)
Lake Tanganyika *Africa*	4,800 ft (1,464 m)
Caspian Sea *Asia Europe*	3,363 ft (1,025 m)
Lake Nyasa (Malawi) *Africa*	2,317 ft (706 m)
Lake Issyk Kul *Asia*	2,303 ft (702 m)

Lake Michigan

water remains in Lake Superior (detention time) is 191 years.

Lake Superior does not move by tides, but by weather. A combination of winds and high air pressure produces a tidal-like rise and fall called a seiche (saysh).

World Wise

A precious lake
Lake Vostok is a liquid water lake located under the East Antarctic Ice Sheet on the continent of Antarctica. The lake is 140 miles (224 km) long and 30 miles (48 km) wide. For the last million years, this lake has been sealed off from the rest of the world under a layer of ice 2 miles (3.2 km) thick. Scientists believe Lake Vostok may contain organisms that are very different from those found elsewhere on Earth. By using the technology of Radarsat pictures, scientists are studying the lake and looking for ways to gain access to it without contaminating it.

State of lakes
The state of Minnesota in the United States has more than 11,000 lakes. They were formed by glacier erosion. In the northern part of the state, near the border of Canada, there is an area of lakes known as the Boundary Waters. Within this million acres of wilderness, there are no roads or buildings. All motors are banned. Explorers and campers paddle the lakes in canoes.

The highest and lowest lakes
Lake Titicaca in South America is the world's highest lake. It is 12,507 feet (3,812 m) above sea level. The world's lowest lake—also the lowest point on Earth—is the Dead Sea, between Israel and Jordan. It lies 1,310 feet (399 m) below sea level.

Reservoirs
These are artificial lakes formed by dams that store fresh drinking water. Many cities get drinking water from cleaner environments outside the area. New York City, for example, uses water from the Catskill Mountains, more than 100 miles (161 km) away from the city.

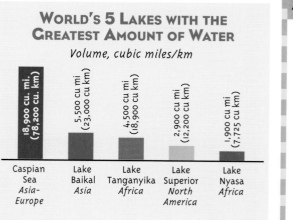

World's 5 Lakes with the Greatest Amount of Water
Volume, cubic miles/km

Lake	Volume
Caspian Sea *Asia-Europe*	18,900 cu. mi. (78,200 cu. km)
Lake Baikal *Asia*	5,500 cu mi (23,000 cu km)
Lake Tanganyika *Africa*	4,500 cu mi (18,900 cu km)
Lake Superior *North America*	2,900 cu mi (12,200 cu km)
Lake Nyasa *Africa*	1,900 cu mi (7,725 cu km)

Rivers

A river is a large body of water that flows over land in a long channel. Rivers are important transportation routes for trade and travel. They deposit fertile soil for farming, and provide valuable water for irrigation.

Channeling rivers

As rain falls to the Earth, the water runs into tiny, narrow channels called rills or rivulets. These crevises then form deeper channels called brooks or creeks, which flow into streams, and then rivers. These channels of water are called the tributaries of a river.

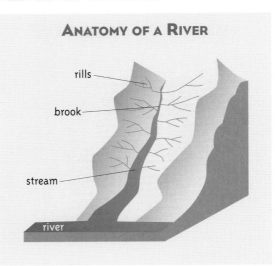

ANATOMY OF A RIVER

rills
brook
stream
river

When streams run into the source of a river, they are called the headwaters. The headwaters are at the highest elevation of a river. Where the river ends is called its mouth. Rivers empty into larger rivers, lakes, or oceans.

Colorado River, Marble Canyon, Arizona

River beginnings and endings

Where a river begins is called its source. The source may be melting snow from a glacier, an overflowing lake, or a spring.

World Wise

The source of the Ganges River of India is an ice cave in the Himalaya Mountain slopes. The Ganges River is considered sacred by the followers of the Hindu religion.

RIVERS WITH THE GREATEST AMOUNT OF WATER

RIVER	LOCATION	FLOW AT THE MOUTH PER SECOND
1. Amazon	South America	6,180,000 cubic feet (174,900 cubic meters)
2. Congo	Africa	1,377,000 cubic feet (39,000 cubic meters)
3. Negro	South America	1,236,000 cubic feet (35,000 cubic meters)
4. Orinoco	South America	890,000 cubic feet (25,200 cubic meters)
5. La Plata-Parana	South America	809,000 cubic feet (22,900 cubic meters)

WORLD'S LONGEST RIVERS

RIVER	CONTINENT	LENGTH
1. Nile	Africa	4,160 miles (1,268 km)
2. Amazon	South America	4,000 miles (1,219 km)
3. Yangtze	Asia	3,964 miles (1,208 km)
4. Huang	Asia	3,395 miles (1,035 km)
5. Ob-Irtysh	Asia	3,362 miles (1,025 km)
6. Amur	Asia	2,744 miles (836 km)
7. Lena	Asia	2,734 miles (833 km)
8. Congo	Africa	2,718 miles (828 km)
9. Mekong	Asia	2,600 miles (792 km)
10. Niger	Africa	2,590 miles (789 km)
11. Parana	South America	2,485 miles (754 km)
12. Mississippi	North America	2,340 miles (713 km)
13. Missouri	North America	2,315 miles (706 km)
14. Murray-Darling	Australia	2,310 miles (704 km)
15. Volga	Europe	2,290 miles (698 km)

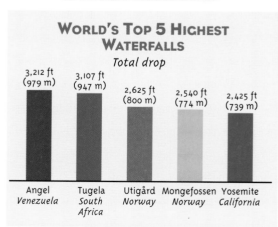

Felucca on Nile, Aswan, Egypt

The continent of Antarctica has no rivers. However, it has a huge network of ice streams that channel their way through surrounding rocks and ice. They travel at speeds of 3,000 feet (915 m) per year, which is 100 times faster than the flow of ice.

Most of Australia's rivers are dry at least part of the year. The Murray River is Australia's longest permanently flowing river. It winds 1,609 miles (2,589 km). During the summer, the Darling River feeds into the Murray. Although its course is dry much of the year, the Darling is Australia's longest river at 1,702 miles (2,739 km).

The Amazon River has a drainage basin of about 2.7 million square miles (7 million sq km).

The Amazon and the Nile rivers are close in length. However, the Nile has only 110,000 cubic feet (3,100 cubic m) of water flow at its mouth.

WORLD'S TOP 5 HIGHEST WATERFALLS
Total drop

	Angel Venezuela	Tugela South Africa	Utigård Norway	Mongefossen Norway	Yosemite California
	3,212 ft (979 m)	3,107 ft (947 m)	2,625 ft (800 m)	2,540 ft (774 m)	2,425 ft (739 m)

GLACIERS—THE WORLD'S LONGEST RIVERS OF ICE

Gigantic glacier

RIVER	LOCATION	LENGTH
1. Lanbert-Fisher	Antarctica	320 miles (512 km)
2. Novaya Zemlya	Russia	260 miles (416 km)
3. Arctic Institute	Antarctica	225 miles (360 km)
4. Nimrod-Lennox-King	Antarctica	180 miles (288 km)
5. Denman	Antarctica	150 miles (240 km)

Earth's greatest river

The Amazon River of South America is the second-longest world river. It is longer than the highway route between New York City and San Francisco. The Amazon carries more water than any other river—more than the Nile, the Mississippi, and the Yangtze rivers, combined! It empties a whopping 6 million cubic feet of water per second into the Atlantic Ocean. The width of the river varies from 1.5 to 6 miles (2.4 to 10 km). The average depth of the Amazon is 40 feet (12 m),

Hut on the bank of the Amazon River

but can be as deep as 300 feet (91 m) in some spots. The Amazon has more than 500 tributaries and provides drainage for more than 40% of South America.

In the 1500s, Spanish explorers were attacked by native warriors—some of whom were female. They called their attackers Amazons, after the female warriors of Greek mythology. Later, the name Amazon was given to the river and the land around it.

World Wise

The world's shortest river is the D River in Oregon, which connects Devil's Lake with the Pacific Ocean. It is only 120 feet (36 m) long!

THE 10 MOST ENDANGERED RIVERS OF THE UNITED STATES, 1998

RIVER	LOCATION	CAUSE OF CONTAMINATION
1. Columbia River	Hanford Reach, WA	Agricultural development and nuclear waste
2. Missouri River	MN, ND, SD, NE, IA, KS, MO	Dams and channelization
3. Pocomoke River	DE, MD, VA	Factory and poultry-farm pollution
4. Blackfoot River	Missoula, MN	Gold mine pollution
5. Colorado River Delta	Baja, CA; Sonora, Mexico	Overuse of water
6. Apple River	WI, IL	Factory hog farms
7. Lower Snake River	WA	Dams
8. Pinto Creek	AZ	Copper mine pollution
9. Kern River	Los Angeles, CA	Small hydropower dams
10. Chattahoochee River	GA, AL, FL	Development and sewage runoff

NO SWIMMING
BY RECOMMENDATION OF COUNTY HEALTH DEPT

RIVER WORDS

bank	The edges of a river.
bed	The bottom of a river channel.
creek	A small tributary; also called a brook, kill, or run.
delta	A deposit of soil at a river's mouth, usually triangular in shape.
drainage basin	The land area drained by a river system.
estuary	A point where the mouth of a river enters the sea. The water is a mix of fresh water and seawater.
exotic river	A river that rises in a humid region and flows downstream through an arid region. Examples are the Nile and the Colorado rivers.
flood plain	The flat area in the middle or lower course of the river that is covered by water during floods.
levee	A buildup of rock and soil that raises up the river's banks.
meanders	Snakelike bends and loops in a river's course.
mouth	The end of a river, the point where it empties into another body of water.
rapids	A place where a river crosses a layer of strong, resistant rocks.
tributary	All of the channels that carry water into a river.

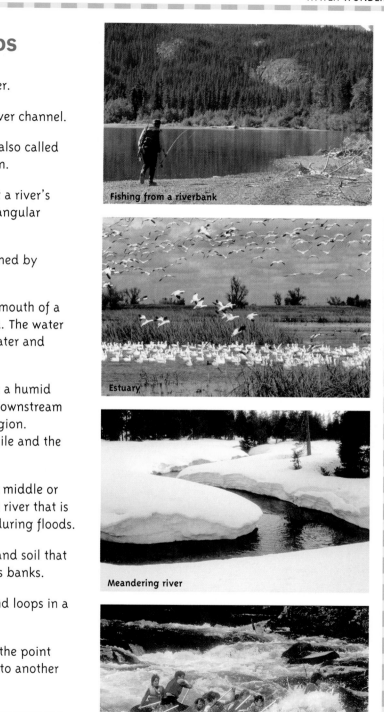

Fishing from a riverbank

Estuary

Meandering river

Rafting through rapids

FAMOUS RIVERS OF THE WORLD

Colorado River

RIVER	LOCATION	IMPORTANCE
Colorado	North America	Its current helped to carve out the Grand Canyon.
Danube	Europe	Inspired the Austrian composer Johann Strauss, Jr., to write the "On the Beautiful Blue Danube" waltz.
Ganges	Asia	Hindu pilgrims believe these waters will wash away sins and cure illnesses. In Hindi, the word *ganga* means "river."
Hudson	North America	Mouth lies at the harbor of New York City. It was named after the English explorer Henry Hudson in 1609.
Indus	Asia	Its source is one of the world's largest irrigation systems.
Jordan	Asia	Mentioned most often in the Bible. It runs through Israel and Jordan.
Niger	Africa	Has the largest delta in Africa.
Potomac	North America	U.S. historic river; it forms a boundary between Maryland, West Virginia, and Virginia.
Rhine	Europe	Most important inland waterway in Europe. It is a transportation way for trade and travel.

Ganges riverfront

Jordan River

Barge on Mississippi River

Alexandre III Bridge over the Seine

Rio Grande	North America	Forms part of the boundary between the United States and Mexico.
St. Lawrence	North America	Links the Great Lakes with the Atlantic Ocean. In 1536, French explorer Jacques Cartier charted this river 1,000 miles (1,609 km) inland to modern-day Montreal, Canada.
Seine	Europe	Flows through the heart of Paris, France, where more than 30 bridges span it.
Thames	Europe	Longest and most important waterway in England. It flows through the city of London.
Zambezi	Africa	Victoria Falls, a natural wonder of the world, is located on this river.

London Bridge over the Thames

Waters Named After Explorers

Bering Sea and Bering Strait
Named after Vitus Jonassen Bering, a Danish navigator in the Royal Russian Navy. He charted the coast of Siberia and explored the Aleutian Islands in 1741.

Hudson Bay and Hudson River
Named after Henry Hudson, an English explorer who found these waters in 1610 and 1611 while attempting to find a northwest passage to Asia.

A mile is 5,280 feet. A nautical mile is 6,076 feet. A knot is one nautical mile per hour. A knot can also mean one nautical mile. A fathom is a depth of 6 feet.

Humboldt Current
This ocean current, also called the Peru Current, is a cold, broad, shallow stream in the Pacific Ocean. Baron von Humboldt was a German geographer who explored South America from 1799 to 1804.

Ferdinand Magellan

Disappointment because he had hoped it would lead to the Pacific Ocean.

Ross Sea
Named after James Clark Ross, an English explorer who chartered this sea and the Ross Ice Shelf of Antarctica in 1841.

Strait of Magellan
This narrow water passageway is located at the tip of South America. It was named after the Portuguese explorer Ferdinand Magellan, who was sponsored by Spain to circumnavigate the globe from 1519 to 1521.

Tasman Sea
Named after Abel Janszoon Tasman, who was sent by the Dutch East India Company to learn more about Australia. He located New Zealand, Tasmania, and the Fiji Islands. His expeditions took place from 1642 to 1643.

Lake Champlain
Named after French explorer Samuel de Champlain, who was called the "Father of New France" because he established the first permanent French colony in North America at Quebec, Canada, in 1608.

Samuel de Champlain

The Grand Canal is the world's oldest and longest canal. It extends 1,000 miles (1,600 km) from a seaport in northern China to the Yangtze River valley in southern China. It was started in the 6th century B.C.

Mackenzie River
Named after Alexander Mackenzie, a Scottish explorer who, in 1789, found the mouth of this river at the Arctic Ocean. Mackenzie called it the River of

WATER WORDS

artesian well A spring of underground pressurized water.

atoll A ringlike coral island that encloses a pool of seawater.

bay A body of water that extends into the land.

beach A rocky or sandy edge of land along a body of water.

canal An artificial waterway.

channel The bed of a stream or river; the deeper part of a river; a broad strait that connects two seas.

coral reef A rocklike wall of coral animals attached to mountains of stony skeletons of dead coral animals. A fringing reef is attached to the shoreline. A barrier reef is separated from the shoreline by a channel of water.

cove An indentation or inlet of water, smaller than a bay.

fjord A long, narrow, deep inlet of the sea between steep land slopes.

geyser A natural hot spring of water that shoots a column of water and steam into the air at intervals.

glacier A huge mass of flowing ice moving slowly over land. It is formed by compacted snow.

gulf A large part of ocean or sea extending into the land, larger than a bay.

ice cap A dome-shaped form of ice and snow.

iceberg A huge, floating body of ice broken away from a glacier.

ice sheet An enormous continental glacier, larger than an ice cap.

key (cay) A low offshore island or reef.

lagoon A shallow body of water separated from the sea by a sandbar or reef.

lake An inland body of fresh water or seawater.

pond A still body of water, smaller than a lake, often artificially made.

reef A strip of rocks, sand, or coral that rises near the surface of a body of water.

sound A long, somewhat wide body of water, larger than a strait, that connects larger bodies of water.

strait A narrow body of water that connects two larger bodies of water.

waterfall A stream of water that falls from a high place.

Beach

Canal

Coral reef

Icebergs

Florida Keys

Waterfall

World Beat
(Music and Dance)

From the beginning of time, the Earth has been alive with a dazzling variety of sounds—from the percussive sounds of exploding volcanoes to the low, bass sounds of gurgling rivers of melting ice. To create music, the earliest humans imitated the sounds of birds' songs, the rustling or whistling of wind moving through branches, and crickets chirping in rhythm. They probably even used rhythmic movements to make stone tools.

Music is a universal need for humans. No matter what the culture—or the period in which it existed—music has played a part in daily life. When humans first gathered to perform rituals, they incorporated dance and song into their activities. Early humans favored the power of singing to express emotions in an uplifting way. The first known instrument was a flute made from hollow bones, which dates back to about 10,000 B.C. Another instrument—the fiddle and bow—evolved from hunting weapons like the bow and arrow.

Today music can be heard everywhere—from hymns sung in churches, to pop tunes played on a car radio, to soothing lullabies sung by parents to their sleepy children. Because music satisfies a basic need, it has become an integral part of our world. From the music played in elevators to the harvest songs of African farmers, music is the rhythm of the universe.

ORIGINS OF SELECTED MUSICAL STYLES AND INSTRUMENTS

Bagpipes
United Kingdom

NORTH AMERICA

EUROPE

ASIA

Kodo drummers
Japan

Cajun/Zydeco
Louisiana

Atlantic Ocean

Balalaika
Russia

Flamenco
Spain

Gong
Tibet

Hula
Hawaii

Salsa
Puerto Rico

Sitar
India

Pacific Ocean

Mariachi
Mexico

Reggae
Jamaica

Talking drum
West Africa

Pacific Ocean

AFRICA

Indian Ocean

Gamelan
Indonesia

SOUTH AMERICA

Didgeridoo
(Aboriginal)

Panpipes
Peru

Samba
Brazil

AUSTRALIA

Mbube
South Africa

Tango
Argentina

Chinese lion dance

Music of the Spheres

The "music of the spheres" refers to beautiful sounds that humans cannot readily hear. The ancient Greeks thought this music was made by the movement of the stars and planets. We know today that the Earth makes its own music. As particles of the sun's rays hit Earth's magnetic field, they cause vibrations of electrical and magnetic energy. The magnetic pulse of this music is translated into sighs, hisses, whistles, and crackles. The area of the aurora borealis, or northern lights, is particularly musical, and scientists have been capturing the "tunes" on sensitive recording devices.

Aurora Borealis

Animals and Music

We know that bears can be trained to dance, that wolves howl in a tuneful song, and that spiders drum on their webs. The first humans to make music probably imitated the animal music they heard around them.

Chinese lion dance

An important tradition in **China** is the Chinese lion dance. Humans take on the animal form of a lion, which is a large puppet with two dancers inside. One person handles the head, and the other handles the body and tail as they perform a dance. Three musicians play a drum, a gong, and cymbals. The Chinese lion dance, which is believed to bring luck and happiness, is usually performed for festivities such as weddings or the Chinese New Year. Lions are not native to China, but were first sent as gifts to the Chinese emperor from rulers in the Middle East around 205 B.C.

Tuareg camel dance

Among the Tuareg nomads of the Sahara Desert, there is a dance in which men on camels make the animals dance. They do this by changing the camels' movements with the changing rhythm of the music. Women beat drums, clap their hands, and sing songs to accompany this special camel dance.

National Dance, Music, and Instruments

Harp

The Celtic harp is the national instrument and the national symbol of Ireland.

Fado

This is the national vocal music of Portugal. *Fado* means "fate" in Portuguese and describes the blues-style music of these mournful songs.

A pedal harp has up to 47 strings and produces the most tones of any stringed instrument.

Kantele

This 40-stringed zither is the national instrument of Finland. In Finnish myth, a hero defeats his enemy by playing a kantele made from the jawbone of a giant fish strung with a young woman's hair.

Morin huur

This lute is the national instrument of Mongolia. The instument, whose name means

Flamenco dancing

"horse's lute," has an ornamental carving of a horse's head at the top of the neck.

Samba

This is the national dance of Brazil. Dancers use forward and backward tilting movements as they dance to syncopated rhythms.

The fiddle is important in Swedish folklore. The Nacken, a troll said to live in streams and lakes, is a master fiddler. Legend says that if a Nacken plays a fiddle, the instrument will become magical.

Samba school

Music and Dance Capitals of the World

Andalusia, Spain, is the heartland of flamenco—a vocal and guitar-based music of gypsy origin. A flamenco singer vocalizes in the voice of a "fractured soul." A flamenco dancer moves from toe to heel, holds the head high, and extends the arms in wavy rhythms.

Chinese dancer

Bali, Indonesia, is known for ancient, local folk dances. Stories or legends are acted out in dance, with intricate hand and arm movements.

Beijing, China, is the home of the Beijing (or Peking) opera, a musical performance that includes acrobatics, dance, dialogue, and music.

Buenos Aires, Argentina, is the the home of the tango. The tapping steps of this dance were based on cowboys dancing the tango with the spurs on their boots.

Indian dancer

Finland is the tango capital of Europe.

India is the birthplace of Bharata Natya, an ancient Hindu dance in which the legends of Hindu gods and goddesses are enacted.

Jamaica is the home of reggae music, which incorporates soul, calypso, and rock 'n' roll with a strong offbeat.

The Beatles, one of the most popular rock 'n' roll bands in history, began their musical career in Liverpool, England.

Mexico is the home of mariachi (brass band music), and the world-renowned folk dance company Ballet Folklorico de Mexico.

Moscow, Russia, is the home of classical ballet and the Bolshoi Ballet. *Bolshoi* means "big" in Russian, a reference to the theater where ballet is performed.

Rajastan, India, is the home of gypsy music accompanied by a violin-like instrument called a *sarangi*.

World Wise

The inventor of recorded music was Thomas Edison, who was deaf when he invented the phonograph.

Sado Island, Japan, is the home of *taiko* drum ensemble music. Professional drummers, such as the Kodo and Ondeko-za, are noted for this style of precision drumming, which combines great physical strength with spirituality.

Ballet Folklorico, Mexico

MUSICAL INSTRUMENTS: KINDS TO KNOW

Electric guitar

Mechanical and electronic

These instruments require electricity for sound or for amplification of sound:

electric organs and guitars

carillon

music box

synthesizer

Synthesizer

Chordophones

These instruments are played by making one or more strings vibrate.

archlute

balalaika

bandore

banjo

banjo-uke (banjo-ukulele)

banjo-zither

banjorine

bass guitar

bouzouki

guitar (centerhole, classical concert, electric F-hole, Hawaiian, Spanish, and steel)

harp

lute

mando-bass

mando-cello

mandolin

mandolute

mandore

oud

pandora

samisen

sitar

tambura

theorbo

troubadour fiddle

ukulele

vina

zither

Guitar

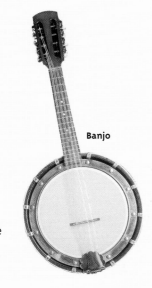
Banjo

Violins

Mandolin

Bowed stringed instruments

These are played by drawing a bow across the strings.

bass
cello
kit
kit violin
pocket fiddle

Presidents Harry S. Truman and Richard Nixon played the piano. President Bill Clinton plays the saxophone.

rebec
trumpet marine
vielle
viola (alto, baritone, bass, treble)
violin or fiddle
violinette
violino piccolo
violotta

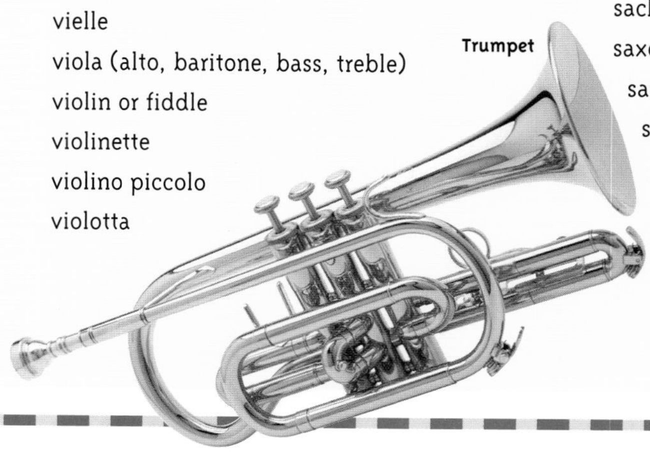

Trumpet

Aerophones

These brass wind instruments are played by blowing into or through a tube.

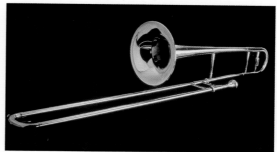

Trombone

alpenhorn
alto horn
ballad horn
baritone horn
bass horn
bombardon
bugle
clarion
cornet
cornopean
double-bell euphonium
flugelhorn
French horn
helicon
mellophone
ophicleide
sackbut
saxcornet
saxtuba
serpent
sousaphone
tenor tuba
trombone
trumpet

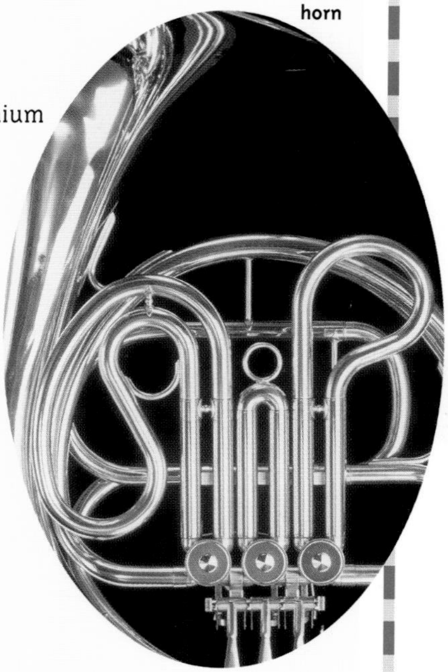

French horn

Woodwinds

These are played by blowing through or into a tube. They are classified together because they were once all made of wood.

bassoon (contra, double)

bombard

clarinet

English horn

fife

flageolet

flute (fipple, multiple, vessel, nose, side-blown, end-blown, and transverse)

hecklephone

hornpipe

krummhorn

musette

oaten reed

oboe

ocarina

Pandean pipe

panpipe

pibgorn

piccolo

pipe

Clarinet

pommer

recorder

saxophone

shawm

shepherd's pipe

sonorophone

syrinx

tabor pipe

tenoroon

tin-whistle (pennywhistle)

whistle

Keyboard stringed instruments

These instruments are played by pressing keys that are connected to strings.

clavichord

clavicymbal

Piano

dulcimer

harmonichord

harpsichord

lyrichord

manichord

melodion

melopiano

monochord

piano (grand, concert, console, cottage, upright, and violin)

spinet

Flutes

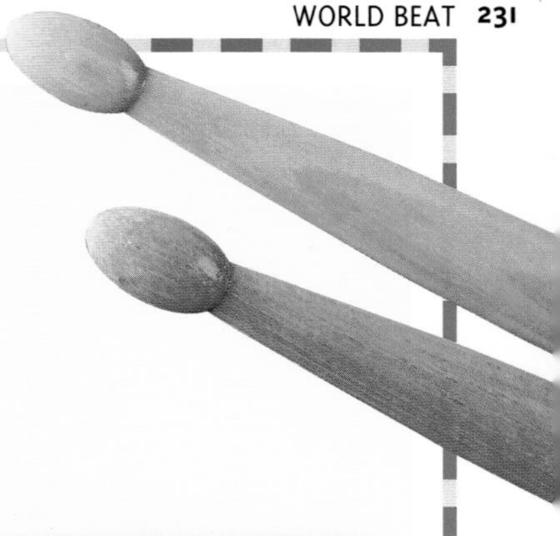

Cymbals

Membranophones and idiophones

Percussion instruments are played by shaking or by tapping with a stick or the hands.

bell

bones

bongo drums

castanets

celesta

chimes

clapper

conga drums

cymbals (crash, finger, highhat, and ride)

glockenspiel

gongs

jingles

kettledrum

lyra

African rattles

nagara

naker

orchestral bell

rattle

rattlebone

side drum

rattle

sizzler

snapper

snare drum

tabor

tambourine

tam-tam

tenor drum

thumb piano

timbrel

timpani (kettledrum)

tintinnabula

triangle

tubular bells

vibraphone

xylophone

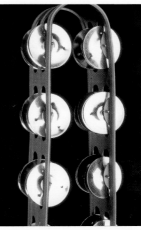

Tambourine

Snare drum

Percussion comes from the Latin word percuss, *which means "to tap."*

World Wise

maraca

marimba

metallophone

Bongo drums

World Music

La musique du monde. Pheeg puv tebchaws. Musica del mundo. Sekai no ongaku. In any language, the spirit of music is alive in people the world over. Here is a sampling of musical styles and instruments from around the world.

Aboriginal music

The music of the Aborigine of Australia is marked by drumming and dancing, and is played in order to honor the spirits of the world. A *corroboree* is a ceremonial gathering of Aboriginal clans. Traditional instruments include the didgeridoo—*Yidaki* in Aborigine—which is a wind instrument made from a hollowed eucalyptus tree, and *bilma*, which are clapsticks and slit log drums.

Berber man playing horn

African music

This is a general term for a wide variety of music found south of the Sahara Desert on the continent of Africa. African music in general is closely linked to all aspects of African life, especially religious ceremonies and festivals. For many Africans, music is the link to the spirit world as well as to the heart of all life—from birth, to rites of passage, to story-telling, to healing, and in preparation for death. Drums are often featured, although flutes, xylophones, and stringed instruments are also important. Complex rhythms are essential to the music. Songs are commonly "call-response," in which a leader sings a phrase and a chorus responds.

Tribal dancers, Kenya

Central and East Africa

• *Bikutsi* is fast and furious dance music from Cameroon. (*Biku* means "to thump," and *tsi* means "the ground.")

• Chakacha is the women's and girls' Swahili wedding dance.

• Danco congo is folk music entertainment from São Tomé.

• *Likembe* is the name of a thumb piano or kalimba from Uganda.

• *Mchiriku* is young, new-style folk music from Tanzania.

• *Ngoma* is drumming, singing, and dancing in the Bantu language.

• *Soukous* is dance music of the Congo and the Democratic Republic of the Congo.

• Tumba are conga drums of Tanzania.

Song and dance festival, Ghana

West African

• *Agidigbo* is a Yoruba dance rhythm named after the thumb piano from Nigeria.

• *Apala* is the Yoruba style of heavy talking-drumming, from Nigeria.

• *Asonko* is an ensemble of large, log xylophones played in Ghana.

• *Banjourou* is a style of rhythmic and melodious songs from Mali.

• A *bala* or *balafon* is an 18- to 21-key xylophone used widely in West Africa.

• *Djembe* is a single-headed, goblet-shaped drum from Senegal and Gambia.

• Donsongoni is a six-stringed hunter's harp from Mali and Guinea.

• *Fle* is a calabash (gourd) strung with beads, which is played in Mali.

• Fuji is a popular Nigerian Yoruba singing and drumming style.

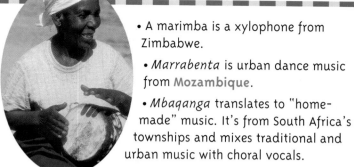
African drummer

• A marimba is a xylophone from Zimbabwe.

• *Marrabenta* is urban dance music from Mozambique.

• *Mbaqanga* translates to "home-made" music. It's from South Africa's townships and mixes traditional and urban music with choral vocals.

• *Mbira* is a hand or thumb piano from Zimbabwe. *Tufo* is women's choral music from Mozambique.

• Talking drums are widely used across West Africa. These drums of communication are pitched for "conversation." The Ashanti of Ghana and the Yoruba and Hausa of Nigeria continue to use these drums to send messages.

For the Mbuti (pygmies) of Africa, everything of importance is expressed in dance, including birth, death, full moon, successful hunt, arrival of friends, relief from worries, and illness.

Southern Africa

• *Chimurenga* is protest music from Zimbabwe.

• *Cothoza mfana* is a smooth style of harmony singing.

• *Hosho* is a gourd rattle from Zimbabwe.

• *Iscathamiya* is traditional Zulu call-response music from South Africa.

• *Jit jive* is fast, hard, percussive dance music from Zimbabwe.

• *Kwela* is a South African pennywhistle music.

• *Marabi* is three-chord music of the townships, which is rooted in the 1930s–1960s and has evolved into African Jazz.

Native American dancer, Canada

Native American music

This is the traditional music of natives of North America. American Indian music is usually associated with an activity, whether it's dancing for rain, hunting, or a religious ceremony. The musical instruments include drums, rattles, and flutes. Dancing and singing are an important part of tribal music. Vocables are the untranslatable sounds and syllables.

Tarahumara Indian dance

The tunes are based on a five-note scale of A C D F G. Two important dances are the stomp dance and the chicken scratch. The stomp dance originated in the southeastern United States among such tribes as the Cherokee, Choctaw, and Chicksaw. It is a heavy-footed, single-file snake dance. The chicken scratch is a modern, popular dance inspired by Spanish-American polkas. A powwow is the ceremonial and musical gathering of American Indians.

Caribbean music

Music from the Caribbean Islands combines native, African, and Spanish influences. Drums, guitars, and rattles are important instruments in this music.

Caribbean dancer, Jamaica

- Beguine is dance music from Martinique.
- Calypso is a traditional song from Trinidad.
- Cha-cha is a mid-tempo dance from Cuba, which was first popularized in the 1940s.
- *Charanga* is an ensemble of violins and flutes from Cuba.
- *Compas* is pop music from Haiti.
- *Conjunto* is a Cuban salsa band with brass, congas, bongo drums, bass, and piano.

- *Cuatro* is a small, four-stringed guitar from Puerto Rico.
- *Deejay* is talk-over, rapping-style music from Jamaica.
- *Gwo ka* is drum and vocal carnival music from Guadeloupe.
- Mambo is Latin-style dance music from Cuba.
- Maracas are a pair of gourd rattles used in the Caribbean.
- Merengue is a style of dance from the Dominican Republic.
- Pans are drums used in a steel band.
- Rumba is Afro-Cuban dance music for percussion and voices.
- Salsa is Latin dance music from Cuba and Puerto Rico. Singers, players, and dancers are known as *salseros*.
- Ska is instrumental music with jazz and rhythm-and-blues influences from Jamaica. Reggae incorporates "soul music" with calypso and rock 'n' roll, for a "cool," easy sound.
- *Tambora* is a double-headed drum used in merengue bands.

Bagpipes

Celtic music

Ceol is the Celtic word for "music." Celtic music originated in Ireland, Scotland, Wales, and the Brittany region of France. Like other music, it traveled with its people. In the Appalachian area of the United States, the Celtic fiddle influenced mountain music.

Irish step dancing, England

Harpist

Music is widely enjoyed and highly revered in Ireland. The gathering of players of traditional music is called a session. The session is the lifeblood of Irish traditional music and usually takes place in pubs and other meeting places. Irish step dancing grew out of Celtic music. There are four basic Irish step dances: reels in 2/4 time, light jigs in 6/8 time, slip jigs in the complex 9/8 time, and hornpipe in 2/4 time. An Irish dance competition is called a *feis* (pronounced fesh). Competitions are held in Canada, Ireland, the United Kingdom, Australia, New Zealand, South Africa, and the United States.

- *Biniou* is a Breton oboe.
- *Bodhran* is a large-frame Irish drum played with a small stick.
- *Bombard* are Breton bagpipes. *Ceili* is a communal dance with traditional music.
- *Clarsach* is a Celtic harp.
- *Eisteddfod* is a music and cultural festival of Wales.
- *Fez-Noz* is a Breton communal dance..

Hungarian dancers

- *Fleadh* is a music festival.
- *Kan ha diskan* is unaccompanied Breton song.
- Mouth music is unaccompanied Scottish dance singing.
- *Pibroch* is the original form of Scottish bagpipe playing.
- *Set* is a traditional group dance of Ireland.
- *Strathspey* is Scottish dance style.
- *Telenn* is a Breton harp.
- Triple harp is the traditional Welsh harp.
- Uilleann pipes are Irish bellows-blown bagpipes.

Lusheng pipes, China

Chinese music

More than 2,000 years old, Chinese music began as an accompaniment to important religious ceremonies and folk festivals. The principal instruments are two plucked string instruments—the *jin* and the *pipa* (a lute with four silk strings). The *qin* is a seven-stringed zither, and the *zheng* is a 13-stringed zither. Flutes, bells, and drums are also used. There is no harmony line in Chinese music. It is based on a five-note scale, F G A C D.

Eastern European music

This is the music of the people from the Baltic Sea to the Balkan Peninsula. The instruments used in this music are common to world music.

A music box has as many as 400 teeth. It is an instrument that plays a tune automatically as pins spin in a cylinder and pluck metal teeth of varying lengths.

- A balalaika is a three-stringed folk instrument from **Russia**.
- *Cimbalom* is a Hungarian hammer dulcimer.
- *Contra* is a three-stringed viola in a Transylvanian band.
- *Csardas* is a paired dance from **Hungary**.
- *Domra* is a Russian three-stringed mandolin, which is an earlier form of the balalaika.
- *Duduk* is an Armenian oboe.
- *Dudy* is a Czech bagpipe.
- *Gadulka* is a Bulgarian fiddle with three to four strings.
- *Gajda* is a Balkan bagpipe.
- *Gusle* is a Serbian and Montenegrin one-stringed fiddle.

Hungarian folk musician

- The hammer dulcimer is an instrument with a trapezoid-shaped sounding box and strings that are struck with two hammers. It is common in Hungary.
- Hora are ring dances of **Romania**, **Bulgaria**, and **Yugoslavia**.

Trumpet players

- *Kaval* is a long wooden flute from Bulgaria.
- *Landler* is a Central European dance in a 3/4 rhythm.
- *Nai* are Romanian panpipes.
- Polka is a dance from **Poland** in 2/4 time.
- *Rebec* is the first known European string instrument, which is similar to a lute.
- *Tapan* is a barrel drum of Bulgaria.
- *Tsambal* is a Romanian hammer dulcimer.
- *Zurna* (also called *surna, zurla, curla, pizge*) is an oboe from **Turkey** that is played throughout the Balkans.

Japanese drummer

Japanese music

This music was influenced by the music of **China**. Like Chinese music, there is no harmony. The basic scales of Japanese music are the minor scale and the major scale with the fourth note raised a half-step. The instruments include the *shakuhachi* (bamboo flutes), *biwa* (a four- to five-stringed lute), koto (a large 13-stringed zither), and the banjolike samisen. Gongs and drums are also important. *Taiko* means "big drum" in Japanese. Many different drums are called *taiko*, including the large, barrel-shaped drum used in *taiko* drum groups. One kind of Japanese vocal music is the *kobushi*, which has a heavy vibrato. *Min'yo* is a Japanese regional folk song.

Hula dancers

Hawaiian music

Hawaiian music is based on traditional Polynesian drum dances and chants. The hula is the dance, and the *mele* is the chant. A sharkskin drum called the *pahu* is a Polynesian drum—it is the oldest instrument of **Hawaii**. The *mele hula pahu* are chants accompanied by drums and dance, and are formal and sacred to Polynesian culture. Settlers brought guitars and ukuleles to Hawaii, and the music evolved to the modern hapa haole songs, written in English and accompanied by steel and slide guitars. Today the slack key guitar is unique to Hawaiian music. The art of playing slack key is in the secret guitar tunings and special thumb picking.

Ukulele player

Indian music

The music of **India** originated in Hindu temples and in the courts of Indian kings. Often, a soloist sings or plays a stringed instrument, such as a sitar. Coconut shell pieces are used to pluck the sarod, an Indian lute. Accompanists may play drums called tablas (a set of two small drums), or *pakhavaj* (drums originally made of clay). Musical patterns called ragas have special meaning and may represent various emotions, moods, seasons, or even the time of day. The underlying drone sound of the tambura is a common element in all traditional Indian music.

Indian folk group

- *Bansuri* is a word for a variety of flutes made from bamboo.
- A *ghazal* is a light classical Indian song.
- *Kriti* is a devotional song from southern India.
- The *shehnai* is a large oboe.
- A *surbahar* is a large bass sitar, and a sarod is a smaller sitar.
- Tambura is a four-stringed lute that provides a dronelike sound to the music.

Ceremonial musicians, Asia

Indonesian dancers

Indonesian music

Orchestras called gamelans are characteristic of music from **Indonesia**. The instruments played in a gamelan are drums, gongs, and xylophones, which all play different melodies and produce a kind of harmony. Gamelan music often accompanies a puppet play. A popular form of Indonesian pop music is called *dangdut*. Indonesian instruments include the *bonang* (a set of knobbed gongs), the *gender* (a bronze xylophone with tubes beneath the bars), and the *saron* (a kind of xylophone).

Latin American music

Latin American music is from the Spanish- or Portuguese-speaking countries south of the **United States**. This music blends the rhythms and instruments of Spanish and Portuguese settlers with native music.

• *Antaras* are panpipes that originated in the Andes Mountains of **Peru**.

• *Bandola* is a small mandolin played in **Brazil**, **Colombia**, and **Venezuela**.

• *Bandoneon* is an accordion used for the tango dance.

• *Bossa nova* means "new wave" and names a style of music from Brazil in the 1950s.

• *Cavaquinho* is a small four-stringed Brazilian guitar.

• Charango is a 10-stringed mandolin made from armadillo or tortoise shell native to the Andes.

• Corridos are Mexican ballads about heroes and revolutions.

• *Cumbia* is the name of Colombia's most popular dance music.

• *Forro* is accordion-led dance music from northeastern Brazil.

• *Gaita* is a traditional Colombian flute.

• Huapango is music and dance from central and eastern **Mexico**.

• *Huayno* is dance music from the Andes.

• Lambada is northern Brazilian dance rhythm that became internationally popular in the 1990s.

• Mariachi is traditional Mexican dance music characterized by trumpets and strings.

• *Milonga* is the traditional song of the gauchos (cowboys) in **Argentina**.

• *Norteña* is accordion-led music of northern Mexico, known as Tex-Mex in the United States.

Peruvian drummers

• *Porro* is festival music played by brass bands of Colombia.

• *Quena* is a bamboo flute from **Peru**.

• *Ranchera* is a Mexican urban song.

• Samba is the most famous dance of Brazil.

• *Zamponas* are bamboo panpipes from the **Andes**.

Music in the United States

Many of the settlers who came to America brought their own style of music and dance to their new land. American music today reflects the rich mix of cultures and ethnic backgrounds that make up American society.

Blues player

• Bluegrass is old-time fiddle and banjo music from the Appalachian Mountains.

• Cajun music is led by the accordion and played by French-speaking settlers of Louisiana.

The song "Dixie" was used to build enthusiasm for the South during the American Civil War. Ironically, it was written in the northern state of New York by Daniel Decatur Empty.

• Gospel is religious, African-American music from spirituals. Southern gospel is gospel music from southern churches.

• Hillbilly is country music from Appalachia.

• Klezmer is Jewish folk music from eastern Europe, which was traditionally played at weddings and other celebrations.

• Rap is a talking-rhyme-based style that was born in the inner city. It often describes and comments on urban life.

• La-La is old-time Creole music from Louisiana.

• Rhythm and blues, or R&B, is music that combines jazz and blues. It is characterized by a strong backbeat.

• Rock 'n' roll is America's most popular musical style. It incorporates many different elements, including R&B, gospel, and jazz.

• Swamp pop is a mix of pop and rock 'n' roll in Louisiana.

• Swing, which originated in Texas, is country music featuring string bands.

• Zydeco is accordion-led music of the Creole communities in Louisiana.

SELECTED MUSIC CAPITALS OF THE UNITED STATES

These cities are known for different types of popular music.

Nashville, Tennessee	Country
Seattle, Washington	Grunge
Los Angeles, California	Surf music
New Orleans, Louisiana	Jazz
Memphis, Tennessee	Blues
Chicago, Illinois	Chicago-style blues
Bronx, New York	Rap
Kansas City, Missouri	Jump jive blues
New Orleans, Louisiana	Zydeco music
Detroit, Michigan	"Motown"

Motown legend, Diana Ross

World Cities
(From Katmandu to Timbuktu)

Cities are probably the most crowded places on Earth—nearly half of the world's population resides there. Cities are centers where people live, work, buy and sell goods, share companionship, and gather to worship. They are the hubs of commerce and culture. Modern cities may be overcrowded, dirty, noisy, and even dangerous. Nonetheless, people are drawn to cities for the job opportunities they offer and for the excitement of fast-paced life.

Katmandu and Timbuktu are two cities that conjure up both the exciting and the exotic qualities of cities. Katmandu is a city nestled in the foothills of the Himalayan Mountains in the country of **Nepal**. This remote city is 2,600 years old and today is a major tourist attraction. Timbuktu was once a rich trading center in **Africa**. It was founded in 1100 in **Mali** at the southern edge of the Sahara Desert. This area, near the Niger River, was a common meeting place for people traveling by camels and canoes. This was where salt, cloth, and copper were exchanged for gold, ivory, and slaves. Today, Timbuktu has declined in importance as a trade center, but the arrival of camel caravans from northern salt mines is still an important event.

SELECTED MAJOR METROPOLITAN AREAS OF THE WORLD
(with populations)

NORTH AMERICA

Toronto
Canada
4.2 million

London
England
7 million

Moscow
Russia
8.5 million

ASIA

Beijing
China
13.3 million

Seoul
Korea
12 million

Los Angeles
U.S.
15.3 million

EUROPE

New York City
U.S.
19.8 million

Rome
Italy
2.7 million

Shanghai
China
16.2 million

Tokyo
Japan
27.3 million

Madrid
Spain
2.9 million

Atlantic
Ocean

Cairo
Egypt
6.8 million

AFRICA

Calcutta
India
12 million

Mumbai
India
16.6 million

Pacific
Ocean

Mexico City
Mexico
24 million

Lagos
Nigeria
1.5 million

Indian
Ocean

Jakarta
Indonesia
12.8 million

Pacific
Ocean

SOUTH AMERICA

AUSTRALIA

Santiago
Chile
4.6 million

São Paulo
Brazil
22 million

Johannesburg
South Africa
1.9 million

Sydney
Australia
3.7 million

Buenos Aires
Argentina
12 million

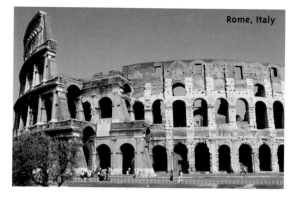
Rome, Italy

Awesome Ancient Cities

Athens, Greece, is the city where western civilization was born. It was the center of culture where great thinkers and writers lived more than 2,500 years ago. The city was first built upon a flat-topped rocky hill on about 10 acres. That site is the Acropolis, which means "high city" in Greek. Gradually, the citizens of Athens moved off the Acropolis. A great temple was built in that location to honor Athena, the patron goddess of the city. In 1833, modern Athens became the capital city of Greece.

Babylon was the ancient capital city of Babylonia. Walls 85 feet (26 m) thick encircled the city. Eight bronze gates allowed entry and exit. The famed Hanging Gardens and Tower of Babel were among the city's most amazing architectural wonders. Around 300 B.C., the capital of Babylonia was moved to Seleucia, and the deserted city of Babylon fell into ruins. Babylon stood near present-day Al Hillah, in Iraq.

Rome was one of the largest ancient cities more than 2,000 years ago. It covered more than 4 square miles (10 sq km), and included one million people. Aqueducts, which looked like walls, carried fresh water in from mountain springs. The city boasted a sewer system, public bathhouses, and huge buildings for public entertainment, including the oblong-shaped Circus Maximus and the Colosseum. Modern Rome is the capital of Italy.

Tenochtitlan, the ancient Aztec capital city, was built on an island in Lake Texcoco in Mexico. Raised roads were built in the lake to connect the city with the mainland. In 1519, the city had a population of 100,000. Great temples, wall carvings, statues, and pottery are artifacts of the once-great city. It was destroyed by Spanish conquistadors in 1521 and replaced with Mexico City.

Athens, Greece

Wailing Wall, Jerusalem

A Tale of Two Cities

Jerusalem, the Holy City

Perhaps more than any other world city, Jerusalem, the capital of Israel, is considered a holy city. Three of the world's major religions—Christianity, Judaism, and Islam—consider Jerusalem to be a center of their faith. An Islamic temple known as the Dome of the Rock contains the footprint of the prophet Muhammad, the founder of Islam. The Western Wall, also called the Wailing Wall, is the holiest site for Jews. Jesus Christ, who lived in Jerusalem, was also crucified there.

New York City, the World City

This famous city in New York state is made up of five boroughs—Bronx, Brooklyn, Queens, Manhattan, and Staten Island. Manhattan is an island and is the center of the city. Its skyline is marked by some of the world's tallest sky-scrapers, including the famous Empire State Building, the Chrysler Building, and the Twin Towers at the World Trade Center.

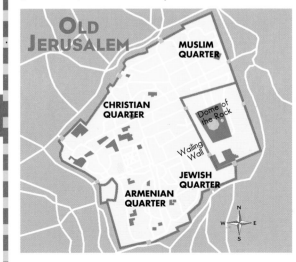

OLD JERUSALEM

MUSLIM QUARTER

CHRISTIAN QUARTER

Dome of the Rock

Wailing Wall

JEWISH QUARTER

ARMENIAN QUARTER

N W E S

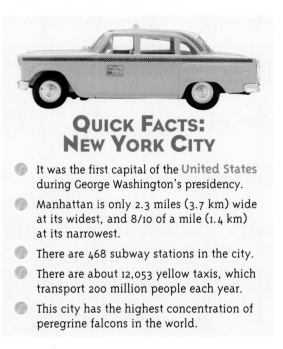

QUICK FACTS: NEW YORK CITY

- It was the first capital of the United States during George Washington's presidency.
- Manhattan is only 2.3 miles (3.7 km) wide at its widest, and 8/10 of a mile (1.4 km) at its narrowest.
- There are 468 subway stations in the city.
- There are about 12,053 yellow taxis, which transport 200 million people each year.
- This city has the highest concentration of peregrine falcons in the world.

Hidden City

The Forbidden City is located within Beijing, China. It includes the palaces of former Chinese emperors. Only members of the emperors' households were allowed to enter this area, and so it became known as the Forbidden City. Today it is preserved as a museum. Surrounding the Forbidden City is the Imperial City, which has lakes, parks, and the homes of modern Chinese leaders. Tiananmen Square is nearby. *Tiananmen* means "the Gate of Heavenly Peace." In the square, parades and fireworks are held annually. Tiananmen Square now symbolizes freedom because of the many

Forbidden City, China

Chinese students who died there, protesting against their non-democratic government in 1989.

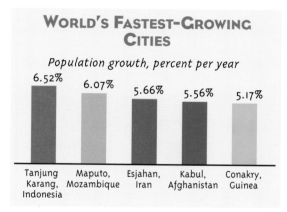

WORLD'S FASTEST-GROWING CITIES

Population growth, percent per year

- 6.52% — Tanjung Karang, Indonesia
- 6.07% — Maputo, Mozambique
- 5.66% — Esjahan, Iran
- 5.56% — Kabul, Afghanistan
- 5.17% — Conakry, Guinea

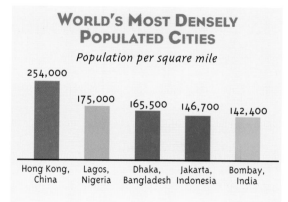

WORLD'S MOST DENSELY POPULATED CITIES

Population per square mile

- 254,000 — Hong Kong, China
- 175,000 — Lagos, Nigeria
- 165,500 — Dhaka, Bangladesh
- 146,700 — Jakarta, Indonesia
- 142,400 — Bombay, India

CITY SPRAWL

As cities have grown in area and size, new words have been created to describe them. Here are a few guidelines for defining cities.

- In the United States, places with populations of 2,500 or more are considered cities.
- The United Nations defines a world city as having a population of more than 20,000.
- *Metropolitan* refers to a large city, its suburbs, and nearby towns.
- A megalopolis is a region made up of several large cities, and their surrounding areas.
- *Urban* refers to a city. *Suburban* refers a residential area around a city. *Rural* refers to the country.
- Communities—in size order from small to large—are as follows: hamlet, village, town, city, metropolis, megalopolis.

Hong Kong

City Highlights

• Agra, a city in India, grew up around the Taj Mahal, a mausoleum that was built to honor one of the wives of Shah Jahan. As many as 20,000 workers were involved in building this world-famous structure.

Taj Mahal, Agra, India

Lhasa, Tibet

• Damascus, Syria, is the oldest existing city. It has been inhabited since prehistoric times.

• Geneva, Switzerland, is a city that is a neutral meeting place for leaders of warring countries. Switzerland has not been at war for over 150 years.

• Hong Kong, China, has more cell phone users than any other city in the world. At least 40% of the population uses cell phones. Hong Kong also has the highest per capita ratio of radio pagers and Rolls Royce cars.

• Istanbul, Turkey, is the only city that spans two continents—Asia and Europe.

• The world's highest railroad runs from Lima, Peru, to Huancayo, Peru, on a single track through the Andes Mountains.

• La Paz, Bolivia, and Lhasa, Tibet, in China are the two highest capital cities. Lhasa is 12,087 feet (3,636 m) above sea level, and La Paz is 11,916 feet (3,632 m) above sea level.

• Monte Carlo, Monaco, is the only city with an orchestra that is larger than its country's army.

Monte Carlo, Monaco

Stockholm, Sweden

• The cities of Moscow and Vladivostok are terminus cities on the world's longest railroad—the Trans-Siberian Railway. It runs through Russia for 5,785 miles (9,310 km).

• Petra, Jordan—a city built in the sandstone cliffs of the desert—was lost by the seventh century only to be rediscovered in 1812. Scenes from the movie *Indiana Jones and The Last Crusade* were filmed in Petra. In 1993, it became a Jordanian national park.

• Quebec City, Canada, is the only walled city in North America north of Mexico. The city is designated as a World Heritage Site.

• Reykjavik, Iceland, is located in a cold northern climate. The buildings are heated by the hot water springs that lie in the ground beneath the city.

A statue of the "Little Mermaid," a character from a tale by Hans Christian Anderson, is located in Copenhagen, Denmark

• Stockholm, Sweden, is the home of the internationally awarded Nobel Peace Prize.

• The entire city of Toledo, Spain, is a Spanish national monument.

• Tokyo, Japan, glows with more neon signs than any other world city.

• Vaduz, Liechtenstein, is the world headquarters for all kinds of dental ware. False teeth and other materials are made and exported to hundreds of places from this tiny country.

• Vatican City is an independent state within Rome, Italy. It is the only city with its own currency and stamps. It also boasts a newspaper and radio station. The population is about 735.

Istanbul, Turkey

CITIES BY WORLD REGIONS

The number of cities—including capital cities and cities with populations of more than 100,000—are listed here by world regions.

REGION	# OF CITIES
Northern Africa	62
Western Africa	58
Eastern Africa	46
Southern Africa	41
Middle Africa	24
Caribbean	42
Central America	92
South America	343
North America	260
Eastern Asia	629
South central Asia	463
Southeastern Asia	165
Western Asia	125
Eastern Europe	332
Northern Europe	275
Western Europe	176
Southern Europe	148
Oceania	36

Bangkok, Thailand

City Nicknames

• Auckland, New Zealand, is known as the "City of Sails" because it is located on two harbors and a gulf that are filled with sailboats.

• Bangkok, Thailand, is called "Venice of the East" because, like Venice, Italy, it once had many water canals that have since been replaced with streets.

More movies are made in Bombay, India than any other place in the world. It was even dubbed "Bollywood," a takeoff on Hollywood, California.

• Mumbai, India—originally called Bombay—is known as the "Gateway to India," after the city landmark completed in 1927. Its airport and seaport are the busiest in India.

• Paris, France, is called the "City of Lights" because it was the first European city to have streetlights.

• Tijuana, Mexico, is called the "Bullring by the Sea" because it is the site of bullfights that attract many tourists to this city near the Pacific Ocean.

• Vancouver, Canada, is called the "Pearl of the Pacific" because it is the busiest port in Canada. Its harbor is connected to the Pacific Ocean and never freezes. Vancouver is the trade center for Canada, Japan, and other Asian countries.

Two Walled Cities

• Carcassonne, France, is a medieval walled city with 52 towers and two concentric walls, which extend for 2 miles (3.2 km) around it. The castle, towers, city walls, and the area between them belong to France, but the rest of the city belongs to the local citizens.

• Jodhpur, India, is located at the edge of the Thar Desert. A massive fort was built on a rocky hill right in the middle of the city. The old city is surrounded by a wall that is 6.2 miles (10 km). This wall was built a century after the city was founded.

Paris, France

City Name Origins

- Bangkok, Thailand

In the Thai language, *bangkok* means "heavenly city."

- Buenos Aires, Argentina

In Spanish, *buenos aires* means "good winds." The city was founded in 1536 by Spanish sailors who needed favorable winds for sailing.

- Canberra, Australia

In the Aborigine language, *canberry* means "meeting place."

Dublin, Ireland

- Dublin, Ireland

In the Gaelic language, *dubh linn* means "black pool," a reference to the Liffey River, which runs through the city.

- Ottawa, Canada

In the Algonquin Indian language, *ottawa* means "to trade."

- Tripoli, Libya

In the Greek language, *tripoli* means "three cities," after the three cities of Oea, Leptis Magna, and Sabrata, which combined to make Tripoli.

World Cities Named After People

- Alexandria, Egypt

Alexander the Great (356–323 B.C.), the king of Macedonia, founded this city in 332 B.C.

Sydney, Australia

- Ho Chi Minh City, Vietnam

Ho Chi Minh (1890–1969) was a Vietnamese leader and first president of North Vietnam.

- Harare, Zimbabwe

Harare was an African ruler whose name means "one who does not sleep."

- St. Petersburg, Russia

Peter the Great (1672–1725), czar of Russia, built this city.

- Sydney, Australia

Lord Sydney (Thomas Townshend Viscount Sydney) was an 18th-century British statesman.

U.S. CITIES BY THE NUMBERS

The following are real cities in the United States:

CITY NAME	STATE
Four Town	Minnesota
Thirtyfour Corner	Missouri
Fiftysix	Arkansas
Eighty Four	Pennsylvania
Eighty Eight	Kentucky
Ninety Six	South Carolina
Hundred	West Virginia
Thousand Sticks	Kentucky

Island Cities

Venice, Italy

• Bangkok, **Thailand**, is built on an island in the Chao Phraya River. Canals, or klangs, were once the city streets. The few canals that remain are used by flatboats, or sampans, to carry and sell fruits and vegetables.

• Brussels, **Belgium**, was founded in A.D. 580 on a marshy island in the Senne River.

• Hong Kong, **China**, is built on 263 islands. It also boasts the world's largest floating restaurant, in Aberdeen Harbor.

• Mumbai, **India**, is built on seven islands. The main island, Mumbadevi, is now called Mumbai. In 1862, the seven islands were converted by the government into one landmass.

• Venice, **Italy**, is well known for its "streets of water." The city is a mere 2 to 4 feet (0.6–1.2 m) above sea level. Built in the Lagoon of Venice, it is held up by wooden timbers that were driven into the floor of the lagoon. The city is built on 118 islands. It has 177 canals and 350 bridges. During the past century, Venice has sunk about 30 inches (76 cm).

World Wise

Some items named after Venice include: Venetian glass, a colorful, fancy glassware; Venetian blue, a strong blue to greenish blue; and Venetian red, a deep, strong reddish brown.

A CITY TAKES SHAPE...

1. The city of Venice, **Italy**—built in the Lagoon of Venice—is shaped like a dolphin. The entire city covers 3 square miles (7.7 sq km).

2. Brasilia became the new capital of **Brazil** in 1960. This futuristic city is laid out in the shape of an airplane.

3. Fez, **Morocco**, is built in the shape of a maze. This Islamic city is characterized by flat-roofed houses, which appear blank and windowless from the streets. The back of these houses face courtyards. The streets appear like mazes, but the entire city is laid out according to the rules of the Koran, the holy book of Islam.

Fez, Morocco

Brussels, Belgium

Confusing Capitals

Belgium and Luxembourg

The administrative capital of the European Union is Brussels, Belgium. The judicial and monetary capital is Luxembourg City, Luxembourg.

Bolivia

La Paz is the seat of government and the official capital. Sucre is the seat of the judiciary and the legal capital.

Cote d'Ivoire

After this country achieved independence from France, the president of this country had the capital moved to his family village at Yamoussoukro.

Kazakhstan

In 1997, the president of this country decided to change the capital city from Almaty to Akmola. *Akmola* means "white tombstone" in Kazakah. The name was later changed to *Astana*, which means "capital."

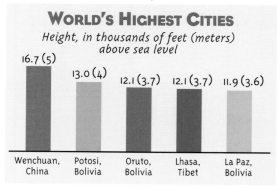

WORLD'S HIGHEST CITIES

Height, in thousands of feet (meters) above sea level

Wenchuan, China	Potosi, Bolivia	Oruto, Bolivia	Lhasa, Tibet	La Paz, Bolivia
16.7 (5)	13.0 (4)	12.1 (3.7)	12.1 (3.7)	11.9 (3.6)

Pakistan

Islamabad is a new capital city, built on the eastern slope of the Margallas Mountains. Taxila, the former capital, was on the western slope.

South Africa

Pretoria is the official capital of this country, but Cape Town is the legislative capital, and Bloemfontein is the judicial capital.

Swaziland

Mbabane is the administrative capital. Loambo is the royal and legislative capital.

Washington, D.C.

This is the capital city of the United States, but unlike other cities in the United States, it is not within a state. It is within its own district—thus the name District of Columbia.

Washington, D.C.

Five World Cities Lend Their Names

Jodhpurs

• Angora cats, goats, and rabbits are distinguished by their long, silky hair. They are named after Angora (now Ankara), Turkey.

Angora cat

• Chihuahua is a breed of dog that is very small, has pointed ears, and is covered by a smooth coat. It is named after Chihuahua, a city in Mexico.

• Jodhpurs are wide-hipped pants with tight-fitting legs from the knee to the ankle. These pants are most commonly worn by horseback riders. They are named after Jodhpur, India.

• Madras is a fine cotton cloth with a plaid or striped pattern. It is named after Madras, a city in southeast India.

• Venetian blinds are window blinds with horizontal slats that overlap when closed. They are named after Venice, Italy.

CITY CELEBRITIES

These notable people are associated with cities in which they lived or worked.

Amsterdam, Netherlands	Anne Frank
Arles, France	Vincent van Gogh
Asbury Park, New Jersey	Bruce Springsteen
Calcutta, India	Mother Teresa
Cape Town, South Africa	Nelson Mandela
Copenhagen, Denmark	Hans Christian Andersen
Florence, Italy	Michelangelo
Orleans, France	Joan of Arc
Philadelphia, Pennsylvania	Ben Franklin
Toledo, Spain	El Greco

Annex where Anne Frank lived, Amsterdam ➤

Xianggang, China

CITY NAME CHANGES

For many reasons—mostly political—some cities have changed their names. A few, such as St. Petersburg, have gone from old to new, then back to old again.

NEW NAME	OLD NAME	COUNTRY
Ankara	Angora	Turkey
Jakarta	Batavia	Indonesia
Mumbai	Bombay	India
Kolkata	Calcutta	India
Guangzhou	Canton	China
Tokyo	Edo	Japan
Istanbul	Constantinople	Turkey
Xianggang	Hong Kong	China
Beijing	Peking	China
Ho Chi Minh City	Saigon	Vietnam
St. Petersburg	Leningrad	Russia
Harare	Salisbury	Zimbabwe

Constantinople, Turkey

Ankara, Turkey

St. Petersburg, Russia

THE CITY OF...

A big city is often identified with a certain characteristic or specialty. Here's a brief list.

CITY	STATE	SPECIALTY
Detroit	Michigan	Automobiles
Hartford	Connecticut	Insurance companies
International Falls	Minnesota	Cold temperatures
Las Vegas	Nevada	Gambling casinos
Los Angeles	California	Movies
Nashville	Tennessee	Country music
New Orleans	Louisiana	Jazz music
New York	New York	Finances
Pittsburgh	Pennsylvania	Steel
Washington	District of Columbia	Government

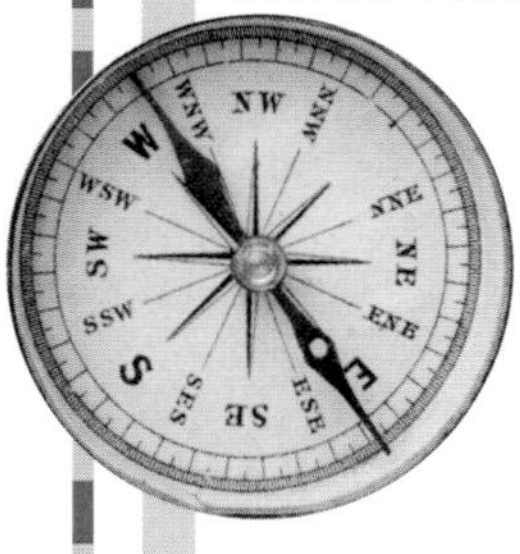

U.S. EXTREMES

Most northern:
Point Barrow,
Alaska

Most western:
Puuwai,
Hawaii

Most eastern:
West Quoddy
Head, Maine

Most southern:
Ka Lae,
Hawaii

TEN MOST POPULAR U.S. CITY NAMES

NAME	# OF U.S. CITIES
1. Midway	180
2. Fairview	163
3. Oak Grove	125
4. Centerville	100
5. Riverside	96
6. Mount Pleasant	79
7. Salem	77
8. Greenwood	72
9. Franklin	52
10. Georgetown	51

TEN BIGGEST U.S. CITIES

These are the largest cities in the United States.

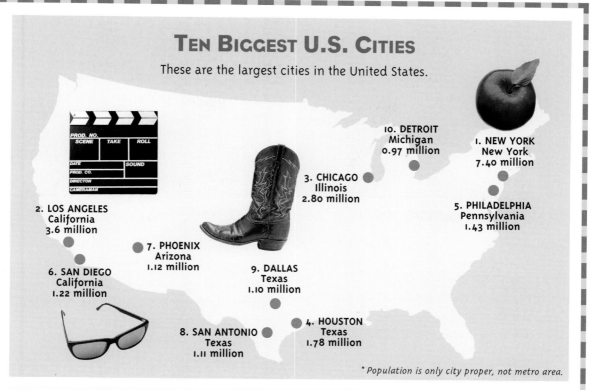

10. DETROIT
Michigan
0.97 million

1. NEW YORK
New York
7.40 million

3. CHICAGO
Illinois
2.80 million

5. PHILADELPHIA
Pennsylvania
1.43 million

2. LOS ANGELES
California
3.6 million

7. PHOENIX
Arizona
1.12 million

6. SAN DIEGO
California
1.22 million

9. DALLAS
Texas
1.10 million

8. SAN ANTONIO
Texas
1.11 million

4. HOUSTON
Texas
1.78 million

* Population is only city proper, not metro area.

COMING TO AMERICA

Many U.S. cities were named after cities in other countries.

Alexandria, Virginia

OLD WORLD NAME	NEW WORLD NAME
Alexandria, Egypt	Alexandria, Virginia
Birmingham, England	Birmingham, Alabama
Jersey Island, England	Jersey City, New Jersey
London, England	New London, Connecticut
Orleans, France	New Orleans, Louisiana
Plymouth, England	Plymouth, Massachusetts
St. Petersburg, Russia	St. Petersburg, Florida
Toledo, Spain	Toledo, Ohio
Woodstock, England	Woodstock, New York
York, England	New York, New York

Atlanta, Georgia

U.S. City Shorts

• Philadelphia, **Pennsylvania**, is the birthplace of the **United States of America**. It was here on July 4, 1776, that the Declaration of Independence was adopted.

• The distance between New York and San Francisco is one-ninth of the way around the world.

• The Twin Cities are located in **Minnesota**. St. Paul is the state capital, and Minneapolis is the state's largest city. The two cities are divided by the Mississippi River.

• Same-name cities that are easily confused are Kansas City, **Missouri**, and Kansas City, **Kansas**.

The cities lie near each other on either side of the border that divides their respective states.

• Atlanta, **Georgia**, was originally named Terminus when it was founded in 1821, because it was the last stop on the Western Atlantic Railroad. It was changed to Marthasville and finally, in 1847, became Atlanta.

• St. Augustine, **Florida**, is the oldest city in the United States.

• Lombard Street in San Francisco, **California**, boasts itself as "the crookedest street in the world."

• Las Vegas, **Nevada**, was built in the grass-lands and gets its name from the Spanish words for "the meadows."

• Seattle, **Washington**, is called the "Emerald City" because of the green vegetation that results from the abundant rain in the area.

World Wise

Chicago earned the nickname "Second City" because for many years it was second in size to New York City.

UNUSUAL U.S. CITY NAMES

Bee Lick, Kentucky	**Peculiar**, Missouri
Burnt Corn, Alabama	**Odd**, West Virginia
Cheesequakes, New Jersey	**Rabbit Hash**, Kentucky
Embarrass, Wisconsin	**Tightwad**, Missouri
Fleatown, Ohio	**Worms**, Nebraska
Gnaw Bone, Indiana	**Yeehaw Junction**, Florida
Hungry Horse, Montana	**Zook**, Kansas
Knockemstiff, Ohio	

Cincinnati, Ohio

"People" Cities

The following U.S. cities were named after people:

• Baltimore, Maryland, is named after the Lords Baltimore, the English family who founded and controlled the Maryland colony.

• Cincinnati, Ohio, is named after Cincinnatus, a Roman statesman, general, and model of patriotism.

• Cleveland, Ohio, is named after Moses Cleaveland, a surveyor who founded the city in 1796. The spelling change was a result of a newspaper misprint.

Seattle, Washington

• Seattle, Washington, is named after Chief Sealth, a Duwamish Indian who befriended the area's first European settlers.

GREAT LAKES CITIES

The following U.S. cities are located on the shores of the Great Lakes.

CITY	STATE	LAKE
Buffalo	New York	Erie
Cleveland	Ohio	Erie
Detroit	Michigan	Erie
Chicago	Illinois	Michigan
Milwaukee	Wisconsin	Michigan
Superior	Wisconsin	Superior
Duluth	Minnesota	Superior
Rochester	New York	Ontario

Detroit, Michigan

Chicago, Illinois

MINNESOTA

WISCONSIN

St.
Paul

Madison

Lansing

MICHIGAN

IOWA

Des
Moines

Springfield   Indianapolis

Columbus

OHIO

MISSOURI

ILLINOIS   INDIANA

Charleston

Jefferson City

Frankfort

WEST   Richmond

KENTUCKY

VIRGINIA   VIRGINIA

Nashville   TENNESSEE

Raleigh

NORTH CAROLINA

ARKANSAS

Little Rock

Columbia

SOUTH CAROLINA

Jackson   Montgomery

Atlanta

LOUISIANA

ALABAMA

GEORGIA

MISSISSIPPI

Baton
Rouge

Tallahassee

FLORIDA

Concord
NEW HAMPSHIRE

MAINE

Montpelier
VERMONT

Augusta

NEW
YORK

Boston
MASSACHUSETTS

Albany

Providence
RHODE ISLAND

PENNSYLVANIA

Hartford, CONNECTICUT

Harrisburg

Trenton, NEW JERSEY

Dover
DELAWARE

Annapolis
MARYLAND

WASHINGTON,
D.C.

U.S. STATE CAPITAL CITIES

World Landmarks
(Natural and Human-Made Wonders)

Do you know where to go if you want to water ski on the world's highest tides? If you were standing on the moon, what great structure on Earth could you see? Where on Earth can you find the only existing remains of one of the Seven Wonders of the World? The Bay of Fundy in Canada has the highest tides, the Great Wall of China can be seen from the moon, and the Great Pyramid in Egypt is the only existing wonder of the world. There are many natural works of wonder on Earth. From early times, humans have built great structures of beauty to add to these natural ones. This chapter provides a whirlwind, worldwide tour of some of the largest, tallest, and most wondrous landmarks on our planet.

Pyramid and Sphinx at Giza, Egypt

WONDERS AND LANDMARKS AROUND THE WORLD

Niagara Falls
Canada/United States

NORTH AMERICA

Bay of Fundy
Canada

Sears Tower
Illinois

Grand Canyon
Arizona

World Trade Center
New York

Golden Gate Bridge
California

Aztec Temple
Mexico

Panama Canal
Panama

Angel Falls
Venezuela

Atlantic Ocean

Pacific Ocean

SOUTH AMERICA

Machu Picchu
Peru

Iguazú Falls
Brazil/Argentina

Stonehenge
England

Red Square
Russia

EUROPE

Parthenon
Greece

Great Pyramid
Egypt

AFRICA

ASIA

Great Wall
China

Mount Everest
Nepal/Tibet

Taj Mahal
India

Petronas Towers
Malaysia

Victoria Falls
Zimbabwe

Indian Ocean

Mount Fuji
Japan

Pacific Ocean

Great Barrier Reef
Australia

Ayers Rock
Australia

AUSTRALIA

Seven Natural Wonders of the World

Here is a modern list of the seven wonders of the natural world.

Angel Falls
South America

This is the highest waterfall in the world. Its total height is 3,212 feet (979 m), and its longest unbroken drop plunges 2,648 feet (807 m). Angel Falls is located on the Auyan-Tepui Mountains of Venezuela. The Churun River flows through this highland region of mesas and tropical rain forests and then cascades down Angel Falls. The waterfall is named after Jimmy Angel, an American pilot who first spotted it from his airplane in 1935.

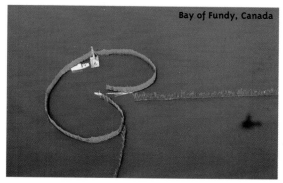
Bay of Fundy, Canada

Bay of Fundy
North America

The highest tides in the world occur in the Bay of Fundy. They rise and fall over a range as great as 50 feet (15 m). The tide rushes into the Petitcodiac River in a wall of water about 2 feet (0.6 m) high. The Bay of Fundy is located in

The Reversing Falls of St. John is a phenomenon created by the high tides of the Bay of Fundy. At high tide, the St. John River is higher than the falls and runs backward up over them.

eastern Canada, where the North Atlantic Ocean fills the gap between New Brunswick and Nova Scotia. The bay is 60 miles (96 km) wide at the mouth, and extends 150 miles (240 km) inland.

Grand Canyon, Arizona

Grand Canyon
North America

This spectacular canyon is located in Arizona. It was formed by the Colorado River, which began to flow here some 6 million years ago. The canyon extends 277 miles (446 km). Parts of the canyon are 1 mile (1.6 km) deep and 18 miles (29 km) wide. The layers of rock carved by the river vary in color and beauty, highlighted by brilliant red tones at sunrise and sunset. The temperatures at the bottom of the canyon may be 25 degrees Fahrenheit (-4° C) higher than at the top. The Grand Canyon was named by an American geologist, John Wesley Powell. In 1869, he led the first successful river expedition through the area.

Great Barrier Reef
Australia

The largest group of coral reefs in the world is found along the northeast coast of Australia. Coral reefs are made of the hardened skeletons of dead water animals called polyps. Billions of living polyps in colors of blue, green, purple, and yellow can also be found on these reefs. The Great Barrier Reef is about 1,250 miles (2,000 km) long. Parts of the reef are only

Victoria Falls, Zimbabwe

10 miles (16 km) from shore, and other parts are more than 100 miles (160 km) from the coast. There are many small islands scattered through the reefs. The Great Barrier Reef is estimated to be 30 million years old.

Mount Everest

Asia

Mount Everest, one mountain in the Himalayan range, is the highest mountain on Earth. It rises about 5.5 miles (8.9 km) above sea level. There is some disagreement on the height of the mountain, but a total of 29,305 feet (8,932 m) is accepted by most people. Mount Everest is located in Nepal and Tibet. The Tibetans call it Chomolungma. The Nopales refer to it as Sagarmatha. The name "Mount Everest" honors Sir George Everest (1790–1866), who was a British surveyor-general of India.

Mount Everest, Nepal/Tibet

Parícutin Volcano

North America

This most recently formed volcano in the Western Hemisphere is located in Mexico. It first appeared in 1943 in a cornfield near the village of Parícutin, when lava began to erupt from a small crack in the Earth. Within one week, a cone formed around the 450-foot- (141-km-) high opening. Within two months, the cone was 1,000 feet (300 m) high! The volcano's activity stopped nine years later, in 1952. Today, Parícutin rises 1,345 feet (410 m) above its base and 9,213 feet (2,808 m) above sea level. Lava from the volcano covers 9 square miles (23 sq km), and sand and ash extend over 7.3 square miles (19 sq km).

Victoria Falls

Africa

Victoria Falls lies between the countries of Zambia and Zimbabwe, and halfway between the source and the mouth of the Zambezi River. The falls range from 256 feet (78 m) to 343 feet (105 m) high. They begin where the Zambezi River is 1 mile (1.6 km) wide, and flow through a 40-mile- (64-km-) long canyon. The roar of water falling can be heard from far away. The people of the area call the falls *Mosi oa Tanya*, which means "smoke that thunders." In 1855, English explorer David Livingstone reached the falls and named them Victoria Falls, in honor of Queen Victoria of England.

FAMOUS MOUNTAINS OF THE WORLD

MOUNTAIN	HEIGHT	LOCATION	FUN FACT
Ararat	17,011 feet (5,185 m)	Turkey, Asia	Formerly Mount Massis, the top of this mountain was supposedly the resting place for Noah's Ark, according to Genesis 6:8 in the Bible.
Kilimanjaro	19,340 feet (5,895 m)	Tanzania, Africa	This highest mountain in Africa has two summits. The highest, Kibo, is always covered with snow and ice. The second, Mawensi, has neither.
Mount Fuji	12,388 feet (3,776 m)	Honshu, Japan, Asia	About 50,000 pilgrims climb to the summit of this sacred mountain in Japan each year. In the winter, it wears a crown of snow, and in the summer, a crown of clouds.
Mount Kenya	17,058 feet (5,199 m)	Kenya, Africa	This mountaintop has glaciers on its slopes, even though its base sits right on the equator (the warmest part of Earth).
Olympus	9,570 feet (2,917 m)	Greece, Europe	The ancient Greeks thought this mountaintop was the center of the universe and home to the palaces of the gods in Greek myths.

Mount Kilimanjaro, Tanzania

Mount Fuji, Japan

Seven Wonders of the Ancient World

The ancient Greeks made many lists of the greatest human-made creations of their world. Few people realize that the seven wonders did not all exist at the same time. The time frame for these structures was 3,000 B.C. to A.D. 476. The real lists of ancient wonders were lost when the great library at Alexandria, **Egypt**, burned down. Scholars of the Middle Ages compiled the list we have today. Incredible structures that currently exist, such as the Great Wall in **China**, are not included because they were not known to the ancient list makers of **Greece**.

Great Pyramid

What: A massive monument built in the deserts of **Egypt** with a rectangular base, four triangular faces, and a single apex. When it was built, the Great Pyramid stood 481 feet (146 m) high. Over time, it lost 30 feet (10 m) off the top and is now only as tall as a 45-story building. The pyramid is made up of 2 million blocks of granite, each weighing over 2 tons. Originally, there was an outer casing of limestone, but it was removed 600 years ago so the stones could be used for other buildings. The Great Pyramid is estimated to weigh 6.5 million tons. The base covers 13 acres, and the mass is estimated at 84 million cubic feet.

Great Pyramid, Giza

Where: Giza, which is 9 miles (14 km) west of Cairo, Egypt. Of the three pyramids at Giza, only the middle one, known as the Great Pyramid, is considered a wonder of the ancient world.

Built: 2613–2494 B.C.

Built by: Pharaoh Khufu (also called Cheops) had it built to eventually serve as his tomb.

> ☛ **Fun Fact:** *The Great Pyramid was the first of the seven wonders to be built, and it is the only one that remains. It took 20 years to build, and it is the most accurately aligned-to-true-north structure in existence. It was also the tallest structure in the world for 43 centuries! The purpose of its many rooms and passageways is still a mystery today.*

Hanging Gardens of Babylon

What: Gardens laid out on brick terraces raised 75 feet (23 m) above ground. Flowers, trees, shrubs, and green grass were planted to cover 400 square feet (37 sq m). The garden featured waterfalls and foliage, which cascaded down the raised terraces.

Where: On the east bank of the Euphrates River, about 31 miles (50 km) south of Baghdad, **Iraq**.

Built: 604–562 B.C.

Built by: King Nebuchadnezzar II, ruler of the ancient kingdom of **Babylon**, built the gardens for one of his wives, who grew up in the mountains. He wanted her to feel at home in this gardenlike setting.

> ☛ **Fun Fact:** *No one knows the exact design of this garden. Most ancient writers who described it had never actually seen it. However, recently discovered walls on the riverbanks of the Euphrates are now thought to be part of the terraces.*

Temple of Artemis

What: One of the largest and most complicated temples built by the Greeks, this served as both a marketplace and a sanctuary. The temple was made entirely of marble. The foundation measured 377 feet by 180 feet (115 m x 55 m). There were 127 columns, which were 40 feet (12 m) high. Great works of art, including bronze statues of Amazons, were housed within the temple.

Where: The former Greek city of Ephesus, now Selcuk, located on the west coast of what is now **Turkey**.

Built: 550 B.C.

Built by: The temple was sponsored by wealthy King Croesus and designed by the architect Cherisphron and his son Metagenes. The temple honored Artemis, the goddess of the moon and hunting.

☛ **Fun Fact:** *The Temple of Artemis was burned down in 356 B.C. by a man named Herostratus, who thought he would become famous for his terrible deed. The temple was rebuilt, but destroyed again in A.D. 262 by the Goths, an invading tribe. Sculptures from the second temple can be found in the British Museum in London, England.*

Statue of Zeus

What: This most famous statue in the ancient world stood 40 feet (12 m) high. It depicted Zeus, the king of the Greek gods, seated on a throne. His robe was made of gold, and his flesh was made of ivory. Zeus held a figure of Nike, his messenger, in his right hand, and a scepter with an eagle in his left hand.

Where: Olympia, **Greece**.

Built: 435 B.C.

Built by: The Greek sculptor Phidias made the statue. It was dedicated by the people to Zeus.

☛ **Fun Fact:** *The statue of Zeus was seen by many Greeks of the time because it was located at the site of the ancient Olympic Games. No part of the statue remains today.*

Mausoleum at Halicarnassus

What: A huge white marble tomb with a statue of a chariot pulled by four horses on the top. Many life-size statues of people, lions, and horses adorned the tomb. The total height of the tomb was 140 feet (43 m). The base was 120 feet by 100 feet (37 m by 30 m).

Where: The city of Bodrum, formerly Halicarnassus, which is located on the Aegean Sea in southwest **Turkey**.

Built: 350 B.C.

Built by: King Mausollos was the ruler of the kingdom of Caria. His wife and his sister ordered the tomb to be built for him when he died. It was started during his lifetime and completed three years after his death. The Greek architects Satyros and Pythios designed the tomb. Many famous sculptors of the time carved the statues.

☛ **Fun Fact:** *The Mausoleum at Halicarnassus was so grand and so famous that all large tombs are now called mausoleums, after Mausollos. The top part of the tomb was destroyed by an earthquake. Statues from the mausoleum are now in the British Museum in London, England.*

Colossus of Rhodes

What: This was a gigantic bronze statue made to honor the Greek sun god, Helios. It had a marble base and stood 120 feet (37 m) high—about the same size as the Statue of Liberty. The statue itself was hollow. About 7.5 tons (6.8 metric tons) of stone blocks were used to support the frame.

Where: At the harbor entrance of the Greek island Rhodes, in the Mediterranean Sea.

Built: 282 B.C.

Built by: The Greek sculptor Chares designed the statue to celebrate the unity of the city-states of Rhodes.

☛ **Fun Fact:** *It took 12 years to build the Colossus. It broke at the knees when Rhodes was damaged by an earthquake in 224 B.C. The huge statue lay in ruins in Rhodes until A.D. 654, when parts of it were transported to Syria on the backs of 900 camels!*

Lighthouse of Alexandria

What: A huge lighthouse built for sailors entering the harbor of Alexandria, Egypt. The three parts of the lighthouse were a square base, an eight-sided middle, and a circular top. The total height was 400 feet (122 m), which is equivalent to a modern 40-story building. During the day, a mirror at the top reflected sunlight. At night, fires were lighted and kept burning until daybreak.

Where: The island of Pharos, now within the city of Alexandria, Egypt.

Built: Sometime between 283–246 B.C.

Built by: The idea for the lighthouse was conceived by Ptolemy I during his reign as king of Egypt. It was completed during the reign of his son, Ptolemy II. The Greek architect Sostratos designed the monument, and it was dedicated to Ptolemy and his wife Berenice.

☛ **Fun Fact:** *This lighthouse on the island of Pharos became so famous that the word* pharos *means "lighthouse" in English, French, Italian, and Spanish. The lighthouse survived two earthquakes, then toppled in a third—1,500 years after it was built.*

Great Spans, Dams, and Canals

The following structures were built for their usefulness rather than for their beauty. The bridges span rivers, the dams make irrigation or hydroelectric energy possible, and the canals connect important waterways.

Channel Tunnel

The "Chunnel" is a tunnel built 130 feet (40 m) beneath the seabed of the English Channel. It connects Folkstone, England, with Coquelles, France. There are three main tunnels—two are 25 feet (7.6 m) in diameter and carry cars, trucks, and buses on high-speed shuttles. The third, smaller tunnel is a service tunnel linked to the others by cross passages. The tunnel extends 31 miles (50 km), some 24 miles (39 km) of which are under water. A trip through the tunnel takes about 35 minutes. The Chunnel was completed in 1994 at a cost of $13.5 billion. It was paid for by the governments of England and France.

WORLD'S LARGEST SPORTS STADIUMS
Seating capacity

Stadium	Capacity
Strahov Stadium, Prague, Czech Republic	240,000
Maracaña Municipal Stadium, Rio de Janeiro, Brazil	205,000
Rungnado Stadium, Pyongyang, South Korea	150,000
Estadio Maghalaes Pinto, Belo Horizonte, Brazil	125,000
Estadio Morumbi, São Paulo, Brazil	120,000
Estadio da Luz, Lisbon, Portugal	120,000
Senayan Main Stadium, Jakarta, Indonesia	120,000
Yuba Bharati Krirangan, Calcutta, India	120,000

Golden Gate Bridge, California

Golden Gate Bridge

The Golden Gate Bridge is one of the world's longest and most famous suspension bridges. Its main span is 4,200 feet (1,280 m) long. The total length of the brick-red structure is 8,981 feet (2,737 m). The bridge crosses over a channel of San Francisco Bay and links the city of San Francisco with Marin County, California.

Hoover Dam

Hoover Dam stands in the Black Canyon of the Colorado River in Arizona. It is one of the world's highest concrete dams, with a height of 726 feet (221 m). A 44-story elevator does not even reach its base, which is 660 feet (200 m) thick. There is enough concrete in the base to pave a two-lane highway from New York City to San Francisco! The dam's reservoir, Lake Mead, is 115 miles (183 km) long and 589 feet (180 m) deep, making it one of the largest artificial lakes in the world. The dam supplies water and power for much of the Pacific Southwest of the United States.

Panama Canal

The Panama Canal is a waterway dug 51 miles (81 km) across the country of Panama, where it links Limon Bay on the Atlantic Ocean to the Bay of Panama on the Pacific Ocean. About 12,000 ships pass through yearly, making it the busiest canal in the world. After it was built, sea travel from New York City to San Francisco was reduced by about 7,800 miles (12,400 km). It was built by the United States at a cost of $380 million, and was completed in 1914, after 10 years. In 1977, treaties signed by the United States returned the canal zone to Panama.

The Grand Canal of China extends over 1,000 miles (1,600 km). Its construction began in 500 B.C. and was not finished until A.D. 1200.

Trans-Alaska Pipeline

When the largest oil field in North America was located at Prudhoe Bay, Alaska, the trans-Alaska pipeline was built to transport the oil for commercial consumption. After the state of Alaska auctioned off the oil reserve to different companies, construction of the pipeline began. It was completed in 1977 at a cost of $9 billion. This 792-mile- (1,260-km-) long structure extends from Prudhoe Bay to Valdez, Alaska. It crosses plains, mountains, and rivers. The pipeline is elevated on a series of stilts, which allows migrating moose and caribou to travel below.

WORLD'S HIGHEST DAMS
Height, in feet (meters)

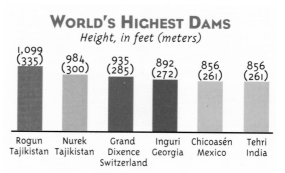

Rogun Tajikistan	Nurek Tajikistan	Grand Dixence Switzerland	Inguri Georgia	Chicoasén Mexico	Tehri India
1,099 (335)	984 (300)	935 (285)	892 (272)	856 (261)	856 (261)

Ayers Rock, Australia

Worldwide Wonders

Ayers Rock, Australia

This natural rock formation in central Australia rises up in the plains. It is about 1.5 miles (2.4 km) long and 1,000 feet (300 m) high. There are many caves within this rock, with paintings made by early native artists. Ayers Rock is considered to be a sacred place for Aborigine people of Australia. Its color changes from orange to gold to brown to red as the sun shines on it throughout the day.

Giants' Causeway, Ireland

This unusual rock formation is located along the north coast of Ireland. About 40,000 basalt columns make up the causeway. Some of the pillars are 20 feet (6 m) high. They range from 15—20 inches (38—51 cm) in diameter. According to Irish folklore, the causeway was built by Finn Mac Cool (Fingal) to bridge Ireland and Scotland so that giants could easily step from one place to the other. Modern geologists say that the unusual rock formation was the result of a lava flow.

Terra-cotta Army, China

The soldiers of the Terra-cotta Army are life-size sculptures that were buried with a Chinese emperor over 2,000 years ago. Buried 16 feet (5 m) underground near Xian, China, the figures were guarding the tomb of Shi Huangdi, the first Qin emperor of the country. The statues include 6,000 life-size soldiers, horses, and chariots. It was Shi Huangdi who ordered the Great Wall of China to be built.

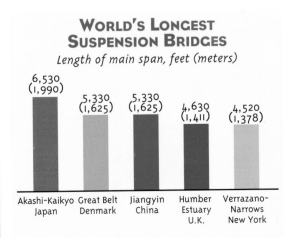

WORLD'S LONGEST SUSPENSION BRIDGES
Length of main span, feet (meters)

6,530 (1,990)	5,330 (1,625)	5,330 (1,625)	4,630 (1,411)	4,520 (1,378)
Akashi-Kaikyo Japan	Great Belt Denmark	Jiangyin China	Humber Estuary U.K.	Verrazano-Narrows New York

Giants' Causeway, Ireland

Mount Rushmore, South Dakota

Mount Rushmore, United States

This monument has the largest carved figures in the world. The busts of four U.S. presidents are chiseled into a granite cliff near Rapid City, **South Dakota**. Rising 5,725 feet (1,745 m) above sea level, the carvings are taller than the Great Pyramid of **Egypt**. In 1927, Gutzon Borglum began drilling and dynamiting the faces of George Washington, Thomas Jefferson, Theodore Roosevelt, and Abraham Lincoln out of the cliffside. He died in 1941, leaving his son Lincoln to finish the job. The head of Washington is 60 feet (18 m) tall, which is equivalent to the height of a five-story building.

Pyramids

The Egyptian pyramids all come to a point at the top because this shape was thought to be sacred. These pyramids were built to protect the bodies of Egyptian kings, and to allow them to climb from the tip of the pyramid to the sky on the slanting rays of the sun. To date, 98 pyramids have been found in **Egypt**.

The pyramids of Egypt may be the most famous in the world, but they are not the only ones constructed by ancient civilizations. In **Central** and **South America**, flat-topped pyramids were built. These pyramid builders used the platform on top as a temple. The Maya of Central America used mounds of earth to build their pyramids.

In **Asia**, particularly **Tibet**, pyramids were also built with flat tops, which allowed space for small temples. On Honshu Island in **Japan**, an ancient pyramid stands only 6.5 feet (2 m) tall. It is made of gray granite and is a smaller version of the Great Pyramid. This pyramid is surrounded by the famed Ena rice terraces.

WORLD CITIES WITH THE MOST SKYSCRAPERS

Number of skyscrapers

New York City, U.S.	Chicago, U.S.	Hong Kong, China	Houston, U.S.	Kuala Lumpur, Malaysia
140	68	36	36	25

Mayan pyramids

Petronas Towers   World Trade Center   Sears Tower

THE 10 TALLEST BUILDINGS IN THE WORLD TODAY

The buildings in this chart seem so high that they scrape the sky. This is why they are commonly known as skyscrapers. The list of tall buildings is continually growing as the race to build higher and higher structures continues throughout the modern world.

BUILDING	LOCATION	YEAR BUILT	HEIGHT
Petronas Tower 1	Kuala Lumpur, Malaysia	1996	1,476 feet (450 m)
Petronas Tower 2	Kuala Lumpur, Malaysia	1996	1,476 feet (450 m)
Sears Tower	Chicago, United States	1974	1,454 feet (443 m)
Jin Mao Building	Shanghai, China	1998	1,379 feet (420 m)
One World Trade	New York, United States	1972	1,368 feet (417 m)
Two World Trade	New York, United States	1973	1,362 feet (415 m)
Empire State	New York, United States	1931	1,250 feet (381 m)
Central Plaza	Hong Kong, China	1992	1,227 feet (374 m)
Bank of China	Hong Kong, China	1989	1,209 feet (369 m)
T and C Tower	Kaoshiung, Taiwan	1997	1,140 feet (347 m)

Two proposed skyscrapers are in the making. They are:

BUILDING	LOCATION	HEIGHT
7 South Dearborn Building	Chicago, United States	1,537 feet (468 m)
São Paulo Tower	São Paulo, Brazil	1,622 feet (494 m)

Lava Beds
National
Monument,
California

Down Below: Notable Caves of the World

Caves are hollow underground areas that are large enough for people to enter. They range from small pockets to huge underground networks of crevices, cavities, and tunnels. Here, for spelunkers (cave explorers) and others, are some distinctive caves of the world.

World's largest cave

The Mammoth-Flint Caves of Kentucky are the world's largest explored caves. They are carved out beneath a limestone plateau that has more than 60,000 sinkholes, through which surface water drains down. There are 190 miles (306 km) of passageways and chambers in the cave. Some 30 miles (48 km) of the passageways are continuous. Lakes and rivers abound within the cave, and flowing water empties into the Echo River valley.

Cave of color

On the Isle of Capri in the Bay of Naples, Italy, there is a sea cave known as the Blue Grotto. When the sun shines through the water, the cave is illuminated with a sapphire blue light. The Blue Grotto was carved out by waves.

A cave that glows

Thousands of tiny glowworms cling to the ceiling of the Waitomo Cave located on the North Island of New Zealand. Inside the cave, these "stars" light up the ceiling like a night sky.

Caves of lava

In the Lava Beds National Monument in northern California, there are more than 300 caves that have been formed by lava, or molten rock, that poured out of volcanoes.

Caves of paintings

The Lascaux Cave of southwestern France is covered with paintings done tens of thousands of years ago by early humans.

The Altamira Cave of northern Spain has 30,000-year-old paintings of bison, boars, and deer.

International Icons

Some structures of the world are so closely connected to their location that they have become high-profile symbols for their countries. Following are some countries and their notable human-made icons.

Australia	Sydney Opera House
Austria	Schonbrunn Palace in Vienna
Brazil	Statue of Christ the Redeemer in Rio de Janeiro
Cambodia	Ancient temple of Angkor, or Angkor Wat
Canada	CN Tower in Toronto
Chile	Moai statues in Rapa Nui, or Easter Island
China	Great Wall; Forbidden City, Beijing
England	Clock tower known as Big Ben in London; Stonehenge on the Salisbury Plains
Ethiopia	Rock-hewn churches of Lalibela
Ghana	Ashanti National Building at Volta, Greater Accra
Greece	Parthenon in Athens
Guatemala	Mayan temples of Tikal
India	Taj Mahal in Agra

CN Tower

Sydney Opera House

Big Ben

Taj Mahal

Parthenon

Indonesia	Borobudur Temple (8th-century Buddhist) in Java
Italy	Leaning Tower of Pisa; the Colosseum in Rome
Jordan	Petra, the rock-carved city
Mexico	Aztec temple in Tenochtitlan, Mexico City
Netherlands	Windmills (1,000 remain from the 18th and 19th centuries)
Norway	Wooden stave churches built between A.D. 1000 and 1300 (Fantoft Church in Bergen and 24 others remaining today)
Peru	Machu Picchu, ancient Inca city
Portugal	Tower of Belem in Lisbon
Russia	Red Square with St. Basil's Church; Spasskaya Tower; the Kremlin in Moscow
Spain	Alhambra, Moorish palace and fortress in Granada
Tibet	Potola Palace (17th-century home of the Dalai Lama, Buddhist leader of Tibet) in Lhasa (China)
Tunisia	Great Mosque of Kairouan (9th-century Muslim holy place)
Ukraine	St. Sophia Cathedral at Kiev; Swallows Nest Castle at Yalta
United States	Statue of Liberty in New York Harbor, New York City

Statue of Liberty

Machu Picchu

Statue of Christ the Redeemer

Potola Palace

Red Square

World Religions
(Spiritual Beliefs and Practices)

Religion is a specific set of beliefs and practices that usually focuses on the nonphysical world, or the world of the spirit. From earliest times, humans from all civilizations and eras have believed that something exists beyond the world they experience with their senses—that is, the spiritual world. Many religions seek to provide answers to fundamental human questions, such as: How was the world created? What is the purpose of life? What happens after death? In searching for answers to these questions, people have developed ideas about the sacred and the spiritual. Worship is the practice of these ideas through ritual, honor, and prayer.

The word *religion* comes from the Latin *religare*, which means "to tie fast." Worship connects a person with the sacred. Worshiping together ties people to a community of common beliefs.

RELIGION AROUND THE WORLD

Key

- Roman Catholic
- Eastern Orthodox
- Protestant
- Mormon
- Mixed Christian
- Jewish
- Sunni Muslim
- Shiite Muslim
- Hindu
- Buddhist
- Buddhist and Shintoist
- Buddhist, Confucianist, Taoist
- Native
- Information unavailable

Burmese worshipers

Sikh performers, India

MAJOR WORLD RELIGIONS

The following religions are considered to be major religions because they have the largest number of known followers. The numbers are based on estimates because it is difficult to count the number of people who hold certain religious beliefs—of the many people who belong to a religion, not all actually practice that religion.

Christianity	1.9 billion members
Islam	1.1 billion members
Hinduism	752 million members
Sikhism	19 million members
Judaism	18 million members
Confucianism	6.2 million members

Jews at the Wailing (Western) Wall, Jerusalem

◄ Roman Catholic priest

WORLD'S LARGEST RELIGION

Christianity, the world's largest religion, can actually be broken into the following subgroups.

Roman Catholic	1 billion members
Protestant	383 million members
Other	343 million members
Eastern Orthodox	174 million members

Understanding Religious Calendars and Dates

The Gregorian calendar was introduced by Pope Gregory XIII in 1582. It is the calendar that is generally used throughout the world. It is also the calendar of the Christian Church. This calendar is solar, which means it is based on the time it takes Earth to go around the sun. The term B.C. stands for "before Christ," a reference to the birth of Jesus Christ, the founder of Christianity. The term A.D. stands for the Latin words *anno domini*, which mean "in the year of the Lord," a reference to the year Jesus Christ was born. Dates in the B.C. period are counted backward. Dates in the A.D. period are counted forward.

The designations B.C.E and C.E are sometimes used, but they are not based on any one religion. B.C.E. is similar to B.C. and stands for "before the common era." C.E. is similar to A.D. and stands for "common era."

The Jewish calendar

The Jewish calendar begins at creation, which is equivalent to 3761 B.C. The Jewish year is divided into twelve months.

THE JEWISH CALENDAR

1. Tishri (Sept.–Oct.)
2. Heshvan (Oct.–Nov.)
3. Kislev (Nov.–Dec.)
4. Tebet (Dec.–Jan.)
5. Shebat (Jan.–Feb.)
6. Adar (Feb.–Mar.)
7. Nisan (March–April)
8. Iyar (April–May)
9. Sivan (May–June)
10. Tammuz (June–July)
11. Av (July–Aug.)
12. Elul (Aug.–Sept.)

Stained glass, Israel

Ancient Mayan calendar

The Islamic calendar

The journey Muhammad made to Medina in A.D. 622 is known as the *Hijrah,* or migration. This event is so important that Muslims date their calendar from it. In the Islamic calendar, it is now the 15th century. That is, the years 2000–2001 are equivalent to 1421 in the Islamic calendar. The calendar is based on a lunar year of 12 months, shown below.

THE ISLAMIC CALENDAR

1. Muharram
2. Safar
3. Rabi I
4. Rabi II
5. Jumada I
6. Jumada II
7. Rajab
8. Shaban
9. Ramadan
10. Shawwal
11. Dhu'l-Qa'dah
12. Dhu'l-hijjah

Mosque, India

The Christian Calendar

The Church calendar combines dates set by both the sun and moon. Some dates, such as Christmas, are fixed dates based on the solar calendar. Other dates, such as Easter, are based on the lunar calendar and change from year to year.

TIMELINE OF WORLD RELIGIONS, 3500 B.C.–A.D. 1

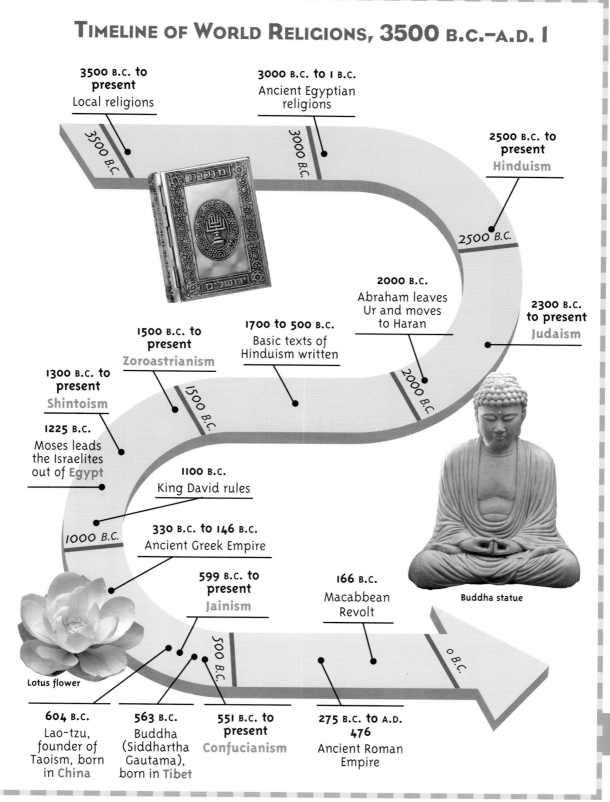

3500 B.C. to present
Local religions

3000 B.C. to 1 B.C.
Ancient Egyptian religions

2500 B.C. to present
Hinduism

3500 B.C.

3000 B.C.

2500 B.C.

2000 B.C.
Abraham leaves Ur and moves to Haran

2300 B.C. to present
Judaism

1500 B.C. to present
Zoroastrianism

1700 to 500 B.C.
Basic texts of Hinduism written

2000 B.C.

1300 B.C. to present
Shintoism

1500 B.C.

1225 B.C.
Moses leads the Israelites out of Egypt

1100 B.C.
King David rules

330 B.C. to 146 B.C.
Ancient Greek Empire

1000 B.C.

599 B.C. to present
Jainism

166 B.C.
Macabbean Revolt

Buddha statue

500 B.C.

0 B.C.

Lotus flower

604 B.C.
Lao-tzu, founder of Taoism, born in China

563 B.C.
Buddha (Siddhartha Gautama), born in Tibet

551 B.C. to present
Confucianism

275 B.C. to A.D. 476
Ancient Roman Empire

TIMELINE OF WORLD RELIGIONS, A.D. 1–A.D. 1000

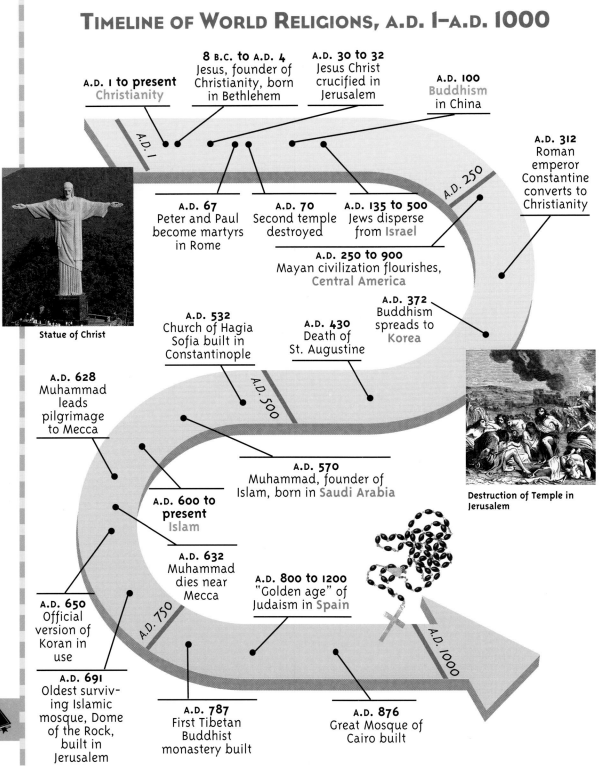

A.D. 1 to present
Christianity

8 B.C. to A.D. 4
Jesus, founder of
Christianity, born
in Bethlehem

A.D. 30 to 32
Jesus Christ
crucified in
Jerusalem

A.D. 100
Buddhism
in China

A.D. 312
Roman
emperor
Constantine
converts to
Christianity

A.D. 1

A.D. 250

A.D. 67
Peter and Paul
become martyrs
in Rome

A.D. 70
Second temple
destroyed

A.D. 135 to 500
Jews disperse
from Israel

A.D. 250 to 900
Mayan civilization flourishes,
Central America

A.D. 372
Buddhism
spreads to
Korea

A.D. 532
Church of Hagia
Sofia built in
Constantinople

A.D. 430
Death of
St. Augustine

Statue of Christ

A.D. 628
Muhammad
leads
pilgrimage
to Mecca

A.D. 500

A.D. 570
Muhammad, founder of
Islam, born in Saudi Arabia

Destruction of Temple in
Jerusalem

**A.D. 600 to
present**
Islam

A.D. 632
Muhammad
dies near
Mecca

A.D. 800 to 1200
"Golden age" of
Judaism in Spain

A.D. 650
Official
version of
Koran in
use

A.D. 750

A.D. 1000

A.D. 691
Oldest surviv-
ing Islamic
mosque, Dome
of the Rock,
built in
Jerusalem

A.D. 787
First Tibetan
Buddhist
monastery built

A.D. 876
Great Mosque of
Cairo built

TIMELINE OF WORLD RELIGIONS, A.D. 1001–A.D. 2000

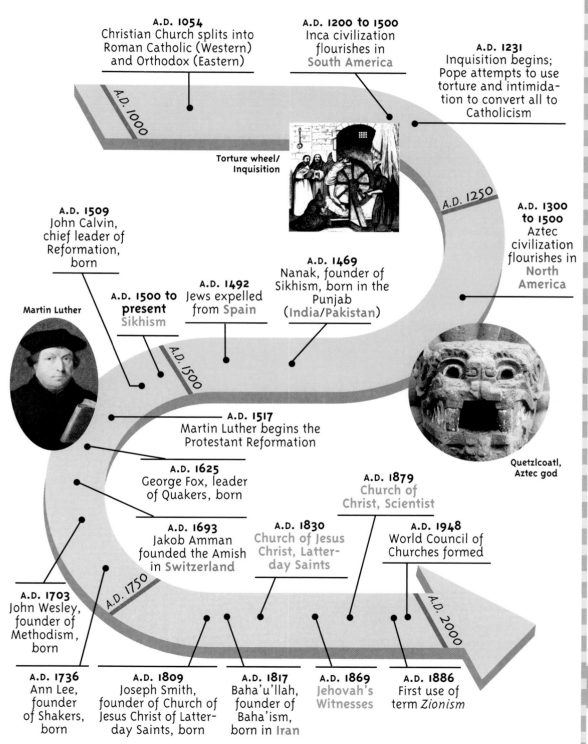

A.D. 1054
Christian Church splits into Roman Catholic (Western) and Orthodox (Eastern)

A.D. 1200 to 1500
Inca civilization flourishes in South America

A.D. 1231
Inquisition begins; Pope attempts to use torture and intimidation to convert all to Catholicism

Torture wheel/ Inquisition

A.D. 1000

A.D. 1250

A.D. 1300 to 1500
Aztec civilization flourishes in North America

A.D. 1509
John Calvin, chief leader of Reformation, born

A.D. 1469
Nanak, founder of Sikhism, born in the Punjab (India/Pakistan)

A.D. 1500 to present
Sikhism

A.D. 1492
Jews expelled from Spain

Martin Luther

A.D. 1500

A.D. 1517
Martin Luther begins the Protestant Reformation

Quetzlcoatl, Aztec god

A.D. 1625
George Fox, leader of Quakers, born

A.D. 1879
Church of Christ, Scientist

A.D. 1693
Jakob Amman founded the Amish in Switzerland

A.D. 1830
Church of Jesus Christ, Latter-day Saints

A.D. 1948
World Council of Churches formed

A.D. 1703
John Wesley, founder of Methodism, born

A.D. 1750

A.D. 2000

A.D. 1736
Ann Lee, founder of Shakers, born

A.D. 1809
Joseph Smith, founder of Church of Jesus Christ of Latter-day Saints, born

A.D. 1817
Baha'u'llah, founder of Baha'ism, born in Iran

A.D. 1869
Jehovah's Witnesses

A.D. 1886
First use of term *Zionism*

THE GOLDEN RULE

The concept of The Golden Rule is a common one that is taught in many world religions. Here is a sample of some religions, each with its own version of this basic, ideal rule.

RELIGION	RULE	WRITTEN SOURCE
Brahmanism	This is the sum of duty: Do naught unto others which would cause you pain if done to you.	Mahabharata 5:1517
Buddhism	Hurt not others in ways that you yourself would find hurtful.	Udana-Varga 5:18
Christianity	All things whatsoever ye would that men should do to you, do ye even so to them; for this is the law and the prophets.	Matthew 7:12
Confucianism	Surely it is the maxim of loving-kindness: Do not unto others what you would not have them do unto you.	Analects 15:23
Islam	No one of you is a believer until he desires for his brother that which he desires for himself.	Sunnah
Judaism	What is hateful to you, do not to your fellow man. That is the entire Law: all the rest is commentary.	Talmud, Shabbat 31a
Taoism	Regard your neighbor's gain as your own gain and your neighbor's loss as your own.	T'ai Shang Kan Ying P'ien
Zoroastrianism	That nature alone is good which refrains from doing unto another whatsoever is not good for itself.	Dadistan-i-dinik 94:5

Quawat, Islam Mosque, New Delhi

Taoist temple, Kunming

MAJOR RELIGIOUS BOOKS

Hinduism

The Vedas

The Vedas consist of four books written in Sanskrit around 1700–500 B.C. *Veda* means "knowledge." The writings tell of many gods, and deal with questions of creation and the universe. The Upanishads (1000–300 B.C.) are writings about the Vedas. The Bhagavad Gita, meaning "Song of the Blessed One" (1st millennium B.C.), is an important book that contains teachings and theories of Hinduism.

Hebrew Torah

Buddhism

Sutras

The Buddha left no writings. The written record of his sermons and conversations are known as sutras. The sutras contain the words of the Buddha, as recalled and passed on orally by his disciples and later written down. In written form, each sutra begins with the phrase "Thus have I heard." The original sutras were divided into five collections called the *nikayas*.

Confucianism

The Analects (Lung-yu)

Confucius (551–479 B.C.) was a Chinese philosopher who left no written books. *The Analects* is a collection of his sayings and dialogues that were recorded by his followers.

Judaism

The Hebrew Bible, or Tanakh

Buddhist
sutras ➤

Tanakh in Hebrew stands for the law, prophets, and writings. The 39 books of the Hebrew Bible contain the sacred texts and correspond to the Old Testament. The earliest Old Testament writings date back to 1000 B.C.

Christianity

The New Testament and the Old Testament (Hebrew Bible)

These two books make up the Bible, which is the sacred text of Christianity. The New Testament was written in Greek from A.D. 49–125. The four Gospels are attributed to Matthew, Mark, Luke, and John. The New Testament includes 27 books.

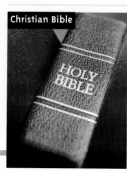

Christian Bible

Islam

The Koran (Qur'an)

The Koran was written in Arabic. The official version dates to A.D. 650. It contains everything that Allah told the Prophet, Muhammad. It is arranged in 114 sutras, or chapters, which are arranged in order of their length rather than in chronological order.

Christianity

The religion of Christians is called Christianity. The followers of this religion believe in the teachings of Jesus Christ. His followers gave him the name *Christ*, which is a Hebrew word for "Messiah." *Messiah* means "one sent by God to establish an age of peace." *Jesus* means "savior." Christians believe Jesus is the Son of God sent to save humans from their sins. Christianity began in what is now Israel. Today, there are 1.9 billion Christians living all over the world—especially in Europe, North America, South America, Australia, and New Zealand.

Shrine marking Jesus' birth

How Christianity began

About 2,000 years after Abraham lived, the land of Judea was governed by Rome. According to Christian sacred writings, the angel Gabriel was sent to a Jewish woman named Mary. Gabriel told Mary she would be the mother of the Messiah, and he would be named Jesus. Mary and her husband, Joseph, had to travel to the town of Bethlehem for the Roman census. The town was overcrowded with people, and Mary and Joseph had to stay in a stable. There, Mary gave birth to Jesus. Soon after the birth, three wise men, who had followed a star, brought gifts of gold, frankincense, and myrrh for the baby Jesus. The gold was for a king, the frankincense for a holy man, and the myrrh for one who would suffer and die.

Jesus was raised in the religion of Judaism in the town of Nazareth where he lived with Joseph and Mary. When he was about 30 years old, he asked his cousin, John, to baptize him. Baptism meant being immersed in water to wash away sins and to start a new spiritual life.

Jesus then chose 12 men as followers, or apostles. He and his apostles traveled for three years to teach people about God. Jesus spoke of God as his Father and told people they were all children of God. He taught his followers to love their enemies as well as their friends. Jesus became a famous healer and miracle worker. He worked especially hard to help the poor and the outcasts of society.

The Jewish religious authorities became upset with Jesus because he spoke of God as his Father. When Jesus went to Jerusalem for the Passover festival, he was arrested for blasphemy, which is the crime of treating God's name with disrespect. He was handed over to

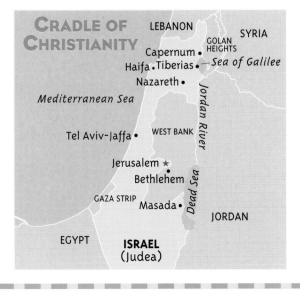

CRADLE OF CHRISTIANITY

LEBANON
SYRIA
GOLAN HEIGHTS
Capernum •
Haifa • Tiberias • — Sea of Galilee
Nazareth •
Mediterranean Sea
Jordan River
Tel Aviv-Jaffa • WEST BANK
Jerusalem ★
Bethlehem
Dead Sea
GAZA STRIP Masada •
JORDAN
EGYPT **ISRAEL** (Judea)

THE SERMON ON THE MOUNT

In the Gospel of St. Matthew in the New Testament, Jesus made the following statements in one of his most influential sermons, known as the Sermon on the Mount. These ideas form the foundation of some of the teachings of Jesus.

- Blessed are the poor in spirit, for theirs is the kingdom of heaven.

- Blessed are they who mourn, for they shall be comforted.

- Blessed are the meek, for they will inherit the Earth.

- Blessed are they who hunger and thirst for justice, for they shall be satisfied.

- Blessed are the merciful, for they shall obtain mercy.

- Blessed are the pure of heart, for they shall see God.

- Blessed are the peacemakers, for they shall be called children of God.

- Blessed are they who suffer persecution for justice's sake, for theirs is the kingdom of heaven.

Statue of Jesus ➤

Pontius Pilate, a Roman authority, ordered Jesus to be crucified (hung on a cross until he died). Jesus was buried in a tomb after his death. Three days later, the tomb was found empty. An angel told his followers that he had been resurrected (risen from the dead). Jesus appeared to his disciples several times after his resurrection. Then, 40 days after his resurrection, he ascended into heaven. Christians believe in the Trinity of one God. The Trinity is God the Father, Jesus the Son, and the Holy Spirit.

Mosaic of Jesus raising the dead

Holy book

The Bible is the holy book of Christianity. It is in two parts, the Old Testament and the New Testament. The Old Testament is almost the same as the Jewish *Tanakh*. The New Testament was written in Greek. It is made up of four Gospels (good news) written by Matthew, Mark, Luke, and John, in which they tell of Jesus' life and teachings. It also includes epistles (letters) written by Paul, and the book of Revelation.

CHRISTIAN HOLY DAYS

- **Sunday** is the Christian sabbath, or day of rest, prayer, and spiritual observance.

- **Christmas** is the celebration of the birth of Jesus on December 25. In the Christian Orthodox Church, it is celebrated on January 7. No one knows the exact date of Jesus' birth.

- **Good Friday** is the day of Jesus' crucifixion. It is observed with fasting and mourning.

- **Easter**, which is held in March or April, is the most important holy day in Christianity because it marks the resurrection of Jesus.

- **Pentecost** is the seventh Sunday after Easter. It commemorates the descent of the Holy Spirit upon the apostles.

The Apostles

The word *apostle* means "one who is sent." The original followers and disciples of Jesus Christ were called the Apostles. According to the New Testament, Jesus sent the 12 apostles forth to spread his teachings. They were instructed not to take money or unnecessary clothing with them because they would be fed and given shelter by people who heard their words.

Shrine marking Jesus' birth

THE TWELVE APOSTLES

1. Simon, called Peter, the leader of the apostles who was a fisherman by trade
2. Andrew, a fisherman and the brother of Peter
3. James a fisherman and the son of Zebedee
4. John, a fisherman and brother of James, and a Gospel writer
5. Matthew, a tax collector and Gospel writer
6. Simon, the Canaanite or the zealot
7. Bartholomew, also called Nathaniel
8. Thaddeus, also called Jude
9. Judas Iscariot, the apostle who betrayed Jesus
10. Philip, a native of Bethsaida
11. James, the son of Alpheus
12. Thomas, also called Didymus

St. Thomas ➤

Catholic and Orthodox

In the 5th century, the Roman Empire split in two. At that time, Constantinople became the center of the Eastern, or Byzantine, Empire. Rome remained the center of the Western Empire. In 1054, the patriarch, who was the leader of the Church in Constantinople, was in dispute with the Pope, who was the head of the Church in Rome. This caused a division between Eastern and Western Christianity. This split, called the Great Schism, took place in 1054. The Western church became known as Roman Catholic. The Eastern church became known as Orthodox. Differences in belief and worship grew between the two groups.

Eastern Orthodox Priest

Orthodox Christians do not recognize the Pope as the church leader. Orthodox priests are allowed to marry and have families, but Roman Catholic priests must remain single.

Other Christian Groups

Church of Christ, Scientist

Founder: Mary Baker Eddy

Year founded: 1879

Headquarters: Boston, Massachusetts

Sacred books: Science and Health with Key to the Scriptures, the Bible

Teachings:

The goal of Christian Scientists is to seek spiritual healing. They feel that God is divine, but often distant and impersonal. Christian Scientists believe that Jesus is a human who understands the divine mind. Humans have an imperfect understanding of God and the divine. They see healing as a way to understand God better. Christian Scientists believe that evil and sickness can be eliminated by prayer and spiritual insights.

Jehovah's Witnesses

Founder: Charles Taze Russell

Year founded: 1869

Headquarters: Brooklyn, New York

Sacred books: Scripture studies, the Bible

Teachings:

The name of the group comes from a Bible verse in Isaiah: "Ye are my witnesses, saith Jehovah, and I am God." Jehovah's Witnesses believe Earth will be rid of evil in the Battle of Armageddon. Abel, son of Adam, is considered to be the first witness.

Joseph Smith ➤

Church of Jesus Christ, Latter-Day Saints

Founder: Joseph Smith

Year founded: 1830

Headquarters: Salt Lake City, Utah

Sacred Books: The Book of Mormon: Another Testament of Jesus Christ, The Doctrine and Covenants, The Pearl of Great Price, The Bible

Teachings:

Mormons believe that the Mormon church is the restored original Christian church. They believe that God the Father, Son, and Holy Spirit all have the same purpose but are separate beings. They also believe that God continually reveals himself through ongoing revelations. On Earth, Mormons come to understand God's plan of salvation. This prepares them for eternity, where believers will be part of eternal family relationships.

THE ORDER OF ANGELS

In Christianity, Islam, and Judaism there is a belief in heavenly beings called angels. They often represent virtues, such as mercy. They are also considered messengers of God.

Seraphim, Cherubim, Thrones	Highest group, closest to God
Dominions, Virtues, Powers	Second-highest group
Angels, Archangels, Principalities	Angels directly connected to humans

Society of Friends

Founder: George Fox

Year founded: 1650

Sacred book: The Bible

Teachings:

The group began in England. Their informal name is the Quakers. They believe in Jesus' teachings in the New Testament. Quakers believe that everyone is equal so there are no religious leaders. In their meetings, all members agree to participate. Friends have few rituals. They feel most religions have placed too much emphasis on rituals and sacraments. Quakers are also opposed to war.

Amish

Founder: Jacob Ammann

Year founded: 1690 in Switzerland; 1728 in North America

Headquarters: Pennsylvania

Sacred book: The Bible

Teachings:

The Amish religion was founded in Switzerland by Jacob Ammann, who led a group that broke away from the Swiss Mennonites. Amish people that came to the United States settled in Pennsylvania. They believe in a strict interpretation of the New Testament and its teachings. They also believe in separating themselves from "worldy" ways. They live a very simple life without modern conveniences, such as cars or electricity. Education is limited to grade 8.

Seventh-Day Adventist

Founder: Ellen G. White

Year founded: 1863

Headquarters: Washington, D.C.

Sacred book: The Bible

Teachings:

The early Adventists began in the 1840s in the Millerite movement, which observed a Saturday sabbath. Ellen White and her

Amish sign

husband James founded the first Seventh-Day Adventist church in 1863 in Battle Creek, Michigan. Adventists believe in salvation by faith. They also believe in the importance of exercise and a vegetarian diet, and they do not use alcohol or tobacco.

The Flow of Religions

Many religions have grown out of each other. Judaism began between 3,000 to 4,000 years ago in the Middle East. Eventually, Christianity grew out of Judaism. The religion of Islam then grew out of Judaism and Christianity. Hinduism began in India thousands of years ago. Buddhism grew out of Hinduism about 2,500 years ago. In China, the teachings of Confucianism and Taoism were written down around the same time as Buddhism. Jainism, which was established in India at about the same time, shares many beliefs with Hinduism and Buddhism.

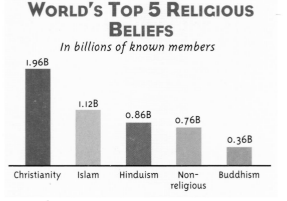

WORLD'S TOP 5 RELIGIOUS BELIEFS

In billions of known members

Christianity	Islam	Hinduism	Non-religious	Buddhism
1.96B	1.12B	0.86B	0.76B	0.36B

Celtic cross

The Protestant Reformation

The Reformation began in Europe in the 1500s as a religious revolt against the Catholic church. The Catholic Church claimed the authority to interpret the Bible. Not everyone agreed with this point of view. John Wycliffe, a priest in England in the 14th century, believed that individuals should be able to read the Bible and interpret it for themselves. Wycliffe's teachings influenced Martin Luther, a leader for reform in the Catholic Church in Germany.

Religious stained glass

In 1517, Luther spoke out against indulgences, a practice where the Catholic church sold "pardons" for sins. The rebellion eventually led to a break with the Catholic church. The word "protestant" was first used in 1529. The Catholic church in Germany issued an order that their authority be respected. Those who disagreed signed a "protest." Other important leaders in the Reformation were John Calvin, John Knox, and Huldrych Zwingli.

Greek Orthodox church

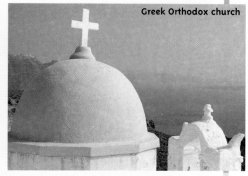

◄ Westminster Abbey, London, England

FIVE "ISMS" OF RELIGION

1. **Monotheism**   A belief in one God.

2. **Polytheism**   A belief in many gods.

3. **Pantheism**   A belief that all things in nature and in the universe are divine or godlike.

4. **Atheism**   Disbelief in the existence of a God or gods.

5. **Agnosticism**   A belief that there can be no proof that God exists or does not exist.

Michelangelo's depiction of God (Sistine Chapel)

Judaism

Judaism is the faith of Jewish people. Unlike people of other religions, Jews are born into their faith. Anyone born of a Jewish mother is considered a Jew, whether or not the person practices the religious beliefs of Judaism. There are about 18 million Jews—half of them live in the United States, a quarter live in Israel, and a quarter live in countries in Europe.

Bar Mitzvah in Israel

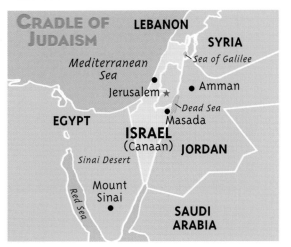

CRADLE OF JUDAISM

LEBANON
SYRIA
Mediterranean Sea
Sea of Galilee
Jerusalem ★
Amman
Dead Sea
EGYPT
Masada
ISRAEL (Canaan)
JORDAN
Sinai Desert
Red Sea
Mount Sinai
SAUDI ARABIA

How Judaism Began

The history of Judaism goes back about 4,000 years to a group of nomadic people called Hebrews who lived in what is now Iraq. At this time, people believed in many gods. Abraham,

In 587 B.C. the temple of Jerusalem, built by King Solomon, was destroyed by the Babylonians. The exiled Israelites were called Jews because Jerusalem was in an area called Judah/Judea.

World Wise

a Hebrew, said there was only one God. This was a completely new idea and the beginning of Judaism, the first religion of one God. Abraham is known as the father of Judaism. Abraham and his wife Sarah had a son named Isaac. God told Abraham to move to new place called the "Promised Land," which was Canaan. There, Isaac's son, Jacob, who was later called Israel, was born.

The descendants of Abraham were eventually called Israelites after his grandson Jacob, or Israel. After living in Canaan for about 500 years, the Israelites moved to Egypt, where food was more plentiful. The Israelites were enslaved in Egypt. Moses, a leader of the Israelites, led his followers out of Egypt. Egyptian soldiers pursued the Israelites to the Red Sea. Moses asked for God's help, and the waters of the Red Sea parted for the Israelites' safe escape. For 40 years, Moses and his people wandered in the desert. There, God gave Moses 10 laws for living, the Ten Commandments. These laws were carved in stone and taken back to Canaan (Israel), the land to which the Israelites returned after Moses died.

THE TEN COMMANDMENTS

1. Thou shalt have no other gods before me.
2. Thou shalt not make thyself a graven image.
3. Thou shalt not take the name of the Lord thy God in vain.
4. Remember the Sabbath day, to keep it holy.
5. Honor thy father and mother.
6. Thou shalt not murder.
7. Thou shalt not commit adultery.
8. Thou shalt not steal.
9. Thou shalt not bear false witness against thy neighbor.
10. Thou shalt not covet.

About 200 years later, Canaan became an Israelite kingdom under David. King David made Jerusalem a capital city in 993 B.C. David's son, Solomon, built a great temple in Jerusalem.

Torah covers

Holy book

The Holy Book of Judaism is the *Tanach*, *Tenakh*, or Bible. The first five books of the Bible are called the Torah. *Torah* means "teaching." These five books tell the history of the Jewish people and how the people should live a religious life. The Ten Commandments given to Moses are the core of the Torah.

The language of Judaism

Ancient Hebrew is the language of the Torah. Modern Hebrew is a living language revived early in the 20th century by Ben Yehuda in Palestine. Today, modern Hebrew is the official language of Israel. Yiddish is a mixture of the ancient Hebrew language and a form of German spoken during the Middle Ages.

COUNTRIES WITH THE LARGEST JEWISH POPULATIONS

Population, in millions

United States	Israel	France	Russia	Ukraine
6.10M	4.40M	0.60M	0.46M	0.42M

Diaspora

During the first century, the Romans ruled Israel. They destroyed the second temple and outlawed Jewish education. Many Jews left Israel to join Jewish communities around the Mediterranean Sea and in Europe. This scattering or dispersion of Jews from their "Promised Land" is called the Diaspora. To this day, the Diaspora refers to all Jews living outside of Israel.

HOLY DAYS

Hanukkah dreidel ➤

• The **Sabbath** (*Shabbat* in Hebrew) is the Jewish holy day. It begins each week at sundown on Friday and ends at sundown on Saturday. It is a day for rest and prayer, and is the most important holy day of Judaism.

• **Rosh Hashanah**, the Jewish New Year, is also called the Day of Judgment and Remembrance. Rosh Hashanah falls in September or October. The main ceremony is the sounding of the ram's horn, or shofar, which is blown to remind Jews to lead holy lives.

• **Yom Kippur** is the Day of Atonement. It occurs 10 days after Rosh Hashanah. This most sacred and serious day in the Jewish year is a time for fasting, prayer, and asking God for forgiveness.

• **Hanukkah,** the Festival of Lights, is held in November or December. It commemorates the first war fought for religious freedom.

• **Passover** (*Pesach* in Hebrew) takes place in March or April. It commemorates the exodus of the Israelites from Egypt. Passover recalls the night when Israelite children were spared death, or "passed over," during the plagues in Egypt. A special meal, called a seder, is prepared. Each ingredient in the seder holds special significance.

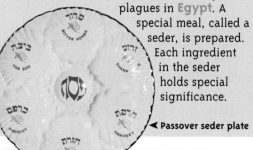
◄ Passover seder plate

Five Women of the Old Testament

Esther

An orphan, who was brought up by her cousin, Mordecai, and who married Xeres, the king of Persia. As queen, she saved the Hebrews from cruel persecution.

Rachel

The second wife of Jacob and the mother of Joseph and Benjamin.

Ruth

The great-grandmother of King David, who was known for her kindness and faithfulness. She was not an Israelite, but married one. When her husband died, she accompanied her mother-in-law, Naomi, back to her people, saying, "Wherever you go, I will go."

Sarah

The wife of Abraham and the mother of Isaac. She is considered to be the "mother of Judaism."

Sheba

The queen of lands in southwestern Arabia. She went to visit and question King Solomon. She traveled with a train of camels laden with precious spices and gold.

Old Testament Pairs

Adam and Eve

In the Book of Genesis, Adam was the first man and Eve was the first woman created by God.

Cain and Abel

In the Book of Genesis, Cain and Abel were the first children of Adam and Eve. When they were grown, Cain killed Abel out of jealousy. For his crime, Cain was exiled to a life of wandering in a distant land.

Ten Commandments in Hebrew

David and Goliath

David was a shepherd in his youth. He asked King Saul's permission to fight the Philistine giant, Goliath. David, who was small, was unafraid of fighting Goliath. David killed the giant by hitting him on the forehead with a stone flung from a sling. David became Israel's second king.

Jacob and Esau

These were the twin sons of Isaac, who was the son of Abraham. Esau, the eldest son, traded his birthright to Jacob for food. The feud between the brothers ended many years later. The night before the reconciliation, Jacob wrestled with God and asked God to bless him. God gave Jacob the name Israel, which means one who has been strong against God.

Samson and Delilah

Samson was a strong and wise man, who fought against the Philistines (a group that was at war with the Jews). He loved Delilah, who tricked Samson into telling her

Menorah ➤

that the secret of his strength was in his hair. Delilah betrayed Samson. She cut his hair while he was asleep and told the Philistines to capture him. The Philistines overcame Samson and blinded him. During his captivity, Samson's hair grew back and he had strength enough to pull the banquet hall of the Philistines down on their heads.

Other Notable Old Testament Characters

Daniel
He was a prophet who continued to pray to his God, even though it was against the king's wishes. He was thrown into a den of lions to be eaten alive. God sent an angel to protect him and he survived, unharmed.

Elijah
He was a prophet who was against the worship of idols. Jezebel, the queen of Israel, despised Elijah and tried to have him killed. Elijah was taken up to heaven in a chariot of fire.

Job
He was a man whose faith in God was tested by much suffering. After losing everything, he continued to praise God and, as a reward, all things were restored to him.

Joshua
He led the Israelites into the Promised Land after the death of Moses. He destroyed the city of Jericho, after which the walls of the city fell.

Noah
God spared Noah and his family from the great flood because of Noah's goodness. God commanded Noah to build an ark (a ship) and to take his family and pairs of all living creatures aboard. After 40 days of rain, the ark came to rest on Mount Ararat, and everyone within the great ship was saved.

Solomon
This Hebrew king was the son of David. He was known for his wealth and splendor and his great wisdom. He built the Temple of Jehovah.

Jerusalem

THE GEOGRAPHY OF JUDAISM

Mesopotamia (now Iraq)	Abraham was born.
Canaan (now Israel)	The "Promised Land."
Nile River	The river in which Moses was found floating.
Mt. Sinai	The place where Moses was given the Ten Commandments.
The Red Sea	Moses led his people through this sea to escape slavery in Egypt.
Jerusalem	The capital city of the Israelite kingdom 993 B.C.
Judah/Judea	The area in which Jerusalem was located.
The Western Wall	The only remaining part of a second temple built in Jerusalem but destroyed by the Romans. Also known as the Wailing Wall, because people mourn the destruction of the temple at this site.
Palestine	In 1948, Palestine was divided and the modern country of Israel was created.

Islam

The followers of Islam are called Muslims, which means "obedient ones." *Islam* means "peace through obedience to the will of Allah." *Allah* means "God" in Arabic. The founder of Islam was born about 600 years after Jesus. His name was Muhammad. He lived in the city of Mecca in Arabia, now called Saudi Arabia. Muslims share cerain beliefs about God with Jews and Christians. The followers of Islam live mainly in the Middle East, northern Africa, and parts of Asia. Islam is the second-largest religion in the world, after Christianity.

CRADLE OF ISLAM

After Muhammad's death, caliphs, or successors, led Islam. The caliphs waged wars to spread Islam. Islam spread quickly, resulting in three powerful Islamic empires.

How Islam began

Muhammad was born in Mecca, a city in pres-ent-day Saudi Arabia, in about A.D. 570. He was orphaned when he was a child. He was raised by his uncle and became a camel driver and trader. Muhammad was a husband and a father and was well respected in his community. At that time, the people of Arabia believed in many gods and not the single God of the Jewish and Christian religions.

Muhammad was not happy with his life in Mecca. He was disturbed by the behavior of the people who cared too much about money and worshiped many idols. He spent many hours alone in the mountains, where he prayed and asked for understanding of the things that troubled him. When he was about 40 years old, he received his first revelation. He was in a cave near Mecca when God spoke to him through the angel Jibril (Gabriel). It was revealed to Muhammad that Allah was the one and only God.

Muhammad began to preach this message of God. Throughout his life Muhammad contin-ued to receive revelations from God. For about 20 years, Muhammad spoke about God to the people of Mecca. As Muhammad's influence and power grew, the leaders and merchants in Mecca became fearful of the new leader. Muhammad was threatened with death many times. In 628, Muhammad fled to the city of

Muslim women praying

Medina. The journey was dangerous and difficult. In Medina, Muhammad gained many followers and built the first mosque, a place to worship.

Eventually Muhammad and an army of followers returned to Mecca, where Muhammad was accepted as the Prophet of God. The Muslims destroyed the idols in Mecca and built a mosque dedicated to Allah. By the time Muhammad died, the people of Arabia had embraced Islam.

Muslim head coverings

Holy book of Islam

The Koran, or Qur'an, is the holy book of Muslims. The writings of the Koran are the words of Allah revealed to Muhammad. The author therefore is Allah, not Muhammad. The revelations were first passed on by word of mouth, then written down in Arabic, and eventually collected into one volume after Muhammad's death. A collection of writings called the *Sunnah* tells about the words and deeds of Muhammad.

THE FIVE PILLARS

Mosque Dome

These show how Muslim beliefs should be practiced in daily life.

1. The Shahadah

This is a declaration of faith repeated several times a day. "There is no God but Allah, and Muhammad is his Prophet and Messenger."

2. The Salat (Salah)

Every Muslim must pray at least five times a day: at dawn, noon, midafternoon, after sunset, and before bed. Worshipers must face Mecca, Islam's holiest city.

3. The Zakat (Zakah)

This is the Muslim obligation to give money to the poor if they can afford to.

4. The Sawm

This means fasting. Adult Muslims do not eat or drink during the daylight hours of the holy month of Ramadan.

5. Hajj

This is the pilgrimage or special journey to a sacred place. All Muslims hope to make a pilgrimage to the holy city of Mecca once in their lifetime.

The Jihad

The jihad is a person's struggle to live a good life. For many Muslims, the jihad includes the holy duty to win others over to Islam by setting good examples.

HOLY DAYS OF ISLAM

- **Friday** is the holy day of the week. Muslims attend mosques at noon.

- **Ramadan** is the ninth month of the Islamic year. It is the holiest period because it commemorates the month the Koran was revealed.

- **Id al-Fitr** is a festival that takes place at the end of the fast of Ramadan. Muslims attend the mosque to pray, to give food to the poor, and to eat celebratory meals.

- **Id al-Adha** is the Feast of the Sacrifice, which takes place during the last month of the year and the season of hajj, or pilgrimage.

Mosque window

Muslims praying

Sunni and Shi'ah Islam

Sunni means "the path shown by Muhammad."
About 90 percent of the world's Muslims are
known as Sunni Muslims. The Shi'ah,
or Shi'ites, are a much smaller
movement of Islam. They are dom-
inant in Iran and exist in Iraq,
Lebanon, and Bahrain, in particular. The main difference
between Sunni and Shi'ah traditions is that Shi'ism does not
recognize the first three caliphs
or successors of Muhammad
and sees the fourth, Alit, as
Muhammad's first true suc-
cessor. In Iran, leaders of
Shi'ism are called ayatollahs,
meaning "a sign of Allah."
Because Iran is a theocracy—a
government centered around
religion—the most powerful
ayatollah is often the country's
political leader as well.

Muslim writings inside a mosque

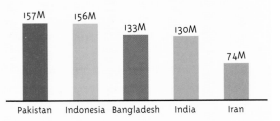

COUNTRIES WITH THE LARGEST MUSLIM POPULATIONS

Population, in millions

Pakistan	Indonesia	Bangladesh	India	Iran
157M	156M	133M	130M	74M

Buddhism

Statue of Buddha ➤

Buddhism is a religion developed by a man named Siddhartha Gautama, who was raised as a Hindu in Nepal about 2,500 years ago. He became known as the Buddha, or "enlightened one," because of his wisdom. Gautama was born a prince, and was sheltered from the suffering of the world. When he discovered that people suffered from illness, age, and death, he tried to learn the reasons. He became a wandering holy man searching for the answer to the problem of suffering.

After years of contemplation, he became enlightened. His new understanding developed into a religion that emphasizes physical

Reclining Buddha ▼

and spiritual discipline as a means of release from the physical world. More than 500 million people practice Buddhism, mainly in countries of eastern Asia.

The statues of Buddha

A reclining statue of Buddha represents the position he took before entry into Nirvana at death. The faces of Buddha statues are made to look peaceful or serene. The long earlobes symbolize the wisdom of Buddha.

PLACES IN BUDDHIST HISTORY

The main places of Buddhist history are places associated with the Buddha's life. These places are also the main locations to which Buddhist pilgrims journey for spiritual fulfillment.

Lumbini Grove, Tibet
The birthplace of Siddhartha Gautama, who later became known as the Buddha.

Bodh Gaya, India (Deep Park)
The place of Buddha's enlightenment.

Sarnath, India
The place of Buddha's first teaching.

Kusinara, India
The place of Buddha's death. This is where Buddha reclined before death and entry into Nirvana, which is the Buddhist equivalent of heaven.

Painting in temple at Sarnath, India

Buddhist monks

COUNTRIES WITH THE LARGEST BUDDHIST POPULATIONS

Population, in millions

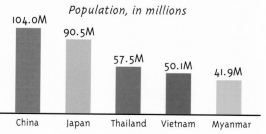

China	Japan	Thailand	Vietnam	Myanmar
104.0M	90.5M	57.5M	50.1M	41.9M

KEY TERMS OF BUDDHISM

Enlightenment	A state of understanding the meaning of all things.
Dharma	Understanding of suffering and of detachment from worldly desires.
Nirvana	The freedom from the cycle of rebirth and suffering achieved at enlightenment.
Tipitaka	A collection of Buddha's sayings and rules for monks, first written on palm leaves, which were collected in baskets. *Tipitaka* means "three baskets."

Buddhist monk, Tokyo

THE NOBLE EIGHTFOLD PATH

Buddha statue, Burma

These are the eight rules of Buddhism:

1. **Right understanding:** Be aware of Buddha's teachings.
2. **Right intentions:** Follow the teachings.
3. **Right speech:** Say nothing to hurt others.
4. **Right action:** Do nothing to harm any living creature.
5. **Right livelihood:** Choose a job that hurts no living thing.
6. **Right effort:** Strive for goodness in living.
7. **Right mindfulness:** Control thoughts and emotions for a quiet mind.
8. **Right concentration:** Practice meditation, which leads to enlightenment.

THE FOUR NOBLE TRUTHS OF BUDDHISM

- All lives are filled with suffering.
- Suffering comes from a desire for worldly things.
- Suffering can be overcome when desire ends.
- The way to overcome suffering is to follow the Eightfold Path.

World's largest Buddha, Japan ➤

Buddhist Festivals

Thailand

Vaisakha, or *Wesak,* is the most sacred festival, celebrated on the full moon in May. It honors the birth, enlightenment, and death of Buddha.

People clean and decorate their houses. They visit temples to make offerings and receive blessings. Statues of Buddha are washed with scented water. Sacred books are dusted. The celebration ends with candlelit processions to the temples.

Sri Lanka

Poson is a festival that takes place on the full moon in June. It is a celebration of the bringing of Buddhism to Sri Lanka. The two ancient cities of Mihintale and Anuradhapura are lit up with brilliant illuminations. Ancient historical events involving the missionary Mahinda, are reenacted, along with other religious ceremonies.

Tibet

Losar is the Tibetan New Year festival. Before this festival takes place, all the bad and

Buddhist temple

unhappy memories of the old year must be chased away. Houses are cleaned and purified. On the last day of the old year, people visit monasteries and make offerings. Rituals are performed to drive out evil spirits. Alms are given to the poor. On Losar, the first day of the New Year, everyone rises early, collects water, and places it along with food on the household shrines. Special foods and drinks are prepared for Losar, and families exchange gifts, dances, and festivals are held.

THE DALAI LAMA OF TIBET

Dalai Lama

The word *dalai* is Mongolian for "ocean." *Lama* is a Tibetan word meaning "teacher." The fourteenth Dalai Lama of Tibet was born in 1935 in the village of Takster in the Amdo province of eastern Tibet to peasant parents shortly after the thirteenth Dalai Lama died.

A search team found him as a two-year-old infant named Lhamo Thondup. He was renamed Tenzin Gyatso and proclaimed to be the fourteenth reincarnation of the Dalai Lama. It took two years before the Chinese (who were in control of Tibet), allowed the Dalai Lama to travel to Lhasa, the capital of Tibet.

The Dalai Lama officially lived at Potala Palace, where he was educated as a Buddhist monk. In 1950, the Dalai Lama was in political control of Tibet when Chinese Communists invaded his tiny country. By 1959, he was forced to flee to India as China took complete control of Tibet. He lives in exile to this day.

Hinduism

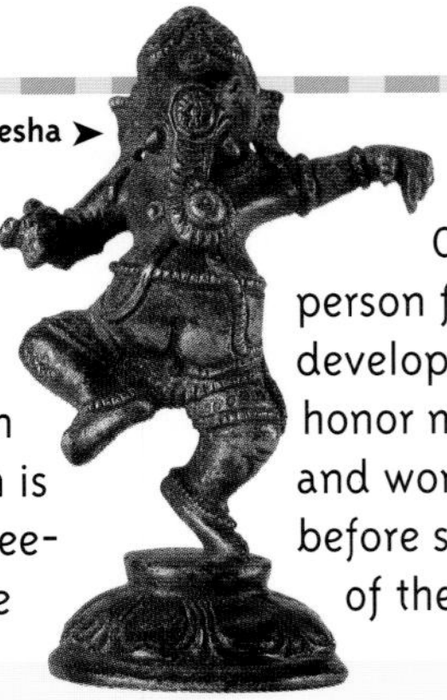

Ganesha ➤

Hinduism is considered the oldest living religion. It originated in the culture of the Indus valley civilization, which flourished between 3500 and 1500 B.C. in **India**. Hinduism is a religion of India that emphasizes freedom from the material world. It is the third-largest religion, after Christianity and Islam. No single person founded this religion, but rather it developed over a long period of time. Hindus honor more than 300 gods and goddesses, and worship takes place mainly in the home before shrines that contain various objects of the senses.

THE LANGUAGE OF HINDUISM

The sacred writings are in Sanskrit, which is the language of ancient **India**.

Hindu praying to Buddha

Atman	The soul of an individual.
Brahman	The "World-Soul" or the Absolute.
Ganesha	A minor god, thought to remove obstacles. Ganesha is pictured with the head of an elephant and a potbelly, representing wealth and success.
Karma	The good and bad actions performed by individuals.
Krishna	A popular god known for his mischievous nature.
Samsara	The continuing cycle of life, death, and rebirth.
Shiva	The destroyer or liberator, a god that combines both male and female qualities.
Upanishads	The sacred writings and teachings about Brahman.
Vedas	These "books of knowledge" contain wisdom of the universe.
Vishnu	The preserver; a main god.
Yoga	A set of mental and physical exercises aimed at spirituality.

Sacred Vishnu elephant

Washing in the Ganges

Shiva temple

Hindu Beliefs

Birth, death, and rebirth

According to Hinduism, living things do not have just one life, but are all part of an endless cycle of life, death, and rebirth. This cycle is called *samsara*. The word for rebirth is reincarnation. Hindus hope to be relieved from the difficulties of samsara. Release from the cycle of suffering and rebirth is called *moksha*. Moksha can be achieved only when someone replaces ignorance with wisdom. *Maya*, or illlusion, prevents people from doing this. *Maya* prevents people from seeing the unchanging reality of *atman*, the individual soul.

Sacred cow

Duty

Hindus are expected to live according to their *dharma,* or the code of behavior, which governs their lives. The code of behavior is determined by the social group, or *varna,* to which the people belong. The four varnas are: priests and teachers, who are called brahmin; members of the military and rulers; merchants; and manual workers.

Four stages of life

The four stages of life are: the student, the family man, the recluse, and the wandering holy man, who lives without family, owns nothing, and lives by begging. These four stages represent how people ought to live as an ideal.

Yoga

Yoga is a discipline that involves exercise of the body, mind, and heart (emotions). In Hinduism, four main types of yoga

Hindu statue

are practiced. *Karma* yoga is the discipline of action, working hard to fulfill dharma. *Bhakti* yoga is the discipline of devotion, where offerings of wholehearted love and prayers are given to God. *Jnana* yoga is the quest for knowledge. *Raja* yoga involves practicing techniques of mental self-control, which include meditation.

Worship

Hindu worship takes place mainly in the home and is focused on a shrine. The images of gods are the ones that are important to the family. The shrine contains objects that match the five senses of sight, hearing, smell, taste, and touch. A statue of a god may focus the sight; a bell is rung to help focus the mind; incense is burned for the smell; fruits are laid out for taste; and prayer beads may be used for touch.

Sacred animals

All life is considered sacred by Hindus. The cow is a highly revered animal and is not killed for beef. Cows are great providers of milk, butter, and dung, which is used for fertilizer and fuel.

Hindu Festivals

• *Diwali,* or *Dival,* is the Hindu Festival of Lights. It is held at the Hindu New Year, which falls in November. The goddess Lakshmi is associated with this festival. Light represents knowledge, and lamps and candles are lit everywhere. People exchange gifts and cards.

• *Dassehra* is a yearly festival that commemorates the god Rama's victory over the evil king Ravan. The story of Rama and his wife, Sita, is retold in dances and plays.

• *Holi* is a spring festival celebrating the playful tricks of the god Krishna. Processions, bonfires, and dancing mark the celebration. People squirt water and colored powder over each other.

World Wise
The most sacred river to Hindus is the Ganges River which flows for 1,500 miles through Varanasi, the center of Hinduism.

Diwali, or festival of lights

Festival boat

◄ Hindu temple

TRANSCENDENTAL MEDITATION

This movement has its origins in a simplified form of Hinduism that has been adapted by western people who do not wish to fully embrace the Hindu culture.

The movement was founded in 1956 by Maharishi Mahesh Yogi, who learned about meditation from his guru. Transcendental meditation is not considered a religion as much as a science by those who practice it. Some of its goals are to promote health and inner happiness and to increase an individual's creativity.

Other Religions in Brief

Baha'ism

This is a religion that began in Iran (formerly Persia). Baha'u'llah was a prophet born in 1817. His name means "Glory of God." Followers of Baha'ism see him as the latest and most important prophet in a line of prophets including Adam, Moses, Krishna, Buddha, Zoraoaster, Jesus Christ, and Muhammad. The symbol of Baha'ism is a nine-pointed star. This religion includes prayer, fasting, and no alcohol. The headquarters are in Haifa, Israel, where Bab, "gate to the truth," is buried. "Bab" was Mirza Ali Muhammad, who predicted that Baha'u'llah would come as a prophet.

Jain priests

Confucianism

Statue of Confucius

A Chinese philosopher named K'uang Fu-Tzu, or Confucius, wrote advice for the rulers of China. He believed in the dignity of people and in kindness toward others. The teachings of Confucianism strive for "beautiful conduct," which means respecting ancestors, considering the feelings of others, and working toward harmony and balance in life.

Jainism

Mahavira, the founder of this religion, lived in India in the 6th century B.C. He lived at the same time as Buddha. He was said to be the twenty-fourth in a chain of great spiritual teachers. He taught respect for all forms of life. Those who follow Jainism have very few possessions and are strict vegetarians. Jains will not eat root vegetables because the whole plant dies when the root is pulled. Followers who achieve a spirituality called "release" are named *jinas,* or "those who overcome." Today there are about 3 million Jains who live mainly in western India.

Baha'i temple

The Nation of Islam

This religious group began in Detroit, Michigan in a mosque that was founded by Wali Farad. Most people who attended the mosque were African Americans, and they believed that Farad was the reincarnation of Allah. They felt their church was the lost nation of Islam in the West. Through Farad, people believed they would find freedom from prejudice and from their daily economic struggles. One of the later leaders of this church was Malcolm X. After his assassination, the Nation of Islam

Malcolm X

went through many changes and became part of the Orthodox Islamic community. Their sacred text is the Koran.

Rastafarianism

This religion was founded in the 1930s when a man from Jamaica, Marcus Garvey, predicted there would be an African savior to follow Jesus Christ. When Ras (Prince) Tafari of Ethiopia became Emperor Haile Selassie, he was hailed as the new savior.

Rastafarians

Rastafarians accept some of the teachings of the Bible. They live close to nature, and grow their own food. Many do not drink alcohol or coffee or smoke tobacco. There are about 100,000 Rastafarians living in Jamaica, Europe, and the United States.

The Church of Scientology

The Church of Scientology was founded by L. Ron Hubbard in 1954. The sacred text of the group, written by Hubbard, is *Dianetics: The Modern Science of Mental Health*. They also rely on the teachings of the Old Testament. The beliefs combine psychoanalysis with eastern philosophies. Members join the organization at different levels. Scientology Mission International (SMI) provides most of the primary Scientology services.

Shinto shrine

Shinto

The word *Shinto* means "the way of the Gods." There are about 5 million people in Japan who practice Shintoism today. In this religion, the gods are called *Kami*. They exist in the natural world: in trees, the wind, stones, animals, and humans. Shinto buildings of worship are called shrines. To purify themselves, believers wash their hands and rinse their mouths before entering these shrines.

Sikh Temple

Sikhism

This religion was founded about 500 years ago in the Punjab region of Asia by Guru Nanak. *Guru* means teacher. Followers of Sikhism are *Sikhs,* which means "disciples." Sikhism combines elements of Hinduism and Islam but stresses that faith in one God is more important than the outward differences in religions. There are about 12 million Sikhs in the world today.

Taoism

In this religion, Tao or "the Way" is the spiritual force of the universe, and believers try to merge with this spirit through meditation and contemplation. T'ai chi ch'uan (known commonly to westerners as tai chi) is a series of body movements that are a form of Taoist meditation. About 5 million people in China practice this religion, along with Confucianism and Buddhism.

Unitarian Universalism

Unitarian Universalism was founded in Transylvania in 1638. Followers use no primary sacred texts, but consider all religious books worthwhile. Unitarianism comes out of a belief that there should be religious tolerance. Early congregations of Universalist groups began in England. In 1779, John Murray became the first minister of a Universalist church in the United States, in Gloucester, Massachusetts. Joseph Priestly, a Unitarian minister, established the

first church in 1979. Unitarians believe in the worth of every person. Individual beliefs can be very diverse, and they practice acceptance in relationships with others. They also believe that each individual should search for truth. They believe in equality for all, regardless of race or gender.

Zoroastrianism

The founder of this religion was a prophet named Zoroaster who lived in ancient Persia (now Iran) around 600 B.C. Followers are called Parsis, and most of them live near Bombay, India, today. The belief of this religion is that there is an ongoing struggle between the forces of good and evil in the world. Fire is sacred in Zoroastrianism, and a flame is always kept burning in the temples. Parsis place their dead at the top of "towers of silence" for birds of prey to consume. They believe Earth has been contaminated by burial, and sacred fire may not be used for cremation. About 150,000 Parsis practice this religion.

China is known as the Land of the Three Teachings. Buddhism, Confucianism, and Taoism all originated in China. Many people practice a combination of these three religions.

World Wise

Indigenous Religions

Many different kinds of religions practiced in particular regions of the world are grouped together as native religions. Many of these religions have no writings. The beliefs are passed down through storytelling, oral traditions, and generations of practicing families. Local religions are the oldest forms of religion. Today, local religions are found among native peoples in North America, South America, Australia, Africa, and the Arctic regions of Asia.

Dreamtime

In Australia, among the Aboriginal peoples, there is a religious idea called Dreamtime. It describes the period of creation when spirits in the form of humans and then animals brought order into the world. Each tribe has its own "Dreaming"—a plant, animal, or natural force to which it is connected. Places connected to Dreamtime spirits are sacred sites.

Cerroboree Aborigines, Uluru, Northwest Territories, Australia

Sedna

Sedna is a goddess of the Inuit, a people who live in the Arctic. The Inuit believe that Sedna will punish people who abuse their natural surroundings. Hunters, in particular, will not be able to find animals needed to survive.

Shamans

Shamans are people with special spiritual powers of healing. In religions of native North Americans and in northern Asia, shamans use rattles and other musical instruments to accompany religious singing and dancing.

Voodoo

First developed in Haiti, voodoo combines traditions from religions of Africa with elements of Christianity.

Voodooists believe the world is filled with demons and spirits of the dead. Charms and spells are used to cure illnesses, ward off diseases, and also to bring love.

Ceremonies in Indigenous Religions

Native American ceremonies

Native American religion can be traced back to the arrival of people from Asia almost 60,000 years ago. Most Native American religions have ceremonies that involve animals that they hunt. They are careful to be respectful of the animals and not offend them.

Native Americans place great importance on rituals. Most ceremonies are adapted to local plants and animals—even to weather conditions. A ceremony in the desert, for example, might be to bring rain. A different ceremony, used in polar regions, might be centered around being spared from a snowstorm.

VOODOO BELIEFS

Voodoo is mainly a religion that is found in Haiti, but it is also practiced in Buca, Trinidad, and Brazil. In the United States, some groups in Louisiana practice voodoo.

Voodoo rituals are led by a houngan (priest) or mambo (priestess). Worshipers dance and sing to the beat of drums and seem to enter a trance before they are overcome by a spirit. The religion mixes parts of Roman Catholicism with African tribal religions. Gods of Africa work alongside Catholic saints. Worshipers also use crosses, bells, and candles.

Apache

New Mexico, U.S.A

Among the Apache tribes of New Mexico, a girl who reaches puberty is honored with a four-day ceremony. Throughout the days of the ceremony, the girl must behave in a proper way and think positive thoughts about her future. She is thought to have special powers of healing during this time. On the first day, a special shelter made from four spruce saplings is made for the ritual. A buckskin is placed on the ground to provide a floor for dancing. The girl wears a yellow cloth dress to represent corn pollen. A godmother is chosen to help the girl during the ceremony. Each night a bonfire is lit, and visitors perform dances in the firelight. One dance, called Mountain Spirit Dance, represents the sacred spirits of the mountain.

The dancers' bodies are painted with symbols. The dance itself is meant to drive away sickness and misfortune and to bring blessings to the ceremony. After four days, the guests leave. The girl and her family remain for a total of nine days. The girl is then purified in a bath of suds made from yucca plants. After the nine days, she is considered to be a woman of the Apache nation.

Masai ceremony

Kwakiutl

British Columbia, Canada

The Hamatsa is a secret society of the Kwakiutl tribe of Canada. A boy, or sometimes a girl, is initiated into this society during a potlatch. A potlatch is a ceremony held to mark important tribal events. It involves feasting, speeches, and gift giving. In the past, the ceremony lasted four days.

Today, the ceremony takes place in one day. It begins with the sounds of whistling from all directions. The older members of the society approach the boy and put a ring of cedar bark around his neck. The boy begins to act wild and ferocious. He acts as if he is possessed by a supernatural creature called the Cannibal. As the dance continues, a female relative helps to calm him down. Other dancers enter wearing large painted carved masks with beaks of supernatural birds. At the end of the ritual, the boy is tame and puts on a special garment to show he is now a member of the Hamatsa Society.

Masai

Kenya-Tanzania, Africa

The initiation ceremony for the Masai warriors is called Eunoto. It marks the end of life as a warrior of Africa and the beginning of status as an elder. The four-day ceremony begins when the mothers of the warriors build a *manyatta*, which is a circle of huts made from cow dung and branches.

The most sacred building within the *manyatta* is the *osingira*. Warriors who are permitted to enter the *osingira* will be blessed by senior elders who will ask the Masai god to protect them. On the second day, the young men travel to a sacred chalk bank to paint their bodies with white designs. The designs represent achievements. At a final gathering, those who are being initiated are blessed and sprayed with mouthfuls of honey, beer, and milk by the senior elders. Then they are told to use their minds and wisdom instead of their weapons.

WORLD RELIGIOUS CENTERS

The Vatican

Roman Catholicism: Vatican City, Italy
The center of Roman Catholicism, where the Pope resides, is located within Rome, Italy.

Judaism: Jerusalem, Israel
In 1948, after the Holocaust, Palestine was divided up, and the modern state of Israel was founded. Jews from all over the world made Israel their home.

Hinduism: India
Hinduism traces its history to the Indus valley civilization. The Indus River valley is in India. The seven sacred cities of Hinduism are: Varanasi, Hardwar, Ayodhya, Dwarka, Mathura, Kanchipuram, and Ujjain. They are all located in India.

Buddhism: India in an area which is now Tibet, Nepal
Spread through India south to Sri Lanka into southeast Asia on to Java and Sumatra, north to China, Tibet, Korea, and Japan. In the 19th century, it spread to Europe and the U.S.

Islam: Mecca, (Saudi Arabia)
Muhammad was born in Mecca. Muslims face the city of Mecca during prayers and travel to Mecca on pilgrimages. The Kaaba, a place of worship for Allah, is located there. Medina is the city where Muhammad lived before returning to Mecca.

Eastern Orthodox Christianity: Istanbul, Turkey
This city is home to what was once the world's largest Christian church. Though most of the city's inhabitants are Muslim, Istanbul is still considered to be the most important religious center for Eastern Orthodoxy. Other major centers include Alexandria, Egypt; Damascus, Syria; and Jerusalem, Israel.

10 RELIGIOUS CENTERS OF THE WORLD

PLACES OF RELIGION AND WORSHIP

This listing names the buildings in which people worship, as well as the names given to the homes of devotees of religions.

Abbey	A monastery where a group of religious people live. Also a church that was once part of a monastery or convent.
Cathedral	An especially large and important church—often highly decorated.
Chapel	A place of worship that is smaller than a church.
Church	A building for public worship, especially Christian.
Convent	A building occupied by a group of nuns (women who live a religious life), especially Christian.
Monastery	A home for a community of monks who live a religious life.
Mosque	A place of worship for followers of Islam.
Pagoda	A sacred building, often in the form of a tiered tower, for Buddhists.
Rectory	A house in which a Christian priest or minister lives.
Seminary	A school where ministers, priests, and rabbis are trained.
Shrine	A sacred place where a holy person is honored. Also a place where holy objects are kept.
Stupa	A structure built by Buddhists to house relics or holy items.
Synagogue	A building for worship and religious instruction for the Jewish religion.
Temple	A building dedicated to religious ceremonies or worship.

Zarcero's Church, Costa Rica

Sacred places may include mountains and rivers. Buddhists and Shintoists in Japan consider Mt. Fuji a sacred mountain. Hindus in India consider the Ganges a sacred river.

Batalha Abbey, Portugal

Pagoda, Burma

PEOPLE OF RELIGION

Abbess	The female head of a monastery of Christian nuns.
Abbot	The male head of a monastery of Christian monks.
Ascetic	A religious person who lives without material comforts in order to grow in spirituality.
Bishop	A high-ranking Christian leader (cleric).
Cantor	A singing leader in Jewish worship.
Cardinal	A high-ranking Roman Catholic priest, just below the Pope.
Clergy	A group of people who have been ordained for religious service.
Congregation	Members of a religious group who regularly worship at a church or synagogue.
Devout	Word used to describe a person who is dedicated to his or her religion and strictly follows its teachings.
Druid	A holy man of ancient Celtic religions. Celts lived in Ireland, Scotland, Wales, and parts of France.
Guru	A religious leader or teacher, particularly in Hinduism and Sikhism.
Imam	A leader of prayers in a mosque in the Islam religion.
Martyr	A person who is tortured or killed for his or her religious beliefs.

Buddhist monks

Indian sadhu

Monk	A man who is a member of a brotherhood of followers of a religion.
Mullah	A teacher or lawyer in the Islam religion.
Muezzin	A caller who summons followers of Islam to prayer.
Nun	A woman who is a member of a sisterhood of religious followers.
Order	A group of monks or nuns who follow the same religious rules.
Patriarch	The highest church leader of the Orthodox Christian religion.
Pope	The head of the Roman Catholic religion. Also the head of some non-Christian religions such as Taoism.
Priest	A person with the authority to perform religious rites.
Prophet	A person said to have been chosen by God to reveal God's word to the world.
Rabbi	A person trained in Jewish law, ritual, and tradition and ordained to lead a Jewish congregation.
Sadhu	A holy person, usually male, in the Hindu religion.
Sangha	A community of Buddhist monks or nuns.
Saint	A person who is officially recognized as one who lived a life of holiness on Earth.
Shaman	A person with great spiritual and healing powers. Shamans are found in the local religions of Africa, Asia, and North American Indians.
Vicar	A priest in the Anglican (Christian) religion.

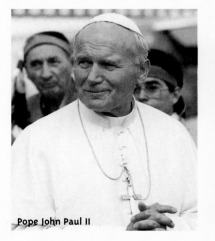

Pope John Paul II

Ascetic priest, Nepal

World Weather
(Winds, Currents, and Storms)

The world's weather engine is fueled by the sun. Every day 160 trillion tons of sunlit energy hit Earth. About half of this energy is absorbed, and the other half is reflected back into the atmosphere. This cycle of energy creates constant movement. The energy builds up and forms clouds. At its most powerful point, the energy is released as weather—thunderstorms, for example. It can be in the form of sunshine, rain, snow—and even violent weather such as cyclones or hurricanes.

View of a hurricane from space

Earth's air-conditioning system is a combination of air movement, air temperature, air pressure, and air moisture. These are the elements of weather. Weather shapes the landscape and helps determine where and how we live, what we eat, what we wear, and how we feel.

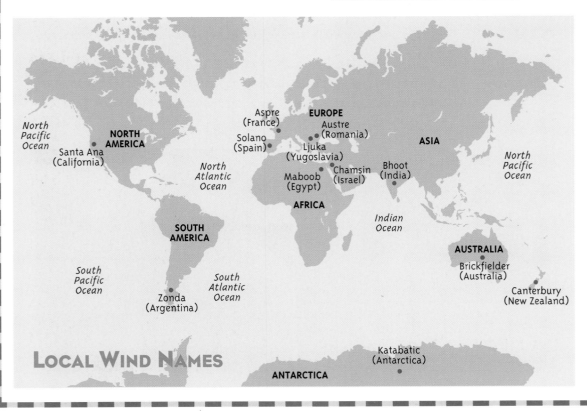

LOCAL WIND NAMES

North Pacific Ocean

NORTH AMERICA
Santa Ana (California)

North Atlantic Ocean

Aspre (France)

EUROPE
Austre (Romania)

Solano (Spain)
Ljuka (Yugoslavia)

Maboob (Egypt)
Chamsin (Israel)

AFRICA

ASIA

Bhoot (India)

North Pacific Ocean

SOUTH AMERICA

South Pacific Ocean

Zonda (Argentina)

South Atlantic Ocean

Indian Ocean

AUSTRALIA
Brickfielder (Australia)

Canterbury (New Zealand)

Katabatic (Antarctica)

ANTARCTICA

Cumulus clouds

ATMOSPHERE

Earth is surrounded by air that extends 434 miles (700 km) above the global surface. This is called the atmosphere. There are four main layers of air within the atmosphere. However, there is no clear boundary to mark the end of the atmosphere and the beginning of space.

NAME	DISTANCE ABOVE EARTH	CHARACTERISTICS
Troposphere	0–6 miles (0–10 km)	Contains vapor and dust.
Stratosphere	6–30 miles (10–50 km)	Dry and warm.
Mesosphere	30–50 miles (50–80 km)	As cold as -1,845° Fahrenheit (-1,205° C).
Ionosphere	30 miles and above	Contains several regions with high electron and ion content.
Thermosphere	Above 50 miles (80 km)	Thin; as hot as 36,325° Fahrenheit (20,005° C). Most weather occurs here; location of the ozone layer.

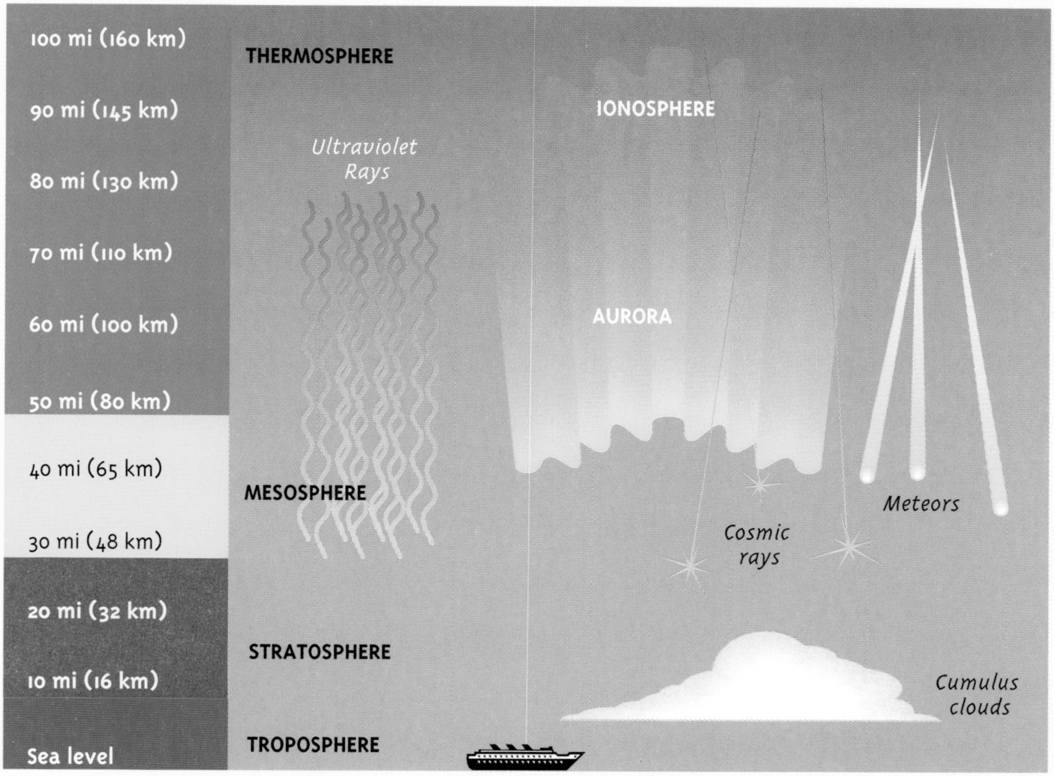

100 mi (160 km)

THERMOSPHERE

90 mi (145 km)

IONOSPHERE

Ultraviolet Rays

80 mi (130 km)

70 mi (110 km)

60 mi (100 km)

AURORA

50 mi (80 km)

40 mi (65 km)

MESOSPHERE

30 mi (48 km)

Cosmic rays

Meteors

20 mi (32 km)

STRATOSPHERE

10 mi (16 km)

Cumulus clouds

Sea level

TROPOSPHERE

Winds

Wind is air moving across the surface of Earth. Air moves because the sun heats Earth's surface unevenly. Hot air expands and rises, and cool air flows in to replace it. This circulation of air is what creates wind.

The general circulation of winds around the globe is called prevailing winds. Earth spins toward the east, causing Earth's air to move eastward with our planet's rotation. Prevailing winds vary with differences in latitude. They resemble wide belts of wind encircling Earth.

The Earth's spin causes the winds to curve. This is known as the Coriolis effect.

Wind Belts

Calm belt

An area called doldrums circles the equator and extends 700 miles (1,100 km) on either side of it. There are no prevailing winds. The air is hottest here because of the direct sun rays. Hot air rises to about 60,000 feet (18,290 m). It does not move across Earth. The narrow intertropical convergence zone (ITCZ) is a region within this belt where winds may converge.

Trade winds belt

These two belts lie between the calm belt and about 30 degrees latitude north and south. Here, cooler air moves in to replace the hot air rising from the equator. These prevailing winds were named because sailors relied on them to sail their trade ships.

Horse latitudes

Around 30 degrees north and south of the equator, there are two narrow belts of calm air. Some of the hot air that rises from the equator falls back down to Earth here. When sailing ships stalled here, many horses on board died. This is why the area is called the horse latitudes.

Prevailing westerlies belt

These westerly belts are located between 30 and 60 degrees latitude north and south. These winds result from surface air moving away from the equator.

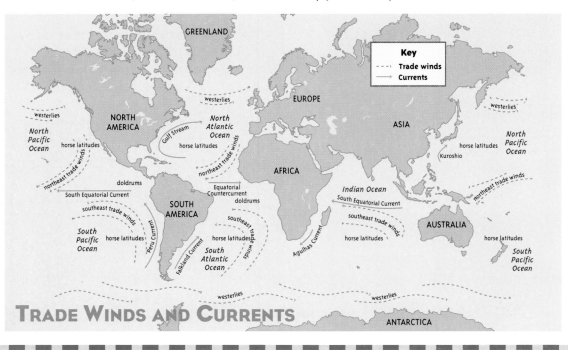

TRADE WINDS AND CURRENTS

Prevailing easterlies belt

These polar belts are located between 60 degrees north and south latitude and the two poles. They move somewhat from east to west, away from the poles.

Regional Winds

These winds form in regions within the prevailing winds. They are also called synoptic-scale circulations because their movement is circular around low- and high-pressure air. There are two kinds of synoptic-scale circulations.

Cyclones or lows

These are airflows that move toward low-pressure regions. In the Northern Hemisphere, they circle counterclockwise. In the Southern Hemisphere, they circle clockwise.

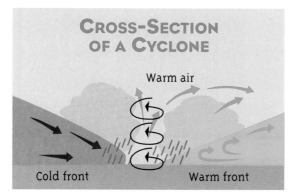

CROSS-SECTION OF A CYCLONE

Warm air

Cold front

Warm front

Anticyclones or highs

These are airflows that move away from high-pressure regions. In the Northern Hemisphere, they spin clockwise. In the Southern Hemisphere, they spin counterclockwise.

Local Winds

Local winds are the seasonal winds that blow in specific areas of the world.

Monsoons control much of the climate of Asia.

Santa Ana winds are named for the Santa Ana Canyon in California. These strong, hot, dusty winds occur from October through February.

Wet winds

Monsoons that blow from the ocean to inland areas during the summer create wet weather. Monsoons that blow toward the ocean during winter make dry weather.

Dry mountain winds

Chinook is the name for these winds in the Rocky Mountains in North America. *Chinook* is an American Indian word meaning "snow eater." *Foehn* is the name for similar winds in the Alps Mountains in Europe.

Desert winds

Harmattan is the name for a cool westerly wind that blows across the Sahara Desert in Africa. This local wind carries a great deal of desert dust, but it also brings cooling relief.

Sirocco comes from the Italian word for a warm wind that blows northward from the Sahara Desert. This wind often picks up moisture from the Mediterranean Sea, which produces a warm damp wind in southern Europe. This wind also carries dust and may darken the sky with its fine sand.

Chinook winds, North America

Wind turbines

Measuring Winds

Weather vanes or wind vanes have been used for thousands of years to show which way the wind blows. The narrow point of the arrow on the vane points into the wind. Today, vanes in use at weather stations are equipped with electrical connections, which record wind direction.

An anemometer measures wind speed. Created in the 15th century, this device has three cups that catch the wind, causing the anemometer to rotate. Today, these devices are connected to computers to increase their accuracy.

Scatterometers are mounted on Earth-orbiting satellites. They map winds by measuring how radar signals bounce off ocean waters. Because the ocean's waves are caused by winds, scientists can tell how strong the wind is by measuring the size of the waves. A scatterometer displays arrows for wind direction and colors for wind strength. Strong winds are shown in orange; medium winds are shown in red and purple; and calmer winds are shown in blue.

Rawinsondes (ra = radar, win = wind , sondes = radios) measure the speed and direction of upper-level winds. They are located in weather balloons stationed at 100,000 feet (30 km.) in the atmosphere.

Gathering weather data

WIND FACTS

- Winds are named for the direction from which they blow. For instance, a north wind comes from the north.
- Downslope winds blow downhill and warm the air.
- Upslope winds blow uphill and bring fog and rain.
- Sea breezes are winds that blow inland from large bodies of water.
- Jet streams are currents of eastbound air—a few hundred miles wide—which flow in the upper atmosphere 20,000 feet (6,000 m) above ground level.
- Jet streaks are high-speed winds within the jet stream.
- Wind shear is the sudden change in the speed or direction of the wind.
- Ocean waves and ripples are caused by the wind pushing the water.

ANATOMY OF A SEA BREEZE

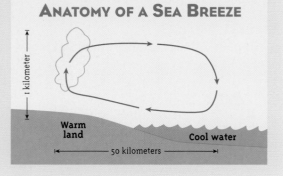

1 kilometer

Warm land

Cool water

50 kilometers

BEAUFORT WIND SCALE

In 1805, an English admiral, Sir Francis Beaufort, devised a scale for measuring wind speed on water. This scale, based on observation, has been adapted to also measure wind speed on land. The Beaufort scale is still used today.

FORCE	WIND SPEED (miles/hour)	(km/hour)	DESCRIPTION
0	1	1.6	Calm. Smoke will rise vertically.
1	1-3	1.6-4.8	Light air. Rising smoke drifts.
2	4-7	6.4-11.3	Light breeze. Can feel wind on the face.
3	8-12	12.9-19.3	Gentle breeze. Leaves and twigs move.
4	13-18	20.9-29	Moderate breeze. Raises dust.
5	19-24	30.6-38.6	Fresh breeze. Small trees sway.
6	25-31	40.2-50	Strong breeze. Large branches move.
7	32-38	51.5-61.2	Moderate gale. Large trees sway.
8	39-46	62.8-74	Fresh gale. Twigs and branches break.
9	47-54	75.6-86.9	Strong gale. Slight damage to buildings.
10	55-63	88.3-101.4	Whole gale. Trees are uprooted.
11	64-72	103-115.9	Storm. Widespread damage.
12	73+	115.9+	Hurricane.

Aftermath of gale winds and an ice storm

EL NIÑO AND LA NIÑA

Both El Niño and La Niña are ocean-atmosphere cycles that affect weather globally. Normally, winds travel west across the Pacific. When El Niño happens, the air-sea relationship becomes unstable, and the ocean warms. This brings heavy rains to South America and drought to places like India.

La Niña is the opposite of El Niño. La Niña brings cold ocean temperatures, dry conditions on the Pacific coast, and heavy rains and flooding in Asia. El Niño means "little child" because the conditions were first seen around Christmas, the time Christians celebrate Christ's birth.

A KID'S SCALE FOR MEASURING WIND SPEED

This is a simplified Beaufort Scale— an easy way to judge wind speed.

DESCRIPTION	WIND SPEED
You can feel wind on your face.	10 mph (16 kph)
Small branches move, dust blows.	20 mph (32 kph)
Large branches move.	30 mph (48 kph)
Whole trees bend.	40 mph (64 kph)

WIND WORD BANK

- The word *hurricane* is from the Taino word *hurakán* which means "evil spirit." The Taino are native people of the Caribbean.

- The word *typhoon* is a mispronunciation of a Chinese word, ta-feng, which means "violent winds."

Hurricane winds

Wind chill index

Wind chill describes how cold wind feels. The wind chill factor combines air temperature with wind speed. As the wind blows against your body, it draws heat away from you. The stronger the wind blows, the faster the heat is withdrawn. When wind causes the body to lose heat faster than it can replace it, the body temperature can drop dangerously low, and hypothermia can result. Meteorologists report wind chill when it is 35 degrees Fahrenheit (1.6° C) or lower.

In Canada, wind chill figures are given in watts of heat loss per square meter on the body. Temperatures are measured in degrees Celsius. Wind speeds are expressed in kilometers.

STORM DEGREES

Meteorologists describe tropical storms in the following ways.

Tropical disturbance
Weak but notable winds

Tropical depression
Winds less than 39 miles (62.4 km) per hour

Tropical storm
Winds from 39—74 miles (62.4 —118.4 km) per hour

Hurricane
Winds greater than 74 miles (118.4 km) per hour

TROPICAL STORMS

Severe winds over tropical and subtropical water are called tropical cyclones. In the Northern Hemisphere these winds blow in a counterclockwise direction. In the Southern Hemisphere these winds blow in a clockwise direction. Names for tropical cyclones vary according to the geographic location.

NAME	LOCATION
Hurricane	Atlantic Ocean, Caribbean Sea, Gulf of Mexico, Northeast Pacific Ocean (east of the International Date Line)
Typhoon	Northeast Pacific Ocean (west of the International Dateline)
Cyclone	Indian Ocean and Southwest Pacific Ocean

THE WORLD'S DEADLIEST TROPICAL CYCLONES

The combination of strong winds, flooding, and storm surges have taken a greater toll in human lives throughout history than earthquakes and volcanoes. Deaths are claimed mostly by water rather than wind.

- In 1737, in the Bay of Bengal, 300,000 people died when a storm surge with 40-foot- (12-m-) high waves crashed along the shoreline.

- In 1881, a cyclone along the coast of China killed 300,000 people.

- In 1970, approximately 500,000 people died on the coastal islands of Bangladesh, as the result of a cyclone.

- In 1991, 125,000 people died from a cyclone in Bangladesh.

- In 1999, about 2,000 people died from a cyclone in Vietnam.

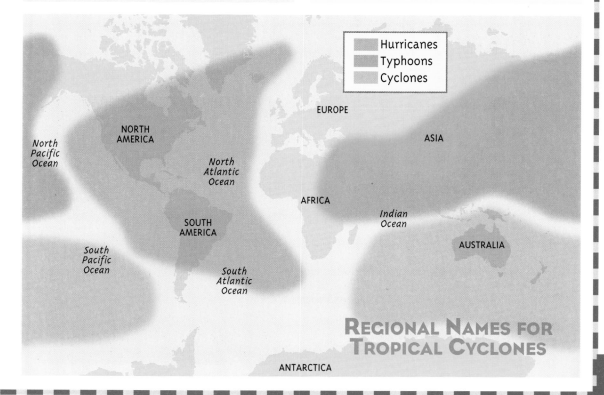

Hurricanes
Typhoons
Cyclones

EUROPE

NORTH AMERICA

North Pacific Ocean

ASIA

North Atlantic Ocean

AFRICA

SOUTH AMERICA

Indian Ocean

South Pacific Ocean

AUSTRALIA

South Atlantic Ocean

ANTARCTICA

REGIONAL NAMES FOR TROPICAL CYCLONES

Tropical storm

Hurricane Hunters

In the United States, specially equipped airplanes are used to track hurricanes to determine the size and direction of the storm. Up to 15 people may be on board the plane. This includes aircraft crew as well as meterologists and scientists who measure the storm's size and development. They obtain information that cannot be taken from weather satellites. The information is then radioed back to the National Hurricane Center in Florida.

Naming Hurricanes

The practice of naming hurricanes may have begun as early as the 19th century, when hurricanes were named after saints. In the early part of the 20th century, a meterologist from Australia named hurricanes after politicians he disliked. During World War II, U.S. military meterologists named Pacific storms for their wives and girlfriends back home.

Naming all hurricanes began in 1950. Names were given in order to reduce confusion and to distinguish one storm from another. By 1977, an official naming system had begun. By 1979, both female and male names were given to hurricanes.

The National Weather Center names Atlantic Ocean hurricanes. The names are in alphabetical order, skipping the letters Q ,U, X, Y, and Z. The Central Pacific Hurricane Center names the Pacific Ocean hurricanes. They use the letters X, Y, and Z.

There are six lists of alphabetized names. Each year, one of the six lists is used. After each six-year cycle, the lists are reused from the beginning.

HURRICANE FACTS

- The lifespan of a hurricane is typically 10 days.
- Hurricanes are almost always born in the summer or fall, between the latitudes 5 and 20 degrees north and south of the equator.
- A full-grown hurricane can have more power than any other force of nature—one trillion pounds of pressure.
- The "eye" of the hurricane is the center of the storm. This low-pressure, calm area is where air sinks. The eye is encircled by high-speed winds.
- In the United States the official hurricane season is from June 1 to November 30.

Hurricane hunter

Atlantic Ocean names
Year 2000

Alberto, Beryl, Chris, Debby, Ernesto, Florence, Gordon, Helene, Isaac, Joyce, Keith, Leslie, Michael, Nadine, Oscar, Patty, Rafael, Sandy, Tony, Valerie, William.

Year 2001

Allison, Barry, Chantal, Dean, Erin, Felix, Gabrielle, Humberto, Iris, Jerry, Karen, Lorenzo, Michelle, Noel, Olga, Pablo, Rebekah, Sebastian, Tanya, Van, Wendy.

Year 2002

Arthur, Bertha, Cristobal, Dolly, Edouard, Fay, Gustav, Hanna, Isidore, Josephine, Kyle, Lili, Marco, Nana, Omar, Paloma, Rene, Sally, Teddy, Vicky, Wilfred.

Eastern North Pacific hurricane names
Year 2000

Aletta, Bud, Carlotta, Daniel, Emilia, Fabio, Gilma, Hector, Ileana, John, Kristy, Lane, Miriam, Norman, Olivia, Paul, Rosa, Sergio, Tara, Vicente, Willa, Xavier, Yolanda, Zeke.

Year 2001

Adolph, Barbara, Cosme, Dalilia, Erick, Flossie, Gil, Henriette, Israel, Juliette, Kiko, Lorena, Manuel, Narda, Octave, Priscilla, Raymond, Sonia, Tico, Velma, Wallis, Xina, York, Zelda.

Year 2002

Alma, Boris, Cristina, Douglas, Elida, Fausto, Genevieve, Hernan, Iselle, Julio, Kenna, Lowell, Marie, Norbert, Odile, Polo, Rachel, Simon, Trudy, Vance, Winnie, Xavier, Yolanda, Zeke.

Retired hurricane names

Storms that have caused severe damage or taken many lives often go into hurricane history. The country most affected by the storm can have the storm's name retired. The following are some names that have been retired.

Alicia (1983)	Cesar (1996)	Fran (1996)
Allen (1980)	David (1979)	Frederic (1979)
Andrew (1992)	Diana (1990)	Gilbert (1988)
Anita (1977)	Edna (1968)	Hortense (1996)
Beulah (1967)	Eloise (1975)	Hugo (1989)
Bob (1991)	Fifi (1974)	Joan (1988)

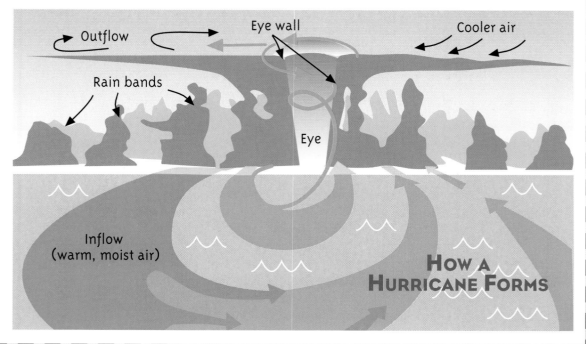

Outflow · Eye wall · Cooler air · Rain bands · Eye · Inflow (warm, moist air)

HOW A HURRICANE FORMS

THE FIVE DEADLIEST HURRICANES IN THE CONTINENTAL UNITED STATES, 1900–1999

RANK	NAME	LOCATION	YEAR	CATEGORY	DEATHS
1	Unnamed	Galveston, TX	1900	4	6,000 +
2	Unnamed	Lake Okeechobee, FL	1928	4	1,836 +
3	Unnamed	Florida Keys	1919	4	600–900
4	"New England"	New England states	1938	3	600
5	"Labor Day"	Florida Keys	1935	5	408

THE FIVE COSTLIEST HURRICANES IN THE CONTINENTAL UNITED STATES, 1900–1999

RANK	NAME	LOCATION	YEAR	CATEGORY	DAMAGE
1	Andrew	FL, LA	1992	4	$30 billion
2	Hugo	SC	1989	4	$7.2 billion
3	Betsy	FL, LA	1965	3	$6.5 billion
4	Agnes	Northeast U.S.	1972	1	$6.4 billion
5	Camille	LA, MS	1969	5	$5.2 billion

THE FIVE MOST INTENSE HURRICANES IN THE ATLANTIC OCEAN, 1900–1999

(Based on the Saffir-Simpson Hurrican Scale. The Saffir-Simpson table is used to estimate the potential flooding and property damage of a given hurricane.)

Hurricane damage

RANK	NAME	LOCATIONS	YEAR	CATEGORY
1	"Labor Day"	Florida Keys	1935	5
2	Camille	MS, VA, WV	1969	5
3	Andrew	FL, LA	1992	4
4	Unamed	Florida Keys	1919	4
5	Unamed	Lake Okeechobee, FL	1928	4

GLOBAL WARMING

Human activities have added chemicals to the atmosphere that have heat-trapping qualities. The added chemicals are primarily carbon dioxide, methane, and nitrous oxide. Together they create a "greenhouse effect," trapping added heat in the atmosphere. These gases occur naturally, but they have entered the atmosphere as byproducts of certain industries, such as those that make foam for insulation and refrigeration.

Surface temperatures on Earth have increased in the last century, and the 10 warmest years of the 20th century have occurred since 1985.

Tornadoes

Tornadoes come from a storm called a super-cell. Supercells are huge thunderstorms with winds spinning in a circle. When the spinning winds form a funnel shape and drop to the ground, the result is called a tornado. Tornadoes occur on land all over the world.

Deadly tornado outbreaks in North America

Tornadoes cause 70 to 80 deaths a year in the United States. Here is a description of the two deadliest tornado outbreaks in the 20th century. On March 18, 1925, deadly tornadoes ripped through Missouri, Illinois, and Indiana. One, about three-quarters of a mile wide, covered 219 miles (352 km) in three and a half hours. This set records for speed, path length, and loss of life. In all, 695 people died. Murphysboro, Illinois, suffered the worst death toll. In that city, 234 people died, including two dozen schoolchildren who were crushed by collapsing school brick walls.

TORNADO FACTS

- Tornado Alley is a strip of the Midwestern United States between the Rocky Mountains and the Mississippi River. More than 700 tornadoes touch down in Tornado Alley each year.

- Some tornadoes stand still. Other tornadoes move along the ground at speeds up to 60 miles (100 km) per hour.

- Most tornadoes touch down for less than five minutes, then rise or dissipate.

- Destruction from tornadoes is mostly due to objects lifted by funnels and then propelled as high-speed missiles.

The largest tornado outbreak on record took place within 24 hours during April 3–4, 1974. More than 148 twisters raced through 13 southern and midwestern U.S. states and parts of Canada, killing 316 people.

HOW A TORNADO FORMS

Rising warm air is sometimes trapped by a higher layer of cool air. As the warm air pushes upward, it can suddenly break through, causing thunderclouds to form. The combination of these clouds and strong winds can make the rising air start to spin. As this column of spinning air becomes wider, it grows into a tornado.

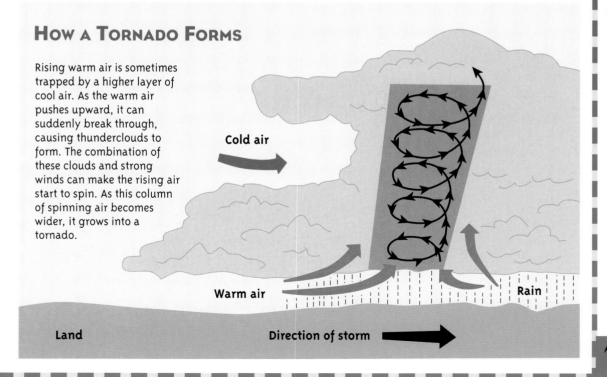

Cold air

Warm air

Rain

Land

Direction of storm

MEASURING TORNADOES

Tornadoes and other severe local windstorms are classified according to the Fujita Tornado Scale (F-Scale). This scale is named after Theodore Fujita, the scientist who developed it. The scale is based on wind damage.

CATEGORY	STRENGTH	DESCRIPTION
F 0	Weak	Winds at 40–73 miles (64–116 km) per hour. Light damage.
F 1	Weak	Winds at 74–112 miles (117–180 km) per hour. Moderate damage.
F 2	Strong	Winds at 113–157 miles (181–252 km) per hour. Considerable damage.
F 3	Strong	Winds at 158–206 miles (254–332 km) per hour. Severe damage.
F 4	Violent	Winds at 207–260 miles (333–418 km) per hour. Devastating damage.
F 5	Violent	Winds at 261–318 miles (420–512 km) per hour. Incredible damage.*

* Rare

Tornado chasers

People who chase tornadoes usually live in southern or midwestern states, where tornadoes are most common. Tornado chasers listen for weather reports of severe thunderstorms or tornado watches. Then they load their equipment in a van and head for the tornado area. Using radar equipment, weather instruments, video cameras, and computers, they detail what they find and report the information to weather stations.

TORNADO SAFETY TIPS

- If you are inside a building, go to the basement and duck under the stairs or a heavy table.

- If you are inside a building without a basement, get down on the floor in a protected place. Stay away from windows.

- If you are outside, lie down and cover your head.

Approaching tornado

WORLD WEATHER EXTREMES

Most extreme temperature range
Verkhoyansk, Siberia

Winters average -90° Fahrenheit (-68° C); Summers reach 98° Fahrenheit (37° C).

Hottest place
Dallol, Denakil Depression, Ethiopia

Annual average temperature 94° Fahrenheit (34° C).

Hottest recorded temperature
Al' Aziziyah, Libya

136.4° Fahrenheit (58° C) on September 13, 1922.

Coldest place
Plateau Station, Antarctica

Annual average temperature -72° Fahrenheit (-58° C).

Coldest recorded temperature
Vostok Base, Antarctica

-128.6° Fahrenheit (-89° C) on July 21, 1983.

Driest place
Atacama Desert, Chile

Annual average rainfall is less than 1/1250 inch (0.1 mm).

Wettest place
Mount Wai'ale'ale, Hawaii

Average annual rainfall is 486 inches (1,234 cm). Rain falls 350 days a year!

Windiest place
Cape Denison, Adélie Land, Antarctica

Extrordinary katabatic winds rage at high speeds for weeks.

Campsite on sea ice, Antarctica

Fastest recorded winds
Mount Washington, New Hampshire

230 miles (368 km) per hour on April 12, 1934.

Greatest recorded snowfall
Silver Lake, Colorado

In this region, 75 inches (193 cm) fell in a 24-hour period between April 14–15, 1921.

Largest hailstone
Coffeyville, Kansas

On September 3, 1970, a hailstone weighed 1.67 pounds (0.75 kg) and measured 17.5 inches (44 cm) in circumference.

Tallest waterspout
Coast of New South Wales, Australia

On May 16, 1898, it was 5,012 feet (1,528 m) high and 10 feet (3 m) in diameter.

APPENDIX

Telephone Numbers

When Alexander Graham Bell called to his assistant, "Watson, come here I want to see you," he sent his voice through a telephone wire a room away. Today, people talk to each other a world away. Satellite connections, fiber optics, and millions of miles of telephone wires blanket the earth. It is possible, simply by pressing a few buttons, to be in touch with someone clear on the other end of the planet. Here's some general information about telephone communication.

 The first commercial trans-Atlantic telephone service was established on January 7, 1927, between New York City and London. The charge was $75 for three minutes.

Dial-A-Bird
614-221-9736

The Audubon Society provides information on bird watching and migration.

Dial-A-Phenomenon
202-357-2000

The Smithsonian Institute in Washington D.C. provides news about earthquakes, volcanoes, and the movement of the stars, planets, and moon.

 *The area code 818, which is located in San Gabriel Valley, California, is a prized area code for Chinese immigrants because it contains two 8's. They believe that 8 is a lucky number because it sounds like their word for prosperity.*

Dial Local Information
555-1212

When you want the telephone number of someone living in your area, dial this number.

Dial Toll Free
800-555-1212

This provides directory assistance for toll-free numbers.

 *In the United States, there are 970 million miles of wire on 20 million poles, 500,000 miles of underground cable, 250,000 miles of micro-wave relay stations, 180 million phones, and dozens of satellites.*

CALLING THE WORLD

- In order to call another country in the world, you must use the international access telephone code. You can find a complete listing of country and city codes in the front section of your phone book. From the United States, this code is 011. Every country has its own code. Many cities within the countries have a code, too. Here are three examples of how it works:

- Is the Queen at home? To reach Buckingham Palace, dial the international access code (011) plus the country code for England (44) plus the city code for London (71) plus the number: 011 + 44 + 1 + 930 - 4832.

- What's happening in Tokyo? Do you want to know the day's events in Tokyo, Japan? For a listing, in English, dial 011 + 81 + 3 + 503 - 2911.

- How's the weather in Bangkok? You can find out about the weather in Bangkok, Thailand, by calling this number. However, if you can't speak Thai, you won't understand what's being said. The number is 011 + 66 + 2 + 392 - 9000.

Zip Codes

Number codes used to sort and speed the delivery of mail in the United States are called ZIP Codes. ZIP stands for Zoning Improvement Plan.

The former Postmaster General, J. Edward Day, created the ZIP Code in 1963 to deal with the high volume of mail in the United States.

How ZIP Codes Work

The first digit of the five-number ZIP Code divides the country into 10 large groups of states from 0 in the Northeast to 9 in the West. The second and third digits divide each state into 10 smaller geographic areas. The fourth and fifth digits identify a post office, or local delivery area.

A nine-number ZIP Code, introduced in 1983, is used by high-volume business mailers.

One of the richest ZIP Code areas is 10021 in Manhattan. During a recent presidential campaign, more than 7.8 million dollars came from this ZIP Code area.

Famous ZIP Code Numbers

- The lowest ZIP Code number is 01001, for Agawam, Massachusetts.
- The highest ZIP Code number is 99929, for Wrangell, Alaska.
- The ZIP for Zap, North Dakota, is 58580.
- America's most famous ZIP Code is 90210 for Beverly Hills, California.
- The most exclusive ZIP Code in the country belongs to the U.S. President. It is a nine-digit number used by a select few. This secret ZIP separates the most confidential mail from the rest of the mail. The President receives as many as 15,000 letters a day.

Looking Up Zip Codes

http://www.framed.usps.com/ncsc/lookups/lookup_ctystzip.html

Using this United States Postal Service site, type in the city and state and get the zip code for that location.

Postal Abbreviations for States and Territories

In 1963, the Post Office came up with two-letter abbreviations for each of the 50 U.S. states. These are space savers created when the ZIP Code was introduced. Here are the abbreviations to use when you send mail.

Northern Mariana Islands	CM
Puerto Rico	PR
Trust Territory of the Pacific	TT
Virgin Islands	VI

Time Zones

Probably at least once a day—or more often—someone asks you what time it is. What exactly is time and how is it measured? Time is hard to define, but it is basically a way to measure events.

Events on Earth can happen at exactly the same time. A parade in Madrid, **Spain**, can take place at the exactly same time people in New Delhi, **India**, are eating dinner or people in Perth, **Australia**, are watching a movie. Because the sun changes its position in the sky, all three of these events don't happen when the sun is at exactly the same position. When the parade in Madrid takes place at noon, it is 5:00 P.M. in New Delhi and 9:00 P.M. in Perth.

For every place on Earth, every day, once a day, the sun is directly overhead. At this point, the local time is noon. However, it would be too confusing if every place used local time! That's why standard time zones were established.

Earth is divided by imaginary circles. Those that run east and west are called parallels of latitude.

THE INTERNATIONAL DATE LINE

- The International Date Line is the place where the 12 zones east and the 12 zones west of Prime Meridian meet.

- If you travel west of this line, you "lose" a day. If you travel west, you "gain" a day.

- The first place to see the sunrise each day is Caroline Island, **Kiribati**, in the South Pacific.

The equator is at 0 degrees latitude. Those that run north are south are called meridians of longitude.

Worldwide time zones were established in 1884 in order to standardize time. The starting point is the Greenwich Observatory in Greenwich, **England**, which is at 0 degrees longitude. There are 12 time zones east of Greenwich and 12 time zones west of Greenwich. Each zone is 15 degrees of longitude, but the zones are jagged in places in order to include important cities or an entire country or state within a time zone. For example, all of **Argentina** is in the same zone.

INTERNATIONAL TIME ZONES

Can you find where you live on the time zone map? How many hours are you from the prime meridian?

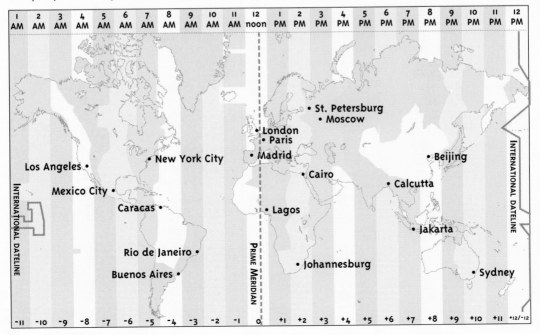

FOR MORE INFORMATION

Internet Sites

Do you want to travel the world on the electronic highway? Would you like to meet someone in cyberspace? Are there exotic places you want to learn about? Here are some of the geography-related sites you might like to visit.

Asiaville
http://www.asiaville.com

Explore the countries of Asia. This site features links to Asian culture, current events, and travel.

Arctic to Amazon Project
http://www.mukilteo.wednet.edu/msd/HsPages/CyberSchool/Arctic_To_Amazon/ArcticTo Amazon.html

Learn about explorers Helen and Bill Thayer's trip from the Artic region of Canada to the Amazon rain forest in Brazil. See photos of different plants and animals in the areas.

The Explorers Club
http://www.explorers.org

Get a sampling of sights of expeditions from all over the world.

Geo-Globe
http://library.thinkquest. org/10157

Explore the world and learn about its famous landmarks, animals, plants, oceans, and land features at this interactive site.

Glacier
http://www.glacier.rice.edu

Learn about Antarctica and the role it has in world weather.

GlobaLearn
http://www.globalearn.org

Take a trip around the world. This site has a special students' section.

Learning Web
http://www.usgs.gov/education

This United States government site links to resources on maps, geography, and the environment.

National Geographic
http://www.nationalgeographic.com

Discover the world. This site features maps and a kids' section.

PBS
http://www.pbs.org/neighborhoods/travel

Visit places around the world and learn about different cultures.

Rand McNally
http://www.randmcnally kids.com

See maps of places around the world. This site has a special trivia section just for kids.

Where in the World?
http://www.geographygames.com/ index.html

This site features geography quizzes and games for students, and provides information on world current events and weather.

World Wildlife Fund
http://www.world wildlife.org

Learn about wildlife found all over the world. Has a kids' page full of fun activities.

Organizations

This is a list of organizations dedicated to exploring, enjoying, and protecting the wildlife and wild places on Earth. Write to them for information on their programs, and learn how you can get involved.

AFS International Intercultural Programs
313 East 43rd Street, New York, NY 10017

American Geographers Society
156 Fifth Avenue, New York, NY 10021

The Institute for Earth Education
PO Box 288, Warrenville, IL 60555

Information Center on Children's Cultures
332 East 38th Street, New York, NY 10016

Izaak Walton League of America
1701 North Fort Myer Drive , Suite 1100, Arlington, VA 22209

National Arbor Day Foundation
211 North 12th Street , Lincoln, NE 68508

National Audubon Society
613 Riversville Road, Greenwich, CT 06831

National Geographic Society
1145 17th Street NW, Washington, D.C. 20036-4688

National Oceanic and Atmospheric Administration
U.S. Department of Commerce
14th Street and Constitution Avenue NW, Room 6013
Washington, D.C. 20230

National Register of Big Trees
American Forestry Association
P.O. Box 2000, Washington, D.C. 20013

National Wildlife Federation
1400 16th Street NW, Washington, D.C. 20036

Royal Canadian Geographic Society
39 McArthur Avenue, Vanier ON KIL 8L7

Sierra Club
730 Polk Street, San Francisco, CA 94109

Society of Women Geographers
415 East Capitol Street S. E., Washington, D.C. 20003

Wilderness Society
900 17th Street NW, Washington, D.C. 20006

Wildlife Conservation Society
2300 Southern Boulevard, Bronx, NY 10460-1099

World Wildlife Fund
1250 Twenty-Fourth Street, N.W.
P.O. Box 97180, Washington, D.C. 20037

Books

Arnold, Caroline. *El Nino: Stormy Weather for People and Wildlife.* New York, NY: Clarion Books, 1998.

Ash, Russell. *Factastic Millennium Facts.* New York, NY: Dorling Kindersley, 1999.

Barnes, Trevor. *Kingfisher Book of Religions: Festivals, Ceremonies, and Beliefs from Around the World.* New York, NY: Larousse Kingfisher Chambers, 1999.

Bergamini, Andrea. *The History of Rock Music* (Masters of Music). Hauppauge, NY: Barrons Juveniles, 2000.

Elsom, Derek M. *Weather Explained: A Beginner's Guide to the Elements* (Your World Explained). New York, NY: Henry Holt and Company, Inc., 1997.

Fontanel, Beatrice. *Monsters: The World's Most Incredible Animals.* New York, NY: NTC Contemporary Publishing Company, 2000.

Haduch, Bill. *Twister!* (Discovery Kids). New York, NY: Dutton Books, 1999.

Jones, Charlotte Foltz. John O'Brien (illustrator). *Eat Your Words: A Fascinating Look at the Language of Food.* New York, NY: Delacorte Press, 1999.

Kerrod, Robin. *Wild Weather* (The Investigations Series). New York, NY: Lorenz Books, 2000.

Kindersley, Anabel (contributor). Barnabas Kindersley (photographer). *Children Just Like Me: Celebrations!* New York, NY: Dorling Kindersley, 1997.

Lorenz, Albert. Joy Schleh. *House: Showing How People Have Lived Throughout History With Examples from the Lives of Legendary Men and Women.* New York, NY: Harry N Abrams, 1998.

Lugira, Aloysius Muzzanganda. *African Religions* (World Religions). New York, NY: Facts on File, Inc., 1999.

MacQuitty, Miranda. *Inside Oceans.* Buffalo, NY: Firefly Books Limited, 1999.

McElrath, William N. *Ways We Worship.* Hauppauge, NY: Barrons Juveniles, 1997.

Miles, Lisa. *Atlas of 20th Century* (History Atlases). Tulsa, OK: EDC Publications, 1997.

National Geographic Society. *National Geographic Book of Mammals.* Washington, D.C.: National Geographic Society, 1998.

National Geographic Society. *National Geographic United States Atlas for Young Explorers.* Washington, D.C.: National Geographic Society, 1999.

Pandell, Karen. Art Wolfe (photographer). Denise Y. Takahashi (illustrator). *Journey Through the Northern Rainforest.* New York, NY: Dutton Books, 1999.

Rand McNally and Company. *Children's Millennium Atlas of the United States.* Skokie, IL: Rand McNally and Company, 1999.

Ruiz, Andres Llamas. *Rain* (Sequences of Earth and Space). New York, NY: Sterling Publications, 1997.

Stack, Peggy Fletcher. Kathleen B. Peterson (illustrator). *A World of Faith.* Salt Lake City, UT: Signature Books, 1998.

Walter, Mildred Pitts. Cheryl Carrington (illustrator). *Kwanzaa: A Family Affair.* New York, NY: Lothrop Lee and Shepard, 1995.

Wood, Tim. *Houses and Homes* (See Through History Series). New York, NY: Viking Childrens Books, 1997.

Wyatt, Valerie. Brian Share (illustrator). *Weather Faq: Frequently Asked Questions.* Nashville, TN: Kids Can Press, 2000.

Videos

Amazing Wonders of the World - The Island Continent: Australia. Questar, Inc., 1999.

Baby Animals, Mammals and More! Tapeworm Video, 1996.

Flags of the United States. Tapeworm Video, 1999.

Israel Folk Dance Festival. Kultur Video, 2000.

National Geographic Kids Video Series: Really Wild Animals - Adventures in Asia. National Geographic Kids Video, 1997.

Peru: Spirits of the Amazon. Fox Lorber, 1998.

Really Wild Animals: Amazing North America. National Geographic Kids Video, 1994.

Really Wild Animals: Totally Tropical Rainforest. National Geographic Kids Video, 1994.

Secrets of the Tornado. Tornado Project, Inc., 2000.

CD Roms

A World of Animals. CounterTop Software.
Learn about the world's animals in this nature encyclopedia.

Amazing Animals Activity Center. DK Multimedia.
Learn about animal behavior, appearance, and habitat.

Birds of the World. CounterTop Software.
Learn the about the habitats, features, and sounds of the world's birds.

Carmen Sandiego Junior Detective Edition. The Learning Company.
Discover the world while solving crime.

My First Amazing History Explorer. DK Multimedia.
Learn about the history of the world's most famous cities.

My First Amazing World Explorer. DK Multimedia.
Take a world tour across the continents.

Oceans. CounterTop Software.
Discover the ocean and its underwater life.

20th Century Day by Day. DK Multimedia.
Learn the history of the past century.

Where in the World is Carmen Sandiego? Mindscape.
Help solve a mystery while learning geography.

INDEX

Aborigines, 50, 107, 108, 224, 232, 266, 302
Abyssal plain, 204
Accordion, 238, 239
Accra, 194, 270
Achiote, 150, 151
Acid rain, 164, 165
Acropolis, 241
A.D., 274
Adornments, 120-131
Aerial map, 191
Afghanistan, 8, 76, 243
Africa, 8, 9, 11, 16, 29, 34, 35, 40, 50, 107, 134, 149, 212, 215, 245, 261, 290, 311
   animals, 6, 7, 11, 13
   biomes, 163, 164
   clothing and adornment, 122, 125, 131
   food, 149, 154, 157, 158, 161
   map, 41, 53
   music, 232-233
   people, 107, 108, 110, 111, 116
   rivers, 216, 217, 220, 221
   trees, 170, 171
African Americans, 239, 300
Afrikaans language, 137
Afro-Asian languages, 134
Agra, 244, 270
Agulhas Current, 210
Air pressure, 311
Alabama, 138, 253, 254
Alaska, 16, 17, 42, 111, 118, 179, 193, 207, 213, 252 , 265
Albania, 48, 67, 77, 133, 159
Aleut, 109
Aleutian Islands, 222
Alexandria, 191, 247, 253, 262, 264
Algeria, 116, 194
Algonquin language, 139
Alhambra, 271
Al Hillah, 241
Al Idrisi, 190
Allah, 290, 291
Almond, 167
Al Murrah, 115
Alps, 48
Altamira Cave, 269
Altiplano, 117
Altitude, 201
Amazon rain forest, 165
Amazon River, 44, 216, 217, 218
American Samoa, 76, 110
Amish, 284
Amphibians, 7, 8, 12

Amsterdam, 250
Amur River, 217
Anaconda, 8
Ancient cities, 241
Ancient world, seven wonders, 262-264
Andalusia, 227
Andersen, Hans Christian, 245, 250
Andes Mountains, 18, 44, 117, 238, 244
Anemometer, 312
Angel Falls, 217, 258, 259
Angkor, 270
Angola, 163
Angora, 250, 251
Animals, 6-21, 69, 225, 250
Ankara, 250, 251
Antarctica, 9, 15, 34, 35, 44, 46, 47, 50, 52, 153, 203, 215, 217, 218, 222, 321
Antarctic Circle, 193
Anteater, 44
Anticyclone, 311
Antipode, 194
Ants, 19, 154
Apache, 109, 303
Apennine Peninsula, 48
Appalachian Mountains, 42, 239
Apple River, 218
April, 88-89
Aqueducts, 241
Aquifer, 196
Arabian Desert, 115
Arabian Peninsula, 77
Arabian Sea, 213
Arabic language, 135, 136, 137
Arachnids, 12, 14, 155
Arafura Sea, 213
Aral Sea, 214
Aran Islands, 121
Ararat, 261
Arawak, 67
Archipelago, 140, 196, 211
Arctic, 15, 19, 118-119
Arctic Circle, 112, 193
Arctic Institute Glacier, 218
Arctic Islands, 211
Arctic Ocean, 47, 48, 203, 206, 211, 222
Argentina, 14, 15, 67, 72, 78, 138, 150, 156, 159, 224, 238, 247, 258
Arizona, 16, 138, 171, 172, 179, 253, 259, 265
Arkansas, 247
Armenia, 78, 79, 133, 236
Artemis, Temple of, 263

Artesian well, 223
Ascension Island, 208
Ashanti, 122, 233
Ash tree, 165
Asia, 9, 29, 34, 35, 36, 38, 48, 109, 121, 123, 134, 165, 169, 215, 217, 220, 261, 290
   animals, 6, 11, 13
   biomes, 164, 166
   climate, 311, 313
   food, 154, 157, 158
   map 39, 54
Astrolabe, 201
Atacama Desert, 44
Athens, 241, 270
Atlanta, 254
Atlantic Intracoastal Waterway, 209
Atlantic Ocean, 34, 48, 203, 206, 208, 209, 265, 316, 318
Atlas, 189
Atmosphere, 309
Atoll, 196, 223
Auckland, 246
August, 96-97
Augustus, 190
Aurora borealis, 225
Australia, 9, 15, 17, 34, 35, 50, 51, 67, 69, 71, 72, 74, 76, 107, 108, 129, 170, 179, 212, 217, 222, 247, 266, 270, 321
   animals, 6, 11, 13
   biomes, 163, 164
   food, 154, 156
   landmarks, 258, 259, 259-260
   language, 137, 145
   music, 224, 232
Austria, 67, 73, 270
Austro-Asiatic languages, 134
Auyan-Tepuli Mountain, 259
Ayatollah, 292
Ayers Rock, 50, 258, 266
Azerbaijan, 76, 79
Azores, 208
Aztecs, 31, 78, 241, 258, 271
Azucena, 154

Babel, Tower of, 241
Babylon, 241, 262
Babylonia, 188, 241, 286
Baghdad, 262
Bagpipes, 224, 235, 236
Baha'ism, 277, 299
Bahrain, 75, 292

Bajau, 113
Balalaika, 224, 228, 236
Bald eagle, 6, 18, 19
Bali, 152
Balkan Peninsula, 48, 77, 235, 236
Balsam fir, 164
Baltimore, 255
Balto-Slavic languages, 133
Bamboo, 236, 237, 238
Bangkok, 247, 248
Bangladesh, 69, 71, 72, 73, 152, 243, 292, 315
Banjo, 228, 239
Bank (river), 219
Bantu, 110, 232
Baobab tree, 164, 170
Barbados, 159
Barents Sea, 213
Barley, 152, 157, 158
Basalt, 266
Basin, 196
Batavia, 251
Bats, 6, 8, 19, 154
Battle Creek, 284
Bay, 140, 196, 212, 213, 223, 259
Bay of Bengal, 213, 315
Bay of Fundy, 258, 259,
B.C., 274
Beach, 71, 196, 223
Bears, 6, 11, 13, 17, 18, 154
Beaufort wind scale, 313
Bed (river), 219
Beef, 155, 159
Beijing, 240, 243, 251, 270
Belarus, 75, 76, 79, 159
Belgium, 67, 75, 248, 249
Belize, 68, 78, 156
Benchmark, 201
Bengali language, 133, 136
Benguela Current, 209
Benham, Martin, 191
Berbers, 108, 116
Beret, 127
Bering Sea, 18, 213, 222
Bering Strait, 222
Berlin Wall, 79
Bermuda, 16, 208
Bermuda Triangle, 209
Bhutan, 76, 151
Bible, 279, 281, 283, 284, 285, 287
Bicycle, 71
Big Ben, 270
Bight, 196
Bilima, 116
Billionaires, 33
Bills (money), 30, 33
Bindi, 129

Biomes, 162, 163-166
Birds, 7, 8, 9, 12, 13, 18, 154
Birmingham, 253
Bison, 125
Bit, 33
Black, 122, 129
Black African languages, 134
Blackfoot River, 218
Blubber, 154
Blue, 122
Blue Grotto, 269
Body decorating, 120, 129-130, 131
Bog, 196
Bolivia, 67, 70, 78, 106, 108, 117, 156, 244, 249
Bombay, 243, 246, 251, 301
See also Mumbai
Bonin Trench, 204
Boreal forest, 164
Borglum, Gutzon, 267
Borneo, 106, 117, 131
Bosnia, 74, 77
Boston, 192, 283
Botswana, 74
Boundary Waters, 215
Bow, 229
Brahmanism, 278
Brasilia, 248
Brass instruments, 229
Brazil, 14, 33, 72, 108, 123, 159, 169, 179, 212, 224, 226, 238, 248, 258, 264, 268, 270
Brazil Current, 209
Breakfast, 156-157
Breton language, 133
Brides, 122, 123, 126
Bridges, 248, 264-265, 266
British Columbia, 303
British Guiana, 68
British Honduras, 68
British Isles, 208
Bronx, 16, 239, 242
Brook, 216, 219
Brooklyn, 242, 283
Brown, 122
Brunei, 33
Brussels, 248, 249
Bucks, 22
Budapest, 180
Buddha, 275, 293, 295, 299
Buddhism, 123, 131, 272, 276, 278, 279, 284, 293-295, 301, 304, 305, 307
Buenos Aires, 240, 247
Buffalo, NY, 161, 255
Bugle, 229
Buildings, 268
Bulgaria, 48, 77, 133, 156, 236
Bullfighting, 122, 246
Burma, 68, 78

Burundi, 74
Bushmen, 107
Butte, 197
Butterflies, 11, 17

Cactus, 163, 171
Cairo, 240, 276
Cajun, 224, 239
Cake, 149
Calcutta, 240, 250, 251, 264
Calendars, 10, 80, 81, 274
Calendula, 100
California, 17, 42, 169, 172, 179, 217, 252, 253, 254, 258, 265, 269, 311
California Current, 207
Calligraphy, 131
Calypso, 234
Cambodia, 78, 155, 270
Camels, 14, 115, 225, 240
Cameroon, 232
Canaan, 286, 289
Canada, 15, 17, 42, 68, 70, 71, 72, 73, 74, 111, 138, 148, 181, 193, 211, 212, 214, 245, 246, 247, 258, 259, 270
food, 148, 152
indigenous peoples, 108, 118-119
language, 136, 137
Canadian shield, 211
Canals, 214, 223, 246, 248, 264-265
Canary Islands, 192, 208
Canberra, 247
Cancer, Tropic of, 40
Canton, 198, 251
Canyon, 197, 259
Cape, 140, 196
Cape Horn, 44
Cape Town, 249, 250
Cape Verde Islands, 208
Capital cities, 59-66, 244, 249, 256-257
Capri, Isle of, 269
Capricorn, Tropic of, 40
Capybara, 6
Carcassonne, 246
Cardinal direction, 200
Carib, 108
Caribbean Islands, 108, 128, 157, 234, 245
Caribbean Sea, 213
Caribou, 11, 18, 118, 119
Carillon, 228
Cartier, Jacques, 221
Cartography, 188
Caspian Sea, 38, 214, 215
Cassava, 157, 161
Cassini, Jean-Dominique, 191
Catholics, 128, 277, 285
Catskill Mountains, 215

Cattle, 14, 31
Caves, 266, 269
Cay, 223
Cell phones, 244
Celtic languages, 133
Celtic music, 234-235
Central America, 42, 108, 245, 267, 276
Century, 80
Cereal, 149, 152-153, 164
Ceremonies, 120, 130, 232, 233, 234, 235, 302-303
Ceylon, 68
Chad, 74
Champlain, Samuel de, 222
Channels, 140, 197, 214, 216, 218, 219, 223
Chao Phraya River, 248
Chaparral, 162, 163
Chattahoochee River, 218
Cheetah, 6, 8, 13
Cherokee, 234
Cheyenne, 109
Chiba, 212
Chicago, 138, 161, 239, 254, 255, 267, 268
Chickens, 154, 155
Chile, 18, 67, 78, 108, 111, 117, 212, 270, 321
China, 8, 10, 14, 15, 16, 17, 19, 33, 37, 38, 52, 68, 69, 71, 72, 73, 76, 78, 108, 123, 127, 130, 169, 170, 176, 190, 212, 222, 243, 265, 266, 268, 270, 315
food, 149, 150, 152, 155, 156, 158
landmarks, 258, 266
languages, 134, 135, 137
money, 29, 31
music, 225, 235, 236
religion, 275, 276, 284, 293, 295, 299, 301
China Sea, 213
Chinese New Year, 123, 225
Chinook, 311
Chipaya, 106, 108, 117
Chocolate, 158, 166, 167
Choctaw, 138, 139, 234
Christianity, 242, 273, 274, 276, 277, 278, 279, 280-285, 283, 284, 296, 305, 306
Christian Science, 192
Christmas Island, 210
Chronometer, 201
Chrysanthemum, 102
Chrysler Building, 242
Chunnel, 264
Church of Christ, Scientist, 277, 283
Church of Jesus Christ, Latter-day Saints, 277,

283
Church of Scientology, 300
Churun River, 259
Cincinnati, 255
Cities, 240-255
capitals, 59-66, 249, 256-257
maps, 198
names, 246, 247, 250-251, 252-257
skyscrapers, 267, 268
smallest, 48
world, 243, 245-255
City, 198
Civilization, western, 241
Cleveland, 255
Cliff, 197
Climate, 42, 48, 163, 164, 165 166, 197, 308-321
Clinton, Bill, 229
Cloth, 125
Clothing, 120-131, 250
Clouds, 308
CN Tower, 270
Coastline, 48, 71, 140, 212
Cocoa beans, 29
Cocos Islands, 210
Code, 187
Coffee, 150, 156, 157, 158
Coins, 31, 33
Colombia, 18, 37, 78, 179, 238
Color, 122-123
Colorado, 138, 321
Colorado River, 218, 219, 220, 259, 265
Colosseum, 241, 271
Colossus of Rhodes, 263
Columbia River, 218
Columbus, 191
Comanche, 109
Communication, 132-147
Comoros Islands, 75, 129
Compass, 200
Compass rose, 189
Computers, 199, 312
Comstat, 199
Conakry, 243
Confucianism, 272, 273, 275, 278, 279, 284, 299, 301
Congo, 67, 74, 111, 232
Congo River, 216, 217
Conifer trees, 164, 165, 169, 172
Connecticut, 138, 252, 253
Constantinople, 251, 276, 282
Continental drift, 35
Continental movement, 37
Continental shelf, 204
Continental slope, 204
Continents, 34-51, 59-66
Contours, 196

Copenhagen, 245, 250
Coral, 7, 18
Coral island, 205, 223
Coral reefs, 50, 196, 223, 259
Coral Sea, 213
Coriolis effect, 310
Cork oak, 163, 170
Corn, 149, 152, 153, 157, 158
Cosmetics, 120, 122
Costa Rica, 138, 159
Cote d'Ivoire, 75
Cotton, 121, 171
Council oak, 172
Countries of the world, 23–28, 52–79, 137, 145, 156–161, 181–186, 198
Country, 198
Country music, 239, 252
County, 198
Cove, 223
Cows, 154, 297
Cree, 108, 139
Creek, 216, 219
Creole, 136, 239
Crime, 199
Croatia, 77
Crocodile, 8, 11, 13
Crow, 109
Crust, earth's, 35, 36
Crustaceans, 7, 12, 14
Cuba, 8, 160, 179, 181, 234
Cuna language, 139
Cuneiform, 38
Currency, 22, 23–28, 32
Currents, air, 312
Currents, ocean, 205, 207, 209, 210
Currents, wind, 310
Cyclones, 149, 308, 311, 315
Czechoslovakia, 79, 133, 236
Czech Republic, 79, 264

Daju, 131
Dakota, 138
Dalai Lama, 271, 295
Dallas, 253
Damascus, 244
Dams, 196, 215, 218, 264–265
Dance, 224–239
Dangle, 197
Danube River, 48, 220
Dead language, 136
Dead Sea, 36, 38, 214, 215
Death Valley, 42
December, 104–105
Deciduous forest, 165
Deforestation, 149, 164, 165, 166
Degree, 192
Dell, 197
Delta, 219, 220
Democratic Republic of the Congo, 68, 75

Denali National Park, 179
Denman Glacier, 218
Denmark, 48, 73, 74, 77, 133, 180, 245, 250, 266
Desert, 40, 41, 44, 50, 140, 162, 163, 179, 197, 321
    See also Specific desert, i.e. Sahara, Gobi
Desertification, 149, 163
DeSoto oak tree, 172
Destruction of animal habitats, 11, 15
Detroit, 252, 255, 300
Devil's Triangle, 209
Dhaka, 243
Dharma, 294
Diamond Coast, 212
Diamonds, 40, 88, 129
Diatom, 203
Dike, 196
Dinosaurs, 15
Direction, 200
District of Columbia, 249, 252
Djibouti, 40
Dogs, 10, 154, 250
Doldrums, 310
Dome of the Rock, 242, 276
Dominican Republic, 160, 234
Dover, England, 212
Drainage basin, 219
Dravidian languages, 134
Dreamtime, 302
Drinking water, 202, 215
Drinks, 150
D River, 218
Drought, 149, 313
Drums, 224, 225, 231, 232, 233, 234, 235, 236, 237, 238
Dublin, 247
Duluth, 255
Dune, 50, 197
Dutch language, 133

Eagles, 6, 18, 19
Earth, 34–47, 203, 207
Earthquakes, 34, 37, 149, 204, 263, 264, 315
East, 200
East Australian Current, 207
Easter Island, 270
Easterlies, 311
Eastern hemisphere, 194
Eastern Orthodox, 272, 273, 277, 282, 304
East Germany, 79
East Indies, 151
East Pacific Rise, 207
East Siberian Sea, 213
East Timor, 52
Ecosystems, 11
Ecuador, 18, 78, 127, 138,

179
Edo, 251
Education, 74
Eel, 9
Egypt, 15, 16, 31, 71, 78, 111, 121, 150, 171, 247, 253, 258, 262, 264, 267, 275, 286, 289
Eire, 67
Elephants, 7, 9, 11, 13, 16, 19, 68
Elevation, 197
El Greco, 250
El Nino, 313
El Salvador, 18, 74, 78
Emerald City, 254
Emerald Isle, 68
Empires, ancient, 78
Empire State Building, 242, 268
Endangered animals, 11–15, 16
Endangered parks, 179
Endangered rivers, 218
Endangered treasures, 71
England, 17, 31, 50, 69, 70, 79, 126, 130, 192, 194, 212, 253, 258, 264, 270
    See also United Kingdom
English Channel, 264
English language, 133, 135, 136, 137, 142–144, 145, 146
Ephesus, 263
Equator, 40, 44, 165, 192, 193, 194, 195, 261, 310
Equatorial Current, 207
Eratosthenes, 190, 191
Erie, Lake, 214, 255
Erosion, 163
Eritrea, 67, 74
Escarpment, 197
Esjahan, 243
Eskimos, 118–119, 126
    See also Inuit
Espana, 67
Esperanto, 134
Estonia, 75, 76, 79
Estuary, 140, 219
Ethiopia, 67, 74, 138, 160, 270, 321
Ethnocide, 106
Eucalyptus tree, 170, 232
Euphrates River, 262
Eurasia, 34, 48
Europe, 6, 11, 13, 31, 34, 48, 49, 56, 77, 112, 121, 158, 163, 166, 165, 176, 215, 217, 220, 221, 245, 261, 286
Everest, Mount, 36, 38, 258, 260
Everglades National Park, 179
Exotic river, 219

Extinction, 11–15, 179

Fabrics, 121
Falcon, peregrine, 9, 13, 242
Falkland Current, 209
Falkland Islands, 208
Famine, 149
Farsi language, 133
Fathom, 222
February, 84–85
Fertile Crescent, 38
Festivals, 148, 149, 225, 232, 235, 238, 291, 295, 298
Fiddle, 224, 226, 228, 229, 234, 236, 239
Fiji Islands, 29, 76, 137, 222
Finland, 68, 73, 76, 112, 126, 160, 226
Fires, 110–111, 163, 173
Fish, 7, 8, 9, 12, 18
Fjord, 212, 223
Flag code, international, 187
Flags, 180–187
Flat map, 195
Flood plain, 219
Floods, 163, 196, 219, 313, 315
Florida, 138, 161, 172, 179, 253, 254, 316
Flowers, 163, 173, 176, 177
Flute, 224, 230, 232, 233, 236, 237, 238
Foehn, 311
Folk music, 232, 235, 236, 239
Food, 148–161, 166, 167
Footwear, 126
Forbidden City, 243, 270
Foreign words and phrases, 146–147
Forests, 48, 162, 164, 165, 197
France, 33, 69, 70, 73, 74, 78, 127, 133, 191, 212, 249, 264, 269
    cities, 246, 250, 253
    food, 148, 152, 160
    music, 234–235
    religion, 287, 306
Freeze-dried food, 149
French Equatorial Africa, 68
French Guiana, 165
French language, 133, 135, 136, 137, 146
French Polynesia, 76
Fresh water, 46
Friday, 287, 291
Friends, Society of, 284
Fuji, Mount, 258, 261, 305
Fujita Tornado Scale, 320
Funerals, 122

Gabon, 68
Gaelic, 133

Galapagos Islands, 44
Galilee, Sea of, 214
Gallery of Maps, 192
Gambia, 233
Gandhi, Mahatma, 128
Ganges River, 216, 220, 298, 305
Gan language, 137
Gao, 194
Gardens, 262
GDP, 33
Geneva, 244
Genista Shallow, 210
Geodolite, 201
Geographical terms, 140-141, 196, 197, 198
Geography, 190, 191
Geophagy, 149
Georgia, 254
Georgia (country), 76, 79, 265
German language, 133, 136, 137
Germany, 14, 33, 67, 69, 70, 73, 74, 79, 124, 148, 159, 160
Geyser, 223
Ghana, 149, 194, 233, 270
Giants' Causeway, 266
Gibson Desert, 50
Giraffe, 6, 7, 19
Giza, 262
Glaciers, 202, 211, 214, 215, 216, 218, 223, 261
Global Positioning System, 201
Global warming, 166, 318
Globe, 191, 192, 195
Glowworm, 269
Gnaw Bone, 254
Goats, 10, 250
Gobi Desert, 163
God, 285, 290
Gold, 40
Golden Gate Bridge, 258, 265
Golden Rule, 278
Gondwana, 50
Gongs, 224, 225, 231, 236, 238
Gorge, 197
Goths, 263
GPS, 201
Grains, 31, 149, 152-153
Granada, 271
Grand Canal, 49, 222, 265
Grand Canyon, 179, 220, 258, 259
Grass, 152, 163, 164, 173, 197
Grasslands, 40, 44, 162, 163, 164
Gravity, 205
Great Barrier Reef, 50, 258, 259-260

Great Britain, 79, 145
Great European Plain, 48
Great Lakes, 42, 214, 221, 255
Great Pyramid, 258, 262, 267
Great Rift Valley, 40, 209
Great Sandy Desert, 50
Great Seal of the United States, 32
Great Smoky Mountains National Park, 179
Great Victoria Desert, 50
Great Wall of China, 190, 258, 262, 266, 270
Greece, 16, 48, 67, 70 75, 77, 78, 133, 241, 258, 261, 263, 270
Greece, ancient, 176, 275
Greek language, 133, 138, 139
Green, 180
Greenhouse effect, 318
Greenland, 42, 67, 68, 118, 148, 193, 203, 208, 211
Greenland problem, 195
Greenland Sea, 213
Greenwich, 192, 194
Gregorian calendar, 80, 81, 274
Grenada, 148
Gross Domestic Product, 33
Guam, 76
Guangzhou, 251
Guatemala, 78, 121, 270
Guinea, 18, 233, 243
Guitar, 228, 234, 237, 238
Gulch, 197
Gulf, 140, 212, 213, 223
Gulf of Alaska, 213
Gulf of Guinea, 213
Gulf of Mexico, 8, 42, 213
Gulf Stream, 16, 48, 203, 209
Gully, 197
Guyana, 68, 165, 181
Guyot, 205
Gypsies, 107

Habitat destruction, 11, 15
Hagia Sofia, 276
Hail, 321
Hair, 128
Haiti, 234, 302
Hakka language, 137
Haleakala National Park, 179
Halicarnassus, 263
Hallbank Shallow, 210
Hamlet, 243
Hanging Gardens of Babylon, 241, 262
Harare, 247, 251
Harmattan, 311

Harp, 226, 228, 233, 235
Hartford, 252
Harvest festivals, 148, 149
Hats, 127-128
Hawaii, 134, 179, 224, 237, 252, 321
Headwater, 216
Healing plants, 176
Hebrew language, 137, 287
Hebrews, 81, 286
Hemisphere, 192
Hemlock tree, 165, 176
Henna, 129
Hereford Mappa Mundi, 191
Hibernia, 67
Highest
  cities, 249
  lake, 44, 215
  mountain range, 38
  plateau, 38
  point in the world, 38
  point on land, 36
  waterfalls, 217
Highland, 197
Hill, 140, 197
Himalayan Mountains, 35, 38, 39, 216, 240, 260
Hindi language, 136, 137
Hindu calendar, 81
Hinduism, 124, 129, 133, 216, 220, 237, 272, 273, 275, 278, 279, 284, 296-298, 304, 305, 306, 307
Ho Chi Minh City, 247, 251
Holidays and events, 82-105, 124, 126
Holy City, 242
Holy days, 281, 287, 291
Honduras, 78
Hong Kong, 124, 212, 243, 244, 248, 251, 267, 268
Honshu Island, 267
Hoofed animals, 17
Hoover Dam, 265
Hopi, 109
Horse latitudes, 310
Horses, 10, 14, 29
Houston, 253, 267
Huang River, 217
Hudson Bay, 211, 213, 222
Hudson River, 220, 222
Hula, 224, 237
Humboldt Current, 207, 222
Hungarian language, 137
Hungary, 151, 160, 180, 236
Hunting, 11, 119
Huron, Lake, 214
Hurricanes, 308, 314, 315, 316, 317, 318
Hydroelectricity, 264
Hydrosphere, 202
Hypothermia, 314

Iban, 107, 109, 131
Iberian Peninsula, 48, 77
Iceberg, 211, 223
Ice cap, 46, 202, 203, 223
Ice cream, 149, 155
Iceland, 73, 127, 133, 193, 208, 209, 245
Ice sheet, 223
Ice stream, 217
Icons, 270-271
Idaho, 138, 179
Iguazu Falls, 258
Illinois, 138, 161, 254, 255, 258, 319
Imperial City, 243
Incas, 31, 78, 117, 271, 277
Inclinometer, 201
India, 8, 14, 15, 35, 37, 50, 67, 68, 70, 71, 72, 76, 78, 107, 109, 129, 169, 170, 171, 176, 179, 212, 216, 243, 250, 264, 265, 270, 313
  cities, 244, 246, 248, 250, 251
  clothing and adornment, 122, 124, 127, 128, 129
  food, 149, 151, 152, 154, 156, 166
  languages, 134, 137
  music, 224, 237
  religion, 284, 292, 293, 296, 299, 304, 305
Indiana, 254, 319
Indian Ocean, 50, 203, 206, 210
Indies, East, 151
Indigenous peoples, 106, 108-109, 130
Indo-European languages, 133
Indo-Iranian languages, 133
Indonesia, 33, 37, 38, 52, 69, 71, 72, 76, 109, 134, 152, 169, 170, 212, 224, 237, 238, 243, 251, 264, 271, 292
Indus River, 220
Indus Valley, 296
Inlet, 212
Insects, 7, 8, 12, 154
Instruments, mapping, 201
Instruments, musical, 171, 224, 226, 228-229, 230, 231, 236, 237
Intermediate direction, 200
International Date Line, 194
International Falls, 252
International flag code, 187
Intertropical convergence zone, 310
Intracoastal Waterway, Atlantic, 209

Inuits, 108, 109, 118-119, 131, 154, 188, 302
Inupiat, 118
Iowa, 172
Iran, 8, 70, 78, 121, 127, 243, 292, 299
Iraq, 18, 33, 241, 262, 286
Ireland, 67, 68, 69, 73, 79, 121, 129, 133, 145, 156, 181, 226, 234-235, 247, 266, 306
Iroquois language, 138-139
Irrigation, 220, 264
Islam, 128, 180, 242, 273, 274, 276, 278, 283, 284, 290-292, 296, 304, 305, 307
Islamabad, 249
Islands, 42, 71, 76, 140, 196, 204, 205, 208, 210, 248
Isle of Capri, 269
Israel, 38, 67, 73, 78, 137, 214, 215, 220, 242, 276, 280, 286, 287, 289, 299, 304
Istanbul, 244, 251
Isthmus, 77, 196
Italian language, 133, 137, 146
Italy, 37, 48, 70, 71, 73, 75, 78, 129, 132, 149, 152, 158, 181, 192, 246, 248, 250, 269, 271, 304
Ituri Forest, 107, 110-111
Ivory Coast, 249

Jainism, 275, 284, 299
Jakarta, 240, 243, 251, 264
Jakobshavns glacier, 211
Jamaica, 17, 67, 179, 224, 234, 300
January, 82-83
Japan, 15, 33, 37, 38, 67, 68, 69, 72, 73, 74, 76, 109, 123, 138, 179, 181, 212, 258, 261, 266, 267
    cities, 245, 251
    clothing and adornment, 122, 126, 130
    food, 148, 150, 152, 156
    languages, 132, 134
    music, 224, 236
    religion, 293, 300, 305
Japan, Sea of, 213
Japanese language, 136
Java, 271
Jazz, 233, 234, 239, 252
Jefferson, Thomas, 149, 267
Jehovah's Witnesses, 277, 283
Jersey City, 253
Jersey Island, 253
Jerusalem, 242, 289, 304
Jesus Christ, 242, 276, 280

Jet stream, 312
Jewel in the Crown, 68
Jewelry, 129
Jodhpur, 246, 250
Johannesburg, 240
Jordan, 38, 215, 220, 244, 271
Jordan River, 220
Judaism, 128, 239, 242, 272, 273, 274, 275, 277, 278, 279, 283, 284, 286-289, 304, 305, 306, 307
Judea, 289
July, 94-95
June, 92-93
Jungle, 165
Jutland Peninsula, 48

Kabul, 243
Kalahari, 107
Kamchatka Current, 207
Kangaroo, 6, 11, 13, 50, 154
Kansas, 138, 254, 321
Kansas City, 239, 254
Kara Sea, 213
Katmandu, 240
Kaya, 131
Kazakhstan, 68, 72, 76, 79, 150, 249
Kente cloth, 125
Kentucky, 247, 254, 269
Kenya, 261, 303
Kermadec Trench, 204
Kern River, 218
Kew Seed Bank, 179
Key, 223
Keyboard instruments, 230
Khoisan languages, 134
Kilimanjaro, 40, 261
Kill, 219
Kirghiz, 29
Kiribati, 76
Knot, 222
Koala bear, 6, 11, 170
Kobe, 212
Kolkata, 251
Komodo Island, 69
Koran, 248, 276, 279, 291
Korea, 73, 78, 134, 160, 276
Korean language, 136
Krakatau, 37
Kuala Lumpur, 267, 268
Kuroshio Current, 207
Kuwait, 33, 77
Kyrgyzstan, 76, 79

Labrador Current, 209
Lagoon, 141, 223
Lagoon of Venice, 248
Lagos, 240, 243
Lake Assal, 40
Lake Baikal, 214, 215
Lake Champlain, 222
Lake Erie, 214, 255

Lake Huron, 214
Lake Issyk Kul, 215
Lake Mead, 265
Lake Michigan, 255
Lake Nyasa, 215
Lake Ontario, 255
Lake Superior, 214, 215, 255
Lake Tanganyika, 215
Lake Texcoco, 241
Lake Titicaca, 44, 215
Lake Victoria, 214
Lake Vostok, 215
Lakes, 38, 42, 44, 202, 214-215, 223, 265
    See also Seas
    See also Specific names
Lanbert-Fisher Glacier, 218
Land, 36
Land down under, 51
Landmarks, world, 258-271
Landmasses, 34-47
Land of the Midnight Sun, 68
Land of the Rising Sun, 68
Languages, world, 132-147, 287
La Nina, 313
Laos, 18, 76
La Paz, 244, 249
Lapland, 112, 160
La Plata-Parana River, 216
Lapps, 107, 109, 112, 122
Largest
    animals, 7
    archipelago, 211
    desert, 40
    island, 42, 208
    lakes, 38, 42, 214
    river, 44
    tropical area, 40
    tropical rainforest, 44
Lascaux Cave, 269
Laser, 201
Las Vegas, 252, 254
Latin America, 157, 238
Latin language, 146
Latitude, 190, 191, 192, 193, 195
Latvia, 75, 76, 79, 133
Lauca River, 117
Laurentian Divide, 211
Lava, 266
Lava Beds National Monument, 269
Leaning tower of Pisa, 271
Lebanon, 160, 292
Legend, 189
Lemon, 148, 158, 167
Lena River, 217
Leningrad, 251
Leopards, 6, 11, 13, 15
Levee, 219
Lewis and Clark, 172
Lhasa, 244, 249, 271

Liberia, 110, 160
Libya, 116, 180, 247, 321
Liechtenstein, 33, 74, 76, 245
Lighthouse of Alexandria, 264
Lima, 244
Linen, 121, 126
Lion, 13, 18, 225
Lisbon, 264, 271
Lithuania, 75, 76, 79, 133
Livestock, 153
Livingston, David, 260
Locks, 214
London, 194, 199, 221, 240, 253, 270
Longest
    canal, 222
    coastline, 212
    mountain chain, 44
    rivers, 40, 217
Longitude, 190, 191, 192, 194, 195, 201
Los Angeles, 239, 240, 252, 253
Louisiana, 152, 161, 170, 224, 239, 252, 253
Lower Snake River, 218
Lowest
    lake, 215
    points in the world, 36, 38
Lute, 226, 228, 236, 237
Luxembourg, 33, 74, 249

Macedonia, 77, 78
Machu Picchu, 258, 271
Mackenzie River, 222
McKinley, Mt., 42
Madagascar, 50, 68, 134, 156, 169, 210
Madeira, 208
Madras, 250
Madrid, 240
Magellan, Ferdinand, 206, 222
Magical Lagoon, 209
Magnetic field, 200, 201
Mahogany, 163, 166
Maine, 16, 252
Malagasy Republic, 68
Malay/Indonesian language, 136
Malayo-Polynesian languages, 134
Malaysia, 17, 109, 125, 170, 258, 268
Maldives, 67, 74, 210
Mali, 74, 116, 194, 233, 240
Malta, 74, 124
Mammals, 7, 8, 9, 12, 13, 14, 19, 154
Mammoth-Flint Caves, 269
Mandarin language, 136,

137, 138
Mandolin, 228, 236, 238
Manhattan, 242
Manitoba, 17
Maori, 109, 130
Map grid, 189
Map index, 189, 190
Maple tree, 165, 167
Mapmaking, 190-191
Mapparium, 192
Maps, 188-201
  Africa, 41, 53
  Al Murrah, 115
  ancient empires, 78
  Antarctica, 47
  Asia, 39, 54
  Australia, 51
  Bajau areas, 113
  calendars of the world,
    80
  clothing, 120
  collections and museums,
    192
  countries of the world,
    52, 76
  currency, 22
  cylones, 315
  earth's tectonic plates, 34
  elements of , 189
  endangered species, 13
  Europe, 49, 56
  indigenous peoples, 106
  instruments, 201
  Inuits, 118
  kinds of , 191, 195, 196-199
  landmarks, 258
  languages, 32, 136
  Lapps, 112
  Mbuti, 110
  nomads, 110, 112, 113, 114,
    115, 116, 118
  North America, 43, 57
  Oceania, 55
  oceans of the world, 202
  peninsular neighbors, 77
  religions, 272, 286, 304
  South America, 45, 58
  tradewinds and currents,
    310
  Tuaregs, 116
  winds, 308
  world biomes, 162
  world population
    density, 72
Maputo, 243
March , 86-87
Marco Polo, 188
Mariachi, 224, 238
Mariana Trench, 36, 204,
  207
Marshall Islands, 76, 188
Martinique, 37, 234
Maryland, 255
Masai, 107, 108, 303

Massachusetts, 33, 172 ,
  253, 301
Massis, 261
Mauritania, 14
Mausoleum, 244
Mausoleum at
  Halicarnassus, 263
May, 90-91
Mayas, 31, 78, 108, 109, 131,
  267, 270, 276
Mbube, 224
Mbuti, 108, 110-111, 233
Meanders, 219
Meat-eating plants, 178
Mecca, 276, 290, 291, 304
Medicine, 166, 176-177
Mediterranean Sea, 48, 212,
  213, 311
Megalopolis, 243
Mekong River, 217
Memphis, TN, 239
Men, 75
Mennonites, 284
Mercator, 191, 195
Merengue, 234
Meridian, 192, 194
Mesa, 197, 259
Mesopotamia, 289
Methodism, 277
Metropolitan areas, 240,
  243
Mexico, 14, 15, 17, 33, 42,
  70, 78, 109, 123, 131, 176,
  179, 209, 238, 241, 258,
  260, 265, 271
  cities, 246, 250
  clothing, 127
  food, 150, 151, 155, 160
  music, 224, 238
Mexico City, 240, 241
Miami language, 138
Michigan, 252, 253, 255
Micmac, 108
Micronesia, 76
Mid-Atlantic Ridge, 209
Middle East, 149, 157, 158,
  173, 284, 290
Midway Island, 17
Mile, 222
Millet, 157, 158
Milwaukee, 255
Minbei language, 137
Minnan language, 137
Minneapolis, 254
Minnesota, 152, 179, 215,
  247, 252, 254, 255
Minute, 192
Mississippi River, 42, 217,
  218, 254
Missouri, 247, 254, 319
Missouri River, 42, 217, 218
Mixed forest, 197
Mohican language, 138
Mojave National Preserve,

179
Moldova, 79
Molleweid map, 195
Monaco, 74, 244
Money, 22-33
Mongefossen Falls, 217
Mongol, 78, 107, 108
Mongolia, 76, 111, 226
Monkeys, 10, 13
Mon-Khmer languages, 134
Monsoon, 311
Montana, 179, 254
Monte Carlo, 244
Montenegro, 77
Months, 81, 82-105, 274
Montreal, 221
Moon, full, 82, 84, 86, 88,
  90, 92, 94, 96, 98, 100,
  102, 104, 295
Moors, 124
Mormon, 272
Morocco, 248
Moscow, 240, 244, 271
Moses, 275, 286, 289
Mosque, 271, 276, 291, 300,
  305
Mountains, 38, 42, 44, 46,
  141, 197, 260, 261
  See also Specific names,
    i.e. Kilimanjaro
Mount Everest, 36, 38, 258,
  260
Mount Fuji, 258, 261, 305
Mount McKinley, 42
Mount Rushmore, 267
Mount Sinai, 289
Mount Washington, 321
Mouth (of river), 216, 219
Movement of the conti-
  nents, 37
Movies, 71, 252
Mozambique, 232, 243
Muhammad, 242, 274, 276,
  290, 291, 304
Mumbai, 240, 246, 248, 251
  See also Bombay
Mummies, 71, 122
Municipality, 198
Murray-Darling River, 217
Museums, 180, 192, 243
Musical instruments, 171,
  224, 226, 228, 229, 230,
  231, 237
Music box, 228, 236
Music of the spheres, 225
Music of the world, 224 -
  239, 252
Muslims, 81, 127, 128, 272,
  290, 291, 292
Myanmar, 67, 68, 76, 110,
  293

Namibia, 74, 163
NASA, 149

Nashville, TN, 239, 252
National Hurricane Center,
  316
Nationality, 59-66
National Parks, United
  States, 179
National Weather Center,
  316
Nation of Islam, 300
Native Americans, 29, 109,
  119, 122, 123, 125, 129, 302
  food, 148, 153, 155
  languages, 134, 138-139
  music, 233, 234
  plants, 173, 176
Natural wonders of the
  world, 221
Nauru, 76
Nautical mile, 222
Navajo, 109
Ndebele language, 137
Nebraska, 254
Negro River, 216
Neighbors, 76-77
Nepal, 38, 76, 120, 151, 240,
  258, 304
Nests, 19, 154
Netherlands, 67, 70, 73,
  126, 127, 156, 160, 212,
  250, 271
Nevada, 172 , 252, 254
New Caledonia, 18, 76
Newfoundland, 71
New Guinea, 8, 18, 130, 173
New Hampshire, 321
New Hebrides, 68
New Jersey, 253, 254
New London, 253
New Mexico, 303
New Orleans, 161, 239, 252,
  253
New South Wales, 321
Newspapers, 71
New Testament, 279, 281,
  284
New World, 191
New York, 16, 161, 252, 253,
  255
New York City, 220, 240,
  242, 252, 253, 254, 258,
  266, 267, 268, 271
New Zealand, 37, 50, 76,
  109, 130, 134, 212, 222,
  246, 269
Nez Perce, 109
Niagra Falls, 42, 258
Nicknames, 68, 246
Niger, 74, 75, 116
Nigeria, 40, 72, 73, 124,
  232, 233, 243
Niger-Kordofanian lan-
  guages, 134
Niger River, 217, 220, 240
Nile River, 40, 217, 218, 219,

289
Nilo-Saharan languages, 134
Nimrod-Lennox-King Glacier, 218
Nixon, Richard, 229
Noah's Ark, 261
Nobel Peace Prize, 245
Nomads, 106-119, 130, 225
Norden, 77
North, 200
North America, 6, 8, 9, 11, 13, 29, 34, 35, 37, 42, 43, 57, 158, 163, 164, 165, 166, 188, 217, 220, 221, 245
North Atlantic Drift, 209
Northern Hemisphere, 192, 193, 311, 315
Northern Ireland, 79
Northern lights, 225
Northern Mariana Islands, 76
Northern Rhodesia, 68
North Korea, 76
North Pacific Drift, 207
North Pole, 47, 193, 194, 201
Norway, 8, 33, 48, 68, 69, 73, 74, 75, 76, 77, 112, 133, 148, 160, 193, 212, 217, 271
Norwegian Sea, 213
Novaya Zemlya Glacier, 218
November, 102-103
Nuclear waste, 218
Nutmeg, 151, 167
Nyasat, Lake, 215

Oak tree, 165, 172
Oasis, 163
Ob-Irtysh River, 217
Oboe, 230, 235, 236, 237
Oceania, 29, 55, 76, 245
Oceans, 13, 36, 162, 202, 204-205, 206, 210, 211, 312
    See also Specific names
October, 100-101
Oglala, 109
Ohio, 253, 254, 255
Ohio River, 42
Oil, 265
Ojibwa language, 139
Old Testament, 279, 281, 287, 288, 289, 300
Old World, 191
Olympia, 263
Olympic Games, 263
Olympus, 261
Omaha language, 139
Oman, 74, 75, 77
Orange, 167
Oregon, 218
Origins of city names, 247

Orinoco River, 216
Orleans, 250, 253
Orthodox Christian, 307
Ottawa, 247
Oxygen, 162
Oyashio Current, 207
Ozone, 11, 309

Pacific Ocean, 37, 50, 188, 193, 194, 203, 204, 206-207, 265, 316
Painting, 269
Painting, body, 120, 129-130
Pakistan, 14, 67, 68, 72, 157, 171, 249, 292
Palau, 29, 76
Palestine, 287, 289, 304
Palm tree, 163, 164, 166, 169
Pampa, 164
Panama, 42, 127, 179, 258
Panama Canal, 258, 265
Panda bear, 6, 11, 13, 17
Pangaea, 34, 35
Panpipes, 224, 230, 236, 238
Papago language, 138
Paper, 31, 166
Papua New Guinea, 76, 110, 165
Parallel, 192, 193
Parana River, 217
Paricutin Volcano, 260
Paris, 221, 246
Parrot, 11, 13
Parsis, 301
Parthenon, 258, 270
Pashto language, 133
Pass, 141
Pawnee, 109
Peak, 141
Pedi language, 137
Peking, 251
Pelee, Mt., 37
Penan, 106, 109, 117
Peninsula, 48, 77, 141, 196
Pennsylvania, 247, 252, 253, 254, 284
Percussion instruments, 231
Periods of time, 81
Permafrost, 166
Persia, 70, 301
    See also Iran
Peru, 31, 37, 78, 111, 117, 148, 149, 150, 151, 154, 179, 224, 238, 244, 258, 271
Peru Current, 207, 222
Peter Stuyvesant pear tree, 172
Petitcodiac River, 259
Petra, 244, 271
Petronas Towers, 258, 268
Pharos, 264
Philadelphia, 253, 254
Philippine Islands, 8, 29,

37, 38, 113, 134, 137, 150, 154, 155
Philippine Sea, 213
Philippine Trench, 204
Phoenix, 253
Phones, 244
Physical maps, 196-197
Piano, 229, 230
Pidgin English, 136
Pigs, 10, 14, 18, 29, 154
Pilipino language, 137
Pine tree, 164, 165, 169, 172
Pinto Creek, 218
Pisa, 271
Pitcairn Islands, 76
Pittsburg, 252
Place names, 138-139
Plain, 141, 197
Plants, 11, 12, 162-179
Plateau, 38, 141, 197
Plates, earth, 35, 37
Plate tectonics, 35
Plymouth, 253
Poaching, 15
Pocomoke River, 218
Point Barrow, 252
Poisonous animals, 9, 19
Poisonous plants, 176-177
Poland, 14, 67, 73, 76, 133, 236
Polar bears, 13, 17, 19, 154
Polar desert, 166
Polar regions, 42
Polawatomi language, 138
Political maps, 198
Pollution, 30, 166, 179, 218
Polo, Marco, 188
Polynesia, 237
Pond, 223
Pongola Reserve, 16
Population, 50, 72, 75, 240, 243, 253
Ports, 141, 212, 246
Portugal, 48, 73, 77, 123, 170, 226, 264, 271
Portuguese language, 133, 135, 136
Possession, 198
Potatoes, 148, 149, 155, 157, 158, 159
Potomac River, 220
Power generation, 202
Powwow, 234
Prague, 264
Prairie, 164, 197
Preservatives, 151
Pretoria, 249
Prevailing winds, 310
Prime Meridian, 192, 194
Prince Edward Island, 210
Projection, 195
Protestants, 272, 273, 277, 285
Province, 198

Prudhoe Bay, 265
Ptolemy, 31, 190, 192, 264
Puerto Rico, 224, 234
Puerto Rico Trench, 208
Punjabi language, 136
Purple, 122, 123
Pygmies, 107, 110-111, 233 108
Pyongyang, 264
Pyramids, 262, 267
    See also Great Pyramid
Pyrenees Mountains, 48

Qatar, 33, 75, 77
Quadrant, 201
Quakers, 277, 284
Quebec, 127, 136, 222, 245
Queens, NY, 242
Quoddy Head, 252
Qur'an, 279, 291

Rabbits, 10, 250
Rachel Carson National Wildlife Reserve, 16
Radar, 312
Railroad, 244
Rain, 308, 313
Rainfall, 110, 111, 321
Rain forest, 117, 162, 165
    See also Tropical rain forest
Rapid City, 267
Rapids, 219
Rastafarian, 128, 300
Ravine, 197
Rawinsondes, 312
Recordholders, 7-9, 19
Red, 123, 129
Red list, 179
Red Sea, 286, 289
Red Square, 258, 271
Redwood tree, 165, 169
Reefs, 18, 223
Reformation, 277, 285
Reggae, 224, 234
Reggane, 194
Reindeer, 17, 112, 160
Reliefs, 196
Religions, world, 38, 128, 272-307
Religious music, 239
Reptiles, 7, 8, 9, 12, 13, 18
Republic of Ireland, 79
Reservoir, 215
Reversing Falls, 259
Revolution of the earth, 36
Reykjavik, 245
Rhine River, 48, 220
Rhinoceros, 11, 13, 15
Rhodes, 263, 264
Rhythm, 232, 233
Rhythm-and-blues, 234, 239
Rialto Bridge, 49

Rice, 149, 150, 152, 157, 158
Rill, 216
Ring of Fire, 37
Rio de Janeiro, 264, 270
Rio Grande River, 221
Rituals, 120
Rivers, 40, 42, 44, 48, 141, 202, 216-217, 218, 219, 220-221
  See also Specific names
Rivulet, 216
Roads, 190
Robinson map, 195
Rochester, 255
Rock, 50, 266
Rock 'n 'roll, 234, 239
Rocky Mountains, 18, 42, 311
Roman Catholic, 272, 273, 277, 282, 304, 306, 307
Romance languages, 133
Roman empire, 78
Romania, 133, 137, 161, 180, 236
Romansh language, 137
Rome, 31, 192, 240, 241, 245, 271
Rome, ancient, 70, 128, 176, 275
Rooftop of the World, 68
Roosevelt, Theodore, 267
Ross Sea, 222
Rotation of the earth, 36
Rotterdam, 212
Rub' al Khali, 115
Run, 219
Rural area, 243
Rushmore, Mount, 267
Russia, 15, 17, 29, 33, 68, 72, 73, 75, 76, 78, 79, 111, 112, 133, 193, 212, 218, 258, 271, 287
  cities, 244, 247, 251, 253
  food, 152, 157, 160, 161
  music, 224, 236
Russian language, 136
Rwanda, 74
Ryuku Islands, 70

Sagarmatha, 260
Sago, 117
Sahara Desert, 40, 41, 116, 149, 225, 232, 240, 311
Saigon, 251
St. Augustine, 254
St. Helena, 208
St. John, 259
St. Lawrence River, 221
St. Lawrence Seaway, 214
St. Paul, 254
St. Petersburg, 247, 251, 253
St. Vincent and the Grenadines, 181
Salisbury, 251
Salsa, 224, 234

Salt Lake City, 283
Salt water, 212
Samba, 224, 226, 238
Sami, 109, 112
Samoa, 131
San Antonio, 253
Sand, 50, 204
San Diego, 253
San Francisco, 254, 265
Sanskrit, 39, 296
Santa Ana winds, 308, 311
Santiago, 240
Sao Paulo, 240, 264, 268
Sarawak, 107, 117
Sargasso Sea, 212
Satellites, 201, 312, 316
Saudi Arabia, 33, 75, 77, 290, 304
Savanna, 164, 197
Saxophone, 229, 230
Scale, 199
Scale bar, 189
Scandinavia, 109, 130
Scandinavian Peninsula, 48, 77
Scarification, 131
Scatterometer, 312
Scientology, 300
Scotland, 16, 69, 70, 79, 121, 122, 124, 161, 234-235, 306
Scrubland, 197
Sea, 212, 213
  See also Lakes
  See also Specific name
Sea anemone, 19
Sea breeze, 312
Sea level, 196, 203
Seals, 19, 154
Sea of Galilee, 214
Sea of Japan, 213
Sea of Okhotsk, 213
Sears Tower, 258, 268
Seattle, 239, 254, 255
Seawater, 204, 205
Second, 192
Second City, 254
Seeds, 179
Seiche, 215
Seine River, 221
Selcuk, 263
Seleucia, 241
Senegal, 18, 233
Senne River, 248
Seoul, 240
September, 98-99
Sequoia tree, 165, 169
Serbia, 77, 79, 236
Serbo-Croatian language, 133
Seven natural wonders of the world, 259-260
Seven seas, 206
Seventh-Day Adventist, 284

Seven wonders of the ancient world, 262-264
Sewage, 179
Sextant, 201
Seychelles, 40, 169, 210
Shakers, 277
Shallows, 210
Shaman, 302, 307
Shanghai, 240, 268
Shetland Islands, 69
Shifting cultures, 107
Shi Huangdi, 266
Shintoism, 272, 275, 300, 305
Ships and flags, 187
Shoes, 126
Shoreline, 204, 214
Shoshone, 109, 138
Siam, 68
Siberia, 17, 68, 118, 222, 321
Sierra Nevada Mountains, 169
Sikhism, 128, 273, 277, 301, 306
Silk, 121, 126
Simpson Desert, 50
Singapore, 76, 124, 212
Sino-Tibetan languages, 134
Sioux City, Iowa, 172
Sioux Indians, 109, 138, 139, 172
Sirocco, 311
Sitar, 224, 228, 237
Skyscrapers, 242, 267, 268
Sloth, 9, 11, 13
Slovakia, 79, 133
Slovenia, 133
Snails, 12, 14, 160
Snakes, 8, 9, 10, 19, 176
Snow, 308, 321
Snowmobiles, 179
Society of Friends, 284
Soil erosion, 163
Solomon Islands, 76, 136, 165
Solstice, 193
Somalia, 14, 74, 108
Sotho language, 137
Source (river), 216
South, 200
South Africa, 40, 129, 137, 179, 217, 224, 233, 249, 250
South America, 8, 9, 29, 31, 34, 35, 37, 44, 50, 67, 70, 109, 121, 165, 171, 176, 215, 222, 245, 259, 313
  animals, 6, 11, 13
  biomes, 163, 164
  food, 154, 158, 166
  highlights, 44-45
  map, 45, 58
  rivers, 216, 217, 218

South Carolina, 152, 247
South Dakota, 267
Southeast Asia, 8
Southern hemisphere, 50, 193, 311, 315
South Georgia Islands, 208
South Korea, 149, 181, 264
South Pacific Islands, 154
South Pole, 46, 47, 193, 194
Spain, 48, 73, 77, 78, 122, 179, 161, 170, 245, 250, 253, 269, 271, 276
Spanish language, 133, 135, 136, 138, 139
Species, 7, 12, 13
Spelunker, 269
Spices, 31, 148, 151
Sports, 70, 168, 264
Sri Lanka, 18, 19, 38, 67, 68, 134, 151, 169, 170, 210, 295
Stadiums, 264
Starvation, 149
State animals, 20-21
Staten Island, 242
States, U.S., 174-175, 198, 256-257
Statue of Liberty, 271
Statue of Zeus, 263
Statues, 263, 266, 270
Steppe, 164
Stockholm, 245
Stonehenge, 258, 270
Storms, 181, 314, 315-320
Storm surge, 315
Strait, 141, 223
Strait of Magellan, 222
Streets, 254
Stringed instruments, 226, 228, 229, 235, 236, 237
Suburban area, 243
Subway, 242
Sudan, 14, 40, 72
Sumerians, 38
Summer solstice, 193
Sun, 201, 308
Sunday, 281
Supercell, 318
Supercontinent, 35
Superior, 255
Suriname, 107, 165
Suspension bridge, 265, 266
Svalbard, 193, 208, 211
Swamp, 197
Swaziland, 74, 249
Swazi language, 137
Sweden, 48, 68, 69, 73, 74, 75, 77, 112, 133, 160, 161, 226, 245
Sweet potatoes, 157, 158
Switzerland, 33, 69, 73, 137, 181, 244, 265
Sydney, 240, 247, 270

Symbols, 18
Synoptic-scale circulations, 311
Syria, 78, 244

Tahiti, 130
Tai Chi, 301
Taiga, 162, 164, 165
Taiwan, 38, 76, 268
Tajikistan, 74, 76, 79, 265
Taj Mahal, 244, 258, 270
Tamil language, 134, 137
Tanganyika, 79
Tango, 224, 238
Tanjung Karang, 243
Tanzania, 15, 40, 79, 232, 261, 303
Taoism, 272, 275, 278, 284, 301, 307
Tasmania, 8, 69, 222
Tasmanian devil, 69
Tasmanian tigers, 11, 69
Tasman Sea, 222
Tattooing, 120, 129, 130
Tea, 29, 150
Tectonic plates, 34
Teeth, 29
Telephone, 132
Televisions, 74
Telugu language, 134
Temperate forest, 162, 165
Temperature, 111, 252, 314, 321
Temple of Artemis, 263
Ten Commandments, 286, 287, 289
Tennessee, 179, 252
Tenochtitlan, 241, 271
Terrace, 197
Terra-cotta army, 266
Territorial waters, 212
Territory, 198
Texas, 239, 253
Thailand, 8, 68, 78, 123, 129, 152, 154, 170, 246, 247, 248, 293, 295
Thames River, 221
Thematic maps, 199
Thousand Islands, 148
Threatened species, 11, 13, 14, 179
Three dog night, 50
Thunderstorms, 318, 320
Tiananmen Square, 243
Tibet, 19, 52, 68, 108, 123, 224, 244, 249, 258, 260, 267, 271, 275, 276, 293, 295, 304
Tidal waves, 34, 204
Tides, 205, 258, 259
Tidewater, 196
Tierra del Fuego, 67
Tigers, 13, 1011
Tijuana, 246

Timber, 169, 170
Timbuktu, 240
Time, 81, 194
Timeline
    continental drift, 35
    world religions, 275-277
Titicaca, Lake, 44
Tokyo, 240, 245, 251
Toledo, 245, 250, 253
Tomb, 263
Tonga, 76, 125
Tonga Trench, 204
Topographical maps, 196-197
Torah, 287
Tornadoes, 318, 320
Toronto, 240, 270
Torrid zone, 193
Tortoise, 9, 44
Tourists, 179
Tournachon, Gaspard-Felix, 191
Tower of Babel, 241
Town, 243
Trade winds, 310
Trans-Alaska Pipeline, 265
Transantarctic Mountains, 46
Transcendental meditation, 298
Transportation, 202, 209, 216, 220, 264
Trans-Siberian Railway, 244
Transylvania, 236
Treasures, endangered, 71
Trees, 164, 165, 166, 167, 169, 170, 172, 173, 174-175
Trench, 204
Triangulation, 191
Tribal movement, 119
Tributary, 216, 219
Triceratops, 15
Trinidad, 150, 234
Tripoli, 247
Tristan de Cunha, 208
Tromelin Island, 210
Tropical area, 40
Tropical grassland, 164
Tropical rain forest, 40, 44, 110, 111, 165, 166, 169, 259
    See also Rain forests
Tropical storms, 314, 315
Tropic of Cancer, 40, 193
Tropic of Capricorn, 40, 193
Truman, Harry S., 229
Trumpet, 229, 238
Tsunami, 204, 205
Tuareg, 108, 116, 225
Tugela Falls, 217
Tundra, 162, 166, 197
Tunisia, 271
Tunnels, 264
Turkestan, 78
Turkey, 8, 31, 37, 48, 69,

77, 152, 157, 161, 179, 236, 244, 250, 251, 261, 263, 304
Turkmenistan, 79
Turtles, 8, 9, 11, 17
Tuvalu, 76
Twin Cities, 254
Typhoon, 314, 315

Uganda, 75, 232
Ukraine, 75, 76, 79, 133, 271, 287
Union of Soviet Socialist Republics, 52, 79
Unitarian Universalism, 301
United Arab Emirates, 74, 75, 77
United Kingdom, 70, 73, 79, 137, 181, 224, 266
    See also England
United Nations, 180
United States, 9, 14, 15, 18, 33, 37, 42, 68, 69, 70, 72, 73, 74, 76, 109, 128, 169, 170, 171, 172, 179, 181, 212, 214, 217, 218, 239, 258, 268, 271, 318
    cities, 243, 247, 249, 252-257, 254
    clothing and adornments, 122, 127, 130
    food, 149, 150, 152, 153, 155, 157, 159
    language, 137, 145, 146
    money, 30, 32
    religion, 286, 287
    state animals, 20-21
Upland, 197
Uralic-Altaic languages, 134
Urban area, 243
Urdu language, 133, 136, 137, 139
USSR See Union of Soviet Socialist Republics
Utigard Falls, 217
Uzbekistan, 74, 76, 79, 171

Vaduz, 245
Valdez, 265
Valley, 141, 197, 202
Vancouver, 246
Vanuatu, 18, 29, 68, 76
Vatican City, 48, 67, 192, 245, 304
Vegetation, 197
Veld, 164
Venda, 137
Venezuela, 67, 114, 130, 217, 238, 258, 259
Venice, 49, 246, 248, 250
Verrazano Narrows Bridge, 266
Vespucci, Amerigo, 191
Vesuvius, 37

Victoria Falls, 221, 258, 260
Vienna, 161, 270
Vietnam, 76, 78, 151, 152, 157, 247, 251, 293, 315
Village, 243
Virginia, 31, 253
Vladivostok, 244
Volcanoes, 34, 37, 205, 260, 269, 315
Volga River, 217
Voodoo, 302
Voyageurs National Park, 179

*W*ailing Wall, 242, 289
Waitomo Cave, 269
Wales, 79, 133, 157, 234-235, 306
Walled city, 245, 246
Walnut tree, 165, 167
Walrus, 154
Walvis Ridge, 209
Wampum, 29, 33
War, 149
Washington, 17, 254, 255
Washington, D.C., 192, 249, 252, 284
Washington, George, 172, 242, 267
Water, 196, 215, 202-223
Waterfalls, 42, 44, 217, 223, 258, 259, 260
Waterfowl, 8, 16
Water pollution, 179
Waterspout, 321
Water transportation, 216, 220
Waves, 204
Wealth, 33
Weather, 308-321
Weather map, 191, 199
Weather vane, 312
Weaving, 121, 125
Well, artesian, 223
West, 200
West Africa, 224
West Australian Current, 210
Westerlies, 310
Western civilization, 48, 241
Western hemisphere, 194
Western Samoa, 76
Western Wall, 242, 289
West Germany, 79
West Indies, 8, 208
West Virginia, 247, 254
West Wind Drift, 207
Wetland, 196
Whales, 7, 8, 9, 11, 13, 17, 18, 154, 209
Wheat, 149, 152, 153, 157, 158
White, 122
White Cliffs of Dover, 212
Wigs, 127, 128
Wildflowers, 163

Wildlife education, 16
Wildlife refuges, 14
Wind, 204, 308, 310-314, 321
Wind chill, 314
Wind instruments, 229
Windmills, 271
Wind shear, 312
Wine, 150
Winter solstice, 193
Wisconsin, 152, 254, 255
Women, 75, 288
Wonders of the world, 221, 258
Woodstock, 253
Woodwind instruments, 230
Words, borrowed, 142-144
Words and phrases, foreign, 146-147

World countries, 52-79
World cities, 240-255
World Conservation Society, 16
World Conservation Union, 179
World Council of Churches, 277
World languages, 140-141
See also Languages, world
World music, 232-239
World records, 110, 111, 169, 169, 170, 172 , 173
World religions, 272-307
World Trade Center, 242, 258, 268
Worms (city), 7, 254
Wu language, 137

Wyoming, 179

Xianggang, 251
Xiang language, 137
Xylophone, 231, 232, 233, 238

Yalta, 271
Yam, 157, 158, 176
Yangtze River, 217, 218, 222
Yellow, 123
Yellowstone National Park, 179
Yemen, 77
Yoga, 296, 297
York, 253
Yosemite Falls, 217
Yue language, 137
Yugoslavia, 48, 79, 236

Yuit, 118
Yupik, 118

Zaire, 68
Zambezi River, 221, 260
Zambia, 68, 260
Zanzibar, 79
Zebra, 13
Zeus, Statue of, 263
Zimbabwe, 67, 74, 137, 233, 247, 251, 260
Zionism, 277
Zither, 226, 228, 236
Zoos, 16, 16-17
Zoroastrianism, 275, 278, 301
Zulu, 137, 233
Zuni, 109
Zydeco, 224, 239

Photo credits:

Page 85 (Lincoln): © National Portrait Gallery, Smithsonian Institution; page 87 (Einstein): © National Archive; pages 101 (Columbus), 105 (Franklin), 190 (map of pilgrim routes), 200 (early compass), 201 (early quadrant, astrolabe, and sextant), 222 (Magellan), 276 (destruction of temple), 277 (Martin Luther, Inquisition): © North Wind Picture Archives; page 110 (Pygmy hut): © John Moss; page 111 (Pygmies): © E.E. Kingsley; page 113 (Bajau boats): © Fritz Prenzel; page 116 (Tuaregs): © Victor Englebert; pages 172 (Hernando de Soto), 222 (de Champlain), 300 (Malcolm X): © Library of Congress; page 268 (Petronas Towers): © J. Apicella/Cesar Pelli & Associates; page 283 (Joseph Smith): © RLDS Archives; page 299 (Diwali): © Air India Library; page 302 (Aborigines): © Australian Tourist Commission; pages 312 (weather data), 316 (hurricane hunter): © R. Scott Martin. All other photos: Blackbirch Press Photo Bank.